HOW TO
SPELL IT

A Dictionary of
Commonly Misspelled Words

by HARRIET WITTELS &
JOAN GREISMAN

Publishers · GROSSET & DUNLAP · New York

Library of Congress Catalog Card No. 80-83937
ISBN: 0-448-14756-4
Copyright © 1973 by Harriet Wittels and Joan Greisman.
All rights reserved.
Published simultaneously in Canada.
Printed in the United States of America.
(Originally published as *The Perfect Speller.*)

INTRODUCTION

There never has been a complete spelling reference book. When one couldn't spell a word, the advice was always, "Look it up in the dictionary." But how does one find the word in a dictionary if one can't spell it? There are several books on the market that simply discuss the many spelling rules we all learned in school. That's the trouble! There are too many rules and even more exceptions to those rules.

Here at last is a complete reference book that is as easy to use for spelling as a dictionary is for definitions, or a thesaurus for synonyms.

On the pages that follow are thousands of words listed in alphabetical order. Simply look up a word any way that you think it is spelled. If it is a common error or a phonetic error (spelled exactly the way the word sounds), you will find it entered in the left-hand column in black. In the right-hand column you will find the correct spelling printed in red. If you should look up the word correctly, you will find it entered on the left, in alphabetical order, in red. Remember: correct spellings are always printed in red.

acored	accord
acorn	
acount	account
acownt	account

If you happen to look up another form of a root word—that is, a word with a suffix—you might not find it listed incorrectly at all. In that case, you will have to look up the root word itself, any way that you think it is spelled. You would have passed the root word in your search, anyway. For example, if you thought *recently* was spelled *resintly,* you would have passed *resint* in your search. Of course, you simply add the suffix *ly* to the root.

How to Spell It will be **usefull too peeple** of all **agez; their shood** be one on **evory** desk!

HOW TO SPELL IT

A

abace	abase	abdemen	abdomen	abolish	
aback		abdicate		abolition	
abackus	abacus	abdickate	abdicate	abominable	
abacus		abdikate	abdicate	abored	aboard
abait	abate	abdomen		abound	
abak	aback	abdominal		about	
abakus	abacus	abee	abbey	above	
abandon		abel	able	abownd	abound
abandoned		abey	abbey	abowned	abound
abase		abgeckt	abject	abowt	about
abashed		abgect	abject	abreast	
abasht	abashed	abgekt	abject	abrest	abreast
abate		abhor		abreviate	abbreviate
abbate	abate	abide		abridge	
abbee	abbey	abideing	abiding	abroad	
abbey		abiding		abrupt	
abbide	abide	ability		absalute	absolute
abbis	abyss	abillity	ability	abscess	
abbode	abode	abis	abyss	abscure	obscure
abbreviate		abjeckt	abject	abselute	absolute
abbreviation		abject		absence	
abby	abbey	abjekt	abject	absense	absence
abbys	abyss	ablaiz	ablaze	absent	
abcent	absent	ablaze		absents	absence
abcents	absence	able		aberve	observe
abcess	abscess	abley	ably	absess	abscess
abcint	absent	ablige	oblige	absince	absence
abcints	absence	abliterate	obliterate	absinse	absence
abdacate	abdicate	ablivion	oblivion	absint	absent
abdackate	abdicate	ably		absints	absence
abdakate	abdicate	abnormal		absird	absurd
abdamen	abdomen	abnoxious	obnoxious	absolute	
abdecate	abdicate	aboad	abode	absolutely	
abdeckate	abdicate	aboard		absolve	
abdekate	abdicate	abode		absorb	

1

absorbtion	absorption	accidentally		acheeve	achieve
absorption		acclaim		acheive	achieve
abstain		acclame	acclaim	achieve	
abstainance	abstinence	accommodate		achievement	
abstainence	abstinence	accomodate	accommodate	achievment	achievement
abstinence		accompaniment		acid	
abstrackt	abstract	accompany		ackcelerator	accelerator
abstract		accomplice		ackcellerator	accelerator
abstrakt	abstract	accomplish		ackcent	accent
abstruct	obstruct	accomplished		ackcept	accept
absurd		accomplishment		ackcesible	accessible
absurdity		accord		ackcesory	accessory
abtain	obtain	accordance		ackcess	access
abtuse	obtuse	accordingly		ackcessory	accessory
abundance		accordion		ackcident	accident
abundant		accored	accord	ackin	akin
abuse		account		ackme	acme
abuv	above	accownt	account	acknoledge	acknowledge
abuze	abuse	accummulate	accumulate	acknowledge	
abyss		accumpany	accompany	acknowledgment	
abzolve	absolve	accumulate		ackommodate	accommodate
abzorb	absorb	accumulation		ackomodate	accommodate
academy		accur	occur	ackompany	accompany
accademy	academy	accuracy		ackomplish	accomplish
accasion	occasion	accurate		ackord	accord
accelerator		accusation		ackordion	accordion
accellerator	accelerator	accuse		ackored	accord
accent		accustom		ackrid	acrid
accept		accustomed		ackrobat	acrobat
acceptable		accute	acute	ackross	across
acceptance		accuze	accuse	acks	ax
accesible	accessible	accwaint	acquaint	ackselerator	accelerator
accesory	accessory	accwies	acquiesce	acksellerator	accelerator
access		accwire	acquire	acksent	accent
accessible		accwit	acquit	acksept	accept
accessory		ace		acksesory	accessory
accident		ache		acksess	access
accidental		acheave	achieve	acksessory	accessory

ackshun	action	acord	accord
acksident	accident	acordion	accordion
acksis	axis	acored	accord
acksle	axle	acorn	
ackt	act	acount	account
acktion	action	acownt	account
acktive	active	acquaduct	aqueduct
acktivity	activity	acquaint	
acktor	actor	acquaintance	
acktress	actress	acquarium	aquarium
acktriss	actress	acqueduct	aqueduct
acktual	actual	acquiesce	
acktually	actually	acquire	
ackuies	acquiesce	acquisition	
ackummulate	accumulate	acquit	
ackumpany	accompany	acquizition	acquisition
ackumulate	accumulate	acrabat	acrobat
ackurate	accurate	acrage	acreage
ackuse	accuse	acre	
ackute	acute	acreage	
ackuze	accuse	acreidge	acreage
ackwaduct	aqueduct	acribat	acrobat
ackwaint	acquaint	acrid	
ackwarium	aquarium	acridge	acreage
ackweduct	aqueduct	acrobat	
ackwies	acquiesce	acros	across
ackwisition	acquisition	across	
ackwizition	acquisition	acselerator	accelerator
a'clock	o'clock	acsellerator	accelerator
acme		acsent	accent
acnoledge	acknowledge	acsept	accept
acnowledge	acknowledge	acsesory	accessory
acommodate	accommodate	acsess	access
acomodate	accommodate	acsessory	accessory
acompany	accompany	acshun	action
acomplice	accomplice	acsident	accident
acomplis	accomplice	act	
acomplish	accomplish	acter	actor

action	
active	
activity	
actor	
actress	
actriss	actress
actual	
actually	
acuaint	acquaint
acuies	acquiesce
acummulate	accumulate
acumpany	accompany
acumulate	accumulate
acurate	accurate
acuse	accuse
acustom	accustom
acute	
acuze	accuse
acwaduct	aqueduct
acwaint	acquaint
acwarium	aquarium
acweduct	aqueduct
acwies	acquiesce
acwire	acquire
acwisition	acquisition
acwit	acquit
acwizition	acquisition
ad	add
adabt	adapt
adacwit	adequate
adakwit	adequate
adamant	
adapt	
adaptable	
adaptation	
adaquate	adequate
add	
addition	

additional	
address	
ade	aid
adebt	adept
adecwit	adequate
adekwit	adequate
adept	
adequate	
adgective	adjective
adgictive	adjective
adhear	adhere
adhere	
adhesive	
adhezive	adhesive
adimant	adamant
adition	addition
adjacent	
adjasent	adjacent
adjective	
adjictive	adjective
adjoin	
adjourn	
adjoyn	adjoin
adjurn	adjourn
adjust	
adjustment	
admerable	admirable
admeral	admiral
admeration	admiration
admier	admire
administer	
administration	
admirable	
admiral	
admiration	
admire	
admirer	
admision	admission

admission	
admit	
admition	admission
admonish	
admonition	
ado	
adobe	
adobt	adopt
adobtion	adoption
adopt	
adoption	
ador	adore
adorable	
adoration	
adore	
adoreable	adorable
adorn	
adornment	
adress	address
adrift	
adult	
advacate	advocate
advakate	advocate
advance	
advanced	
advancement	
advanse	advance
advansed	advanced
advantage	
advantageous	
adventure	
adventurer	
adventurous	
adverb	
adverce	adverse
adversary	
adverse	
adversity	

advertise	
advertisement	
advice	
advirb	adverb
advirce	adverse
advirsary	adversary
advirse	adverse
advirtise	advertise
advisable	
advise	
advise	advice
adviser	
advisor	
advizable	advisable
advize	advise
advocate	
advurce	adverse
advurse	adverse
aereal	aerial
aerial	
aeriel	aerial
afable	affable
afair	affair
afar	
afare	affair
afeald	afield
afeckt	affect
afeckt	effect
afecktion	affection
afect	affect
afect	effect
afection	affection
afeeld	afield
afekt	affect
afekt	effect
afektion	affection
afend	offend
aferm	affirm

affable		afield		aggravate	
affair		afier	afire	aggreave	aggrieve
affare	affair	afire		aggreeve	aggrieve
affeald	afield	afirm	affirm	aggregate	
affeckt	affect	aflaim	aflame	aggreive	aggrieve
affect		aflame		aggresion	aggression
affect	effect	aflickt	afflict	aggresive	aggressive
affected		aflict	afflict	aggresor	aggressor
affection		aflikt	afflict	aggression	
affectionate		afloat		aggressive	
affeeld	afield	aflote	afloat	aggressor	
affekt	affect	afluent	affluent	aggretion	aggression
affektion	affection	afoot		aggreve	aggrieve
affend	offend	aford	afford	aggrieve	
afferm	affirm	afrade	afraid	aggrigate	aggregate
affible	affable	afraid		aggrivate	aggravate
afficient	efficient	afront	affront	aghast	
affield	afield	afta	after	agid	aged
affier	afire	aftanoon	afternoon	agil	agile
affire	afire	aftaward	afterward	agile	
affirm		after		agility	
affirmative		afternoon		agillity	agility
afflaim	aflame	afterward		agincy	agency
afflame	aflame	afurm	affirm	agint	agent
afflickt	afflict	again		agitate	
afflict		against		ago	
affliction		agast	aghast	agonizing	
afflikt	afflict	agatate	agitate	agony	
affloat	afloat	agate		agraculture	agriculture
afflote	afloat	age		agravate	aggravate
affluent		aged		agreave	aggrieve
affoot	afoot	agen	again	agree	
afford		agency		agreeable	
affrade	afraid	agenst	against	agreement	
affraid	afraid	agent		agreeve	aggrieve
affront		aget	agate	agregate	aggregate
affurm	affirm	aggate	agate	agreive	aggrieve
afible	affable	agget	agate	agresion	aggression

agresive	aggressive	airport		akomodate	accommodate
agresor	aggressor	airy		akompany	accompany
agression	aggression	aisle		akomplish	accomplish
agressive	aggressive	ait	eight	akor	acre
agressor	aggressor	ajar		akord	accord
agreve	aggrieve	ajatate	agitate	akordion	accordion
agricultural		aje	age	akorn	acorn
agriculture		ajency	agency	akount	account
agrieve	aggrieve	ajent	agent	akownt	account
agrigate	aggregate	ajile	agile	akrabat	acrobat
agrivate	aggravate	ajincy	agency	akribat	acrobat
aground		ajint	agent	akrid	acrid
agrowned	aground	ajitate	agitate	akrobat	acrobat
aguny	agony	ajoin	adjoin	akross	across
ahead		ajourn	adjourn	aks	ax
ahed	ahead	ajoyn	adjoin	akselerator	accelerator
ahms	alms	ajurn	adjourn	aksellerator	accelerator
ahoy		ajust	adjust	aksent	accent
ail		ajustment	adjustment	aksept	accept
ail	ale	akar	acre	aksesory	accessory
ailein	alien	akasion	occasion	aksess	access
ailien	alien	akcelerator	accelerator	aksessory	accessory
ailment		akcellerator	accelerator	aksesury	accessory
aim		akcent	accent	akshun	action
aimeable	amiable	akcept	accept	aksident	accident
aimiable	amiable	akcesory	accessory	aksil	axle
ain't		akcess	access	aksis	axis
air		akcessory	accessory	akt	act
air	heir	akcident	accident	akter	actor
airaplane	airplane	ake	ache	aktion	action
aircraft		aker	acre	aktive	active
airea	area	aker	occur	aktivity	activity
airial	aerial	akin		aktor	actor
airkraft	aircraft	akir	acre	aktress	actress
airline		a'klock	o'clock	aktriss	actress
airoplane	airplane	akme	acme	aktual	actual
airplain	airplane	aknoledge	acknowledge	akuaint	acquaint
airplane		aknowledge	acknowledge	akuies	acquiesce

akummulate	accumulate	alement	ailment	allmanac	almanac
akumpany	accompany	alemint	ailment	allmighty	almighty
akumulate	accumulate	alert		allmost	almost
akur	acre	alertness		allood	allude
akur	occur	alewd	allude	alloor	allure
akurate	accurate	aley	alley	alloosion	allusion
akuse	accuse	alfabet	alphabet	alloozion	allusion
akustom	accustom	aliance	alliance	allot	
akute	acute	alide	allied	allow	
akuze	accuse	alied	allied	allowance	
akwaduct	aqueduct	alien		alloy	
akwaint	acquaint	aligator	alligator	allready	already
akwarium	aquarium	alike		allso	also
akweduct	aqueduct	alimpic	olympic	alltar	altar
akwies	acquiesce	alirt	alert	alltar	alter
akwire	acquire	alive		allter	altar
akwisition	acquisition	alkahol	alcohol	allter	alter
akwit	acquit	alkohol	alcohol	allternate	alternate
akwizition	acquisition	alkove	alcove	alltho	although
alarm		all		allthough	although
alas		all	awl	alltogether	altogether
alay	allay	allay		allude	
album		alleagiance	allegiance	allued	allude
alcahol	alcohol	alleajiance	allegiance	allure	
alcohol		alledge	allege	allusion	
alcoholic		alleegiance	allegiance	alluzion	allusion
alcove		alleejiance	allegiance	allways	always
ale		allege		ally	
ale	ail	allegiance		almanac	
aleagiance	allegiance	allejiance	allegiance	almand	almond
aleajiance	allegiance	allert	alert	almend	almond
aledge	allege	allewd	allude	almighty	
aleegiance	allegiance	alley		alminac	almanac
aleejiance	allegiance	alliance		almind	almond
alege	allege	allide	allied	almity	almighty
alegiance	allegiance	allied		almond	
alein	alien	alligator		almost	
alejiance	allegiance	allirt	alert	alms	

almunac	almanac	alto		ambulance	
almund	almond	altoe	alto	ambur	amber
aloan	alone	altogether		ambush	
aloft		altow	alto	ame	aim
alone		alturnate	alternate	ameable	amiable
along		alude	allude	amen	
alood	allude	alued	allude	amend	
aloof		alufe	aloof	amendment	
aloominum	aluminum	aluminum		amends	
alot	allot	alure	allure	America	
aloud		alurt	alert	American	
alow	allow	alusion	allusion	amethyst	
alowance	allowance	alwaize	always	amfibious	amphibious
alowd	aloud	alwaze	always	amiable	
aloy	alloy	aly	ally	amid	
alphabet		alympic	olympic	amidst	
alphabetical		amaize	amaze	amis	amiss
alphabetically		amas	amass	amiss	
alphabetize		amass		ammas	amass
alphebet	alphabet	amateur		ammass	amass
alphibet	alphabet	amathyst	amethyst	ammend	amend
alphobet	alphabet	amayze	amaze	ammends	amends
alphubet	alphabet	amaze		ammid	amid
already		amazement		ammidst	amidst
alredy	already	ambal	amble	ammiss	amiss
also		ambar	amber	ammong	among
altar		ambasador	ambassador	ammongst	amongst
altar	alter	ambassador		ammonia	
altarnate	alternate	ambel	amble	ammount	amount
altatude	altitude	amber		ammownt	amount
alter		ambil	amble	ammunition	
alter	altar	ambir	amber	ammuse	amuse
alteration		ambition		amond	almond
alternate		ambitious		among	
alternative		amble		amongst	
altho	although	ambol	amble	amonia	ammonia
although		ambor	amber	amount	
altitude		ambul	amble	amownt	amount

ampal	ample	anecdote		anihilate	annihilate
ampel	ample	aneckdote	anecdote	anihliate	annihilate
amphibian		anecks	annex	anikdote	anecdote
amphibious		anekdote	anecdote	aniks	annex
ampil	ample	aneks	annex	aniliate	annihilate
ample		anemal	animal	animal	
amply		anemosity	animosity	animate	
ampol	ample	anew		animated	
ampul	ample	anex	annex	animation	
amung	among	angal	angel	animosity	
amungst	amongst	angal	angle	aniversary	anniversary
amunition	ammunition	angar	anger	anix	annex
amuse		angel		anjal	angel
amusement		angel	angle	anjel	angel
amuze	amuse	angelic		anjil	angel
an		angellic	angelic	anjol	angel
anadomy	anatomy	anger		anjul	angel
analysis		angil	angel	ankal	ankle
analyze		angil	angle	ankel	ankle
anamal	animal	angir	anger	anker	anchor
anamate	animate	angle		ankil	ankle
anamosity	animosity	angle	angel	ankle	
anatomy		angol	angel	anklet	
ancar	anchor	angol	angle	anklit	anklet
ancesstor	ancestor	angor	anger	ankol	ankle
ancestor		angrily		ankor	anchor
ancestral		angry		anksious	anxious
anchent	ancient	angryly	angrily	ankul	ankle
anchient	ancient	anguish		ankur	anchor
anchint	ancient	angul	angel	annadomy	anatomy
anchor		angul	angle	annalysis	analysis
ancient		angular		annalyze	analyze
anckle	ankle	angur	anger	annatomy	anatomy
ancklet	anklet	angwish	anguish	annecdote	anecdote
anckor	anchor	angziety	anxiety	annecks	annex
ancor	anchor	anicdote	anecdote	anneks	annex
ancur	anchor	anickdote	anecdote	annew	anew
and		anicks	annex	annex	

annexation		ansor		answer		antilope	antelope
annialate	annihilate	ansur		answer		antipathy	
annicks	annex	answer				antiquated	
annihilate		ant				antique	
annihilation		ant	aunt			antiquity	
annihliate	annihilate	antagonism				antiroom	anteroom
anniks	annex	antagonist				antiseptic	
anniversary		antagonistic				antisipate	anticipate
annix	annex	antagonize				antissipate	anticipate
annoint	anoint	antalope	antelope			antitoxin	
announce		anteak	antique			antlar	antler
announcement		antebiotic	antibiotic			antler	
announcer		antebody	antibody			antlir	antler
announse	announce	antedote	antidote			antlor	antler
annownce	announce	anteek	antique			antlur	antler
annownse	announce	anteke	antique			antolope	antelope
annoy		antelope				antulope	antelope
annoyance		antena	antenna			anual	annual
annual		antenna				anumal	animal
annually		antequated	antiquated			anumosity	animosity
annuwal	annual	anteque	antique			anuther	another
anoint		anteroom				anxiety	
anomosity	animosity	antetoxin	antitoxin			anxious	
another		antham	anthem			anxiously	
anounce	announce	anthem				anxous	anxious
anounse	announce	anthim	anthem			any	
anownce	announce	anthom	anthem			anybody	
anownse	announce	anthum	anthem			anyhow	
anoy	annoy	antibiotic				anyone	
anoynt	anoint	antibody				anything	
ansar	answer	anticeptic	antiseptic			anyware	anywhere
anser	answer	anticipate				anyway	
ansesstor	ancestor	anticipation				anywear	anywhere
ansestor	ancestor	antics				anywhere	
anshent	ancient	anticks	antics			anywon	anyone
anshient	ancient	antidote				apal	appall
anshint	ancient	antiks	antics			apal	apple
ansir	answer	antikwity	antiquity			apall	appall

apall	apple	aposle	apostle	applause	
aparatus	apparatus	apossum	opossum	applawd	applaud
aparel	apparel	apostle		applawse	applause
aparent	apparent	apostrophe		apple	
aparition	apparition	apothecary		applecation	application
aparrel	apparel	apothy	apathy	appleckation	application
aparrent	apparent	appal	appall	applekation	application
apart		appall		appliance	
apartment		apparatus		applicant	
apathy		apparel		application	
apature	aperture	apparent		applickant	applicant
ape		apparently		applickation	application
apeal	appeal	apparition		applikant	applicant
apear	appear	apparrel	apparel	applikation	application
apease	appease	apparrent	apparent	applord	applaud
apecks	apex	appatite	appetite	applorse	applause
apeks	apex	appeal		applucation	application
apel	apple	appear		appluckation	application
apendage	appendage	appearance		applukation	application
apendix	appendix	appease		apply	
aperture		appeel	appeal	applyance	appliance
apethy	apathy	appeer	appear	appoint	
apetite	appetite	appeese	appease	appointment	
apex		appel	apple	apponent	opponent
aphor	abhor	appendage		appose	oppose
apinion	opinion	appendix		appoynt	appoint
apithy	apathy	apperatus	apparatus	apprahend	apprehend
aplaud	applaud	appere	appear	appreciate	
aplause	applause	apperition	apparition	appreciation	
aple	apple	appese	appease	appreciative	
apliance	appliance	appetite		apprehend	
aplicant	applicant	appil	apple	apprehension	
aplication	application	appirition	apparition	apprehensive	
aply	apply	appitite	appetite	apprentice	
apoint	appoint	applacation	application	apprenticeship	
apologetic		applackation	application	appress	oppress
apologize		applakation	application	appricot	apricot
apology		applaud		apprihend	apprehend

approach		aputhy	apathy	arck	ark		
approch	approach	aquaduct	aqueduct	arckipelago	archipelago		
approove	approve	aquaint	acquaint	arckitect	architect		
appropriate		aquaintance	acquaintance	arcktic	arctic		
appropriation		aquarium		ardar	ardor		
approval		aqueduct		ardent			
approve		aquiduct	aqueduct	arder	ardor		
approximate		aquiesce	acquiesce	ardint	ardent		
approximately		aquire	acquire	ardir	ardor		
appruhend	apprehend	aquisition	acquisition	ardor			
appul	apple	aquit	acquit	arduous			
appurition	apparition	aquoduct	aqueduct	ardur	ardor		
apputite	appetite	ar	are	area			
apracot	apricot	Arab		areana	arena		
aprahend	apprehend	arad	arid	Areb	Arab		
Apral	April	arange	arrange	ared	arid		
apran	apron	aray	array	areena	arena		
apreciate	appreciate	arbar	arbor	arena			
aprecot	apricot	arber	arbor	aren't			
aprehend	apprehend	arbir	arbor	arest	arrest		
aprekot	apricot	arbitrary		argew	argue		
Aprel	April	arbitrate		argue			
apren	apron	arbitration		arguement	argument		
aprentice	apprentice	arbor		argument			
aprikot	apricot	arbur	arbor	ari	awry		
April		arc		aria	area		
aprin	apron	arc	ark	Arib	Arab		
aproach	approach	arch		arid			
Aprol	April	archary	archery	arie	awry		
apron		archery		ariginal	original		
apropriate	appropriate	archipelago		arise			
aprove	approve	archiry	archery	aristocracy			
aproximate	approximate	architect		aristocrat			
aprucot	apricot	architecture		aristocratic			
aprukot	apricot	archory	archery	arithmetic			
Aprul	April	archury	archery	arive	arrive		
aprun	apron	arcitect	architect	arize	arise		
apt		arck	arc	ark			

ark	arc	arrangement		artful	
arkipelago	archipelago	arrangment	arrangement	artichoke	
arkitect	architect	arratic	erratic	artickle	article
arktic	arctic	array		article	
arm		arrest		artifice	
armada		arrid	arid	artificial	
armament		arrigant	arrogant	artikle	article
armar	armor	arrival		artilery	artillery
armement	armament	arrive		artillery	
armer	armor	arro	arrow	artiry	artery
armiment	armament	arrogant		artisan	
armir	armor	arrow		artist	
armisstice	armistice	arrugant	arrogant	artistic	
armistice		arsanal	arsenal	artless	
armoment	armament	arsanic	arsenic	artliss	artless
armor		arsenal		artocle	article
armorry	armory	arsenic		artockle	article
armory		arsonal	arsenal	artofice	artifice
arms		arsonic	arsenic	artoficial	artificial
armument	armament	arsunal	arsenal	artokle	article
armur	armor	arsunic	arsenic	artory	artery
army		art		artuckle	article
armz	arms	artachoke	artichoke	artucle	article
arn't	aren't	artackle	article	artufice	artifice
Arob	Arab	artacle	article	artuficial	artificial
arod	arid	artafice	artifice	artukle	article
arogant	arrogant	artaficial	artificial	artury	artery
aroma		artakle	article	artusan	artisan
around		artary	artery	Arub	Arab
arouse		artasan	artisan	arud	arid
arouze	arouse	artechoke	artichoke	ary	awry
arow	arrow	arteckle	article	as	
arownd	around	artecle	article	asail	assail
arowse	arouse	artefice	artifice	asassin	assassin
arowze	arouse	arteficial	artificial	asault	assault
arragant	arrogant	artekle	article	asbestos	
arrainge	arrange	artery		ascend	
arrange		artesan	artisan	ascent	

ascertain		asparagus		assignment	
ascribe		asparant	aspirant	assilum	asylum
ase	ace	asparation	aspiration	assimilate	
asemble	assemble	aspeckt	aspect	assimmilate	assimilate
asend	ascend	aspect		assine	assign
asent	ascent	aspekt	aspect	assirt	assert
asent	assent	asperant	aspirant	assist	
asert	assert	asperation	aspiration	assistance	
asertain	ascertain	asphalt		assistant	
aset	asset	aspier	aspire	associate	
asfalt	asphalt	aspirant		association	
ash		aspiration		assoom	assume
ashaimed	ashamed	aspire		assorted	
ashamed		ass		assortment	
ashes		assail		assosiate	associate
ashez	ashes	assailant		assuage	
ashis	ashes	assale	assail	assume	
ashiz	ashes	assalt	assault	assumption	
ashoar	ashore	assasin	assassin	assumtion	assumption
ashor	ashore	assassin		assunder	asunder
ashore		assassinate		assurance	
Asia		assassination		assure	
asid	acid	assault		assured	
aside		assawlt	assault	asswage	assuage
asign	assign	assemble		assylum	asylum
asilum	asylum	assembly		astonish	
asimilate	assimilate	assend	ascend	astound	
asist	assist	assent		astownd	astound
ask		assent	ascent	astranaut	astronaut
askance		assert		astray	
askanse	askance	assertain	ascertain	astrenaut	astronaut
askribe	ascribe	assertion		astride	
asleap	asleep	asset		astrinaut	astronaut
asleep		assewm	assume	astronaut	
aslepe	asleep	asshoor	assure	astronomer	
asociate	associate	assid	acid	astronomy	
asorted	assorted	asside	aside	astrunaut	astronaut
asortment	assortment	assign		asuage	assuage

asume	assume	atoan	atone	attoon	attune
asunder		atom		attorney	
asure	assure	atomic		attrackt	attract
asylum		atone		attract	
at		atonement		attraction	
atach	attach	atonment	atonement	attractive	
atack	attack	atorney	attorney	attrakt	attract
atain	attain	atract	attract	attribute	
atam	atom	atribute	attribute	attrocious	atrocious
ate		atrocious		attune	
ate	eight	attac	attack	atturney	attorney
atem	atom	attach		atum	atom
atempt	attempt	attachment		atune	attune
atend	attend	attack		aucktion	auction
atention	attention	attain		auction	
atentive	attentive	attainment		audable	audible
atest	attest	attak	attack	audacious	
athleat	athlete	attane	attain	audacity	
athleet	athlete	attatch	attach	audeble	audible
athlete		attempt		audible	
athletic		attemt	attempt	audit	
athletics		attend		auditor	
atic	attic	attendance		auditorium	
atim	atom	attendant		audoble	audible
atire	attire	attention		auduble	audible
atitude	attitude	attentive		Augast	August
Atlantic		atterney	attorney	Augest	August
atlas		attest		Augist	August
atless	atlas	attic		augment	
atlis	atlas	attick	attic	Augost	August
atlos	atlas	attier	attire	augsiliary	auxiliary
atlus	atlas	attik	attic	August	
atmasphere	atmosphere	attire		auktion	auction
atmesphere	atmosphere	attirney	attorney	aunt	
atmisphere	atmosphere	attittude	attitude	aunt	ant
atmosphere		attitude		auspaces	auspices
atmospheric		attoan	atone	auspases	auspices
atmusphere	atmosphere	attone	atone	auspeces	auspices

auspeses	auspices
auspices	
auspises	auspices
ausposis	auspices
auspusis	auspices
austear	austere
austeer	austere
austere	
Austrailia	Australia
Australia	
autacrat	autocrat
autagraph	autograph
autamatic	automatic
autamobile	automobile
autecrat	autocrat
autegraph	autograph
autematic	automatic
autemobile	automobile
authar	author
authentic	
auther	author
authir	author
author	
authoritative	
authority	
authorize	
authur	author
auticrat	autocrat
autigraph	autograph
autimatic	automatic
autimobile	automobile
auto	
autocrat	
autograph	
autokrat	autocrat
automatically	
automobile	

autucrat	autocrat
autugraph	autograph
autum	autumn
autumatic	automatic
autumn	
autumobile	automobile
auxiliary	
auxilliary	auxiliary
avad	avid
avail	
available	
avalanche	
avale	avail
avanue	avenue
avarice	
avaricious	
aveary	aviary
aveation	aviation
aveator	aviator
aved	avid
avelanche	avalanche
avenge	
avenue	
average	
averice	avarice
averse	
aversion	
avert	
aviary	
aviation	
aviator	
avid	
avilanche	avalanche
avinue	avenue
avirice	avarice
avirse	averse
avirsion	aversion

avirt	avert
avocation	
avod	avid
avoid	
avokation	avocation
avolanche	avalanche
avonue	avenue
avorice	avarice
avow	
avoyd	avoid
avrage	average
avud	avid
avulanche	avalanche
avunue	avenue
avurice	avarice
avurse	averse
avursion	aversion
avurt	avert
aw	awe
awaik	awake
awair	aware
await	
awake	
awaken	
awakening	
award	
aware	
awate	await
away	
awb	orb
awbit	orbit
awchard	orchard
awchestra	orchestra
awchid	orchid
awcktion	auction
awckward	awkward
awction	auction

awdacious	audacious	awnate	ornate	awspices	auspices
awdacity	audacity	awning		awspicious	auspicious
awdain	ordain	awoak	awoke	awstere	austere
awdeal	ordeal	awoke		Awstralia	Australia
awder	order	awored	award	awt	ought
awdible	audible	awphan	orphan	awthentic	authentic
awdience	audience	awr	oar	awthodox	orthodox
awdinance	ordinance	awr	or	awthor	author
awdinary	ordinary	awr	ore	awthority	authority
awdit	audit	awracle	oracle	awto	auto
awe		awral	oral	awtocrat	autocrat
awear	aware	awration	oration	awtograph	autograph
aweful	awful	awrb	orb	awtomatic	automatic
awf	off	awrbit	orbit	awtomobile	automobile
awfan	orphan	awrchard	orchard	awtumn	Autumn
awful		awrchestra	orchestra	awxiliary	auxiliary
awfully		awrchid	orchid	ax	
awgan	organ	awrdain	ordain	axal	axle
awgandy	organdy	awrdeal	ordeal	axe	
awganism	organism	awrder	order	axel	axle
awganize	organize	awrdinance	ordinance	axelerator	accelerator
awgment	augment	awrdinary	ordinary	axent	accent
awgsiliary	auxiliary	awrfan	orphan	axept	accept
Awgust	August	awrgan	organ	axess	access
awhere	aware	awrgandy	organdy	axessory	accessory
awhile		awrganism	organism	axident	accident
awile	awhile	awrganize	organize	axil	axle
awkestra	orchestra	awri	awry	axis	
awkid	orchild	awrient	orient	axle	
awktion	auction	awrifice	orifice	axol	axle
awkward		awriole	oriole	axul	axle
awkwardly		awrkestra	orchestra	az	as
awkwood	awkward	awrkid	orchid	azailea	azalea
awl		awrnament	ornament	azalea	
awl	all	awrnate	ornate	Azia	Asia
awnament	ornament	awrphan	orphan	azure	
		awrthodox	orthodox		

B

ba	bay	bacteeria	bacteria	bagonia	begonia
babal	babble	bacteria		bagpipe	
babbal	babble	bacun	bacon	bahm	balm
babbel	babble	bad		baid	bade
babbil	babble	bade		baik	bake
babble		badge		bail	
babbol	babble	badger		bail	bale
babboon	baboon	badgir	badger	bair	bare
babbul	babble	badjer	badger	bair	bear
babe		badly		bairing	bearing
babel	babble	bafal	baffle	bais	base
babil	babble	bafel	baffle	bais	bass
bable	babble	baffal	baffle	baised	baste
babol	babble	baffel	baffle	baist	baste
baboon		baffil	baffle	bait	
babul	babble	baffle		baithe	bathe
babune	baboon	baffol	baffle	bak	back
baby		bafful	baffle	bakan	bacon
bac	back	bafil	baffle	bake	
bacan	bacon	bafle	baffle	baken	bacon
bace	base	bafol	baffle	baker	
bace	bass	bafore	before	bakery	
bach	batch	bafour	before	bakin	bacon
bachelor		baful	baffle	bakir	baker
bachlor	bachelor	bag		bakon	bacon
back		bagage	baggage	bakteria	bacteria
background		baggadge	baggage	bakun	bacon
backgrownd	background	baggage		balad	ballad
backround	background	baggedge	baggage	balance	
backrownd	background	baggege	baggage	balanse	balance
backteria	bacteria	baggidge	baggage	balast	ballast
backwad	backward	baggige	baggage	balcany	balcony
backward		baggodge	baggage	balcony	
backwood	backward	baggoge	baggage	balcuny	balcony
bacon		baggudge	baggage	bald	
bactearia	bacteria	bagguge	baggage	bale	

bale	bail	banc	bank	baptisem	baptism
balence	balance	banck	bank	baptisim	baptism
baligerent	belligerent	banckwet	banquet	baptism	
balince	balance	bancwet	banquet	baptisom	baptism
balk		band		baptisum	baptism
balkony	balcony	bandadge	bandage	baptize	
ball		bandage		bar	
ball	bawl	bandana		baracade	barricade
ballad		bandanna		barackade	barricade
ballast		bandedge	bandage	baracks	barracks
ballid	ballad	bandege	bandage	barakade	barricade
balligerent	belligerent	bandidge	bandage	baraks	barracks
ballod	ballad	bandige	bandage	baral	barrel
balloon		bandit		baran	baron
ballot		baner	banner	baran	barren
ballroom		banevolent	benevolent	barax	barracks
ballsa	balsa	bang		barbacue	barbecue
ballsam	balsam	banish		barbakue	barbecue
ballud	ballad	banishment		barbaque	barbecue
ballune	balloon	banjo		barbar	barber
balm		bank		barbarian	
balm	bomb	banker		barbaric	
balmy		bankwet	banquet	barbearian	barbarian
baloon	balloon	bannana	banana	barbecue	
balot	ballot	bannar	banner	barbekue	barbecue
balsa		banner		barbeque	barbecue
balsam		bannish	banish	barber	
balsar	balsa	bannor	banner	barbicue	barbecue
balser	balsa	banoculars	binoculars	barbikue	barbecue
balsim	balsam	banquet		barbique	barbecue
balsom	balsam	banquit	banquet	barbocue	barbecue
balsome	balsam	bantar	banter	barbokue	barbecue
balsum	balsam	banter		barbor	barber
bamboo		bantir	banter	barbucue	barbecue
bambu	bamboo	bantor	banter	barbukue	barbecue
ban		bantur	banter	barbur	barber
banana		baptisam	baptism	barc	bark
bananna	banana	baptise	baptize	barck	bark

bard		barocade	barricade	barrocade	barricade
bare		barockade	barricade	barrockade	barricade
bare	bear	barocks	barracks	barrocks	barracks
bareave	bereave	barokade	barricade	barrokade	barricade
barecade	barricade	baroks	barracks	barroks	barracks
bareckade	barricade	barol	barrel	barrol	barrel
barefoot		barometer		barron	baron
barefut	barefoot	baron		barron	barren
barekade	barricade	baron	barren	barrox	barracks
bareks	barracks	barox	barracks	barrucade	barricade
barel	barrel	barracade	barricade	barruckade	barricade
barely		barrackade	barricade	barrucks	barracks
baren	baron	barracks		barrukade	barricade
baren	barren	barrakade	barricade	barruks	barracks
barex	barracks	barraks	barracks	barrul	barrel
bargain		barral	barrel	barrun	baron
bargan	bargain	barran	baron	barrun	barren
barge		barran	barren	barrux	barracks
bargen	bargain	barrax	barracks	bartar	barter
bargin	bargain	barrecade	barricade	barter	
bargon	bargain	barreckade	barricade	bartor	barter
bargun	bargain	barrecks	barracks	barucade	barricade
baricade	barricade	barrekade	barricade	baruckade	barricade
barickade	barricade	barreks	barracks	barucks	barracks
baricks	barracks	barrel		barukade	barricade
barier	barrier	barren		baruks	barracks
barikade	barricade	barren	baron	barul	barrel
bariks	barracks	barrex	barracks	barun	baron
baril	barrel	barricade		barun	barren
barin	baron	barrickade	barricade	barux	barracks
barin	barren	barricks	barracks	bas	bass
baring	bearing	barrier		basan	basin
barix	barracks	barrikade	barricade	basc	bask
bark		barriks	barracks	bascat	basket
barley		barril	barrel	basck	bask
barly	barley	barrin	baron	bascket	basket
barn		barrin	barren	bascot	basket
barnyard		barrix	barracks	bascut	basket

base		bath		baubil	bauble
base	bass	bathe		bauble	
baseball		bathroom		baubol	bauble
based	baste	batil	battle	baubul	bauble
basement		batir	batter	baught	bought
basemint	basement	batiry	battery	bawble	bauble
basen	basin	batle	battle	bawk	balk
bashful		batol	battle	bawl	
basic		baton		bawl	ball
basick	basic	bator	batter	bawt	bought
basik	basic	batory	battery	bay	
basin		battal	battle	bayanet	bayonet
basis		battalion		bayenet	bayonet
bask		battar	batter	bayinet	bayonet
baskat	basket	battary	battery	bayonet	
basket		battel	battle	bayunet	bayonet
basketball		batter		bazaar	
baskit	basket	battery		bazaar	bizarre
baskot	basket	battil	battle	bazar	bazaar
baskut	basket	battir	batter	bazar	bizarre
bason	basin	battiry	battery	bazarre	bazaar
bass		battle		bazarre	bizarre
bassis	basis	battle-ax		be	
baste		battle-axe		be	bee
basun	basin	battlefield		bea	be
bat		battleship		bea	bee
batal	battle	battol	battle	beacan	beacon
batalion	battalion	batton	baton	beach	
batanical	botanical	battor	batter	beacon	
batar	batter	battory	battery	beacun	beacon
batary	battery	battul	battle	bead	
batch		battur	batter	beaf	beef
batchelor	bachelor	battury	battery	beagal	beagle
batchlor	bachelor	batul	battle	beagel	beagle
bate	bait	batur	batter	beagil	beagle
batel	battle	batury	battery	beagle	
bater	batter	baubal	bauble	beagol	beagle
batery	battery	baubel	bauble	beagul	beagle

beak		beaver		beed	bead
beakan	beacon	beavir	beaver	beef	
beakar	beaker	beavor	beaver	beegle	beagle
beaken	beacon	beavur	beaver	beehive	
beaker		becaim	became	beek	beak
beakin	beacon	became		beekon	beacon
beakir	beaker	becan	beckon	beem	beam
beakon	beacon	beckan	beckon	been	
beakor	beaker	becken	beckon	been	bean
beakun	beacon	beckin	beckon	beer	
beakur	beaker	beckon		beer	bier
beam		beckun	beckon	beerd	beard
bean		become		beest	beast
bear		becomeing	becoming	beet	
bear	bare	becoming		beet	beat
bear	beer	becon	beckon	beetal	beetle
bear	bier	becum	become	beetel	beetle
beard		becun	beckon	beetil	beetle
bearing		becweath	bequeath	beetle	
beast		bed		beetol	beetle
beastly		bedding		beetul	beetle
beat		bede	bead	beever	beaver
beat	beet	beding	bedding	befall	
beaten		bedlam		befit	
beatle	beetle	bedlem	bedlam	befor	before
beau		bedlim	bedlam	before	
beautaful	beautiful	bedlom	bedlam	beforehand	
beautafy	beautify	bedlum	bedlam	befour	before
beauteful	beautiful	bedraggle		befreind	befriend
beautefy	beautify	bedragle	bedraggle	befrend	befriend
beautiful		bedroom		befriend	
beautify		bedspread		beg	
beautoful	beautiful	bedspred	bedspread	began	
beautofy	beautify	bedtime		begar	beggar
beautuful	beautiful	bee		beger	beggar
beautufy	beautify	bee	be	beggar	
beauty		beech	beach	begger	beggar
beavar	beaver	beecon	beacon	beggor	beggar

begiel	beguile	beleive	believe	beneeth	beneath
begile	beguile	belfree	belfry	benefactor	
begin		belfry		benefit	
beginer	beginner	belie		benevolence	
begining	beginning	belief		benevolent	
beginner		believe		benidiction	benediction
beginning		beligerent	belligerent	benifactor	benefactor
begonia		belitle	belittle	benifit	benefit
begor	beggar	belittle		bennana	banana
beguile		bell		benoculars	binoculars
begun		bellfry	belfry	benodiction	benediction
behaf	behalf	belligerent		benofactor	benefactor
behaive	behave	bellijerent	belligerent	benofit	benefit
behalf		bello	bellow	bent	
behave		belly		benudiction	benediction
behavior		belo	bellow	benufactor	benefactor
behead		belo	below	benufit	benefit
behed	behead	belong		bequeath	
behind		belongings		bequeeth	bequeath
behold		beloved		berait	berate
being		below		berate	
beir	bier	below	bellow	berch	birch
bekaim	became	belt		berd	bird
bekame	became	beluved	beloved	berden	burden
bekan	beckon	bely	belie	bere	beer
beke	beak	bely	belly	bere	bier
beken	beckon	beme	beam	bereave	
bekin	beckon	benadiction	benediction	bereeve	bereave
bekon	beckon	benafactor	benefactor	bereft	
bekun	beckon	benafit	benefit	berglar	burglar
bekweath	bequeath	benana	banana	berial	burial
bel	bell	benanna	banana	berlap	burlap
belaited	belated	bench		berly	burly
belated		bend		bern	burn
belch		bene	bean	bernish	burnish
beleaf	belief	beneath		berrial	burial
beleave	believe	benedicshun	benediction	berry	
beleif	belief	benediction		berry	bury

berst	burst	bettir	better	bias	
berth		bettor	better	biased	
berth	birth	bettur	better	biast	biased
bery	berry	betur	better	bib	
bery	bury	betwean	between	bibal	bible
beschal	bestial	between		bibel	bible
beschel	bestial	betwene	between	bibil	bible
beschil	bestial	betwickst	betwixt	bible	
beschol	bestial	betwikst	betwixt	bibol	bible
beschul	bestial	betwixt		bibul	bible
beseach	beseech	beval	bevel	bicarbonate	
beseage	besiege	bevarage	beverage	bicicle	bicycle
beseech		bevel		bicuspid	
beseege	besiege	beverage		bicweath	bequeath
beseige	besiege	bevil	bevel	bicycle	
beset		bevirage	beverage	bid	
beside		bevol	bevel	bidding	
besides		bevorage	beverage	bide	
besiege		bevul	bevel	biding	bidding
best		bevurage	beverage	bied	bide
bestial		bevy		bier	
besto	bestow	bevvy	bevy	biess	bias
bestow		bewail		bifore	before
bet		bewale	bewail	big	
betanical	botanical	beware		bigonia	begonia
betar	better	bewear	beware	bihead	behead
bete	beat	bewhere	beware	bihind	behind
bete	beet	bewhich	bewitch	bihold	behold
beter	better	bewich	bewitch	bikarbonate	bicarbonate
betir	better	bewilder		bike	
betor	better	bewilderment		bikuspid	bicuspid
betray		bewilleder	bewilder	bikweath	bequeath
betroath	betroth	bewitch		bil	bill
betroth		beyond		bilated	belated
betrothal		bezaar	bazaar	bild	build
bettar	better	bezaar	bizarre	bile	
better		bi	buy	biliards	billiards
betterment		bi	by	bilie	belie

bilief	belief	bind		bisicle	bicycle		
bilieve	believe	bineath	beneath	biside	beside		
biligerent	belligerent	binevolent	benevolent	bisides	besides		
bilion	billion	binnana	banana	bisiege	besiege		
bilittle	belittle	binockulars	binoculars	bisin	bison		
bill		binoculars		bisiness	business		
billboard		binokulars	binoculars	biskit	biscuit		
billbored	billboard	biography		biskut	biscuit		
billed	build	biology		bison			
billian	billion	bios	bias	bistander	bystander		
billiards		bipass	bypass	bistow	bestow		
billien	billion	biproduct	byproduct	bisun	bison		
billierds	billiards	biqueath	bequeath	bisy	busy		
billigerent	belligerent	birate	berate	bisycle	bicycle		
billion		birch		bit			
billiords	billiards	bird		bitanical	botanical		
billiun	billion	birden	burden	bite			
billiurds	billiards	bireave	bereave	biteing	biting		
billo	billow	birglar	burglar	biten	bitten		
billow		birlap	burlap	biter	bitter		
billyan	billion	birly	burly	biting			
billyards	billiards	birn	burn	bitray	betray		
billyen	billion	birnish	burnish	bitroth	betroth		
billyerds	billiards	birst	burst	bittar	bitter		
billyin	billion	birth		bitten			
billyirds	billiards	birth	berth	bitter			
billyon	billion	birthday		bittir	bitter		
billyords	billiards	bisan	bison	bittor	bitter		
billyun	billion	biscuit		bittur	bitter		
billyurds	billiards	biscut	biscuit	bitween	between		
bilong	belong	biseech	beseech	bitwixt	betwixt		
biloved	beloved	bisen	bison	bius	bias		
bilow	below	biset	beset	bivewac	bivouac		
bilow	billow	bishap	bishop	bivouac			
bilt	built	bishep	bishop	bivuac	bivouac		
bin		biship	bishop	biwail	bewail		
bin	been	bishop		biware	beware		
binana	banana	bishup	bishop	biway	byway		

biwilder	bewilder	bleach	
biwitch	bewitch	bleack	bleak
biyond	beyond	blead	bled
bizaar	bazaar	blead	bleed
bizaar	bizarre	bleak	
bizarre		bled	
biziness	business	blede	bleed
bizy	busy	bleech	bleach
black		bleeck	bleak
blackboard		bleed	
blackbored	blackboard	bleek	bleak
blacksmith		blemish	
bladdar	bladder	blend	
bladder		bler	blur
bladdir	bladder	blert	blurt
bladdor	bladder	bless	
bladdur	bladder	blessed	
blade		blessid	blessed
blader	bladder	blessing	
blaid	blade	blew	
blaim	blame	blew	blue
blair	blare	blight	
blaize	blaze	blinck	blink
blak	black	blind	
blame		blindfold	
blameless		blindly	
blameliss	blameless	blindness	
blanch		blindniss	blindness
blanck	blank	blined	blind
blancket	blanket	blink	
bland		blir	blur
blank		blirt	blurt
blanket		bliss	
blankit	blanket	blissful	
blare		blistar	blister
blassed	blast	blister	
blast		blistir	blister
blaze		blistor	blister

blistur	blister
blite	blight
blithe	
blizard	blizzard
blizerd	blizzard
blizird	blizzard
blizord	blizzard
blizurd	blizzard
blizzard	
blizzerd	blizzard
blizzird	blizzard
blizzord	blizzard
blizzurd	blizzard
blo	blow
bloan	blown
bloat	
blob	
bloc	
bloc	block
blocade	blockade
bloch	blotch
block	
block	bloc
blockade	
blockaid	blockade
blodder	blotter
bloder	blotter
blok	bloc
blok	block
blokade	blockade
blond	
blonde	
blone	blown
blood	
bloodgeon	bludgeon
bloodshead	bloodshed
bloodshed	
bloodthersty	bloodthirsty

bloodthirsty		bludjun	bludgeon	boald	bold
bloodthursty	bloodthirsty	blue		boalder	boulder
bloody		blue	blew	boalster	bolster
bloom		blueberd	bluebird	boalt	bolt
blosom	blossom	bluebird		boan	bone
blossam	blossom	blueburd	bluebird	boany	bony
blossem	blossom	bluf	bluff	boaquet	bouquet
blossim	blossom	bluff		boar	
blossom		blugean	bludgeon	boar	bore
blossum	blossom	blugein	bludgeon	board	
blot		blugen	bludgeon	boardar	boarder
blotch		blugeon	bludgeon	boarder	
blote	bloat	blugeun	bludgeon	boarder	border
bloter	blotter	blugin	bludgeon	boarding	
blottar	blotter	blujan	bludgeon	boardir	boarder
blotter		blujen	bludgeon	boardor	boarder
blottir	blotter	blujin	bludgeon	boardur	boarder
blottor	blotter	blujon	bludgeon	boarn	born
blottur	blotter	blujun	bludgeon	boast	
blouce	blouse	blume	bloom	boastful	
blouse		blundar	blunder	boat	
blow		blunder		boath	both
blower		blundir	blunder	boatsan	boatswain
blown		blundor	blunder	boatsen	boatswain
blowout		blundur	blunder	boatsin	boatswain
blowse	blouse	blunt		boatson	boatswain
blubbar	blubber	blur		boatsun	boatswain
blubber		blurt		boatswain	
blubbir	blubber	blush		boatswane	boatswain
blubbor	blubber	blustar	bluster	bob	
blubbur	blubber	bluster		bocks	box
bluber	blubber	blustir	bluster	bodily	
blud	blood	blustor	bluster	body	
bludgeon		blustur	bluster	bodygard	bodyguard
bludjan	bludgeon	blythe	blithe	bodygod	bodyguard
bludjen	bludgeon	bo	beau	bodyguard	
bludjin	bludgeon	bo	bow	bodyly	bodily
bludjon	bludgeon	boal	bowl	bofore	before

bog	
bogonia	begonia
boil	
boistarous	boisterous
boisterous	
boistirous	boisterous
boistorous	boisterous
boisturous	boisterous
boks	box
bold	
bolder	boulder
boldness	
boldniss	boldness
bole	bowl
boled	bold
boleder	boulder
bolegged	bowlegged
boligerent	belligerent
boling	bowling
bolligerent	belligerent
bolm	balm
bolm	bomb
bolstar	bolster
bolster	
bolstir	bolster
bolstor	bolster
bolstur	bolster
bolt	
bom	balm
bom	bomb
bomb	
bomb	balm
bombard	
bonana	banana
bond	
bondadge	bondage
bondage	
bondedge	bondage

bondege	bondage
bondidge	bondage
bondige	bondage
bondodge	bondage
bondoge	bondage
bondudge	bondage
bonduge	bondage
bone	
bonet	bonnet
bonevolent	benevolent
boney	bony
bonfier	bonfire
bonfire	
bonit	bonnet
bonnana	banana
bonnet	
bonnit	bonnet
bonoculars	binoculars
bony	
book	
bookace	bookcase
bookase	bookcase
bookcace	bookcase
bookcase	
booklet	
booklit	booklet
boom	
boon	
booquet	bouquet
boosh	bush
booshel	bushel
boosom	bosom
boost	
boot	
booth	
booty	
boozom	bosom
bor	bore

bordar	border
border	
bordir	border
bordor	border
bordur	border
bore	
bore	boar
boreave	bereave
bored	board
boreder	border
born	
borough	
borow	borrow
borro	borrow
borrow	
bosam	bosom
bosem	bosom
bosim	bosom
bosom	
boss	
boste	boast
bosum	bosom
boswain	boatswain
botal	bottle
botam	bottom
botanical	
botany	
bote	boat
boteny	botany
both	
bothar	bother
bother	
bothir	bother
bothor	bother
bothur	bother
botil	bottle
botim	bottom
botiny	botany

botle	bottle	boundory	boundary	bowuls	bowels
botol	bottle	boundry	boundary	bowulz	bowels
botom	bottom	boundury	boundary	box	
botony	botany	bounse	bounce	boxer	
bottal	bottle	bounteful	bountiful	boy	
bottam	bottom	bounteous		boy	buoy
bottel	bottle	bountey	bounty	boyant	buoyant
bottem	bottom	bountiful		boyhood	
bottil	bottle	bountious	bounteous	boyish	
bottim	bottom	bounty		boyl	boil
bottle		bountyful	bountiful	boysterous	boisterous
bottol	bottle	bouquet		brace	
bottom		bout		bracelet	
bottul	bottle	bow		bracelit	bracelet
bottum	bottom	bow	beau	bracket	
botul	bottle	bow	bough	brackit	bracket
botum	bottom	bowals	bowels	brade	braid
botuny	botany	bowalz	bowels	brag	
bough		bowels		braid	
bought		bowelz	bowels	braik	brake
boukay	bouquet	bowils	bowels	braik	break
boulavard	boulevard	bowilz	bowels	brain	
bouldar	boulder	bowl		braisen	brazen
boulder		bowleged	bowlegged	braive	brave
bouldir	boulder	bowlegged		braizen	brazen
bouldor	boulder	bowling		brake	
bouldur	boulder	bownce	bounce	brake	break
boulevard		bownd	bound	braket	bracket
boulivard	boulevard	bowned	bound	brall	brawl
boulovard	boulevard	bownse	bounce	bran	
bouluvard	boulevard	bownteous	bounteous	branch	
bounce		bowntiful	bountiful	brand	
bound		bownty	bounty	brandish	
boundary		bowols	bowels	brandy	
boundery	boundary	bowolz	bowels	brane	brain
boundiry	boundary	bowquet	bouquet	brase	brace
boundless		bowswain	boatswain	braselet	bracelet
boundliss	boundless	bowt	bout	brass	

braught	brought	bredth	breadth	bridesmaid	
brave		breech		bridezmaid	bridesmaid
bravery		breech	breach	bridge	
brawd	broad	breeches		bridil	bridle
brawl		breechez	breeches	bridle	
brawn		breechis	breeches	bridol	bridle
brawny		breechiz	breeches	bridul	bridle
brawt	brought	breed		brief	
brazan	brazen	breef	brief	briefly	
brazen		breese	breeze	brigade	
brazin		breeze		brigaid	brigade
brazon	brazen	breezey	breezy	brigand	
brazun	brazen	breezy		brige	bridge
breach		brefe	brief	briggand	brigand
breach	breech	breif	brief	bright	
breaches	breeches	brekfast	breakfast	brighten	
bread		brest	breast	brightness	
bread	bred	breth	breath	brightniss	brightness
bread	breed	brevaty	brevity	brik	brick
breadth		brevety	brevity	briliant	brilliant
breaf	brief	brevity		brilliance	
break		brevoty	brevity	brillianse	brilliance
break	brake	brevuty	brevity	brilliant	
breakdown		brew		brillient	brilliant
breakfast		brewm	broom	brilliont	brilliant
breakfest	breakfast	brewse	bruise	brilliunt	brilliant
breakfist	breakfast	brewt	brute	brillyant	brilliant
breakfost	breakfast	breze	breeze	brillyent	brilliant
breakfust	breakfast	bribe		brillyint	brilliant
brease	breeze	bribery		brillyont	brilliant
breast		briches	breeches	brillyunt	brilliant
breath		brick		brim	
breathless		bridal	bridle	brinck	brink
breathliss	breathless	bride		brine	
breaze	breeze	bridegroom		bring	
bred		bridegrume	bridegroom	brink	
bred	bread	bridel	bridle	brisal	bristle
brede	breed	bridesmade	bridesmaid	brisel	bristle

brisk		brocade		brothir	brother
brisle	bristle	broccoli		brothor	brother
brisol	bristle	broche	broach	brothur	brother
brissal	bristle	broche	brooch	brought	
brissel	bristle	brockoli	broccoli	brow	
brissil	bristle	brocoli	broccoli	brown	
brissle	bristle	broil		browney	brownie
brissol	bristle	broiler		brownie	
brissul	bristle	brokade	brocade	browny	brownie
bristle		broke		browse	
brisul	bristle	broken		brude	brood
Britain		brokoli	broccoli	bruise	
brital	brittle	broncheal	bronchial	bruize	bruise
Britan	Britain	bronchial		brume	broom
brite	bright	bronckeal	bronchial	brunette	
britel	brittle	bronckial	bronchial	brunt	
Briten	Britain	broncko	bronco	bruse	bruise
britil	brittle	bronco		brush	
Britin	Britain	bronkeal	bronchial	brusk	brusque
British		bronkial	bronchial	brusque	
britol	brittle	bronko	bronco	brutal	
Briton	Britain	bronse	bronze	brutality	
brittal	brittle	bronze		brute	
brittel	brittle	broo	brew	bruteal	brutal
brittil	brittle	brooch		brutel	brutal
brittle		brood		bruther	brother
brittol	brittle	brook		brutil	brutal
brittul	brittle	broom		brutle	brutal
britul	brittle	broonette	brunette	brutol	brutal
Britun	Britain	broose	bruise	brutul	brutal
broacade	brocade	broot	brute	bruze	bruise
broach		brooze	bruise	bubal	bubble
broach	brooch	brored	broad	bubbal	bubble
broad		brorn	brawn	bubbel	bubble
broadcast		broth		bubbil	bubble
broadkast	broadcast	brothar	brother	bubble	
broak	broke	brother		bubbol	bubble
broakade	brocade	brotherhood		bubbul	bubble

bubel	bubble	buffilo	buffalo	bulbous	
bubil	bubble	buffolo	buffalo	bulbus	bulbous
buble	bubble	buffulo	buffalo	bulck	bulk
bubol	bubble	bufilo	buffalo	buldozer	bulldozer
bubul	bubble	bufolo	buffalo	bulet	bullet
bucaneer	buccaneer	bufore	before	buletin	bulletin
buccaneer		bufulo	buffalo	bulevard	boulevard
bucceneer	buccaneer	bug		bulge	
buccineer	buccaneer	bugaboo		buligerent	belligerent
bucconeer	buccaneer	bugal	bugle	bulion	bullion
buccuneer	buccaneer	bugeboo	bugaboo	bulit	bullet
bucher	butcher	bugel	bugle	bulitin	bulletin
buck		buggey	buggy	bulk	
buckal	buckle	buggy		bulky	
buckaneer	buccaneer	bugiboo	bugaboo	bull	
buckel	buckle	bugil	bugle	bulldoazer	bulldozer
bucket		bugle		bulldoser	bulldozer
buckil	buckle	bugoboo	bugaboo	bulldozer	
buckit	bucket	bugol	bugle	bullet	
buckle		bugonia	begonia	bulletin	
buckol	buckle	buguboo	bugaboo	bullevard	boulevard
buckskin		bugul	bugle	bullfight	
bucksom	buxom	bugy	buggy	bullfite	bullfight
buckul	buckle	build		bullian	bullion
bud		building		bullien	bullion
budge		built		bulligerent	belligerent
budget		buk	buck	bullion	
budgit	budget	bukaneer	buccaneer	bullit	bullet
buety	beauty	buket	bucket	bullitin	bulletin
bufalo	buffalo	bukit	bucket	bulliun	bullion
bufay	buffet	bukle	buckle	bullwark	bulwark
bufelo	buffalo	buksom	buxom	bully	
bufet	buffet	bul	bull	bullyan	bullion
buff		bulb		bullyen	bullion
buffalo		bulbas	bulbous	bullyin	bullion
buffay	buffet	bulbess	bulbous	bullyon	bullion
buffelo	buffalo	bulbis	bulbous	bullyun	bullion
buffet		bulbos	bulbous	bulwark	

bulwerk	bulwark	bunoculars	binoculars	burow	bureau
bulwirk	bulwark	bunt		burow	burro
bulwork	bulwark	buny	bunny	burow	burrow
bulwurk	bulwark	buoy		burro	
buly	bully	buoyancy		burro	borough
bumbalbee	bumblebee	buoyant		burro	burrow
bumbelbee	bumblebee	buoyantcy	buoyancy	burrow	
bumbilbee	bumblebee	buoyent	buoyant	burrow	burro
bumblebee		buoyint	buoyant	burst	
bumbolbee	bumblebee	buoyont	buoyant	burth	berth
bumbulbee	bumblebee	buoyunt	buoyant	burth	birth
bume	boom	buquet	bouquet	bury	
bump		burch	birch	buryal	burial
bun		burd	bird	bus	
bunana	banana	burdan	burden	busal	bustle
bunch		burden		busaly	busily
bundal	bundle	burdensome		busel	bustle
bundel	bundle	burdin	burden	busely	busily
bundil	bundle	burdon	burden	buses	
bundle		burdun	burden	bush	
bundol	bundle	bureau		bushal	bushel
bundul	bundle	bureave	bereave	bushel	
bune	boon	burglar		bushey	bushy
bunevolent	benevolent	burglary		bushil	bushel
bungal	bungle	burgler	burglar	bushle	bushel
bungalow		burglir	burglar	bushol	bushel
bungel	bungle	burglor	burglar	bushul	bushel
bungelow	bungalow	burglur	burglar	bushy	
bungil	bungle	burial		busil	bustle
bungilow	bungalow	burlap		busily	
bungle		burly		business	
bungol	bungle	burn		businiss	business
bungolow	bungalow	burnish		busle	bustle
bungul	bungle	buro	borough	busol	bustle
bungulow	bungalow	buro	bureau	busoly	busily
bunk		buro	burro	bussal	bustle
bunnana	banana	buro	burrow	bussel	bustle
bunny		burough	borough	bussil	bustle

bussis	busses	butlur	butler	buy	
bussiz	busses	buton	button	buy	by
bussle	bustle	butor	butter	buyer	
bussol	bustle	butress	buttress	buz	buzz
bussul	bustle	butt		buzaar	bazaar
bust		buttalion	battalion	buzaar	bizarre
bustle		buttan	button	buzard	buzzard
busul	bustle	buttar	butter	buzerd	buzzard
busuly	busily	butten	button	buzird	buzzard
busy		butter		buzord	buzzard
busybody		buttercup		buzurd	buzzard
but		buttermilk		buzy	busy
but	butt	buttin	button	buzz	
butalion	battalion	buttir	butter	buzzard	
butan	button	button		buzzerd	buzzard
butanical	botanical	buttonhole		buzzird	buzzard
butar	butter	buttor	butter	buzzord	buzzard
butchar	butcher	buttress		buzzurd	buzzard
butcher		buttriss	buttress	by	
butchir	butcher	buttun	button	by	buy
butchor	butcher	buttur	butter	byas	bias
butchur	butcher	butun	button	bycicle	bicycle
bute	boot	butur	butter	bycycle	bicycle
buten	button	buty	booty	byke	bike
butin	button	buxam	buxom	byography	biography
butir	butter	buxem	buxom	byology	biology
butlar	butler	buxim	buxom	bypass	
butler		buxom		byproduct	
butlir	butler	buxsom	buxom	bystander	
butlor	butler	buxum	buxom	byway	

C

cab		caban	cabin	cabbige	cabbage
cabage	cabbage	cabanet	cabinet	cabel	cable
cabal	cable	cabbage		caben	cabin

cabenet	cabinet	cafe		caldren	caldron
cabil	cable	cafeine	caffeine	caldrin	caldron
cabin		cafeteria		caldron	
cabinet		caffean	caffeine	caldrun	caldron
cable		caffeen	caffeine	caleco	calico
cabol	cable	caffein		calect	collect
cabon	cabin	caffeine		Calefornia	California
cabonet	cabinet	caffene	caffeine	caleidoscope	kaleidoscope
caboose		cafiteria	cafeteria	calendar	
cabul	cable	cafoteria	cafeteria	calerie	calorie
cabun	cabin	cafuteria	cafeteria	caless	callous
cabunet	cabinet	cage		caless	callus
cabuse	caboose	cahm	calm	calf	
cach	catch	caible	cable	calico	
cache		caidence	cadence	calide	collide
cackal	cackle	caige	cage	California	
cackel	cackle	caike	cake	calindar	calendar
cackil	cackle	cain	cane	calirie	calorie
cackle		caip	cape	calis	callous
cackol	cackle	caipable	capable	calis	callus
cacktus	cactus	cair	care	calkulate	calculate
cackul	cackle	caise	case	call	
cacky	khaki	caive	cave	callapse	collapse
cacoon	cocoon	cake		callas	callous
cactas	cactus	cakle	cackle	callas	callus
cactes	cactus	caktus	cactus	calldron	caldron
cactis	cactus	caky	khaki	callect	collect
cactos	cactus	Calafornia	California	calless	callous
cactus		calako	calico	calless	callus
cadance	cadence	calamity		callico	calico
cadence		calandar	calendar	callide	collide
cadet		calapse	collapse	callis	callous
cadince	cadence	calarie	calorie	callis	callus
cadonce	cadence	calas	callous	callos	callous
cadunce	cadence	calas	callus	callos	callus
caf	calf	calcium		callous	
cafateria	cafeteria	calculate		callus	
cafay	cafe	caldran	caldron	callus	callous

calm		cammand	command
caloco	calico	cammemorate	commemorate
Calofornia	California	cammence	commence
calondar	calendar	cammend	commend
calonial	colonial	cammission	commission
calorie		cammit	commit
calos	callous	cammittee	committee
calos	callus	cammodious	commodious
calossal	colossal	cammodity	commodity
calous	callous	cammotion	commotion
calseum	calcium	cammunicate	communicate
calsium	calcium	cammunion	communion
caluco	calico	cammunity	community
Calufornia	California	cammute	commute
calundar	calendar	camodious	commodious
calurie	calorie	camodity	commodity
calus	callous	camoflage	camouflage
calus	callus	camol	camel
camaflage	camouflage	camora	camera
camal	camel	comotion	commotion
camand	command	camouflage	
camara	camera	camp	
cambine	combine	campaign	
cambustion	combustion	campain	campaign
cameflage	camouflage	campane	campaign
camel		campanion	companion
cameleon	chameleon	campare	compare
camemorate	commemorate	campartment	compartment
camence	commence	campassion	compassion
camend	commend	campatible	compatible
camera		campel	compel
camfor	camphor	campete	compete
camiflage	camouflage	campfier	campfire
camil	camel	campfire	
camira	camera	campfor	camphor
camission	commission	camphar	camphor
camit	commit	campher	camphor
camitee	committee	camphir	camphor

camphor		camphor	
camphur	camphor	camphur	camphor
campile	compile		
camplacent	complacent		
camplain	complain		
camplete	complete		
camplexion	complexion		
camply	comply		
campose	compose		
camposure	composure		
campress	compress		
camprise	comprise		
campulsion	compulsion		
campute	compute		
camra	camera		
camuflage	camouflage		
camul	camel		
camunicate	communicate		
camunion	communion		
camunity	community		
camura	camera		
camute	commute		
can			
Canada			
canal			
canan	cannon		
canan	canon		
canapy	canopy		
canary			
canceal	conceal		
cancede	concede		
canceit	conceit		
canceive	conceive		
cancel			
cancer			
cancern	concern		
cancerto	concerto		
cancession	concession		

cancil	cancel	canfederate	confederate	cannin	canon
canciliate	conciliate	canfer	confer	cannobal	cannibal
cancir	cancer	canfess	confess	cannon	
cancise	concise	canfide	confide	cannon	canon
cancker	canker	canfine	confine	cannubal	cannibal
canclude	conclude	canfirm	confirm	cannun	cannon
cancur	concur	canform	conform	cannun	canon
cancussion	concussion	canfront	confront	canny	
cand	canned	canfuse	confuse	Canoda	Canada
candadate	candidate	cangaroo	kangaroo	canoe	
candal	candle	cangeal	congeal	canon	
candar	candor	cangenial	congenial	canon	cannon
candedate	candidate	cangested	congested	canoo	canoe
candel	candle	cangratulate	congratulate	canopy	
candemn	condemn	canibal	cannibal	cansal	cancel
candense	condense	Canida	Canada	cansar	cancer
cander	candor	canin	cannon	cansecutive	consecutive
candid		canin	canon	cansel	cancel
candidate		canine		cansent	consent
candil	candle	canipy	canopy	canser	cancer
candir	candor	canjecture	conjecture	canservative	conservative
candition	condition	canjunction	conjunction	canserve	conserve
candle		cankar	canker	cansider	consider
candodate	candidate	canker		cansiderable	considerable
candol	candle	cankir	canker	cansiderate	considerate
candor		cankor	canker	cansign	consign
canduct	conduct	cankur	canker	cansil	cancel
candudate	candidate	cannabal	cannibal	cansir	cancer
candul	candle	cannan	cannon	cansist	consist
candur	candor	cannan	canon	cansistent	consistent
candy		cannebal	cannibal	cansol	cancel
cane		cannect	connect	cansole	console
canect	connect	canned		cansolidate	consolidate
Caneda	Canada	cannen	cannon	cansor	cancer
canen	cannon	cannen	canon	canspicuous	conspicuous
canen	canon	canney	canny	canspire	conspire
canepy	canopy	cannibal		canstituent	constituent
canew	canoe	cannin	cannon	canstrain	constrain

canstrict	constrict	cantuloupe	cantaloupe
canstruct	construct	cantur	canter
canstrue	construe	Canuda	Canada
cansul	cancel	canue	canoe
cansult	consult	canun	cannon
cansume	consume	canun	canon
cansur	cancer	canupy	canopy
cantagious	contagious	canvas	
cantain	contain	canvene	convene
cantaloupe		canvenient	convenient
cantaminate	contaminate	canventional	conventional
cantanckerous	cantankerous	canverse	converse
cantankerous		canvert	convert
cantar	canter	canvess	canvas
cantean	canteen	canvey	convey
canteen		canvict	convict
canteloupe	cantaloupe	canvince	convince
cantemporary	contemporary	canvis	canvas
cantempt	contempt	canvos	canvas
cantend	contend	canvulse	convulse
cantene	canteen	canvus	canvas
cantent	content	cany	canny
cantention	contention	canyan	canyon
canter		canyen	canyon
cantest	contest	canyin	canyon
cantiloupe	cantaloupe	canyon	
cantinue	continue	canyun	canyon
cantir	canter	caos	chaos
cantoloupe	cantaloupe	cap	
cantor	canter	capability	
cantort	contort	capable	
cantract	contract	capacity	
cantralto	contralto	capallary	capillary
cantrast	contrast	capar	caper
cantribute	contribute	capatal	capital
cantrite	contrite	Capatol	Capitol
cantrive	contrive	Capatul	Capitol
cantrol	control	capchur	capture

cape	
capeble	capable
capellary	capillary
caper	
capetal	capital
Capetol	Capitol
Capetul	Capitol
capible	capable
capilary	capillary
capillary	
capir	caper
capital	
capitalize	
Capitol	
Capitul	Capitol
capoble	capable
capollary	capillary
capor	caper
capotal	capital
Capotol	Capitol
Capotul	Capitol
capricious	
caprishous	capricious
capsal	capsule
capsel	capsule
capshun	caption
capsil	capsule
capsise	capsize
capsize	
capsol	capsule
capsul	capsule
capsule	
captain	
captan	captain
captar	captor
captavate	captivate
captchur	capture
capten	captain

capter	captor	card		carnaval	carnival
captevate	captivate	cardanal	cardinal	carnaytion	carnation
captin	captain	cardboard		carneval	carnival
caption		cardbored	cardboard	carnige	carnage
captir	captor	cardenal	cardinal	carnival	
captivate		cardinal		carnivorous	
captive		cardonal	cardinal	carnoval	carnival
captivity		cardunal	cardinal	carnuval	carnival
capton	captain	care		carol	
captor		carear	career	carot	carat
captovate	captivate	career		carot	carrot
captun	captain	carefree		carovan	caravan
captur	captor	carefry	carefree	carp	
capture		careful		carpanter	carpenter
captuvate	captivate	carefully		carpenter	
capuble	capable	carel	carol	carpet	
capullary	capillary	careless		carpinter	carpenter
capur	caper	carelessly		carpit	carpet
caputal	capital	carelessness		carponter	carpenter
Caputol	Capitol	careliss	careless	carpunter	carpenter
Caputul	Capitol	carere	career	carrage	carriage
car		caress		carral	corral
caracter	character	caret	carat	carrat	carat
caral	carol	caret	carrot	carrat	carrot
caramel		caretaker		carrect	correct
carat		carevan	caravan	carreer	career
carat	carrot	cargo		carress	caress
caravan		cariage	carriage	carret	carat
carban	carbon	carier	carrier	carret	carrot
carben	carbon	caril	carol	carrey	carry
carbin	carbon	carit	carat	carriage	
carbine		carit	carrot	carrier	
carbohydrate		carivan	caravan	carrige	carriage
carbon		carkass	carcass	carrit	carat
carbun	carbon	carmel	caramel	carrit	carrot
carcass		carnage		carroborate	corroborate
carcos	carcass	carnaition	carnation	carrode	corrode
carcus	carcass	carnation		carrot	

carrot	carat	cash	cache	caste	
carrupt	corrupt	cashear	cashier	castle	
carrut	carat	casheer	cashier	casual	
carrut	carrot	cashere	cashier	casualty	
carry		cashew		casul	castle
carryer	carrier	cashier		casurole	casserole
cart		cashmear	cashmere	cat	
cartalage	cartilage	cashmeer	cashmere	catachism	catechism
cartan	carton	cashmere		catal	cattle
cartelage	cartilage	cashoo	cashew	catalog	
carten	carton	cashue	cashew	catalogue	
cartilage		casil	castle	catapillar	caterpillar
cartin	carton	casirole	casserole	catapult	
cartolage	cartilage	cask		catar	cater
carton		caskade	cascade	cataract	
cartoon		caskaid	cascade	catarpillar	caterpillar
cartridge		casket		catastrophe	
cartrige	cartridge	caskit	casket	catch	
cartulage	cartilage	casle	castle	catcher	
cartun	carton	casm	chasm	catchy	
cartune	cartoon	casol	castle	catechism	
carul	carol	casorole	casserole	catel	cattle
carut	carat	cassal	castle	catelog	catalog
carut	carrot	cassarole	casserole	catepult	catapult
caruvan	caravan	casscade	cascade	cater	
carve		cassed	cast	cateract	cataract
cary	carry	cassel	castle	caterpillar	
casal	castle	casserole		Cathalic	Catholic
casarole	casserole	cassil	castle	catheadral	cathedral
cascade		cassirole	casserole	cathedral	
cascat	casket	cassle	castle	catheedral	cathedral
cascot	casket	cassol	castle	Cathelic	Catholic
cascut	casket	cassorole	casserole	Cathilic	Catholic
case		casstle	castle	Cathlic	Catholic
casel	castle	cassul	castle	Catholic	
casement		cassurole	casserole	Cathulic	Catholic
caserole	casserole	cast		catichism	catechism
cash		cast	caste	catil	cattle

catilog	catalog	cavalier		cayos	chaos
catipult	catapult	cavalry		cayote	coyote
catir	cater	cavarn	cavern	caypable	capable
catiract	cataract	cavaty	cavity	cayse	case
catirpillar	caterpillar	cave		cayve	cave
catle	cattle	cavelcade	cavalcade	cazm	chasm
catochism	catechism	cavelier	cavalier	cazual	casual
catol	cattle	cavelry	cavalry	cazualty	casualty
catolog	catalog	caveman		cead	cede
catopult	catapult	cavern		cealing	ceiling
cator	cater	cavety	cavity	cease	
catoract	cataract	cavilcade	cavalcade	ceaseless	
catorpillar	caterpillar	cavilier	cavalier	ceaseliss	ceaseless
catsup		cavilry	cavalry	cechup	catsup
cattal	cattle	cavirn	cavern	cedar	
cattel	cattle	cavity		cede	
cattil	cattle	cavolcade	cavalcade	ceder	cedar
cattle		cavolier	cavalier	cedir	cedar
cattol	cattle	cavolry	cavalry	cedor	cedar
cattul	cattle	cavorn	cavern	cedur	cedar
catuchism	catechism	cavort		ceed	cede
catul	cattle	cavoty	cavity	ceeling	ceiling
catulog	catalog	cavulcade	cavalcade	ceese	cease
catupult	catapult	cavulier	cavalier	ceiling	
catur	cater	cavulry	cavalry	celabrate	celebrate
caturact	cataract	cavurn	cavern	celar	cellar
caturpillar	caterpillar	cavuty	cavity	celary	celery
caugh	cough	cawf	cough	celebrate	
caught		cawse	cause	celebration	
cauldron	caldron	cawshun	caution	celebrity	
cauliflower		cawt	caught	celer	cellar
cause		cawtion	caution	celery	
caushun	caution	cawtious	cautious	celestial	
caushus	cautious	cawze	cause	celibrate	celebrate
caution		cayak	kayak	celir	cellar
cautious		cayble	cable	celiry	celery
cauze	cause	caydence	cadence	cell	
cavalcade		caynine	canine	cellaphane	cellophane

cellar		cent		cerimony	ceremony
cellebrate	celebrate	centagrade	centigrade	ceromony	ceremony
cellephane	cellophane	centapede	centipede	certain	
celler	cellar	centar	center	certainly	
cellery	celery	centchury	century	certan	certain
celliphane	cellophane	centegrade	centigrade	certen	certain
cellir	cellar	centepede	centipede	certificate	
cellist		centigrade		certify	
cello		centipede		certin	certain
cellophane		centir	center	certon	certain
cellor	cellar	centograde	centigrade	certun	certain
cellulose		centopede	centipede	cerumony	ceremony
celluphane	cellophane	centor	center	cesation	cessation
cellur	cellar	central		cessation	
celo	cello	centrally		cetchup	catsup
celobrate	celebrate	centrel	central	cevilian	civilian
celophane	cellophane	centril	central	chafe	
celor	cellar	control	central	chagrin	
celory	celery	centrul	central	chaif	chafe
celubrate	celebrate	centugrade	centigrade	chaimber	chamber
celulose	cellulose	centupede	centipede	chain	
celur	cellar	centur	center	chainge	change
celury	celery	century		chair	
cematery	cemetery	ceramics		chairman	
cement		ceramony	ceremony	chaise	
cemetery		cercle	circle	chaise	chase
cemitery	cemetery	cercuit	circuit	chaiste	chaste
cemotery	cemetery	cercuitous	circuitous	chalenge	challenge
cemutery	cemetery	cercular	circular	chalice	
cenchury	century	cerculate	circulate	chalis	chalice
censas	census	cercumference	circumference	chalk	
censess	census	cercumstance	circumstance	challange	challenge
censhoor	censure	cercumvent	circumvent	challenge	
censhure	censure	cercus	circus	challenger	
censis	census	cereal		challice	chalice
censos	census	ceremonial		challinge	challenge
censure		ceremony		challonge	challenge
census		cerial	cereal	challunge	challenge

chambar	chamber	chanul	channel	charm	
chamber		chaos		charming	
chambir	chamber	chaotic		charoty	charity
chambor	chamber	chap		charriot	chariot
chambur	chamber	chapal	chapel	chart	
chamealeon	chameleon	chapel		chartar	charter
chameber	chamber	chapil	chapel	charter	
chameeleon	chameleon	chaplain		chartir	charter
chameleon		chaplan	chaplain	chartor	charter
champeon	champion	chaplen	chaplain	chartur	charter
champion		chaplin	chaplain	charuty	charity
championship		chaplon	chaplain	charyot	chariot
chanal	channel	chaplun	chaplain	chasam	chasm
chance		chapol	chapel	chasan	chasten
chancellor		chaptar	chapter	chase	
chancelor	chancellor	chapter		chasem	chasm
chancillor	chancellor	chaptir	chapter	chasen	chasten
chancilor	chancellor	chaptor	chapter	chasie	chassis
chandalier	chandelier	chaptur	chapter	chasim	chasm
chandelier		chapul	chapel	chasin	chasten
chandilier	chandelier	char		chasis	chassis
chandolier	chandelier	character		chasm	
chandulier	chandelier	characteristic		chasom	chasm
chane	chain	characterize		chason	chasten
chanel	channel	charaty	charity	chassie	chassis
changable	changeable	charcoal		chassis	
change		charcole	charcoal	chassy	chassis
changeable		chare	chair	chaste	
chanil	channel	charety	charity	chasten	
channal	channel	charge		chastise	
channel		charickter	character	chastize	chastise
channil	channel	charicter	character	chasum	chasm
channol	channel	charikter	character	chasun	chasten
channul	channel	chariot		chasy	chassis
chanol	channel	charitable		chat	
chanse	chance	charity		chatar	chatter
chansellor	chancellor	charkoal	charcoal	chateau	
chant		charkole	charcoal	chater	chatter

chatir	chatter	**cheet**	cheat	**chete**	cheat
chato	chateau	**cheeze**	cheese	chew	
chator	chatter	**chegrin**	chagrin	**chewse**	choose
chatow	chateau	**cheif**	chief	**chez**	chaise
chattar	chatter	**chek**	check	**cheze**	cheese
chatter		**chekars**	checkers	**chickan**	chicken
chattir	chatter	**cheke**	cheek	chicken	
chattor	chatter	**chekers**	checkers	**chickin**	chicken
chattur	chatter	**chekirs**	checkers	**chickon**	chicken
chatur	chatter	**chekors**	checkers	**chickun**	chicken
chaufar	chauffeur	**chekurs**	checkers	chide	
chaufer	chauffeur	**chello**	cello	**chied**	chide
chaufeur	chauffeur	**chemacal**	chemical	chief	
chauffer	chauffeur	**chemecal**	chemical	chiefly	
chauffeur		chemical		chieftain	
chaufir	chauffeur	chemist		**chieftan**	chieftain
chaufor	chauffeur	chemistry		**chieften**	chieftain
chaufur	chauffeur	**chemocal**	chemical	**chieftin**	chieftain
chawk	chalk	**chemucal**	chemical	**chiefton**	chieftain
chazm	chasm	**chepe**	cheap	**chieftun**	chieftain
cheaf	chief	**cherab**	cherub	**chigrin**	chagrin
cheak	cheek	**cherch**	church	**chiken**	chicken
cheap		**chere**	cheer	**chil**	chill
chear	cheer	**chereb**	cherub	child	
chease	cheese	**cherib**	cherub	childhood	
cheat		cherish		**childhud**	childhood
check		**chern**	churn	childish	
checkars	checkers	**cherob**	cherub	**childran**	children
checkers		**cherrish**	cherish	children	
checkirs	checkers	**cherrub**	cherub	**childrin**	children
checkors	checkers	cherry		**childron**	children
checkurs	checkers	cherub		**childrun**	children
cheef	chief	**chery**	cherry	**chiled**	child
cheek		**ches**	chess	chill	
cheep	cheap	**chese**	cheese	chilly	
cheer		chess		**chily**	chilly
cheerful		chest		**chimaney**	chimney
cheese		chestnut		chime	

chimeney	chimney	chlorean	chlorine	chopy	choppy
chiminy	chimney	chloreen	chlorine	choras	chorus
chimney		chlorene	chlorine	chord	
chimny	chimney	chlorephyll	chlorophyll	chore	
chimony	chimney	chlorine		choress	chorus
chimpanzee		chloriphyll	chlorophyll	choris	chorus
chimuny	chimney	chlorophyll		chork	chalk
chin		chloruphyll	chlorophyll	choros	chorus
china		choak	choke	chorus	
China		choar	chore	chose	
Chinease	Chinese	choase	chose	chosen	
Chineaze	Chinese	choaze	chose	chowdar	chowder
Chineese	Chinese	chocalate	chocolate	chowder	
Chineeze	Chinese	chockolate	chocolate	chowdir	chowder
Chinese		choclate	chocolate	chowdor	chowder
Chineze	Chinese	chocolate		chowdur	chowder
chip		choculate	chocolate	choyce	choice
chipmonk	chipmunk	chogrin	chagrin	choyse	choice
chipmunk		choice		choze	chose
chirch	church	choir		chrisan-	chrysan-
chirn	churn	choise	choice	themum	themum
chisal	chisel	chok	chalk	Christ	
chisel		chok	choke	christan	christen
chisil	chisel	choke		christen	
chisol	chisel	chokolate	chocolate	christening	
chisul	chisel	cholara	cholera	Christian	
chivalrous		cholera		Christianity	
chivalry		cholira	cholera	Christien	Christian
chivelry	chivalry	chollera	cholera	christin	christen
chivilry	chivalry	cholora	cholera	Christion	Christian
chivolry	chivalry	cholura	cholera	Christiun	Christian
chivulry	chivalry	choo	chew	Christmas	
chizal	chisel	choose		Christmes	Christmas
chizel	chisel	chop		Christmis	Christmas
chizil	chisel	choppy		Christmos	Christmas
chizol	chisel	chopsticks		Christmus	Christmas
chizul	chisel	chopstiks	chopsticks	christon	christen
chloraphyll	chlorophyll	chopstix	chopsticks	christun	christen

Christyin	Christian	cifer	cipher	ciramics	ceramics
chromeum	chromium	cigar		circal	circle
chromium		cigarette		circkit	circuit
chronacle	chronicle	cigerette	cigarette	circkle	circle
chronecle	chronicle	cigirette	cigarette	circkuitous	circuitous
chronic		cigorette	cigarette	circkular	circular
chronick	chronic	cigurette	cigarette	circkulate	circulate
chronicle		ciklone	cyclone	circkum-	circum-
chronik	chronic	cilestial	celestial	ference	ference
chronocle	chronicle	cilinder	cylinder	circkumstance	circumstance
chronucle	chronicle	cimbal	cymbal	circkumvent	circumvent
chrysanthemum		ciment	cement	circkus	circus
chubby		cinama	cinema	circle	
chuby	chubby	cinamon	cinnamon	circol	circle
chuckal	chuckle	cinch		circuit	
chuckel	chuckle	cindar	cinder	circuitous	
chuckil	chuckle	cinder		circul	circle
chuckle		cindir	cinder	circular	
chuckol	chuckle	cindor	cinder	circulate	
chuckul	chuckle	cindur	cinder	circulation	
chue	chew	cinema		circulatory	
chugrin	chagrin	cinemon	cinnamon	circumference	
chukle	chuckle	cinima	cinema	circumstance	
chum		cinimon	cinnamon	circumvent	
chunck	chunk	cinnamon		circus	
chunk		cinnimon	cinnamon	circut	circuit
church		cinnomon	cinnamon	cirkit	circuit
churn		cinnumon	cinnamon	cirkle	circle
chuse	choose	cinoma	cinema	cirkuitous	circuitous
chute		cinomon	cinnamon	cirkular	circular
cicle	cycle	cinuma	cinema	cirkulate	circulate
ciclone	cyclone	cinumon	cinnamon	cirkumference	circumference
cidar	cider	ciphar	cipher	cirkumstance	circumstance
cider		cipher		cirkumvent	circumvent
cidir	cider	ciphir	cipher	cirkus	circus
cidor	cider	ciphor	cipher	cirtificate	certificate
cidur	cider	ciphur	cipher	cisstern	cistern
cieling	ceiling	cipress	cypress	cistern	

citadel		clammy		classification	
citation		clamor		classify	
citazen	citizen	clamorous		classik	classic
cite		clamp		classmait	classmate
citedel	citadel	clamur	clamor	classmate	
citezen	citizen	clamy	clammy	classofy	classify
citidel	citadel	clan		classroom	
citisen	citizen	clap		classufy	classify
citizen		clarafy	clarify	clasufy	classify
citizenship		claranet	clarinet	clatar	clatter
citodel	citadel	claraty	clarity	clater	clatter
citozen	citizen	clarefy	clarify	clatir	clatter
citras	citrus	clarenet	clarinet	clator	clatter
citress	citrus	clareon	clarion	clattar	clatter
citris	citrus	clarety	clarity	clatter	
citros	citrus	clarify		clattir	clatter
citrus		clarinet		clattor	clatter
citudel	citadel	clarion		clattur	clatter
cituzen	citizen	clarity		clatur	clatter
city		clarofy	clarify	clause	
cival	civil	claronet	clarinet	claw	
civel	civil	claroty	clarity	clawse	clause
civic		clarufy	clarify	clawth	cloth
civik	civic	clarunet	clarinet	clawze	clause
civil		claruty	clarity	clay	
civilian		clasafy	classify	cleak	clique
civility		clasefy	classify	clean	
civilization		clash		cleanliness	
civilize		clasic	classic	cleanlyness	cleanliness
civol	civil	clasify	classify	cleanse	
civul	civil	clasofy	classify	cleanser	
clad		clasp		cleanze	cleanse
claim		class		clear	
clam		classafy	classify	clearly	
clamar	clamor	classefy	classify	cleat	
clame	claim	classic		cleavage	
clamer	clamor	classical		cleave	
clamir	clamor	classick	classic	cleaveage	cleavage

cleaver		client		close	
cleavige	cleavage	cliff		closely	
cleek	clique	clik	click	closeness	
cleen	clean	climacks	climax	closeniss	closeness
cleer	clear	climaks	climax	closet	
cleet	cleat	climate		closit	closet
cleeve	cleave	climax		clot	
clef		climb		cloth	
cleft		clime	climb	clothe	
cleke	clique	climit	climate	clotheing	clothing
clemancy	clemency	clinch		clothes	
clemency		cling		clothespin	
clemincy	clemency	cliont	client	clothez	clothes
clemoncy	clemency	clip		clothing	
clemuncy	clemency	cliping	clipping	cloud	
clench		clipper		cloudy	
clene	clean	clipping		clout	
clenliness	cleanliness	clique		clovar	clover
clense	cleanse	clirk	clerk	clove	
clenze	cleanse	cliunt	client	clover	
cleracal	clerical	cloak		clovir	clover
clere	clear	cloase	close	clovor	clover
clerecal	clerical	cloave	clove	clovur	clover
clergy		cloaze	close	clowd	cloud
clerical		cloaze	clothes		
clerk		clock		clowt	clout
clerocal	clerical	clod		cloyster	cloister
clerucal	clerical	clog		cloz	clause
clete	cleat	cloistar	cloister	cloze	close
clevar	clever	cloister		cloze	clothes
cleve	cleave	cloistir	cloister	clozet	closet
clever		cloistor	cloister	clozit	closet
clevir	clever	cloistur	cloister	club	
clevor	clever	clok	clock	cluch	clutch
clevur	clever	cloke	cloak	clue	
clew	clue	cloo	clue	clump	
cliant	client	clorine	chlorine	clumsy	
click		clorophyll	chlorophyll	clumzy	clumsy

clung		coastel	coastal
clurk	clerk	coastil	coastal
clustar	cluster	coastol	coastal
cluster		coastul	coastal
clustir	cluster	coat	
clustor	cluster	coave	cove
clustur	cluster	coax	
clutar	clutter	cob	
clutch		cobalstone	cobblestone
cluter	clutter	cobalt	
clutir	clutter	cobbalstone	cobblestone
clutor	clutter	cobbelstone	cobblestone
cluttar	clutter	cobbilstone	cobblestone
clutter		cobblar	cobbler
cluttir	clutter	cobbler	
cluttor	clutter	cobblestone	
cluttur	clutter	cobblir	cobbler
clutur	clutter	cobblor	cobbler
coach		cobblur	cobbler
coacks	coax	cobbolstone	cobblestone
coad	code	cobbulstone	cobblestone
coagulate		cobelstone	cobblestone
coak	coke	cobilstone	cobblestone
coaks	coax	coblar	cobbler
coal		cobler	cobbler
coala	koala	coblestone	cobblestone
coalt	colt	coblir	cobbler
coam	comb	coblor	cobbler
coan	cone	coblur	cobbler
coar	core	cobolstone	cobblestone
coar	corps	cobolt	cobalt
coard	chord	coboose	caboose
coarse		cobra	
coarse	course	cobulstone	cobblestone
coart	court	cobweb	
coartship	courtship	coche	coach
coast		cock	
coastal		cockaroach	cockroach

cockpit	
cockroach	
cockroche	cockroach
cockswain	coxswain
cocky	
coco	cocoa
cocoa	
coconut	
cocoon	
cocune	cocoon
cod	
coddal	coddle
coddel	coddle
coddil	coddle
coddle	
coddol	coddle
coddul	coddle
code	
codet	cadet
codgar	codger
codger	
codgir	codger
codgor	codger
codgur	codger
codle	coddle
coerce	
coerse	coerce
cofan	coffin
cofee	coffee
cofen	coffin
coffan	coffin
coffee	
coffen	coffin
coffey	coffee
coffin	
coffon	coffin
coffun	coffin
cofin	coffin

cofon	coffin
cofun	coffin
cog	
coger	codger
coil	
coin	
coincide	
coincidence	
cok	cock
coke	
cokes	coax
coko	cocoa
cokonut	coconut
cokpit	cockpit
cokroach	cockroach
cokswain	coxswain
coky	cocky
colam	column
colamity	calamity
colan	colon
colany	colony
colapse	collapse
colar	collar
cold	
coldron	caldron
cole	coal
coleague	colleague
colect	collect
colege	college
colem	column
colen	colon
coleny	colony
colera	cholera
colide	collide
colie	collie
coliflower	cauliflower
colige	college
colim	column

colin	colon
coliny	colony
colir	collar
coll	call
collapse	
collar	
colleag	colleague
colleague	
collect	
collection	
collector	
colleeg	colleague
college	
coller	collar
colley	collie
collide	
collie	
colliflower	cauliflower
collige	college
collir	collar
collishun	collision
collision	
collizion	collision
collor	collar
collosal	colossal
collossal	colossal
collumn	column
collur	collar
colly	collie
colom	column
colon	
colonel	
colonial	
colonist	
colony	
color	
Colorado	
colored	

colorful	
coloring	
colossal	
colt	
colum	column
column	
colun	colon
coluny	colony
comady	comedy
coman	common
comand	command
comb	
combat	
combatant	
combination	
combine	
combustible	
combustion	
come	
comedian	
comedy	
comeing	coming
comeley	comely
comeliness	
comely	
comelyness	comeliness
comemorate	commemorate
comen	common
comence	commence
comend	commend
coment	comment
comerce	commerce
comet	
comfart	comfort
comfert	comfort
comfirt	comfort
comfort	
comfortable	

comfurt	comfort
comic	
comical	
comidy	comedy
comik	comic
comin	common
coming	
comission	commission
comit	comet
comit	commit
comittee	committee
comma	
comman	common
command	
commander	
commandment	
commemorate	
commen	common
commence	
commencement	
commend	
commendation	
commense	commence
comment	
commer	coma
commer	comma
commerce	
commercial	
commerse	commerce
commin	common
commirce	commerce
commision	commission
commission	
commissioner	
commit	
committee	
commodious	
commodity	

common	
commonly	
commonplace	
commonwealth	
commotion	
commun	common
communicable	
communicate	
communication	
communion	
community	
commurce	commerce
commute	
commuter	
comodious	commodious
comodity	commodity
comody	comedy
comon	common
comotion	commotion
compact	
compair	compare
compakt	compact
companion	
companionship	
compansate	compensate
company	
comparable	
comparative	
comparatively	
compare	
compareable	comparable
compareson	comparison
comparetive	comparative
comparison	
compartment	
compasion	compassion
compass	
compassion	

compassionate	
compatent	competent
compatible	
compeat	compete
compeet	compete
compel	
compell	compel
compensate	
compensation	
compeny	company
compess	compass
compete	
competent	
competition	
competitive	
competitor	
compile	
compinsate	compensate
compiny	company
compiss	compass
compitent	competent
complacate	complicate
complacency	
complacent	
complain	
complaint	
complament	complement
complament	compliment
complane	complain
compleat	complete
complecate	complicate
complecks	complex
complecktion	complexion
compleet	complete
compleks	complex
complektion	complexion
complement	
complete	

completely	
completion	
complex	
complexion	
complexity	
complicate	
complicated	
complication	
compliment	
compliment	complement
complimentary	
complocate	complicate
comploment	complement
complucate	complicate
complument	complement
complument	compliment
comply	
componsate	compensate
compony	company
compose	
composer	
composite	
composition	
composs	compass
composure	
compotent	competent
compound	
compownd	compound
compoze	compose
compozure	composure
compramise	compromise
comprehend	
comprehension	
comprehensive	
compremise	compromise
compress	
compressor	
comprihend	comprehend

comprihensive	comprehensive
comprimise	compromise
comprise	
comprize	comprise
compromise	
comprumise	compromise
compulsion	
compulsory	
compultion	compulsion
compunsate	compensate
compuny	company
compuss	compass
computation	
compute	
computeation	computation
computent	competent
comrade	
comudy	comedy
comun	common
comunicate	communicate
comunion	communion
comunity	community
comute	commute
con	
conal	canal
conary	canary
concaive	concave
concar	concur
concave	
concead	concede
conceal	
concealment	
conceat	conceit
conceave	conceive
concede	
conceed	concede
conceel	conceal
conceet	conceit

conceeve	conceive
conceit	
conceited	
conceivable	
conceive	
conceiveable	conceivable
concele	conceal
concentrate	
concentration	
concept	
conception	
concern	
concerned	
concert	
concerto	
conceshion	concession
concession	
concete	conceit
conceve	conceive
concherto	concerto
conciet	conceit
concieve	conceive
conciliate	
concintrate	concentrate
concise	
conclude	
conclusion	
conclusive	
concoard	concord
concoarse	concourse
concoct	
concor	concur
concord	
concorse	concourse
concourse	
concreat	concrete
concreet	concrete
concrete	

concur		confiscate	
concushion	concussion	conflagration	
concussion		conflegration	conflagration
concwest	conquest	conflict	
condem	condemn	confligration	conflagration
condemn		conflikt	conflict
condemnation		conflogration	conflagration
condensation		conflugration	conflagration
condense		conform	
condescend		conformity	
condesend	condescend	confound	
condisend	condescend	confownd	confound
condishun	condition	confront	
condition		confrunt	confront
conditional		confurm	confirm
conduct		confuse	
conductor		confusion	
condukt	conduct	confuze	confuse
cone		congeal	
conect	connect	congeanial	congenial
confederacy		congecture	conjecture
confederate		congeel	congeal
confederation		congeenial	congenial
confer		congele	congeal
conference		congenial	
conferm	confirm	conger	conjure
confess		congested	
confession		congrachulate	congratulate
confide		congradulate	congratulate
confidence		congragate	congregate
confident		congratulate	
confidential		congratulation	
confied	confide	congregate	
confine		congregation	
confinement		congress	
confirm		congrigate	congregate
confirmation		congriss	congress
confirmed		congrogate	congregate

congrugate	congregate
conjar	conjure
conjecture	
conjekture	conjecture
conjer	conjure
conjir	conjure
conjor	conjure
conjunction	
conjunktion	conjunction
conjure	
conkar	conquer
conkave	concave
conker	conquer
conkir	conquer
conklude	conclude
conkoct	concoct
conkokt	concoct
conkor	conquer
conkord	concord
conkourse	concourse
conkrete	concrete
conkur	concur
conkur	conquer
conkussion	concussion
conkwest	conquest
connect	
Connecticut	
connection	
connekt	connect
Conneticut	Connecticut
conoe	canoe
conquer	
conqueror	
conquest	
consacrate	consecrate
consal	consul
consammate	consummate
consanant	consonant

consantrate	concentrate	conseve	conceive	consolation	
consaquence	consequence	conshance	conscience	console	
conscience		conshanse	conscience	consolidate	
conscientious		conshas	conscious	consommate	consummate
conscious		conshence	conscience	consonant	
consciousness		conshense	conscience	consontrate	concentrate
conscius	conscious	conshess	conscious	consoom	consume
consead	concede	conshince	conscience	consoquence	consequence
conseal	conceal	conshinse	conscience	consort	
conseat	conceit	conshis	conscious	conspicuous	
conseave	conceive	conshonce	conscience	conspier	conspire
consecrate		conshonse	conscience	conspikuous	conspicuous
consecutive		conshos	conscious	conspiracy	
consede	concede	conshunce	conscience	conspirator	
conseed	concede	conshunse	conscience	conspire	
conseel	conceal	conshus	conscious	constable	
conseet	conceit	consicrate	consecrate	constallation	constellation
conseeve	conceive	consider		constant	
conseit	conceit	considerable		constantly	
conseive	conceive	considerate		constarnation	consternation
consekutive	consecutive	consideration		constatute	constitute
consel	consul	consieve	conceive	consteble	constable
consele	conceal	consign		constellation	
consemmate	consummate	consil	consul	constent	constant
consenant	consonant	consiliate	conciliate	consternation	
consent		consimmate	consummate	constetute	constitute
consentrate	concentrate	consinant	consonant	constible	constable
consept	concept	consine	consign	constichuent	constituent
consequence		consintrate	concentrate	constillation	constellation
consequently		consiquence	consequence	constint	constant
consern	concern	consirvative	conservative	constirnation	consternation
consert	concert	consirve	conserve	constituent	
conserve		consise	concise	constitute	
conservation		consistency		constitution	
conservative		consistent		constitutional	
conseshion	concession	consoal	console	constoble	constable
consession	concession	consocrate	consecrate	constollation	constellation
consete	conceit	consol	consul	constont	constant

constornation	consternation	contamplate	contemplate	contract	
constotute	constitute	contane	contain	contraction	
constrain		contanent	continent	contractor	
constraint		contanuity	continuity	contradict	
constrane	constrain	contemplate		contradiction	
constrew	construe	contemplation		contradictory	
constrict		contemporary		contrakt	contract
constrikt	constrict	contempt		contralto	
construct		contemptible		contrary	
construction		contemptuous		contrast	
constructive		contemt	contempt	contraversy	controversy
construe		contend		contreband	contraband
construkt	construct	contenent	continent	contredict	contradict
constuble	constable	content		contrery	contrary
constullation	constellation	contented		contrerry	contrary
constunt	constant	contention		contreversy	controversy
consturnation	consternation	contentment		contriband	contraband
constutute	constitute	contenuity	continuity	contribute	
consucrate	consecrate	contest		contribution	
consul		contestant		contridict	contradict
consult		contestent	contestant	contrite	
consume		contimplate	contemplate	contrive	
consumer		continent		contriversy	controversy
consummate		continental		controal	control
consummation		continual		controband	contraband
consumption		continually		controdict	contradict
consumtion	consumption	continuation		control	
consunant	consonant	continue		controversy	
consuntrate	concentrate	continuity		contruband	contraband
consuquence	consequence	continuous		contrudict	contradict
consurvative	conservative	continuously		contruversy	controversy
consurve	conserve	contomplate	contemplate	contumplate	contemplate
contact		contonent	continent	contunent	continent
contagious		contonuity	continuity	contunuity	continuity
contain		contort		conture	contour
container		contortion		convalesce	
contakt	contact	contour		convalescent	
contaminate		contraband		convay	convey

convecks	convex	coop		**corgial**	cordial
conveks	convex	cooperate		**corgiel**	cordial
convelesce	convalesce	cooperation		**coril**	coral
convene		cooperative		**corination**	coronation
convenience		**coopon**	coupon	**corinet**	coronet
convenient		coordinate		**corjal**	cordial
convent		**copacity**	capacity	**corjel**	cordial
convention		cope		**corjil**	cordial
conventional		**copeous**	copious	**corjol**	cordial
conversation		copious		**corjul**	cordial
converse		**coppar**	copper	cork	
conversion		copper		corkscrew	
convert		**coppir**	copper	**corkscrue**	corkscrew
convertible		**coppor**	copper	**corkskrew**	corkscrew
convertion	conversion	**coppur**	copper	**corkskrue**	corkscrew
converzion	conversion	**coppy**	copy	corn	
convex		**copricious**	capricious	**cornacopia**	cornucopia
convey		copy		**cornar**	corner
conveyance		coral		cornea	
convict		**coranation**	coronation	**cornecopia**	cornucopia
conviction		**coranet**	coronet	corner	
convilesce	convalesce	cord		**cornfeald**	cornfield
convince		cord	chord	cornfield	
convinse	convince	**cordaroy**	corduroy	**cornia**	cornea
convolesce	convalesce	**corderoy**	corduroy	cornice	
convoy		cordial		**cornicopia**	cornucopia
convulesce	convalesce	cordiality		**cornir**	corner
convulse		**cordiroy**	corduroy	**cornis**	cornice
convulsion		**cordoroy**	corduroy	**cornocopia**	cornucopia
convulsive		corduroy		**cornor**	corner
cood	could	core		cornstarch	
cook		core	corps	cornucopia	
cookie		**cored**	chord	**cornur**	corner
cooky		**coreer**	career	**corol**	coral
cool		**corel**	coral	coronation	
cooley	coolie	**corenation**	coronation	coronet	
coolie		**corenet**	coronet	**corparal**	corporal
cooly	coolie	**coress**	caress	**corparation**	corporation

corpascle	corpuscle	corrudor	corridor	cotton	
corperal	corporal	corrugate		cottun	cotton
corperation	corporation	corrupt		couch	
corpescle	corpuscle	corruption		coud	could
corpiral	corporal	corruspond	correspond	cougar	
corpiration	corporation	corsage		couger	cougar
corpiscle	corpuscle	corsarge	corsage	cough	
corporal		corse	coarse	cought	caught
corporation		corse	course	cougir	cougar
corposcle	corpuscle	corset		cougor	cougar
corps		corsit	corset	cougur	cougar
corpse		cort	court	could	
corpulent		cortship	courtship	couldn't	
corpural	corporal	corul	coral	council	
corpuration	corporation	corunation	coronation	councillor	councilor
corpuscle		corunet	coronet	councilor	
corrador	corridor	corus	chorus	counsal	council
corragate	corrugate	cosmetic		counsel	
corral		cosmic		counsel	council
corraspond	correspond	cosmos		counsellor	counselor
correct		cost		counselor	
correction		coste	coast	counsil	council
correctly		costewm	costume	counsol	council
corredor	corridor	costly		counsul	council
corregate	corrugate	costoom	costume	count	
correkt	correct	costume		countanance	countenance
correspond		cosy	cozy	countar	counter
correspondence		cot		countarfeit	counterfeit
correspondent		cotage	cottage	countenance	
corridor		cotastrophe	catastrophe	counter	
corrigate	corrugate	cote	coat	counteract	
corrispond	correspond	cothedral	cathedral	counterclockwise	
corroad	corrode	cotion	caution	counterfeit	
corroborate		cotious	cautious	counterpart	
corrode		cottage		countersign	
corrodor	corridor	cottan	cotton	countersine	countersign
corrogate	corrugate	cotten	cotton	countess	
corrospond	correspond	cottin	cotton	countinance	countenance

countir	counter	cousun	cousin	cowntess	countess
countirfeit	counterfeit	couzin	cousin	cownty	county
countiss	countess	covanant	covenant	cowoperate	cooperate
countless		cove		cowor	cower
countliss	countless	covenant		coword	coward
countonance	countenance	cover		cowordinate	coordinate
countor	counter	covert		cowur	cower
countorfeit	counterfeit	covet		cowurd	coward
country		covetous		coxsan	coxswain
countunance	countenance	covey		coxsen	coxswain
countur	counter	covinant	covenant	coxsin	coxswain
counturfeit	counterfeit	covit	covet	coxson	coxswain
county		covonant	covenant	coxsun	coxswain
coupal	couple	covort	cavort	coxswain	
coupel	couple	covunant	covenant	coy	
coupil	couple	covy	covey	coyote	
couple		cow		coz	cause
coupol	couple	cowala	koala	cozmetic	cosmetic
coupon		cowar	cower	cozmic	cosmic
coupul	couple	coward		cozmos	cosmos
courage		cowardice		cozy	
courageous		cowardly		crab	
courier		cowboy		crack	
course		cowch	couch	crackal	crackle
course	coarse	cower		crackel	crackle
court		cowerd	coward	cracker	
courtasy	courtesy	cowgirl		crackil	crackle
courteous		cowhand		crackle	
courtesy		cowhide		crackol	crackle
courtious	courteous	cowir	cower	crackul	crackle
courtisy	courtesy	cowird	coward	cradal	cradle
courtosy	courtesy	cowl		cradel	cradle
courtship		cowncil	council	cradil	cradle
courtusy	courtesy	cownsel	counsel	cradle	
cousan	cousin	cownt	count	cradol	cradle
cousen	cousin	cowntenance	countenance	cradul	cradle
cousin		cownter	counter	craft	
couson	cousin	cownterfeit	counterfeit	craftsman	

crafty		crawl		crepe	
crag		crayon		crepe	creep
crain	crane	craze		crepey	creepy
crainium	cranium	crazey	crazy	cresant	crescent
craip	crape	crazy		crescent	
craip	crepe	cread	creed	crese	crease
crait	crate	creak		cresent	crescent
craiter	crater	creak	creek	cresint	crescent
craive	crave	creaky		cresont	crescent
craize	craze	cream		cressent	crescent
craizy	crazy	creamery		crest	
crak	crack	creamy		crestfallen	
crakle	crackle	creap	creep	cresunt	crescent
crall	crawl	creapy	creepy	crevat	cravat
cram		crease		crevice	
cramp		creast	crest	crevis	crevice
cranberry		creatcher	creature	crew	
cranck	crank	create		crewel	cruel
crancky	cranky	creation		crewet	cruet
crane		creative		criate	create
craneum	cranium	creator		crib	
cranium		creature		cricket	
crank		crede	creed	crickit	cricket
cranky		credit		criket	cricket
crape		creditor		crikit	cricket
crape	crepe	credulous		crimanal	criminal
crash		creecher	creature	crime	
cratar	crater	creed		crimenal	criminal
crate		creek		criminal	
crater		creek	creak	crimonal	criminal
cratir	crater	creem	cream	crimsan	crimson
crator	crater	creep		crimsen	crimson
cratur	crater	creepy		crimsin	crimson
craul	crawl	creese	crease	crimson	
cravat		creeture	creature	crimsun	crimson
crave		creke	creak	crimunal	criminal
craveing	craving	creke	creek	crimzon	crimson
craving		creme	cream	crinckle	crinkle

cringe		crocas	crocus	croop	croup
crinkal	crinkle	crocay	croquet	croose	cruise
crinkel	crinkle	croch	crotch	crooshal	crucial
crinkil	crinkle	crochay	crochet	crooshel	crucial
crinkle		crochet		crooze	cruise
crinkol	crinkle	crock		crop	
crinkul	crinkle	crockary	crockery	croquet	
crippal	cripple	crockery		croquet	croquette
crippel	cripple	crockiry	crockery	croquette	
crippil	cripple	crockodile	crocodile	croshay	crochet
cripple		crockory	crockery	cross	
crippol	cripple	crockury	crockery	crossing	
crippul	cripple	crocodile		crotch	
crisanthe-mum	chrysanthe-mum	crocos	crocus	crouch	
		crocudile	crocodile	croup	
criscross	crisscross	crocus		croutch	crouch
crisen	christen	crok	croak	crovat	cravat
crisis		crok	crock	crow	
criskross	crisscross	crokay	croquet	crowch	crouch
crisp		croke	croak	crowd	
crisscross		crokette	croquette	crown	
crissen	christen	crokodile	crocodile	crowquette	croquette
crisskross	crisscross	crokus	crocus	cruch	crutch
Crist	Christ	cromeum	chromium	crucial	
cristen	christen	cromium	chromium	crucifix	
Cristmas	Christmas	croney	crony	crucifixion	
critic		cronic	chronic	crucify	
critical		cronicle	chronicle	crude	
criticism		crony		crue	crew
criticize		croo	crew	cruel	
critik	critic	croocial	crucial	cruelty	
critisize	criticize	crood	crude	cruet	
crivat	cravat	crooet	cruet	cruise	
cro	crow	crook		cruiser	
croak		crooked		cruit	cruet
croany	crony	crookid	crooked	cruize	cruise
croaquette	croquette	crool	cruel	cruk	crook
crocadile	crocodile	croon		cruked	crooked

crukid	crooked	cruze	cruise	culcher	culture
crule	cruel	crysanthe-	chrysanthe-	cule	cool
crullar	cruller	mum	mum	culect	collect
cruller		crysis	crisis	culey	coolie
crullir	cruller	cuboard	cupboard	culide	collide
crullor	cruller	cuboose	caboose	cull	
crullur	cruller	cucoon	cocoon	cullapse	collapse
crum	crumb	cucumber		cullect	collect
crumb		cud		cullide	collide
crumbal	crumble	cudal	cuddle	culmanate	culminate
crumbel	crumble	cuddal	cuddle	culmenate	culminate
crumbil	crumble	cuddel	cuddle	culminate	
crumble		cuddil	cuddle	culmonate	culminate
crumbol	crumble	cuddle		culmunate	culminate
crumbul	crumble	cuddol	cuddle	culonial	colonial
crumpal	crumple	cuddul	cuddle	culor	color
crumpel	crumple	cudel	cuddle	culossal	colossal
crumpil	crumple	cudet	cadet	culpable	
crumple		cudgal	cudgel	culpeble	culpable
crumpol	crumple	cudgel		culpible	culpable
crumpul	crumple	cudgil	cudgel	culpoble	culpable
crunch		cudgol	cudgel	culprit	
crune	croon	cudgul	cudgel	culpuble	culpable
crupe	croup	cudil	cuddle	cultavate	cultivate
crusade		cudle	cuddle	cultcher	culture
crusader		cudol	cuddle	cultevate	cultivate
crusafix	crucifix	cudul	cuddle	cultivate	
crusaid	crusade	cue		cultivation	
cruse	cruise	cue	queue	cultivator	
crush		cuff		cultovate	cultivate
crusifix	crucifix	cugar	cougar	culture	
crusify	crucify	cugel	cudgel	cultured	
crusofix	crucifix	cuk	cook	cultuvate	cultivate
crust		cukie	cookie	culvert	
crustacean		cukumber	cucumber	culvirt	culvert
crusufix	crucifix	cuky	cookie	culvurt	culvert
crutch		culamity	calamity	cum	come
cruvat	cravat	culapse	collapse	cumand	command

cumbarsome	cumbersome	cumpel	compel	cunfer	confer
cumbersome		cumpete	compete	cunfess	confess
cumbine	combine	cumpile	compile	cunfide	confide
cumbirsome	cumbersome	cumplacent	complacent	cunfine	confine
cumborsome	cumbersome	cumplain	complain	cunfirm	confirm
cumbursome	cumbersome	cumplete	complete	cunform	conform
cumbustion	combustion	cumplexion	complexion	cunfront	confront
cumemorate	commemorate	cumply	comply	cunfuse	confuse
cumence	commence	cumpose	compose	cungeal	congeal
cumend	commend	cumposure	composure	cungenial	congenial
cumfort	comfort	cumpress	compress	cungested	congested
cumission	commission	cumprise	comprise	cungratulate	congratulate
cumit	commit	cumpulsion	compulsion	cuning	cunning
cumittee	committee	cumpute	compute	cunjecture	conjecture
cumley	comely	cumunicate	communicate	cunjunction	conjunction
cummand	command	cumunion	communion	cunnect	connect
cummemorate	commemorate	cumunity	community	cunning	
cummence	commence	cumute	commute	cunoe	canoe
cummend	commend	cunal	canal	cunsecutive	consecutive
cummission	commission	cunary	canary	cunsent	consent
cummit	commit	cunceal	conceal	cunservative	conservative
cummittee	committee	cuncede	concede	cunserve	conserve
cummodious	commodious	cunceit	conceit	cunsider	consider
cummodity	commodity	cunceive	conceive	cunsiderable	considerable
cummotion	commotion	cuncern	concern	cunsiderate	considerate
cummunicate	communicate	cuncerto	concerto	cunsign	consign
cummunion	communion	cuncession	concession	cunsist	consist
cummunity	community	cunciliate	conciliate	cunsistent	consistent
cummute	commute	cuncise	concise	cunsole	console
cumodious	commodious	cunclude	conclude	cunsolidate	consolidate
cumodity	commodity	cuncur	concur	cunspicuous	conspicuous
cumotion	commotion	cuncussion	concussion	cunspire	conspire
cumpanion	companion	cundemn	condemn	cunstituent	constituent
cumpany	company	cundense	condense	cunstrain	constrain
cumpare	compare	cundition	condition	cunstrict	constrict
cumpartment	compartment	cunduct	conduct	cunstruct	construct
cumpassion	compassion	cunect	connect	cunstrue	construe
cumpatible	compatible	cunfederate	confederate	cunsult	consult

cunsume	consume	cuple	couple	curont	currant
cuntagious	contagious	cupol	couple	curont	current
cuntain	contain	cupon	coupon	curral	corral
cuntaminate	contaminate	cupricious	capricious	currant	
cuntemporary	contemporary	cupul	couple	currant	current
cuntempt	contempt	cur		currect	correct
cuntend	contend	curage	courage	currency	
cuntent	content	curant	currant	current	currant
cuntention	contention	curant	current	current	
cuntest	contest	curator		currey	curry
cuntinue	continue	curb		currint	currant
cuntort	contort	curcus	circus	currint	current
cuntract	contract	curd		curroborate	corroborate
cuntralto	contralto	curdal	curdle	currode	corrode
cuntrast	contrast	curdel	curdle	curront	currant
cuntribute	contribute	curdil	curdle	curront	current
cuntrite	contrite	curdle		currunt	currant
cuntrive	contrive	curdol	curdle	currunt	current
cuntrol	control	curdul	curdle	currupt	corrupt
cuntry	country	cure		curry	
cunvene	convene	cureer	career	curse	
cunvenient	convenient	curent	currant	curt	
cunventional	conventional	curent	current	curtail	
cunverse	converse	cureous	curious	curtain	
cunvert	convert	curess	caress	curtale	curtail
cunvey	convey	curfew		curtan	curtain
cunvict	convict	curfue	curfew	curtane	curtain
cunvince	convince	curier	courier	curten	curtain
cunvulse	convulse	curint	currant	curtesy	courtesy
cup		curint	current	curtin	curtain
cupacity	capacity	curios	curious	curton	curtain
cupal	couple	curiosity		curtsy	
cupboard		curious		curtun	curtain
cupbored	cupboard	curiousity	curiosity	curunt	currant
cupe	coop	curius	curious	curunt	current
cupel	couple	curl		curve	
Cupid		curly		cury	curry
cupil	couple	curnel	colonel	cushan	cushion

cushen	cushion	cutliss	cutlass	cwarrel	quarrel
cushin	cushion	cutlory	cutlery	cwarry	quarry
cushion		cutloss	cutlass	cwaver	quaver
cushon	cushion	cutlury	cutlery	cwean	queen
cushun	cushion	cutluss	cutlass	cwear	queer
cusin	cousin	cutocle	cuticle	cweary	query
custady	custody	cutting		cween	queen
custam	custom	cutucle	cuticle	cweer	queer
custard		cuvar	cover	cweery	query
custedy	custody	cuvenant	covenant	cwell	quell
custem	custom	cuver	cover	cwench	quench
custerd	custard	cuvert	covert	cwene	queen
custidy	custody	cuvet	covet	cwere	queer
custim	custom	cuvey	covey	cwerey	query
custird	custard	cuvir	cover	cwery	query
custodian		cuvit	covet	cwest	quest
custody		cuvor	cover	cwestion	question
custom		cuvort	cavort	cwick	quick
customary		cuvur	cover	cwier	choir
customer		cuvy	covey	cwiet	quiet
custord	custard	cuzin	cousin	cwik	quick
custudy	custody	cwack	quack	cwill	quill
custum	custom	cwadruped	quadruped	cwilt	quilt
custurd	custard	cwadruplet	quadruplet	cwinine	quinine
cut		cwaff	quaff	cwintet	quintet
cutacle	cuticle	cwaik	quake	cwire	choir
cutastrophe	catastrophe	Cwaiker	Quaker	cwit	quit
cute		cwail	quail	cwite	quite
cutecle	cuticle	cwaint	quaint	cwiver	quiver
cuthedral	cathedral	cwaiver	quaver	cwiz	quiz
cuticle		cwake	quake	cwoat	quote
cutikle	cuticle	Cwaker	Quaker	cwoata	quota
cuting	cutting	cwale	quail	cwodruped	quadruped
cutlary	cutlery	cwalify	qualify	cwodruplet	quadruplet
cutlass		cwality	quality	cwoit	quoit
cutlery		cwam	qualm	cwolify	qualify
cutless	cutlass	cwantity	quantity	cwolity	quality
cutliry	cutlery	cwarantine	quarantine	cwom	qualm

cwontity	quantity	cwoyt	quoit	cylinder	
cworantine	quarantine	cycal	cycle	cylindrical	
cworrel	quarrel	cycle		cylonder	cylinder
cworry	quarry	cycloan	cyclone	cyclunder	cylinder
cwort	quart	cyclone		cymbal	
cworter	quarter	cycol	cycle	cymbel	cymbal
cworts	quartz	cycul	cycle	cymbil	cymbal
cwortz	quartz	cykle	cycle	cymbol	cymbal
cwoshent	quotient	cyklone	cyclone	cymbul	cymbal
cwota	quota	cylander	cylinder	cyote	coyote
cwote	quote	cylender	cylinder	cypress	
cwotient	quotient			czar	

D

da	day	dafadil	daffodil	dail	dale
dab		daffadil	daffodil	daily	
dabal	dabble	daffedil	daffodil	daim	dame
dabbal	dabble	daffidil	daffodil	dain	deign
dabbel	dabble	daffodil		daintily	
dabbil	dabble	daffudil	daffodil	dainty	
dabble		dafidil	daffodil	daintyly	daintily
dabbol	dabble	dafodil	daffodil	dair	dare
dabbul	dabble	daft		dairy	
dabel	dabble	dafudil	daffodil	dais	
dabil	dabble	dagar	dagger	daise	daze
dable	dabble	dagest	digest	daisy	
dabol	dabble	daggar	dagger	dait	date
dabris	debris	dagger		daize	daze
dabul	dabble	daggir	dagger	daizy	daisy
dachshund		daggor	dagger	dakshund	dachshund
dachshunt	dachshund	daggur	dagger	dalapidated	dilapidated
dad		dagir	dagger	dale	
daddy		dagor	dagger	daley	daily
dady	daddy	dagur	dagger	dally	

daly	dally	dapar	dapper	daughtor	daughter
dam		dapir	dapper	daughtur	daughter
damage		daploma	diploma	daunt	
damask		dapor	dapper	dauntless	
dame		dappar	dapper	dauntliss	dauntless
damege	damage	dapper		dauter	daughter
damension	dimension	dappir	dapper	davide	divide
damestic	domestic	dappor	dapper	davine	divine
damige	damage	dappur	dapper	davorce	divorce
daminish	diminish	dapur	dapper	davulge	divulge
daminutive	diminutive	darck	dark	dawdal	dawdle
damm	damn	dare		dawdel	dawdle
damn		darect	direct	dawdil	dawdle
damoge	damage	dareing	daring	dawdle	
damp		darey	dairy	dawdol	dawdle
dampen		daring		dawdul	dawdle
damuge	damage	dark		dawg	dog
dance		darken		dawn	
dancer		darkness		dawnt	daunt
dandalion	dandelion	darkniss	darkness	dawter	daughter
dandelion		darling		daxhund	dachshund
dandilion	dandelion	darn		day	
dondolion	dandelion	dart		daybrake	daybreak
dandulion	dandelion	dasaster	disaster	daybreak	
dandy		dascern	discern	daydream	
dane	deign	dasciple	disciple	dayis	dais
danety	dainty	dasease	disease	daylight	
dangal	dangle	dasern	discern	daylite	daylight
dangel	dangle	dash		daysy	daisy
danger		dasheveled	disheveled	daytime	
dangerous		dashing		dazal	dazzle
dangil	dangle	dasiple	disciple	daze	
dangir	danger	data		dazil	dazzle
dangle		date		dazle	dazzle
dangol	dangle	dater	data	dazol	dazzle
dangul	dangle	daughtar	daughter	dazul	dazzle
dank		daughter		dazy	daisy
danse	dance	daughtir	daughter	dazzal	dazzle

dazzel	dazzle	decade		declair	declare
dazzil	dazzle	decaid	decade	declaration	
dazzle		decarate	decorate	declare	
dazzol	dazzle	decay		decline	
dazzul	dazzle	decease		decompose	
deacan	deacon	deceased		decorate	
deacon		deceave	deceive	decoration	
deacun	deacon	deceese	decease	decorative	
dead		deceeve	deceive	decorum	
dead	deed	deceit		decoy	
deaden		deceitful		decrease	
deadicate	dedicate	deceive		decree	
deadly		decemal	decimal	decreese	decrease
deaf		December		decrese	decrease
deafen		decency		decurate	decorate
deakon	deacon	decent		ded	dead
deal		decentcy	decency	dedacate	dedicate
dealing		decentsy	decency	dede	deed
dealt		deception		dedecate	dedicate
deam	deem	deceptive		dedicate	
deap	deep	decese	decease	dedocate	dedicate
dear		decete	deceit	deducate	dedicate
dear	deer	deceve	deceive	deduct	
dearly		decide		deduction	
dearth		decided		dedukt	deduct
death		decidedly		deecon	deacon
deathly		deciet	deceit	deed	
deaty	deity	decieve	deceive	deel	deal
debais	debase	decifer	decipher	deem	
debait	debate	decimal		deep	
debase		decint	decent	deer	
debate		decipher		deer	dear
debree	debris	decision		def	deaf
debrey	debris	decisive		deface	
debris		deck		defaise	deface
debt		deckade	decade	defanite	definite
debter	debtor	deckorate	decorate	defanition	definition
debtor		decksterity	dexterity	defase	deface

defeat
defect
defective
defeet   defeat
defekt   defect
defence   defense
defend
defender
defenite   definite
defenition   definition
defense
defenseless
defensive
defer
deference
defete   defeat
defiance
defiant
deficent   deficient
deficiency
deficient
defile
define
definite
definitely
definition
defishent   deficient
defonite   definite
defonition   definition
deform
deformity
defraud
defrawd   defraud
deft
defunite   definite
defunition   definition
defy
degest   digest

degrade
degree
deign
deity
dejected
dejekted   dejected
dek   deck
dekade   decade
dekay   decay
deklare   declare
dekline   decline
dekompose   decompose
dekorate   decorate
dekorum   decorum
dekoy   decoy
dekrease   decrease
dekree   decree
deksterity   dexterity
delacate   delicate
delagate   delegate
delapidated   dilapidated
Delaware
delay
dele   deal
delecate   delicate
delegate
delegation
delewd   delude
delewsion   delusion
deliberate
deliberately
deliberation
delicacy
delicate
delicious
delicius   delicious
delicous   delicious
deligate   delegate

delight
delightful
delirious
delirium
delishious   delicious
delishous   delicious
delishus   delicious
delite   delight
deliver
delivery
dellta   delta
delluge   deluge
delocate   delicate
delogate   delegate
delood   delude
deloosion   delusion
delt   dealt
delta
delter   delta
delucate   delicate
delude
delugate   delegate
deluge
delusion
deluzion   delusion
delve
demacrat   democrat
deman   demon
demand
demanstrate   demonstrate
deme   deem
demeanor
demecrat   democrat
demeenor   demeanor
demen   demon
demension   dimension
demenstrate   demonstrate
demestic   domestic

demicrat	democrat	dentul	dental	derizion	derision
demin	demon	deny		derizive	derisive
deminish	diminish	deoty	deity	derizun	derision
deminstrate	demonstrate	depart		derogatory	
deminutive	diminutive	department		derrick	
demoat	demote	departure		derrik	derrick
democracy		depe	deep	dert	dirt
democrat		depend		derth	dearth
democratic		dependence		desalate	desolate
demokracy	democracy	dependent		desaster	disaster
demolish		depict		descend	
demollish	demolish	depikt	depict	descendant	
demon		deploar	deplore	descent	
demonstrate		deploma	diploma	descern	discern
demonstration		deplore		desciple	disciple
demote		depo	depot	describe	
demucrat	democrat	deportment		describtion	description
demun	demon	deposit		description	
demunstrate	demonstrate	depositor		descriptive	
demure		depot		desease	decease
den		depozit	deposit	desease	disease
dence	dense	depress		deseit	deceit
denial		depression		deseive	deceive
denomination		deprive		deselate	desolate
denominator		depth		Desember	December
denote		deputy		desend	descend
denounce		derail		desent	decent
denounse	denounce	derale	derail	deseption	deception
denownce	denounce	derby		desern	discern
denownse	denounce	dere	deer	desert	
dense		derect	direct	desert	dessert
density		derge	dirge	deserter	
dent		derick	derrick	deserve	
dental		deride		desheveled	disheveled
dentel	dental	derik	derrick	deside	decide
dentil	dental	derision		desier	desire
dentist		derisive		design	
dentol	dental	derive		designate	

designing		dessert		detest	
desilate	desolate	**destan**	destine	detestable	
desimal	decimal	**destatute**	destitute	**deth**	death
desine	design	**desten**	destine	dethrone	
desipher	decipher	**destetute**	destitute	**detirmine**	determine
desiple	disciple	**destin**	destine	detour	
desirability		destination		**detur**	detour
desirable		destine		**deturmine**	determine
desire		**destiney**	destiny	**deuty**	deity
desireability	desirability	destiny		**deval**	devil
desireable	desirable	destitute		devastate	
desirous		**deston**	destine	**devel**	devil
desirt	desert	**destotute**	destitute	develop	
desirve	deserve	destroy		**developement**	development
desision	decision	destroyer		development	
desist		destruction		**devestate**	devastate
desk		destructive		device	
deskribe	describe	**destruktive**	destructive	**devide**	divide
desolate		**destun**	destine	devil	
desolation		**destutute**	destitute	**devine**	divine
despair		**desulate**	desolate	devise	
desparate	desperate	**desurt**	desert	**devise**	device
despare	despair	**desurve**	deserve	**devistate**	devastate
despat	despot	**det**	debt	**devize**	devise
desperate		detach		**devoat**	devote
desperation		detachment		devoid	
despet	despot	detail		**devol**	devil
despirate	desperate	detain		devorce	divorce
despise		**detale**	detail	**devostate**	devastate
despit	despot	**detane**	detain	devote	
despite		**detatch**	detach	devoted	
despize	despise	detect		devotion	
despoil		detective		devour	
despondent		**detekt**	detect	devout	
desporate	desperate	deter		**devower**	devour
despot		determination		**devowt**	devout
despurate	desperate	determine		**devoyd**	devoid
desput	despot	determined		**devul**	devil

devulge	divulge	dicay	decay	difacult	difficult
devustate	devastate	dice		difar	differ
dew		diceit	deceit	difeat	defeat
dew	due	diceive	deceive	difect	defect
dewel	dual	Dicember	December	difecult	difficult
dewel	duel	diception	deception	difend	defend
dewk	duke	dich	ditch	difer	defer
dewl	duel	dicide	decide	difer	differ
dewly	duly	dicipher	decipher	diffacult	difficult
dewn	dune	dicision	decision	diffar	differ
dewp	dupe	dicktionary	dictionary	diffecult	difficult
dewplicate	duplicate	diclare	declare	differ	
dewty	duty	dicline	decline	difference	
dexterity		dicorum	decorum	different	
dezert	desert	dicrease	decrease	differently	
dezert	dessert	dicree	decree	difficult	
dezerve	deserve	dicshunary	dictionary	difficulty	
dezignate	designate	dictate		diffir	differ
dezine	design	dictation		diffocult	difficult
di	die	dictator		diffor	differ
di	dye	dictionary		diffucult	difficult
diacese	diocese	did		diffur	differ
diafram	diaphragm	didn't		difiant	defiant
diagnose		diduct	deduct	dificient	deficient
diagnosis		die		dificult	difficult
diagonal		die	dye	difile	defile
diagram		diecese	diocese	difine	define
dial		diegnose	diagnose	difir	differ
dialect		diegram	diagram	difocult	difficult
dialogue		diel	dial	difor	differ
diameter		dielect	dialect	diform	deform
diamond		dielogue	dialogue	difraud	defraud
diaphragm		diephragm	diaphragm	diftheria	diphtheria
diary		dier	dire	difthong	diphthong
diat	diet	diery	diary	difucult	difficult
dibase	debase	diet		difur	differ
dibate	debate	dietitian		dify	defy
dibris	debris	diface	deface	dig	

digest	
digestion	
digestive	
digit	
dignaty	dignity
dignety	dignity
dignified	
dignify	
dignitary	
dignity	
dignoty	dignity
dignuty	dignity
digrade	degrade
digree	degree
dijected	dejected
dijest	digest
dijit	digit
dike	
diktate	dictate
diktionary	dictionary
dilagent	diligent
dilait	dilate
dilapidated	
dilate	
dilay	delay
dilegent	diligent
dilewt	dilute
diliberate	deliberate
dilicious	delicious
diligence	
diligent	
dilight	delight
dilirious	delirious
diliver	deliver
dilly-dally	
dilogent	diligent
diloot	dilute
dilude	delude
dilugent	diligent
dilusion	delusion
dilute	
dily-dally	dilly-dally
dim	
dimand	demand
dime	
dimeanor	demeanor
dimend	diamond
dimension	
dimestic	domestic
dimind	diamond
diminish	
diminutive	
dimocracy	democracy
dimolish	demolish
dimond	diamond
dimote	demote
dimpal	dimple
dimpel	dimple
dimpil	dimple
dimple	
dimpol	dimple
dimpul	dimple
dimund	diamond
dimure	demure
din	
dinamic	dynamic
dinamite	dynamite
dinamo	dynamo
dinar	dinner
dinasaur	dinosaur
dinasty	dynasty
dine	
diner	
diner	dinner
dinesaur	dinosaur
dingey	dinghy
dingey	dingy
dinghy	
dingy	
dingy	dinghy
dinial	denial
dinir	dinner
dinisaur	dinosaur
dinjy	dingy
dinnar	dinner
dinner	
dinnir	dinner
dinnur	dinner
dinominator	denominator
dinor	diner
dinor	dinner
dinosaur	
dinote	denote
dinounce	denounce
dint	
dinur	dinner
dinusaur	dinosaur
diny	deny
diocese	
diocis	diocese
diofram	diaphragm
diognose	diagnose
diogram	diagram
diol	dial
diolect	dialect
diologue	dialogue
diophragm	diaphragm
diophram	diaphragm
diory	diary
diosis	diocese
diot	diet
dip	
dipart	depart
dipartment	department

dipend	depend	dirugible	dirigible	disconnect	
diphtheria		disability		discontent	
diphthong		disable		discontinue	
dipict	depict	disadvantage		discord	
diplamat	diplomat	disagree		discordant	
diplemat	diplomat	disagreeable		discorse	discourse
diplimat	diplomat	disagreement		discount	
diploma		disapline	discipline	discourage	
diplomat		disappear		discouragement	
diplomatic		disappearance		discourse	
diplomer	diploma	disappoint		discourteous	
diplore	deplore	disappointment		discover	
diplumat	diplomat	disapproval		discoverer	
diportment	deportment	disapprove		discovery	
diposit	deposit	disarm		discownt	discount
dipress	depress	disaster		discrace	disgrace
diprive	deprive	disastrous		discreat	discreet
diptheria	diphtheria	disatisfaction	dissatisfaction	discredit	
dipthong	diphthong	disatisfied	dissatisfied	discreet	
diragible	dirigible	disband		discrete	discreet
dirby	derby	disbelieve		discretion	
dire		disbilieve	disbelieve	discribe	describe
direct		disc	disk	discriminate	
direction		discannect	disconnect	discrimination	
directly		discantent	discontent	discualify	disqualify
director		discantinue	discontinue	disculor	discolor
directory		discard		discumfort	discomfort
diregible	dirigible	discend	descend	discunnect	disconnect
direkt	direct	discern		discuntent	discontent
dirge		discharge		discuntinue	discontinue
diride	deride	disciple		discurage	discourage
dirigible		discipline		discurteous	discourteous
dirive	derive	disclaim		discuss	
dirogatory	derogatory	disclame	disclaim	discussion	
dirogible	dirigible	disclose		discuver	discover
dirt		discoarse	discourse	discwiet	disquiet
dirth	dearth	discolor		discwolify	disqualify
dirty		discomfort		disdain	

disdainful		disimilar	dissimilar	dislocate	
disdane	disdain	disinfect		dislodge	
dise	dice	disinfectant		disloge	dislodge
disease		disintegrate		disloyal	
diseased		disinterested		disloyalty	
disect	dissect	disipate	dissipate	dismal	
disedvantage	disadvantage	disiple	disciple	dismantle	
disegree	disagree	disipline	discipline	dismay	
disembark		disippear	disappear	dismel	dismal
disend	descend	disippoint	disappoint	dismil	dismal
disension	dissension	disipprove	disapprove	dismiss	
disent	dissent	disire	desire	dismissal	
disepline	discipline	disist	desist	dismol	dismal
diseppear	disappear	disk		dismount	
diseppoint	disappoint	diskard	discard	dismownt	dismount
disepprove	disapprove	diskerage	discourage	dismul	dismal
disern	discern	disklaim	disclaim	disobedience	
diserve	deserve	disklose	disclose	disobedient	
disfavor		diskolor	discolor	disobey	
disfigure		diskomfort	discomfort	disodvantage	disadvantage
disgise	disguise	diskonnect	disconnect	disogree	disagree
disgize	disguise	diskontent	discontent	disolve	dissolve
disgrace		diskontinue	discontinue	disonest	dishonest
disgraceful		diskord	discord	disonor	dishonor
disgrase	disgrace	diskorse	discourse	disopline	discipline
disguise		diskount	discount	disoppear	disappear
disgust		diskourteous	discourteous	disoppoint	disappoint
dish		diskover	discover	disopprove	disapprove
disharten	dishearten	diskredit	discredit	disorder	
dishearten		diskreet	discreet	disorderly	
disheveled		diskriminate	discriminate	disorganize	
dishonest		diskuler	discolor	disown	
dishonesty		diskumfort	discomfort	dispach	dispatch
dishonor		diskuss	discuss	dispair	despair
dishonorable		diskwiet	disquiet	dispatch	
disidvantage	disadvantage	diskwolify	disqualify	dispel	
disign	design	dislage	dislodge	dispell	dispel
disigree	disagree	dislike		dispence	dispense

dispense		dissent		distribution	
disperse		dissert	dessert	district	
dispirse	disperse	dissimilar		distrikt	district
dispise	despise	dissipate		distroy	destroy
dispite	despite	dissolve		distructive	destructive
displace		dissuade		distrust	
displase	displace	disswade	dissuade	distunce	distance
display		disswaid	dissuade	distunt.	distant
displease		distaff		disturb	
displeasure		distaiste	distaste	disturbance	
displeaze	displease	distance		disuade	dissuade
displeese	displease	distanse	distance	disudvantage	disadvantage
displese	displease	distant		disugree	disagree
dispoase	dispose	distaste		disupline	discipline
dispoil	despoil	distasteful		disuppear	disappear
dispondent	despondent	distence	distance	disuppoint	disappoint
disposal		distend		disupprove	disapprove
dispose		distent	distant	ditach	detach
disposition		disterb	disturb	ditail	detail
dispoze	dispose	distill		ditain	detain
disproove	disprove	distillation		ditch	
disprove		distince	distance	ditect	detect
dispruve	disprove	distinct		diter	deter
dispurse	disperse	distinction		ditermine	determine
dispute		distinctive		ditest	detest
disqualify		distinctly		dithrone	dethrone
disquiet		distinguish		ditty	
disquolify	disqualify	distinguished		dity	ditty
disregard		distinkt	distinct	diucese	diocese
disreputable		distint	distant	diufram	diaphragm
disrespect		distirb	disturb	diugnose	diagnose
disrigard	disregard	distonce	distance	diugram	diagram
disrispect	disrespect	distont	distant	diul	dial
dissatisfaction		distort		diulect	dialect
dissatisfied		distract		diulog	dialogue
dissect		distrakt	distract	diulogue	dialogue
dissekt	dissect	distress		diuphragm	diaphragm
dissension		distribute		diury	diary

diut	diet	dizert	dessert	dodge	
divadend	dividend	dizerve	deserve	doe	
divan		dizign	design	doe	dough
dive		dizire	desire	does	
divedend	dividend	dizmal	dismal	doesn't	
divelop	develop	dizolve	dissolve	doff	
diver		dizy	dizzy	dog	
diverse		dizziness		doge	dodge
diversion		dizzy		doged	dogged
diversity		dizzyness	dizziness	dogest	digest
divert		do		dogged	
diverzion	diversion	do	dew	doggid	dogged
divice	device	do	doe	dogid	dogged
divide		do	dough	doily	
dividend		do	due	doings	
divine		doal	dole	dok	dock
divinity		doam	dome	doktor	doctor
divirse	diverse	doar	door	doktrine	doctrine
divirsion	diversion	doas	dose	dokument	document
divise	devise	doat	dote	dolapidated	dilapidated
divisible		doaze	doze	dolar	dollar
division		dobris	debris	dolarous	dolorous
divisor		docel	docile	doldrams	doldrums
divizible	divisible	docile		doldrems	doldrums
divizion	division	docill	docile	doldrims	doldrums
divodend	dividend	dock		doldroms	doldrums
divoid	devoid	doctar	doctor	doldrums	
divorce		docter	doctor	dole	
divorse	divorce	doctir	doctor	doleful	
divote	devote	doctor		dolerous	dolorous
divour	devour	doctran	doctrine	dolfin	dolphin
divout	devout	doctren	doctrine	dolir	dollar
divudend	dividend	doctrin	doctrine	dolirous	dolorous
divulge		doctrine		doll	
divurse	diverse	doctron	doctrine	dollar	
divursion	diversion	doctrun	doctrine	doller	dollar
dizaster	disaster	doctur	doctor	dollir	dollar
dizease	disease	document		dollor	dollar

dollur	dollar	donate		dosease	disease
dolor	dollar	donation		dosern	discern
dolorous		done		dosheveled	disheveled
dolphan	dolphin	doner	donor	dosile	docile
dolphen	dolphin	donir	donor	dosiple	disciple
dolphin		donkey		dot	
dolphon	dolphin	donky	donkey	dote	
dolphun	dolphin	donor		doubal	double
dolt		don't		doubel	double
dolur	dollar	donur	donor	doubil	double
dolurous	dolorous	dooal	dual	double	
domain		dook	duke	doubley	doubly
domanant	dominant	dool	duel	doubly	
domanate	dominate	dooly	duly	doubol	double
domane	domain	doom		doubt	
domano	domino	doon	dune	doubtful	
dome		doop	dupe	doubtless	
domenant	dominant	dooplicate	duplicate	doubtliss	doubtless
domenate	dominate	door		doubul	double
domeno	domino	dooty	duty	dough	
domension	dimension	doploma	diploma	doughnut	
domestic		dore	door	douse	
domesticate		dorect	direct	dout	doubt
dominant		dormant		dove	
dominate		dormatory	dormitory	dovide	divide
domination		dorment	dormant	dovine	divine
dominion		dormetory	dormitory	dovorce	divorce
dominish	diminish	dormint	dormant	dovulge	divulge
domino		dormitory		dow	doe
dominutive	diminutive	dormont	dormant	dowal	dowel
domonant	dominant	dormotory	dormitory	dowdy	
domonate	dominate	dormunt	dormant	dowel	
domono	domino	dormutory	dormitory	dowil	dowel
domunant	dominant	dorn	dawn	down	
domunate	dominate	dosaster	disaster	downcast	
domuno	domino	doscern	discern	downfall	
don		dosciple	disciple	downkast	downcast
donar	donor	dose		downpore	downpour

downpour		drank		dribal	dribble
downright		drape		dribbal	dribble
downrite	downright	drapery		dribbel	dribble
downstairs		drastic		dribbil	dribble
downstares	downstairs	drastik	drastic	dribble	
downtown		draw		dribbol	dribble
dowol	dowel	draw	drawer	dribbul	dribble
dowry		drawback		dribel	dribble
dowse	douse	drawbak	drawback	dribil	dribble
dowt	doubt	drawer		drible	dribble
dowul	dowel	drawing		dribol	dribble
doyly	doily	drawl		dribul	dribble
dozan	dozen	drawn		dride	dried
doze		drawr	drawer	dried	
dozen		dread		drier	
dozin	dozen	dreadful		drift	
dozon	dozen	dreadfully		drill	
dozun	dozen	dream		drinck	drink
drab		dreamer		drink	
draft		dreamey	dreamy	drip	
drag		dreamt		drive	
dragan	dragon	dreamy		driven	
dragen	dragon	dreary		driver	
dragin	dragon	dred	dread	drizal	drizzle
dragnet		dredge		drizel	drizzle
dragon		dreem	dream	drizle	drizzle
dragun	dragon	dreery	dreary	drizol	drizzle
drain		drege	dredge	drizul	drizzle
drainage		dregs		drizzal	drizzle
draip	drape	dregz	dregs	drizzel	drizzle
drall	drawl	dreme	dream	drizzle	
drama		dremt	dreamt	drizzol	drizzle
dramatic		drench		drizzul	drizzle
dramatically		drerey	dreary	droal	droll
dramatist		dress		droan	drone
dramatization		dresser		droar	draw
dramatize		dressing		droar	drawer
drane	drain	drew		droave	drove

drole	droll	drunkird	drunkard	dule	duel
droll		drunkord	drunkard	duley	duly
dromadary	dromedary	drunkurd	drunkard	dull	
dromedary		drupe	droop	duly	
dromidary	dromedary	dry		dum	dumb
dromodary	dromedary	dryd	dried	dumb	
dromudary	dromedary	dryer		dumbbell	
drone		dryley	dryly	dumbell	dumbbell
droo	drew	dryly		dume	doom
drool		du	do	dumension	dimension
droop		du	due	dumestic	domestic
drop		dual		duminish	diminish
drore	draw	dual	duel	duminutive	diminutive
drore	drawer	dub		dummy	
drought		dubeous	dubious	dump	
drout	drought	dubious		dumy	dummy
drove		duble	double	dun	done
drown		dubris	debris	dunce	
drowse		duchess		dune	
drowsey	drowsy	duchiss	duchess	dungaree	
drowsy		duck		dungeon	
drowt	drought	duckling		dungeree	dungaree
drowze	drowse	due		dungian	dungeon
drudge		due	dew	dungien	dungeon
drudgery		due	do	dungin	dungeon
drue	drew	duel		dungion	dungeon
drug		duel	dual	dungiree	dungaree
druge	drudge	duet		dungiun	dungeon
druggist		dug		dungoree	dungaree
drugist	druggist	dugest	digest	dunguree	dungaree
drule	drool	dugout		dunkey	donkey
drum		dugowt	dugout	dunky	donkey
drumer	drummer	duil	dual	dunse	dunce
drummer		duil	duel	duol	dual
drunck	drunk	duk	duck	duol	duel
drunk		duke		dupe	
drunkard		dulapidated	dilapidated	duplacate	duplicate
drunkerd	drunkard	dule	dual	duplecate	duplicate

duplicate		dusk		dwindul	dwindle
duplocate	duplicate	dust		dworf	dwarf
duploma	diploma	dusty		dy	die
duplucate	duplicate	dutchess	duchess	dy	dye
durable		dutiful		dye	
duration		duty		dying	
durby	derby	dutyful	dutiful	dyke	dike
dureble	durable	duv	dove	dynamic	
durect	direct	duvide	divide	dynamite	
durge	dirge	duvine	divine	dynamo	
durible	durable	duvorce	divorce	dynasty	
during		duvulge	divulge	dynemite	dynamite
duroble	durable	duz	does	dynemo	dynamo
durt	dirt	duzen	dozen	dynesty	dynasty
durth	dearth	dwarf		dynimite	dynamite
duruble	durable	dweling	dwelling	dynimo	dynamo
dusaster	disaster	dwell		dynisty	dynasty
duscern	discern	dwelling		dynomite	dynamite
dusciple	disciple	dwindal	dwindle	dynomo	dynamo
dusease	disease	dwindel	dwindle	dynosty	dynasty
dusern	discern	dwindil	dwindle	dynumite	dynamite
dusheveled	disheveled	dwindle		dynumo	dynamo
dusiple	disciple	dwindol	dwindle	dynusty	dynasty

E

each		eagir	eager	earie	eerie
Eaden	Eden	eagle		earing	earring
eadict	edict	eagol	eagle	early	
eagal	eagle	eagor	eager	earn	
eagar	eager	eagul	eagle	earnest	
eagel	eagle	eagur	eager	earnestly	
eager		Eagypt	Egypt	earnings	
eagerly		eal	eel	earring	
eagerness		ear		earth	
eagil	eagle	eara	era	earthcwake	earthquake

earthkwake	earthquake	ebony		ecspense	expense
earthquake		ebuny	ebony	ecsperience	experience
eary	eerie	eccentric		ecsperiment	experiment
easal	easel	ech	etch	ecspert	expert
easaly	easily	echo		ecspire	expire
ease		ecko	echo	ecsplain	explain
easel		eckonomic	economic	ecsplicit	explicit
easely	easily	eckstasy	ecstasy	ecsplisit	explicit
easier		eckwity	equity	ecsplode	explode
easil	easel	eclipse		ecsploit	exploit
easily		economic		ecsplore	explore
easol	easel	economical		ecsplosion	explosion
easoly	easily	economics		ecsport	export
east		economize		ecspose	expose
eastarn	eastern	economy		ecspound	expound
Easter		ecscavate	excavate	ecspress	express
eastern		ecschange	exchange	ecspulsion	expulsion
eastirn	eastern	ecsclaim	exclaim	ecstasy	
eastorn	eastern	ecsclude	exclude	ecstend	extend
easturn	eastern	ecscurzion	excursion	ecstent	extent
easul	easel	ecscuse	excuse	ecsterior	exterior
easuly	easily	ecscwisite	exquisite	ecsterminate	exterminate
easy		ecsecute	execute	ecsternal	external
easyer	easier	ecseed	exceed	ecstesy	ecstasy
eat		ecsel	excel	ecstinct	extinct
eaten		ecsept	except	ecstisy	ecstasy
eather	either	ecsercise	exercise	ecstol	extol
eave	eve	ecsess	excess	ecstosy	ecstasy
eavesdropper		ecshale	exhale	ecstra	extra
eaze	ease	ecsite	excite	ecstracate	extricate
eazel	easel	ecskwisite	exquisite	ecstract	extract
eazy	easy	ecsodus	exodus	ecstraordinary	extraordinary
eb	ebb	ecspand	expand	ecstravagant	extravagant
ebany	ebony	ecspect	expect	ecstreme	extreme
ebb		ecspedient	expedient	ecstremity	extremity
ebbony	ebony	ecspedition	expedition	ecstricate	extricate
ebeny	ebony	ecspel	expel	ecstrordinary	extraordinary
ebiny	ebony	ecspend	expend	ecstusy	ecstasy

ecwal	equal	Eeden	Eden	eg	egg
ecwator	equator	eedict	edict	ege	edge
ecwilibrium	equilibrium	eeger	eager	egg	
ecwinox	equinox	eegle	eagle	Egipt	Egypt
ecwip	equip	Eegypt	Egypt	egucate	educate
ecwivalent	equivalent	eel		Egypt	
edable	edible	eer	ear	Egyptian	
edafice	edifice	eerie		egzact	exact
Edan	Eden	eese	ease	egzaggerate	exaggerate
eddit	edit	eest	east	egzalt	exalt
eddy		Eester	Easter	egzamine	examine
edeble	edible	eesy	easy	egzample	example
edefice	edifice	eet	eat	egzasperate	exasperate
Eden		eether	either	egzaust	exhaust
edge		eevesdropper	eavesdropper	egzecutive	executive
edgucate	educate	eevning	evening	egzempt	exempt
edible		eface	efface	egzert	exert
edickt	edict	efaice	efface	egzibit	exhibit
edict		efart	effort	egzilarate	exhilarate
edifice		efemeral	ephemeral	egzile	exile
edikt	edict	efert	effort	egzist	exist
Edin	Eden	efface		egzit	exit
edishun	edition	effart	effort	egzorbitant	exorbitant
edit		effase	efface	egzort	exhort
edition		effeckt	effect	egzotic	exotic
editor		effect		egzult	exult
editorial		effective		eight	
edoble	edible	effectual		eighth	
edofice	edifice	effekt	effect	eithar	either
Edon	Eden	effert	effort	either	
eduble	edible	efficient		eithir	either
educate		effirt	effort	eithor	either
education		effort		eithur	either
educational		effurt	effort	ejackulate	ejaculate
edufice	edifice	eficient	efficient	ejaculate	
Edun	Eden	efirt	effort	ejakulate	ejaculate
edy	eddy	efort	effort	ejeckt	eject
eech	each	efurt	effort	eject	

ejekt	eject	ekskwisite	exquisite	ekstract	extract
ejucate	educate	eksocute	execute	ekstraord-	extraordinary
ekceed	exceed	eksodus	exodus	inary	
ekcel	excel	eksorcise	exercise	ekstravagant	extravagant
ekcentric	eccentric	ekspand	expand	ekstreme	extreme
ekcept	except	ekspect	expect	ekstremity	extremity
ekcercise	exercise	ekspedient	expedient	ekstricate	extricate
ekcess	excess	ekspedition	expedition	ekstrordinary	extraordinary
ekcite	excite	ekspel	expel	eksucute	execute
eklipse	eclipse	ekspend	expend	eksurcise	exercise
eko	echo	ekspense	expense	ekwal	equal
ekonomy	economy	eksperience	experience	ekwator	equator
eksacute	execute	eksperiment	experiment	ekwilibrium	equilibrium
eksarcise	exercise	ekspert	expert	ekwinox	equinox
ekscavate	excavate	ekspire	expire	ekwip	equip
ekschange	exchange	eksplain	explain	ekwity	equity
eksclaim	exclaim	eksplicit	explicit	ekwivalent	equivalent
eksclude	exclude	eksplisit	explicit	elaborate	
ekscursion	excursion	eksplode	explode	elacution	elocution
ekscuse	excuse	eksploit	exploit	elagant	elegant
ekscuze	excuse	eksplore	explore	elagible	eligible
ekscwisite	exquisite	eksplosion	explosion	elaited	elated
eksecute	execute	eksport	export	element	element
ekseed	exceed	ekspose	expose	elaphant	elephant
eksel	excel	ekspound	expound	elapse	
eksentric	eccentric	ekspress	express	elaquent	eloquent
eksept	except	ekspulsion	expulsion	elastic	
eksercise	exercise	eksquisite	exquisite	elasticity	
eksess	excess	ekstasy	ecstasy	elated	
ekshale	exhale	ekstend	extend	elation	
eksicute	execute	ekstent	extent	elavate	elevate
eksircise	exercise	eksterior	exterior	elbow	
eksite	excite	eksterminate	exterminate	elck	elk
eksklaim	exclaim	eksternal	external	eldar	elder
eksklude	exclude	ekstinct	extinct	elder	
ekskursion	excursion	ekstol	extol	elderly	
ekskuse	excuse	ekstra	extra	eldest	
ekskuze	excuse	ekstracate	extricate	eldir	elder

eldist	eldest
eldor	elder
eldur	elder
ele	eel
eleckt	elect
elecktric	electric
elect	
election	
electric	
electrical	
electrician	
electricity	
electrify	
electron	
elecution	elocution
elegance	
elegant	
elegible	eligible
elekt	elect
elektric	electric
element	
elementary	
elephant	
elequent	eloquent
elevate	
elevation	
elevator	
eleven	
elf	
elicit	
elicution	elocution
eligant	elegant
eligible	
eliment	element
eliminate	
eliphant	elephant
elipse	ellipse
eliquent	eloquent

elisit	elicit
elivate	elevate
elk	
ellbow	elbow
ellder	elder
ellicit	elicit
ellipse	
ellocution	elocution
elloquent	eloquent
elm	
eloap	elope
elocution	
elogant	elegant
elogible	eligible
eloment	element
elongate	
elood	elude
elope	
elophant	elephant
eloquence	
eloquent	
elovate	elevate
else	
elucution	elocution
elude	
elugant	elegant
elugible	eligible
elument	element
eluphant	elephant
eluquent	eloquent
elusive	
eluvate	elevate
elves	
elvs	elves
elvz	elves
emaciated	
emagrant	emigrant
emagrate	emigrate

emancipate	
emanent	eminent
emarald	emerald
emasiated	emaciated
emassary	emissary
embalm	
embam	embalm
embankment	
embar	ember
embarass	embarrass
embark	
embarrass	
embarrassment	
embassy	
embatled	embattled
embattled	
ember	
embessy	embassy
embezle	embezzle
embezzle	
embir	ember
embissy	embassy
embiter	embitter
embitter	
emblam	emblem
emblem	
emblim	emblem
emblom	emblem
emblum	emblem
embody	
embor	ember
emboss	
embossy	embassy
embrace	
embraice	embrace
embrase	embrace
embreo	embryo
embrio	embryo

embroider		emphatic		enchant	
embroidery		emphatically		enchanting	
embroyder	embroider	emphesize	emphasize	enchantment	
embryo		emphisize	emphasize	enciclopedia	encyclopedia
embur	ember	emphosize	emphasize	encircle	
embussy	embassy	emphusize	emphasize	encloase	enclose
emegrant	emigrant	empier	empire	enclose	
emegrate	emigrate	empire		enclosure	
emenent	eminent	empiror	emperor	encoar	encore
emerald		employ		encompass	
emerge		employee		encore	
emergency		employer		encounter	
emessary	emissary	employment		encourage	
emfasize	emphasize	emporor	emperor	encouragement	
emfatic	emphatic	empower		encownter	encounter
emfesize	emphasize	empriss	empress	encroach	
emfisize	emphasize	emptiness		encroche	encroach
emfosize	emphasize	empty		encumber	
emfusize	emphasize	emptyness	emptiness	encumpass	encompass
emigrant		empuror	emperor	encurage	encourage
emigrate		emugrant	emigrant	encwire	enquire
emigration		emugrate	emigrate	encyclopedia	
eminence		emulate		end	
eminent		emulation		endainger	endanger
emirald	emerald	emulsion		endanger	
emissary		emunent	eminent	endear	
emit		emurald	emerald	endeavor	
emogrant	emigrant	emussary	emissary	endeer	endear
emograte	emigrate	enable		endere	endear
emonent	eminent	enackt	enact	endevor	endeavor
emorald	emerald	enact		endewr	endure
emossary	emissary	enakt	enact	ending	
emotion		enamel		endless	
emotional		enamy	enemy	endoarse	endorse
emparor	emperor	enargy	energy	endoor	endure
emperor		encamp		endorse	
emphasis		encampment		endow	
emphasize		encercle	encircle	endowment	

endurance		enhanse	enhance	enoomerate	enumerate
endure		enigma		enorgy	energy
endurence	endurance	enimy	enemy	enormous	
enemy		enirgy	energy	enough	
energetic		enjan	engine	enquire	
energetically		enjen	engine	enquirey	enquiry
energy		enjender	engender	enquiry	
enewmerate	enumerate	enjin	engine	enrage	
enfoald	enfold	enjoin		enraige	enrage
enfold		enjon	engine	enrich	
enforce		enjoy		enroal	enroll
enforcement		enjoyable		enrole	enroll
enforse	enforce	enjoyment		enroll	
engage		enjoyn	enjoin	ensan	ensign
engaged		enjun	engine	ensen	ensign
engageing	engaging	enkamp	encamp	ensew	ensue
engagement		enklose	enclose	enshewr	ensure
engaging		enkompass	encompass	enshoor	ensure
engaige	engage	enkore	encore	enshrine	
engender		enkounter	encounter	enshur	ensure
engine		enkourage	encourage	ensiclopedia	encyclopedia
engineer		enkroach	encroach	ensign	
engineering		enkumber	encumber	ensin	ensign
England		enkurage	encourage	ensircle	encircle
Englend	England	enkwire	enquire	enslaive	enslave
Englind	England	enlarge		enslave	
English		enlargement		enson	ensign
Englond	England	enlighten		ensoo	ensue
Englund	England	enlist		ensue	
engraive	engrave	enliten	enlighten	ensun	ensign
engrave		enliven		ensure	
engraveing	engraving	enmaty	enmity	ensyclopedia	encyclopedia
engraving		enmety	enmity	entangle	
engroase	engross	enmity		entanglement	
engrose	engross	enmoty	enmity	entar	enter
engross		enmuty	enmity	enter	
engulf		enny	any	enterance	entrance
enhance		enomy	enemy	enterprise	

enterprising		enuf	enough
entertain		enumerate	
entertainment		enumy	enemy
enthewsiasm	enthusiasm	enunciate	
enthoosiasm	enthusiasm	enunciation	
enthooziasm	enthusiasm	enunsiate	enunciate
enthrall		enurgy	energy
enthroan	enthrone	envalope	envelope
enthrol	enthrall	envelop	
enthrone		envelope	
enthusiasm		enviable	
enthusiast		envie	envy
enthusiastic		envilope	envelope
enthusiastically		enviornment	environment
enthuziasm	enthusiasm	envious	
entice		environment	
entier	entire	envolope	envelope
entir	enter	envoy	
entire		envulope	envelope
entirely		envyable	enviable
entirety		envyous	envious
entise	entice	eny	any
entitle		epach	epic
entor	enter	epademic	epidemic
entrance		epak	epic
entranse	entrance	epasode	episode
entreat		epech	epic
entree	entry	epedemic	epidemic
entreet	entreat	epek	epic
entrence	entrance	epesode	episode
entrete	entreat	ephemeral	
entrince	entrance	epic	
entronce	entrance	epich	epic
entrunce	entrance	epick	epic
entrust		epidemic	
entry		epik	epic
entur	enter	episode	
entwine		epoch	

enough	
enemy	

epock	epic
epodemic	epidemic
epok	epic
eposode	episode
epuch	epic
epudemic	epidemic
epuk	epic
epusode	episode
equal	
equalibrium	equilibrium
equality	
equally	
equaly	equally
equanox	equinox
equator	
equatorial	
equaty	equity
equel	equal
equelibrium	equilibrium
equenox	equinox
equety	equity
equil	equal
equilibrium	
equinox	
equip	
equipment	
equitable	
equity	
equivalent	
equl	equal
equlibrium	equilibrium
equnox	equinox
equol	equal
equolibrium	equilibrium
equonox	equinox
equoty	equity
equty	equity
era	

erace	erase	eroad	erode	ese	ease
eradicate		erode		esel	easel
eraice	erase	erond	errand	esence	essence
eraise	erase	eront	errant	esey	easy
erand	errand	eror	error	esince	essence
erant	errant	erosion		Eskamo	Eskimo
erar	error	erozion	erosion	eskape	escape
erase		err		Eskemo	Eskimo
eraser		errand		Eskimo	
eratic	erratic	errant		Eskomo	Eskimo
erb	herb	errar	error	eskort	escort
erban	urban	erratic		Eskumo	Eskimo
erchin	urchin	errend	errand	esofagus	esophagus
ere	ear	errent	errant	esonce	essence
ereckt	erect	errer	error	esophagus	
erect		errind	errand	especially	
erection		errint	errant	espeonage	espionage
erekt	erect	errir	error	espeshally	especially
erend	errand	errond	errand	espionage	
erent	errant	erroneous		essance	essence
erer	error	erront	errant	essay	
erey	eerie	error		essence	
erge	urge	errund	errand	essencial	essential
ergent	urgent	errunt	errant	essense	essence
erind	errand	errur	error	essential	
erint	errant	erth	earth	essentially	
erir	error	erund	errand	essince	essence
erksome	irksome	erunt	errant	essonce	essence
erly	early	erupt		essunce	essence
erman	ermine	eruption		establish	
ermen	ermine	erur	error	establishment	
ermin	ermine	esance	essence	estait	estate
ermine		esay	essay	estamate	estimate
ermon	ermine	escaip	escape	estate	
ermun	ermine	escape		esteam	esteem
ern	earn	escoart	escort	esteem	
ern	urn	escort		estemate	estimate
ernest	earnest	escourt	escort	esteme	esteem

estimate		evakuate	evacuate	evoak	evoke	
estimation		eval	evil	evodent	evident	
estomate	estimate	evalution	evolution	evoke		
estumate	estimate	evan	even	evol	evil	
esunce	essence	evaning	evening	evolution		
etaquette	etiquette	evaporate		evolve		
etch		evaporation		evon	even	
etching		evar	ever	evoning	evening	
ete	eat	evary	every	evor	ever	
etequette	etiquette	eve		evory	every	
eternal		evedent	evident	evudent	evident	
eternity		evel	evil	evul	evil	
ethar	ether	evelution	evolution	evulution	evolution	
ether		even		evun	even	
ethereal		evening		evuning	evening	
ethir	ether	evenly		evur	ever	
ethor	ether	event		evury	every	
ethur	ether	eventful		exact		
etiket	etiquette	eventual		exacting		
etiquette		eventually		exactly		
etirnal	eternal	ever		exacute	execute	
etoquette	etiquette	evergreen		exadus	exodus	
etuquette	etiquette	everlasting		exagerate	exaggerate	
eturnal	eternal	evermore		exaggerate		
eucalyptus		every		exaggeration		
eukalyptus	eucalyptus	everybody		exakt	exact	
Eurap	Europe	everyone		exalt		
Eurep	Europe	everything		examination		
Eurip	Europe	everywhere		examine		
Europ	Europe	evesdropper	eavesdropper	example		
Europe		evidence		exarsize	exercise	
European		evident		exasperate		
Eurup	Europe	evil		exasperation		
evackuate	evacuate	evilution	evolution	exaust	exhaust	
evacuate		evin	even	exawst	exhaust	
evade		evining	evening	excavate		
evadent	evident	evir	ever	excavation		
evaid	evade	eviry	every	exceed		

exceeding
exceedingly
excel
excelent   excellent
excellence
excellency
excellent
except
exception
exceptional
excess
excessive
exchange
excitable
excite
exciteable   excitable
excited
excitedly
excitement
exclaim
exclaimation   exclamation
exclamation
exclamatory
exclame   exclaim
exclude
exclusion
exclusive
exclusively
excovate   excavate
excursion
excuse
excuvate   excavate
excuze   excuse
excwisite   exquisite
execute
execution
executioner
executive

exedus   exodus
exempt
exentric   eccentric
exercise
exert
exertion
exhail   exhale
exhale
exhaust
exhausted
exhaustion
exhawst   exhaust
exhibit
exhibition
exhilarate
exhort
exicute   execute
exidus   exodus
exilarate   exhilarate
exile
exircise   exercise
exist
existence
exit
exkavate   excavate
exkersion   excursion
exklude   exclude
exkuze   excuse
exkwisite   exquisite
exocute   execute
exodus
exorbitant
exorcise   exercise
exort   exhort
exotic
expadition   expedition
expance   expanse
expand

expanse
expansion
expect
expectant
expectation
expedient
expedition
expel
expend
expenditure
expense
expensive
experience
experienced
experiment
experimental
expert
expidition   expedition
expier   expire
expire
explain
explaination   explanation
explanation
explanatory
explane   explain
explicit
explisit   explicit
expload   explode
exploar   explore
explode
exploit
exploration
explore
exploreation   exploration
explorer
explosion
explosive
exployt   exploit

explozion	explosion	exsess	excess	extravagant	
expoase	expose	exsite	excite	extream	extreme
expodition	expedition	extend		extreem	extreme
export		extension		extreme	
expose		extensive		extremely	
exposition		extent		extremity	
exposure		exterior		extricate	
expound		exterminate		extrordinary	extraordinary
expownd	expound	external		exucute	execute
express		extinct		exudus	exodus
expression		extinction		exult	
expressive		extinguish		exultant	
expressly		extoal	extol	exultation	
expudition	expedition	extol		exurcise	exercise
expulsion		extra		eye	
exquisite		extracate	extricate	eyelet	
exquizite	exquisite	extract		eyelit	eyelet
exseed	exceed	extrakt	extract	eyesight	
exsel	excel	extraordinarily		eyesite	eyesight
exsept	except	extraordinary		ezel	easel
		extravagance			

F

fabal	fable	face		factary	factory
fabel	fable	facet		factchual	factual
fabewlous	fabulous	facial		facter	factor
fabil	fable	faciel	facial	factery	factory
fable		facilitate		factir	factor
fabol	fable	facility		factiry	factory
fabric		faciol	facial	factor	
fabrik	fabric	facit	facet	factory	
fabul	fable	faciul	facial	factual	
fabulous		facolty	faculty	factur	factor
facade		fact		factury	factory
facalty	faculty	factar	factor	faculty	

fade	
fag	
fahranheit	fahrenheit
fahrenheit	
fahrinheit	fahrenheit
fahronheit	fahrenheit
fahrunheit	fahrenheit
faible	fable
faice	face
faid	fade
faik	fake
fail	
failing	
failure	
failyur	failure
faim	fame
fain	feign
faint	
faint	feint
fair	
fair	fare
fairly	
fairness	
fairniss	fairness
fairwell	farewell
fairy	
fait	fate
faital	fatal
faith	
faithful	
fake	
fakt	fact
faktory	factory
fakulty	faculty
falcan	falcon
falcon	
falcun	falcon
fale	fail

falicity	felicity
falkan	falcon
falken	falcon
falkin	falcon
falkon	falcon
falkun	falcon
fall	
fallan	fallen
fallen	
fallow	
fallt	fault
fallter	falter
falow	fallow
false	
falsehood	
falsehud	falsehood
faltar	falter
falter	
faltir	falter
faltor	falter
faltur	falter
famaly	family
faman	famine
famas	famous
fame	
famely	family
famen	famine
famess	famous
familiar	
familiarity	
family	
famin	famine
famine	
famis	famous
famish	
famoly	family
famon	famine
famos	famous

famous	
famuly	family
famun	famine
famus	famous
fan	
fanatic	
fanciful	
fancy	
fancyful	fanciful
fane	feign
fang	
fansy	fancy
fantastic	
fantasy	
fantesy	fantasy
fantisy	fantasy
fantom	phantom
fantosy	fantasy
fantusy	fantasy
far	
faran	foreign
Faraoh	Pharaoh
farbid	forbid
fare	
fare	fair
faren	foreign
farenheit	fahrenheit
farest	forest
farever	forever
farewell	
farey	fairy
farget	forget
fargive	forgive
farin	foreign
farist	forest
farm	
farmacy	pharmacy
farmer	

Faro	Pharaoh	fat		favorite	
farocious	ferocious	fatal		favur	favor
farthar	farther	fate		favurite	favorite
farther		fateag	fatigue	fawcet	faucet
farthest		fateeg	fatigue	fawlt	fault
farthir	farther	fatel	fatal	fawn	
farthist	farthest	fatham	fathom	fayn	feign
farthor	farther	fathar	father	faynt	faint
farthur	farther	fathem	fathom	faynt	feint
farun	foreign	father		fayth	faith
fasade	facade	father	farther	faze	phase
fasan	fasten	fathim	fathom	feable	feeble
fasanate	fascinate	fathir	father	feachur	feature
fascenate	fascinate	fathom		fead	feed
fascinate		fathor	father	feal	feel
fascination		fathum	fathom	feald	field
fase	face	fathur	father	fealty	
fase	phase	fatigue		feamale	female
fasen	fasten	fatil	fatal	feand	fiend
fasenate	fascinate	fatol	fatal	fear	
faset	facet	fatty		fearce	fierce
fashan	fashion	fatul	fatal	fearful	
fashen	fashion	faucet		fearless	
fashin	fashion	faucit	faucet	fearliss	fearless
fashion		faught	fought	feasable	feasible
fashionable		fault		feasant	pheasant
fashon	fashion	faultless		feaseble	feasible
fashun	fashion	faultliss	faultless	feasible	
fasility	facility	faulty		feasoble	feasible
fasin	fasten	favar	favor	feast	
fasinate	fascinate	favarite	favorite	feasuble	feasible
fason	fasten	faver	favor	feat	
fasonate	fascinate	faverite	favorite	feat	feet
fast		favir	favor	featchur	feature
fasten		favirite	favorite	feathar	feather
fastidious		favor		feather	
fasun	fasten	favorable		feathir	feather
fasunate	fascinate	favorably		feathor	feather

feathur	feather	feezible	feasible	fere	fear
feature		feign		feret	ferret
feaver	fever	feild	field	ferever	forever
feazible	feasible	feilty	fealty	ferget	forget
February		feind	fiend	fergive	forgive
Febuary	February	feint		ferit	ferret
Feburary	February	feirce	fierce	ferl	furl
fecade	facade	fele	feel	ferlong	furlong
fech	fetch	felicity		ferlough	furlough
fecilitate	facilitate	felisity	felicity	ferm	firm
fed		fell		fermament	firmament
fedaral	federal	fellow		ferment	
fede	feed	felow	fellow	fern	
federal		felt		fernace	furnace
fediral	federal	femail	female	fernish	furnish
fedoral	federal	female		ferniture	furniture
fedural	federal	femanine	feminine	ferocious	
fee		femenine	feminine	ferret	
feebal	feeble	familiar	familiar	ferrit	ferret
feebel	feeble	feminine		ferrow	furrow
feebil	feeble	femonine	feminine	ferry	
feeble		femunine	feminine	ferst	first
feebol	feeble	fenatic	fanatic	fertal	fertile
feebul	feeble	fence		fertel	fertile
feed		fencing		ferther	further
feel		fendar	fender	fertil	fertile
feeld	field	fender		fertile	
feeling		fendir	fender	fertility	
feemale	female	fendor	fender	fertilization	
feend	fiend	fendur	fender	fertilize	
feer	fear	fenomenon	phenomenon	fertilizer	
feerce	fierce	fense	fence	fertive	furtive
feesible	feasible	fents	fence	fertol	fertile
feest	feast	feolty	fealty	fertul	fertile
feet		feord	fiord	fervant	fervent
feet	feat	fer	fir	fervar	fervor
feeture	feature	fer	fur	fervent	
feever	fever	ferbid	forbid	ferver	fervor

fervint	fervent	fevar	fever	fiddler	
fervir	fervor	fever		fiddol	fiddle
fervont	fervent	feverish		fiddul	fiddle
fervor		fevir	fever	fidelity	
fervunt	fervent	fevor	fever	fidellity	fidelity
fervur	fervor	fevur	fever	fidget	
fery	ferry	few		fidgit	fidget
fesant	pheasant	fewd	feud	fidil	fiddle
festaval	festival	fewl	fuel	fidol	fiddle
festeval	festival	fewneral	funeral	fidul	fiddle
festewn	festoon	fews	fuse	field	
festival		fez		fiend	
festive		fial	file	fiendish	
festivity		fib		fier	fire
festoon		fibar	fiber	fierce	
festoval	festival	fiber		fiercely	
festune	festoon	fibir	fiber	fiery	
festuval	festival	fibor	fiber	fiesta	
fet	fete	fibur	fiber	fifteen	
fetar	fetter	ficade	facade	fifth	
fetch		fical	fickle	fifty	
fetching		ficility	facility	fig	
fete		fickal	fickle	figet	fidget
fete	feat	fickel	fickle	fight	
fete	feet	fickil	fickle	fighter	
feter	fetter	fickle		figit	fidget
fether	feather	fickol	fickle	figure	
fetigue	fatigue	ficks	fix	figyer	figure
fetir	fetter	ficktion	fiction	fijet	fidget
fetor	fetter	fickul	fickle	fikal	fickle
fettar	fetter	ficol	fickle	fikel	fickle
fetter		ficshun	fiction	fikil	fickle
fettir	fetter	fiction		fikol	fickle
fettor	fetter	ficul	fickle	fiks	fix
fettur	fetter	fidal	fiddle	fiktion	fiction
fetur	fetter	fiddal	fiddle	fikul	fickle
feud		fiddil	fiddle	fil	fill
feulty	fealty	fiddle		filament	

filanthropist	philanthropist	**financeal**	financial	**firm**	
filay	fillet	**financial**		**firmament**	
filch		**financier**		**firmement**	firmament
file		**finanse**	finance	**firmiment**	firmament
filial		**finary**	finery	**firmness**	
filicity	felicity	**finatic**	fanatic	**firmniss**	firmness
filiment	filament	**finch**		**firmoment**	firmament
filings		**find**		**firmument**	firmament
Filippine	Philippine	**fine**		**firn**	fern
fill		**fined**	find	**firnace**	furnace
fillay	fillet	**finel**	final	**firnish**	furnish
fillet		**finery**		**firniture**	furniture
fillial	filial	**fingar**	finger	**firocious**	ferocious
filling		**finger**		**firrow**	furrow
Fillippine	Philippine	**fingir**	finger	**first**	
fillth	filth	**fingor**	finger	**firther**	further
filly		**fingur**	finger	**firtile**	fertile
film		**finil**	final	**firtive**	furtive
filoment	filament	**finiry**	finery	**firvent**	fervent
filosophy	philosophy	**finish**		**fish**	
filtar	filter	**finol**	final	**fishon**	fission
filter		**finory**	finery	**fishun**	fission
filth		**finul**	final	**fishure**	fissure
filthy		**finury**	finery	**fisical**	physical
filtir	filter	**fiord**		**fisics**	physics
filtor	filter	**fir**		**fisique**	physique
filtur	filter	**fir**	fur	**fission**	
filument	filament	**firarms**	firearms	**fissure**	
fily	filly	**firbid**	forbid	**fist**	
fimiliar	familiar	**fire**		**fit**	
fin		**firearms**		**fite**	fight
final		**firever**	forever	**fitful**	
finale		**firey**	fiery	**fitigue**	fatigue
finaley	finale	**firget**	forget	**fiting**	fitting
finally		**firgive**	forgive	**fitness**	
finaly	finale	**firl**	furl	**fitniss**	fitness
finaly	finally	**firlong**	furlong	**fitting**	
finance		**firlough**	furlough	**five**	

fix		flannul	flannel	fleck	
fixcher	fixture	flanol	flannel	flecks	flex
fixtcher	fixture	flanul	flannel	fled	
fixture		flap		fledgling	
fizical	physical	flare		flee	
fizics	physics	flare	flair	flee	flea
fizique	physique	flash		fleece	
flacks	flax	flask		fleecey	fleecy
flag		flat		fleecy	
flaike	flake	flatar	flatter	fleese	fleece
flail		flater	flatter	fleet	
flaim	flame	flatir	flatter	fleeting	
flair		flator	flatter	flek	fleck
flair	flare	flattar	flatter	fleks	flex
flake		flatter		flemingo	flamingo
flaks	flax	flattery		flerish	flourish
flale	flail	flattir	flatter	flerry	flurry
flamable	flammable	flattor	flatter	flert	flirt
flamboyant		flattur	flatter	flesh	
flame		flatur	flatter	fleshy	
flameble	flammable	flaunt		flete	fleet
flamible	flammable	flavar	flavor	flew	
flamingo		flaver	flavor	flew	flue
flammable		flavir	flavor	flewid	fluid
flammeble	flammable	flavor		flewt	flute
flammible	flammable	flavoring		flex	
flammoble	flammable	flavur	flavor	flexable	flexible
flammuble	flammable	flaw		flexeble	flexible
flamoble	flammable	flawless		flexible	
flamuble	flammable	flawliss	flawless	flexoble	flexible
flanal	flannel	flawnt	flaunt	flexuble	flexible
flanel	flannel	flax		flick	
flanil	flannel	flay		flickar	flicker
flank		flea		flicker	
flannal	flannel	flea	flee	flickir	flicker
flannel		fleace	fleece	flickor	flicker
flannil	flannel	flease	fleece	flickur	flicker
flannol	flannel	fleat	fleet	flier	

flight		flog		flower	
flik	flick	flok	flock	flower	flour
flimingo	flamingo	flomingo	flamingo	flowir	flour
flimsy		flone	flown	flowir	flower
flimzy	flimsy	flont	flaunt	flown	
flinch		floo	flue	flownder	flounder
fling		flood		flowor	flour
flint		flooid	fluid	flowor	flower
flip		floor		flowt	flout
flipant	flippant	floot	flute	flowur	flour
flipar	flipper	flop		flowur	flower
flipent	flippant	flor	floor	flud	flood
fliper	flipper	Florada	Florida	flue	
flipint	flippant	floral		flue	flew
flipir	flipper	flore	flaw	fluf	fluff
flipont	flippant	flore	floor	fluff	
flipor	flipper	Floreda	Florida	fluffy	
flippant		florel	floral	fluid	
flippar	flipper	Florida		flumingo	flamingo
flippent	flippant	floril	floral	flung	
flipper		florist		flurish	flourish
flippint	flippant	Floroda	Florida	flurry	
flippir	flipper	florol	floral	flurt	flirt
flippont	flippant	Floruda	Florida	flury	flurry
flippor	flipper	florul	floral	flush	
flippunt	flippant	flos	floss	flustar	fluster
flippur	flipper	floss		fluster	
flipunt	flippant	flote	float	flustir	fluster
flipur	flipper	flouer	flour	flustor	fluster
flirry	flurry	flouer	flower	flustur	fluster
flirt		flounder		flutar	flutter
flit		flour		flute	
flite	flight	flour	flower	flutir	flutter
floan	flown	flourish		flutor	flutter
floar	flaw	flout		fluttar	flutter
floar	floor	flow		flutter	
float		flowar	flour	fluttir	flutter
flock		flowar	flower	fluttor	flutter

fluttur	flutter	foggy		fomiliar	familiar
flutur	flutter	fogy	foggy	fonatic	fanatic
fly		foibal	foible	fond	
flyer		foibel	foible	fondal	fondle
flying		foibil	foible	fondel	fondle
fo	foe	foible		fondil	fondle
foak	folk	foibol	foible	fondle	
foal		foibul	foible	fondness	
foaliage	foliage	foil		fondniss	fondness
foam		foke	folk	fondol	fondle
foar	for	foks	fox	fondul	fondle
foar	fore	fokus	focus	fone	phone
foar	four	fold		fonetic	phonetic
foaray	foray	foldar	folder	fonograph	phonograph
foarbear	forbear	folder		font	
foarbid	forbid	foldir	folder	food	
foarce	force	foldor	folder	fool	
foarceps	forceps	foldur	folder	foolhardy	
foartify	fortify	fole	foal	foolheardy	foolhardy
foartitude	fortitude	foleage	foliage	foolish	
foartnight	fortnight	foliage		foolishness	
focade	facade	folicity	felicity	foolproof	
focas	focus	folk		foolpruf	foolproof
focility	facility	foll	fall	foot	
focks	fox	foll	foal	footing	
focos	focus	folley	folly	for	
focus		follo	follow	for	fore
fodar	fodder	follow		for	four
foddar	fodder	follower		forage	
fodder		following		foram	forum
foddir	fodder	folly		foran	foreign
foddor	fodder	folow	follow	foray	
foddur	fodder	folse	false	forbade	
fodir	fodder	folt	fault	forbaid	forbade
fodor	fodder	folter	falter	forbair	forbear
fodur	fodder	foly	folly	forbare	forbear
foe		folyage	foliage	forbear	
fog		fome	foam	forbearance	

forbid	
forbidden	
forbidding	
forbiden	forbidden
forbiding	forbidding
forboding	foreboding
forcast	forecast
force	
forceble	forcible
forceful	
forceps	
forcet	faucet
forchune	fortune
forcible	
forck	fork
ford	
fore	
fore	four
foreboading	foreboding
foreboding	
forecast	
forege	forage
forego	
foreground	
forehead	
forehed	forehead
foreign	
foreigner	
forekast	forecast
forelorn	forlorn
forem	forum
foremost	
foremulate	formulate
foren	foreign
foresake	forsake
foresee	
foresight	
foresooth	forsooth

forest	
foresythia	forsythia
foretell	
foreth	forth
foretify	fortify
foretitude	fortitude
forety	forty
forever	
foreward	forward
forfeit	
forfiet	forfeit
forfit	forfeit
forgaive	forgave
forgave	
forge	
forget	
forgetful	
forgive	
forgiven	
forgo	forego
forgot	
forgoten	forgotten
forgotten	
forground	foreground
forhead	forehead
forid	forehead
forige	forage
forim	forum
forin	foreign
forist	forest
fork	
forloarn	forlorn
forlorn	
form	
formadable	formidable
formal	
formality	
formally	

formar	former
formation	
formedable	formidable
formel	formal
former	
formerly	
formidable	
formil	formal
formir	former
formodable	formidable
formol	formal
formor	former
formost	foremost
formudable	formidable
formul	formal
formulate	
formur	former
forocious	ferocious
foroge	forage
forom	forum
forsaik	forsake
forsake	
forsaken	
forse	force
forsee	foresee
forseps	forceps
forsight	foresight
forsithia	forsythia
forsook	
forsooth	
forsuk	forsook
forsuth	forsooth
forsythia	
fort	
fort	fought
fortafy	fortify
fortatude	fortitude
fortchune	fortune

fortefy	fortify	fossol	fossil	fox	
fortell	foretell	fossul	fossil	foxy	
fortetude	fortitude	fostar	foster	foyble	foible
forth		foster		foyl	foil
forthcoming		fostir	foster	fracktion	fraction
forthwith		fostor	foster	frackture	fracture
fortieth		fostur	foster	fracshun	fraction
fortification		fosul	fossil	fractchur	fracture
fortify		fotigue	fatigue	fraction	
fortitude		foto	photo	fracture	
fortnight		fotograph	photograph	fragial	fragile
fortnite	fortnight	fought		fragiel	fragile
fortofy	fortify	foul		fragil	fragile
fortotude	fortitude	foul	fowl	fragile	
fortress		found		fragiol	fragile
fortriss	fortress	foundation		fragiul	fragile
fortufy	fortify	founder		fragment	
fortunate		foundling		fragrance	
fortune		fount		fragranse	fragrance
fortutude	fortitude	fountain		fragrant	
forty		fountan	fountain	fragrence	fragrance
fortyeth	fortieth	founten	fountain	fragrince	fragrance
foruge	forage	fountin	fountain	fragronce	fragrance
forum		founton	fountain	fragrunce	fragrance
forun	foreign	fountun	fountain	frail	
forwad	forward	four		frailty	
forward		four	fore	fraim	frame
forwood	forward	fourgo	forego	frait	freight
forwud	forward	fourteen		frajile	fragile
fosal	fossil	fourth		frakchur	fracture
fosel	fossil	fourtnight	fortnight	fraktion	fraction
fosforus	phosphorus	fourty	forty	frakture	fracture
fosil	fossil	fow	foe	frale	frail
fosol	fossil	fowl		frame	
fosphorus	phosphorus	fowl	foul	franc	
fossal	fossil	fownd	found	France	
fossel	fossil	fowndling	foundling	franck	franc
fossil		fownt	fount	franck	frank

frank		free		friendliness	
frank	franc	freedam	freedom	friendly	
frankferter	frankfurter	freedem	freedom	friendlyness	friendliness
frankfirter	frankfurter	freedim	freedom	friendship	
frankfooter	frankfurter	freedom		frier	friar
frankforter	frankfurter	freedum	freedom	frigat	frigate
frankfurter		freek	freak	frigate	
frankness		freequent	frequent	friget	frigate
frankniss	frankness	freeze		fright	
Franse	France	freezer		frighten	
frantic		freight		frightful	
frantically		freighter		frigid	
franticaly	frantically	freind	friend	frigot	frigate
franticly	frantically	freke	freak	frigut	frigate
frantik	frantic	frekle	freckle	frijid	frigid
frase	phrase	frekwent	frequent	friktion	friction
frate	freight	French		fril	frill
fraternal		frend	friend	frill	
fraternity		frenzied		fringe	
fratirnal	fraternal	frenzy		frior	friar
fraturnal	fraternal	frenzyd	frenzied	frisk	
fraud		frequent		frisky	
fraught		frequently		frite	fright
frawd	fraud	fresh		friternal	fraternal
frawt	fraught	freshet		friur	friar
fray		freshit	freshet	frivalous	frivolous
fraze	phrase	fret		frivelous	frivolous
frea	free	freternal	fraternal	frivilous	frivolous
freak		frewt	fruit	frivolous	
freaquent	frequent	freze	freeze	frivulous	frivolous
freaze	freeze	friar		fro	
freckal	freckle	fricktion	friction	froaze	froze
freckel	freckle	friction		frock	
freckil	freckle	Friday		frod	fraud
freckle		fride	fried	frog	
freckol	freckle	fridgid	frigid	frok	frock
freckul	freckle	fried		frolic	
frecwent	frequent	friend		frolick	frolic

frolicsome		fruternal	fraternal	fumble	
frolik	frolic	fry		fumbol	fumble
frollic	frolic	Fryday	Friday	fumbul	fumble
from		fryed	fried	fume	
front		fual	fuel	fumegate	fumigate
frontear	frontier	fucade	facade	fumigate	
fronteer	frontier	fucher	future	fumiliar	familiar
fronteir	frontier	fucilitate	facilitate	fumogate	fumigate
frontere	frontier	fude	feud	fumugate	fumigate
frontier		fude	food	fun	
froot	fruit	fue	few	funal	funnel
frord	fraud	fuel		funaral	funeral
frort	frought	fugative	fugitive	funatic	fanatic
frost		fugetive	fugitive	funcktion	function
frosting		fugitive		funcshun	function
froternal	fraternal	fugotive	fugitive	function	
froth		fugutive	fugitive	fund	
frought	fraught	fuil	fuel	fundamental	
frow	fro	fujitive	fugitive	fundemental	fundamental
frown		ful	full	fundimental	fundamental
froze		fulcram	fulcrum	fundomental	fundamental
frozen		fulcrem	fulcrum	fundumental	fundamental
frugal		fulcrim	fulcrum	funel	funnel
frugality		fulcrom	fulcrum	funeral	
frugel	frugal	fulcrum		fungas	fungus
frugil	frugal	fule	fool	fungess	fungus
frugol	frugal	fule	fuel	fungis	fungus
frugul	frugal	fulfill		fungos	fungus
fruit		fulfillment		fungus	
fruitful		fulicity	felicity	funil	funnel
fruitless		fulkrum	fulcrum	funiral	funeral
fruitliss	fruitless	full		funktion	function
frum	from	fullfill	fulfill	funnal	funnel
frunt	front	fully		funnel	
fruntier	frontier	fumagate	fumigate	funnil	funnel
frustrait	frustrate	fumbal	fumble	funnol	funnel
frustrate		fumbel	fumble	funnul	funnel
frute	fruit	fumbil	fumble	funny	

funol	funnel	furneture	furniture	furyous	furious
funoral	funeral	furnice	furnace	fus	fuss
funul	funnel	furnis	furnace	fusalage	fuselage
funural	funeral	furnish		fuse	
funy	funny	furniture		fuselage	
fuol	fuel	furnoture	furniture	fusilage	fuselage
fur		furnuture	furniture	fusion	
fur	fir	furo	furrow	fusolage	fuselage
furbid	forbid	furocious	ferocious	fuss	
fureous	furious	furow	furrow	fussy	
furever	forever	furro	furrow	fusulage	fuselage
furget	forget	furrow		fut	foot
furgive	forgive	furst	first	futal	futile
furious		furthar	further	futcher	future
furius	furious	further		futel	futile
furl		furthermore		futigue	fatigue
furlo	furlough	furthest		futil	futile
furlong		furthir	further	futile	
furlough		furthist	furthest	futol	futile
furlow	furlough	furthor	further	futul	futile
furm	firm	furthur	further	future	
furmament	firmament	furtile	fertile	fuze	fuse
furn	fern	furtive		fuzelage	fuselage
furnace		furvent	fervent	fuzion	fusion
furnase	furnace	fury		fyord	fiord
furnature	furniture			fysical	physical

G

ga	gay	gagit	gadget	gainsay	
gadget		gaiety		gaip	gape
gadgit	gadget	gail	gale	gait	
gadjet	gadget	gaila	gala	gait	gate
gag		gaily		gaive	gave
gage	gauge	gaim	game	gaize	gaze
gaget	gadget	gain		gala	

galan	gallon	gallory	gallery	gandur	gander
galant	gallant	gallows		gane	gain
galap	gallop	galloze	gallows	ganesay	gainsay
galary	gallery	gallun	gallon	gang	
gale		gallunt	gallant	gap	
galen	gallon	gallup	gallop	gape	
galent	gallant	gallury	gallery	garage	
galeon	galleon	gally	galley	garantee	guarantee
galep	gallop	galoaze	gallows	garason	garrison
galer	gala	galon	gallon	garb	
galery	gallery	galont	gallant	garbage	
galey	galley	galop	gallop	garbege	garbage
galin	gallon	galory	gallery	garbige	garbage
galint	gallant	galosh		garboge	garbage
galion	galleon	galows	gallows	garbuge	garbage
galip	gallop	galoze	gallows	Gard	God
galiry	gallery	galun	gallon	gard	guard
gall		galunt	gallant	gardan	garden
gallan	gallon	galup	gallop	garden	
gallant		galury	gallery	gardener	
gallantry		gambal	gamble	gardin	garden
gallap	gallop	gambal	gambol	gardon	garden
gallary	gallery	gambel	gamble	gardun	garden
gallen	gallon	gambel	gambol	gareson	garrison
gallent	gallant	gambil	gamble	garet	garret
galleon		gambil	gambol	gargal	gargle
gallep	gallop	gamble		gargel	gargle
gallery		gamble	gambol	gargil	gargle
galley		gambler		gargle	
gallin	gallon	gambol		gargoil	gargoyle
gallint	gallant	gambol	gamble	gargol	gargle
gallion	galleon	gambul	gamble	gargoyle	
gallip	gallop	gambul	gambol	gargul	gargle
galliry	gallery	game		garilla	gorilla
galloaze	gallows	gandar	gander	garintee	guarantee
gallon		gander		garison	garrison
gallont	gallant	gandir	gander	garit	garret
gallop		gandor	gander	garland	

garlend	garland	gaseous		gayity	gaiety
garlic		gaseus	gaseous	gayla	gala
garlik	garlic	gash		gayly	gaily
garlind	garland	gasiline	gasoline	gayoty	gaiety
garlond	garland	gasious	gaseous	gayuty	gaiety
garlund	garland	gasoline		gaze	
garmant	garment	gasp		gazel	gazelle
garment		gastly	ghastly	gazelle	
garmint	garment	gasuline	gasoline	geanial	genial
garmont	garment	gatar	guitar	geanie	genie
garmunt	garment	gate		geanius	genius
garnar	garner	gate	gait	geans	jeans
garner		gathar	gather	gear	
garnet		gather		gease	geese
garnir	garner	gathering		geenial	genial
garnish		gathir	gather	geenie	genie
garnit	garnet	gathor	gather	geenius	genius
garnor	garner	gathur	gather	geep	jeep
garnur	garner	gaudy		geer	gear
garontee	guarantee	gauge		geer	jeer
garoson	garrison	gaunt		geese	
garrason	garrison	gauntlet		gelatin	
garreson	garrison	gauntlit	gauntlet	geletin	gelatin
garret		gauze		gelitin	gelatin
garrison		gaval	gavel	gelly	jelly
garrit	garret	gave		gelotin	gelatin
garroson	garrison	gavel		gelous	jealous
garruson	garrison	gavil	gavel	gelutin	gelatin
gartar	garter	gavol	gavel	gem	
garter		gavul	gavel	genaral	general
gartir	garter	gawdy	gaudy	genarate	generate
gartor	garter	gawl	gall	genarous	generous
gartur	garter	gawnt	gaunt	general	
garuntee	guarantee	gawntlet	gauntlet	generally	
garuson	garrison	gawze	gauze	generate	
gas		gay		generation	
gasaline	gasoline	gayaty	gaiety	generator	
gaseline	gasoline	gayety	gaiety	generous	

geney	genie	gergle	gurgle	gidy	giddy
genial		gerk	jerk	gie	guy
genie		gerl	girl	gient	giant
genious	genius	germ		giffy	jiffy
geniral	general	German		gift	
genirate	generate	germanate	germinate	gifted	
genirous	generous	Germany		giftid	gifted
genius		germenate	germinate	gig	
genoral	general	germinate		gig	jig
genorate	generate	germonate	germinate	gigal	giggle
genorous	generous	germunate	germinate	gigantic	
gental	gentle	gersey	jersey	gigel	giggle
gentel	gentle	gerth	girth	giggal	giggle
gentil	gentle	geschur	gesture	giggel	giggle
gentile		gese	geese	giggil	giggle
gentility		gess	guess	giggle	
gentle		gest	guest	giggle	jiggle
gentleman		gest	jest	giggol	giggle
gentley	gently	gestchur	gesture	giggul	giggle
gently		gesture		gigil	giggle
gentol	gentle	get		gigle	giggle
gentul	gentle	get	jet	gigol	giggle
genuine		getty	jetty	gigsaw	jigsaw
genural	general	gewel	jewel	gigul	giggle
genurate	generate	geysar	geyser	gil	gill
genurous	generous	geyser		gilatine	guillotine
genyal	genial	geysir	geyser	gild	
genyus	genius	geysor	geyser	gild	guild
geography		geysur	geyser	gile	guile
geology		geyzer	geyser	gilitine	guillotine
geometry		ghastly		gill	
Georgia		ghost		gillatine	guillotine
gepardy	jeopardy	ghostly		gilled	gild
geraffe	giraffe	gi	guy	gilletine	guillotine
geranium		giant		gillitine	guillotine
gerder	girder	gibe		gillotine	guillotine
gerdle	girdle	giddy		gillutine	guillotine
gere	gear	gide	guide	gilosh	galosh

gilotine	guillotine	girth		glanse	glance
gilt		gise	guise	glare	
gilt	guilt	giser	geyser	glareing	glaring
gilutine	guillotine	gitar	guitar	glaring	
gimnasium	gymnasium	giunt	giant	glas	glass
gin		give		glashal	glacial
gingam	gingham	given		glasher	glacier
gingem	gingham	gizard	gizzard	glass	
ginger		gize	guise	glassy	
gingham		gizer	geyser	glaze	
gingim	gingham	gizerd	gizzard	gle	glee
gingir	ginger	gizird	gizzard	glea	glee
gingle	jingle	gizord	gizzard	gleam	
gingom	gingham	gizurd	gizzard	glean	
gingum	gingham	gizzard		glee	
ginricksha	jinrikisha	gizzerd	gizzard	gleeful	
giography	geography	gizzird	gizzard	gleem	gleam
giology	geology	gizzord	gizzard	gleen	glean
giometry	geometry	gizzurd	gizzard	gleme	gleam
giont	giant	glacial		glene	glean
gipsey	gypsy	glaciar	glacier	glew	glue
giraffe		glacier		glide	
giranium	geranium	glad		glider	
girdal	girdle	gladeator	gladiator	glimar	glimmer
girdar	girder	gladeolus	gladiolus	glimer	glimmer
girdel	girdle	gladiator		glimir	glimmer
girder		gladiolus		glimmar	glimmer
girdil	girdle	gladness		glimmer	
girdir	girder	gladniss	gladness	glimmir	glimmer
girdle		glair	glare	glimmor	glimmer
girdol	girdle	glaize	glaze	glimmur	glimmer
girdor	girder	glamar	glamour	glimor	glimmer
girdul	girdle	glamer	glamour	glimpse	
girdur	girder	glamir	glamour	glimse	glimpse
girgle	gurgle	glamour		glimur	glimmer
girl		glamur	glamour	glint	
girm	germ	glance		glisan	glisten
Girman	German	gland		glisen	glisten

glisin	glisten	glossy		gobal	gobble
glison	glisten	glosury	glossary	gobbal	gobble
glissen	glisten	glote	gloat	gobbel	gobble
glisten		glove		gobbil	gobble
glisun	glisten	glow		gobble	
glitar	glitter	glue		gobbler	
gliter	glitter	glum		gobbol	gobble
glitir	glitter	glume	gloom	gobbul	gobble
glitor	glitter	glutan	glutton	gobel	gobble
glittar	glitter	gluten	glutton	gobil	gobble
glitter		glutin	glutton	goblan	goblin
glittir	glitter	gluton	glutton	goble	gobble
glittor	glitter	gluttan	glutton	goblen	goblin
glittur	glitter	glutten	glutton	goblet	
glitur	glitter	gluttin	glutton	goblin	
glo	glow	glutton		goblit	goblet
gloab	globe	gluttun	glutton	goblon	goblin
gloat		glutun	glutton	goblun	goblin
globe		gluv	glove	gobol	gobble
gloo	glue	gnarl		gobul	gobble
gloom		gnarled		God	
gloomy		gnash		goddess	
glorify		gnat		goddiss	goddess
glorious		gnaw		gode	goad
glorius	glorious	gnoam	gnome	godess	goddess
glory		gnome		godiss	goddess
gloryfy	glorify	gnor	gnaw	goes	
gloryous	glorious	go		gofer	gopher
glosary	glossary	goad		going	
glosery	glossary	goal		gold	
glosiry	glossary	goar	gore	golden	
glosory	glossary	goard	gourd	gole	goal
gloss		goarge	gorge	golf	
glossary		goargeous	gorgeous	golosh	galosh
glossery	glossary	goas	goes	gon	gone
glossiry	glossary	goast	ghost	gondala	gondola
glossory	glossary	goat		gondela	gondola
glossury	glossary	goaz	goes	gondila	gondola

gondola		gospil	gospel	grade	
gondula	gondola	gospol	gospel	gradgual	gradual
gone		gospul	gospel	gradguate	graduate
gong		gossamer		gradjual	gradual
good		gossemer	gossamer	gradjuate	graduate
good-by		gossimer	gossamer	gradual	
good-bye		gossip		gradually	
goose		gossomer	gossamer	graduate	
gophar	gopher	gossumer	gossamer	graduation	
gopher		gost	ghost	graem	graham
gophir	gopher	gosumer	gossamer	graf	graph
gophor	gopher	got		graffite	graphite
gophur	gopher	gotar	guitar	grafite	graphite
gorage	garage	gote	goat	graft	
gord	gourd	goten	gotten	graham	
gordy	gaudy	gotten		graice	grace
gore		gouge		graid	grade
gored	gourd	goun	gown	graim	graham
gorey	gory	gourd		grain	
gorge		govarn	govern	grainge	grange
gorgeos	gorgeous	govern		graipe	grape
gorgeous		government		grait	grate
gorgeus	gorgeous	governor		grait	great
Gorgia	Georgia	govirn	govern	graive	grave
gorgous	gorgeous	govorn	govern	graize	graze
gorilla		govurn	govern	grajual	gradual
gorjess	gorgeous	gowge	gouge	grajuate	graduate
gorjous	gorgeous	gown		gram	
gorjus	gorgeous	goz	gauze	gramace	grimace
gory		goze	goes	gramar	grammar
gosamer	gossamer	gozelle	gazelle	gramer	grammar
gose	goes	grab		gramir	grammar
gosemer	gossamer	grace		grammar	
gosimer	gossamer	graceful		grammatical	
gosip	gossip	graceous	gracious	grammer	grammar
gosomer	gossamer	gracious		grammir	grammar
gospal	gospel	gracius	gracious	grammor	grammar
gospel		gracous	gracious	grammur	grammar

gramor	grammar	grasp		grayhound	greyhound
gramur	grammar	grass		graze	
granade	grenade	grassy		Greace	Greece
granary		gratafy	gratify	gread	greed
grand		gratatude	gratitude	greaf	grief
grandeur		grate		Greak	Greek
grandgure	grandeur	grate	great	grean	green
grandjur	grandeur	grateful		grease	
grandure	grandeur	gratefully		Grease	Greece
grane	grain	gratefy	gratify	greasey	greasy
granery	granary	grateing	grating	greasy	
granet	granite	gratetude	gratitude	great	
grange		gratification		great	grate
graniry	granary	gratify		great	greet
granit	granite	grating		Great Britain	
granite		gratitude		Grece	Greece
granjur	grandeur	gratofy	gratify	grede	greed
granory	granary	gratotude	gratitude	Greece	
grant		gratufy	gratify	greed	
granury	granary	gratutude	gratitude	greedily	
graom	graham	graum	graham	greedy	
grapal	grapple	graval	gravel	greedyly	greedily
grape		gravaty	gravity	greef	grief
grapel	grapple	grave		Greek	
graph		gravel		green	
graphic		gravety	gravity	greese	grease
graphik	graphic	gravey	gravy	greet	
graphite		gravil	gravel	greeting	
grapil	grapple	gravitate		grefe	grief
graple	grapple	gravitation		greif	grief
grapol	grapple	gravity		Greke	Greek
grappal	grapple	gravol	gravel	gremace	grimace
grappel	grapple	gravoty	gravity	grenade	
grappil	grapple	gravul	gravel	grenaid	grenade
grappol	grapple	gravuty	gravity	grene	green
grappul	grapple	gravy		grese	grease
grapul	grapple	gray		grete	greet
grase	grace	grayam	graham	greve	grieve

grew		grip		grosur	grocer
grewl	gruel	grisal	gristle	grotesk	grotesque
grewp	group	grisel	gristle	grotesque	
grewve	groove	grisil	gristle	groth	growth
greyhound		grisol	gristle	groto	grotto
greyhownd	greyhound	grissle	gristle	grotto	
gridal	griddle	grist		grouch	
griddal	griddle	gristle		grouchy	
griddel	griddle	grisul	gristle	groul	growl
griddle		grit		ground	
griddol	griddle	grizly	grizzly	group	
griddul	griddle	grizzly		groval	grovel
gridel	griddle	gro	grow	grove	groove
gridiron		groan		grovel	
gridle	griddle	groan	grown	grovil	grovel
gridol	griddle	groap	grope	grovol	grovel
gridul	griddle	groas	gross	grovul	grovel
grief		groath	growth	grow	
grievance		groave	groove	growch	grouch
grieve		grocer		growl	
grieveance	grievance	grocery		grown	
grievence	grievance	grocir	grocer	grownd	ground
grievince	grievance	gromace	grimace	growth	
grievonce	grievance	gronade	grenade	grub	
grievunce	grievance	grone	groan	grudge	
gril	grill	grone	grown	grue	grew
grill		groo	grew	gruel	
grim		grool	gruel	gruf	gruff
grimace		groom		gruff	
grimas	grimace	groop	group	gruge	grudge
grimase	grimace	groove		grule	gruel
grime		grope		grumace	grimace
grimey	grimy	grosar	grocer	grumbal	grumble
grimis	grimace	grose	gross	grumbel	grumble
grimy		groser	grocer	grumbil	grumble
grin		grosir	grocer	grumble	
grinade	grenade	grosor	grocer	grumbol	grumble
grind		gross		grumbul	grumble

grume	groom	guilty		gurgel	gurgle
grunade	grenade	guise		gurgil	gurgle
grunt		guitar		gurgle	
gruve	groove	guize	guise	gurgol	gurgle
guage	gauge	gul	gull	gurgul	gurgle
guarantee		gulable	gullible	gurilla	gorilla
guard		gulch		gurl	girl
guardean	guardian	guleble	gullible	gurm	germ
guardian		guley	gully	Gurman	German
guarentee	guarantee	gulf		gurth	girth
guarintee	guarantee	gulible	gullible	guse	goose
guarontee	guarantee	gull		gush	
guaruntee	guarantee	gullable	gullible	gust	
gud	good	gulleble	gullible	gutar	guitar
guess		gulley	gully	gutar	gutter
guest		gullible		gutir	gutter
guidance		gulloble	gullible	gutor	gutter
guide		gulluble	gullible	guttar	guitar
guidence	guidance	gully		guttar	gutter
guidince	guidance	guloble	gullible	gutter	
guidonce	guidance	gulosh	galosh	guttir	gutter
guidunce	guidance	gulp		guttor	gutter
guild		guluble	gullible	guttur	gutter
guile		guly	gully	gutur	gutter
guillatine	guillotine	gum		guvern	govern
guilletine	guillotine	gun		guy	
guillitine	guillotine	gurage	garage	guzelle	gazelle
guillotine		gurder	girder	gymnasium	
guillutine	guillotine	gurdle	girdle	gymnastics	
guilotine	guillotine	gurgal	gurgle	gymnazium	gymnasium
guilt				gypsy	

H

ha	hay	habatat	habitat	habichual	habitual
ha	hey	habetat	habitat	habit	

habitable		
habitat		
habitation		
habitchual	habitual	
habitual		
habotat	habitat	
habutat	habitat	
hach	hatch	
hachet	hatchet	
hachit	hatchet	
hacienda		
hack		
had		
hadn't		
haf	half	
hag		
hagard	haggard	
hagerd	haggard	
haggard		
haggerd	haggard	
haggird	haggard	
haggord	haggard	
haggurd	haggard	
hagird	haggard	
hagord	haggard	
hagurd	haggard	
hail		
hail	hale	
hailo	halo	
hair		
hair	hare	
hairy		
haiste	haste	
hait	hate	
haiven	haven	
haize	haze	
hak	hack	
halabut	halibut	
halalujah	hallelujah	
halarity	hilarity	
hale		
hale	hail	
halebut	halibut	
halelujah	hallelujah	
half		
halibut		
halilujah	hallelujah	
hall		
hall	haul	
hallalujah	hallelujah	
hallarity	hilarity	
hallelujah		
hallilujah	hallelujah	
hallo	hallow	
hallolujah	hallelujah	
hallow		
Halloween		
hallter	halter	
hallulujah	hallelujah	
halo		
halobut	halibut	
halolujah	hallelujah	
halow	hallow	
halt		
haltar	halter	
halter		
haltir	halter	
haltor	halter	
haltur	halter	
halubut	halibut	
halulujah	hallelujah	
halve		
halves		
halvez	halves	
ham		
hamak	hammock	
hamar	hammer	
hamberger	hamburger	
hambirger	hamburger	
hamburger		
hamek	hammock	
hamik	hammock	
hamir	hammer	
hamlet		
hamlit	hamlet	
hammak	hammock	
hammar	hammer	
hammek	hammock	
hammer		
hammik	hammock	
hammir	hammer	
hammock		
hammok	hammock	
hammor	hammer	
hammuk	hammock	
hammur	hammer	
hamock	hammock	
hamok	hammock	
hamor	hammer	
hampar	hamper	
hampir	hamper	
hampor	hamper	
hampur	hamper	
hamuk	hammock	
hamur	hammer	
hanck	hank	
hand		
handal	handle	
handecap	handicap	
handecraft	handicraft	
handel	handle	
handicap		
handicraft		
handil	handle	

handkerchief		happun	happen
handle		happy	
handol	handle	happyly	happily
handriting	handwriting	happyness	happiness
handsome		hapun	happen
handsum	handsome	hapy	happy
handul	handle	harah	hurrah
handwriting		harass	
handy		harbar	harbor
hang		harber	harbor
hangar		harbir	harbor
hangar	hanger	harbor	
hanger		harbur	harbor
hanger	hangar	harck	hark
hanging		hard	
hangir	hangar	harden	
hangkerchief	handkerchief	hardley	hardly
hangor	hangar	hardly	
hangur	hangar	hardship	
hank		hardwair	hardware
hankerchief	handkerchief	hardware	
hansom		hardwear	hardware
hansom	handsome	hare	
hansome	handsome	hare	hair
hansum	handsome	haredity	heredity
hapan	happen	harizon	horizon
haphazard		hark	
haphazzard	haphazard	harken	hearken
hapin	happen	harm	
hapon	happen	harmany	harmony
happan	happen	harmeny	harmony
happen		harmful	
happening		harminy	harmony
happily		harmless	
happin	happen	harmliss	harmless
happiness		harmonica	
happiniss	happiness	harmonious	
happon	happen	harmonize	

harmony	
harmuny	harmony
harness	
harniss	harness
haro	harrow
harow	harrow
harp	
harpest	harpist
harpewn	harpoon
harpist	
harpoon	
harpune	harpoon
harrah	hurrah
harrass	harass
harro	harrow
harrow	
harry	
harsh	
hart	heart
harth	hearth
harvest	
harvist	harvest
hary	harry
has	
hash	
hasienda	hacienda
hasn't	
haste	
hastely	hastily
hasten	
hastily	
hasty	
hastyly	hastily
hat	
hatch	
hatchet	
hatchit	hatchet
hate	

hateful		hay	
hatered	hatred	hay	hey
haterid	hatred	haylo	halo
hatred		haylow	halo
hatrid	hatred	haz	has
haughty		hazal	hazel
haul		hazard	
haunch		hazardous	
haunt		haze	
haunted		hazel	
hauty	haughty	hazerd	hazard
hav	have	hazey	hazy
havac	havoc	hazil	hazel
havak	havoc	hazird	hazard
havan	haven	hazol	hazel
have		hazord	hazard
have	halve	hazul	hazel
havec	havoc	hazurd	hazard
havek	havoc	hazy	
haven		hazzard	hazard
haven't		hazzerd	hazard
havic	havoc	hazzird	hazard
havik	havoc	hazzord	hazard
havin	haven	hazzurd	hazard
havn't	haven't	he	
havoc		Heabrew	Hebrew
havok	havoc	head	
havon	haven	head	heed
havuc	havoc	headache	
havuk	havoc	headaike	headache
havun	haven	headake	headache
Hawaii		headcwarters	headquarters
hawk		headkwarters	headquarters
hawl	haul	headquarters	
hawnch	haunch	heal	
hawnt	haunt	heal	heel
hawry	hoary	health	
hawty	haughty	healthful	

healthy	
heap	
hear	
hear	here
hearby	hereby
heard	
hearkan	hearken
hearken	
hearkin	hearken
hearkon	hearken
hearkun	hearken
hearo	hero
hearsay	
heart	
heartaly	heartily
heartely	heartily
hearth	
heartily	
heartless	
heartliss	heartless
heartoly	heartily
heartuly	heartily
hearty	
heat	
heatar	heater
heater	
heathan	heathen
heathar	heather
heathen	
heather	
heathin	heathen
heathir	heather
heathon	heathen
heathor	heather
heathun	heathen
heathur	heather
heatir	heater
heator	heater

heatur	heater	heffur	heifer
heavan	heaven	hefir	heifer
heave		hefor	heifer
heaven		hefur	heifer
heavenly		hege	hedge
heavin	heaven	heifer	
heavon	heaven	height	
heavun	heaven	heighten	
heavy		heir	
hebitual	habitual	heiress	
Hebrew		heiriss	heiress
hecktic	hectic	heirloom	
hectic		heirlume	heirloom
hectik	hectic	hektic	hectic
hed	head	helacopter	helicopter
hede	heed	helarity	hilarity
hedge		held	
Heebrew	Hebrew	heel	
heed		hele	heal
heedless		hele	heel
heedliss	heedless	helecopter	helicopter
heel		helicopter	
heel	heal	hell	
heep	heap	hellacopter	helicopter
heer	hear	hellarity	hilarity
heer	here	hellecopter	helicopter
heerby	hereby	hellicopter	helicopter
heero	hero	hellmet	helmet
heersay	hearsay	hellmit	helmet
heet	heat	hello	
heethen	heathen	hellocopter	helicopter
heeve	heave	hellow	hello
hefar	heifer	hellucopter	helicopter
hefer	heifer	helm	
heffar	heifer	helmet	
heffer	heifer	helmit	helmet
heffir	heifer	helo	hello
heffor	heifer	helocopter	helicopter

heifer		helow	
heifer		help	hello
heifer		helper	
heifer		helpful	
hedge		helpless	
		helplessness	
heiress		helpliss	helpless
		helth	health
heirloom		helucopter	helicopter
		hem	
hectic		hemasphere	hemisphere
helicopter		hemesphere	hemisphere
hilarity		hemisphere	
		hemlock	
		hemlok	hemlock
		hemosphere	hemisphere
		hemp	
		hemusphere	hemisphere
heal		hen	
heel		hence	
helicopter		henceforth	
		hense	hence
		hepe	heap
helicopter		her	
hilarity		herah	hurrah
helicopter.		herald	
helicopter		heran	heron
helmet		herass	harass
helmet		herasy	heresy
		heratage	heritage
helicopter		herb	
hello		herbivorous	
helicopter		Hercules	
		herd	
		herd	heard
helmet		herdle	hurdle
hello		here	
helicopter		here	hear

hereby		herutage	heritage
hereditary		herz	hers
heredity		hesatate	hesitate
hereld	herald	hesetate	hesitate
heren	heron	hesitate	
heresay	hearsay	hesitation	
heresy		hesotate	hesitate
heretage	heritage	hesutate	hesitate
heretic		hete	heat
herild	herald	hethen	heathen
herin	heron	hether	heather
hering	herring	heve	heave
herisy	heresy	heven	heaven
heritage		hevy	heavy
herizon	horizon	hew	hue
Herkules	Hercules	Hewaii	Hawaii
herl	hurl	hewge	huge
hermet	hermit	hewman	human
hermit		hewmid	humid
hero		hewmility	humility
heroic		hewmor	humor
heroine		hewmus	humus
heroism		hey	
herold	herald	hezitate	hesitate
heron		hi	high
herosy	heresy	hiacinth	hyacinth
herotage	heritage	hiaroglyphic	hieroglyphic
herrah	hurrah	hibarnate	hibernate
herrass	harass	hibernate	
herricane	hurricane	hibirnate	hibernate
herring		hibornate	hibernate
hers		hibrid	hybrid
herself		hiburnate	hibernate
hert	hurt	hicary	hickory
hertle	hurtle	hiccup	
heruld	herald	hich	hitch
herun	heron	hickary	hickory
herusy	heresy	hickery	hickory

hickory	
hickup	hiccup
hickury	hickory
hicory	hickory
hicup	hiccup
hicury	hickory
hid	
hidden	
hide	
hiden	hidden
hideous	
hidious	hideous
hidrant	hydrant
hidrogen	hydrogen
hidrophobia	hydrophobia
hied	hide
hiena	hyena
hier	hire
hieroglyphic	
hifen	hyphen
high	
highly	
Highness	
Highniss	Highness
higiene	hygiene
hikary	hickory
hike	
hikery	hickory
hikory	hickory
hikup	hiccup
hikury	hickory
hil	hill
hilarious	
hilarity	
hill	
hillarity	hilarity
him	
him	hymn

himn	hymn	hirass	harass	hitter	
himself		hirb	herb	hiuroglyphic	hieroglyphic
hind		hird	herd	hive	
hindar	hinder	hirdle	hurdle	Hiwaii	Hawaii
hinder		hire		hiz	his
hinderance	hindrance	hiredity	heredity	ho	hoe
hindir	hinder	hirizon	horizon	hoal	hole
hindor	hinder	hirl	hurl	hoal	whole
hindrance		hirmit	hermit	hoalster	holster
hindranse	hindrance	hiroglyphic	hieroglyphic	hoam	home
hindrence	hindrance	hirrah	hurrah	hoamly	homely
hindrince	hindrance	hirrass	harass	hoap	hope
hindronce	hindrance	hirricane	hurricane	hoard	
hindrunce	hindrance	hirs	hers	hoard	horde
hindur	hinder	hirt	hurt	hoarn	horn
Hiness	Highness	hirtle	hurtle	hoarnet	hornet
hinge		his		hoarse	
hint		hiss		hoarse	horse
hioroglyphic	hieroglyphic	histary	history	hoary	
hip		histearia	hysteria	hoase	hose
hipacrite	hypocrite	histeeria	hysteria	hoast	host
hipapotamus	hippopotamus	histeria	hysteria	hoatel	hotel
hipecrate	hypocrite	histery	history	hoaze	hose
hipepotamus	hippopotamus	histiry	history	hobal	hobble
hiphen	hyphen	historian		hobbal	hobble
hipicrate	hypocrite	historic		hobbel	hobble
hipipotamus	hippopotamus	historical		hobbil	hobble
hipocrite	hypocrite	history		hobble	
hipopotamus	hippopotamus	histury	history	hobbol	hobble
hippapotamus	hippopotamus	hit		hobbul	hobble
hippepotamus	hippopotamus	hitch		hobby	
hippipotamus	hippopotamus	hite	height	hobel	hobble
hippopotamus		hithar	hither	hobgoblin	
hippupotamus	hippopotamus	hither		hobil	hobble
hipucrite	hypocrite	hitherto		hobitual	habitual
hipupotamus	hippopotamus	hithir	hither	hoble	hobble
hir	her	hithor	hither	hobol	hobble
hirah	hurrah	hithur	hither	hobul	hobble

hoby	hobby	holloday	holiday	homoge	homage
hockey		hollow		homony	hominy
hocky	hockey	holluday	holiday	homuge	homage
hodgepodge		holly		homuny	hominy
hodgepoge	hodgepodge	holly	holy	honar	honor
hodjepodge	hodgepodge	holo	hollow	honch	haunch
hoe		holoday	holiday	honer	honor
hog		holow	hollow	honest	
hogepodge	hodgepodge	holstar	holster	honesty	
hogesh	hoggish	holster		honey	
hoggesh	hoggish	holstir	holster	honeymoon	
hoggish		holstor	holster	honir	honor
hogish	hoggish	holstur	holster	honist	honest
hoist		holt	halt	honk	
hojpodge	hodgepodge	holter	halter	honor	
hokey	hockey	holuday	holiday	honorable	
hoky	hockey	holy		honorary	
holaday	holiday	holy	holly	hont	haunt
holarity	hilarity	holyness	holiness	honur	honor
hold		homage		hony	honey
holder		homany	hominy	hoo	who
holding		home		hood	
hole		homege	homage	hoof	
hole	whole	homeless		hook	
holeday	holiday	homeley	homely	hoom	whom
holester	holster	homeliss	homeless	hoop	
holey	holy	homely		hoop	whoop
holiday		homemade		hoose	whose
holiness		homeny	hominy	hoot	
holiniss	holiness	homesick		hooz	whose
holl	hall	homestead		hop	
holl	haul	homested	homestead	hopar	hopper
holladay	holiday	homeward		hope	
hollarity	hilarity	homewood	homeward	hopeful	
holleday	holiday	homework		hopeless	
holley	holly	homewud	homeward	hopeliss	hopeless
holliday	holiday	homige	homage	hopir	hopper
hollo	hollow	hominy		hopor	hopper

hoppar	hopper	horrefy	horrify	hostel	
hopper		horrer	horror	hostel	hostile
hoppir	hopper	horrible		hostess	
hoppor	hopper	horrid		hostige	hostage
hoppur	hopper	horrify		hostil	hostel
hopur	hopper	horrir	horror	hostil	hostile
horable	horrible	horroble	horrible	hostile	
horafy	horrify	horrofy	horrify	hostility	
horah	hurrah	horror		hostiss	hostess
horar	horror	horruble	horrible	hostoge	hostage
horass	harass	horrufy	horrify	hostol	hostel
hord	hoard	horrur	horror	hostol	hostile
horde		horse		hostuge	hostage
horeble	horrible	horse	hoarse	hostul	hostel
hored	hoard	horuble	horrible	hostul	hostile
hored	horde	horufy	horrify	hosury	hosiery
horedity	heredity	horur	horror	hot	
horefy	horrify	hory	hoary	hotel	
horer	horror	hosary	hosiery	hoty	haughty
horey	hoary	hose		houer	hour
horible	horrible	hosery	hosiery	hound	
horid	horrid	hoshary	hosiery	hour	
horify	horrify	hoshery	hosiery	hourly	
horir	horror	hoshiry	hosiery	house	
horizon		hoshory	hosiery	houseing	housing
horizontal		hoshury	hosiery	housing	
horn		hosiery		houzing	housing
hornet		hosiry	hosiery	hoval	hovel
hornit	hornet	hosory	hosiery	hovar	hover
horoble	horrible	hospitable		hovel	
horofy	horrify	hospitably		hover	
horor	horror	hospital		hovil	hovel
horrable	horrible	hospitality		hovir	hover
horrafy	horrify	host		hovol	hovel
horrah	hurrah	hostage		hovor	hover
horrar	horror	hostal	hostel	hovul	hovel
horrass	harass	hostal	hostile	hovur	hover
horreble	horrible	hostege	hostage	how	

how	hoe	huemor	humor	humiliation	
Howaii	Hawaii	huemus	humus	humility	
however		huf	hoof	humin	human
howl		hug		humingbird	hummingbird
hownd	hound	huge		humir	humor
howse	house	huk	hook	humis	humus
hoyst	hoist	hukalberry	huckleberry	hummingbird	
hoze	hose	hukelberry	huckleberry	humon	human
hozery	hosiery	hukilberry	huckleberry	humor	
hoziery	hosiery	hukleberry	huckleberry	humorist	
hu	who	hukolberry	huckleberry	humorous	
hub		hukulberry	huckleberry	humos	humus
hubbub		hul	hull	hump	
hubitual	habitual	hularity	hilarity	humpbacked	
hubub	hubbub	hulk		humun	human
huckalberry	huckleberry	hull		humur	humor
huckelberry	huckleberry	hullarity	hilarity	humus	
huckilberry	huckleberry	hum		hunch	
huckleberry		humain	humane	hunchbacked	
huckolberry	huckleberry	human		hundred	
huckulberry	huckleberry	humane		hundrid	hundred
hud	hood	humanity		huney	honey
hudal	huddle	humar	humor	hung	
huddal	huddle	humas	humus	hungar	hunger
huddel	huddle	humbal	humble	hunger	
huddil	huddle	humbel	humble	hungir	hunger
huddle		humbil	humble	hungor	hunger
huddol	huddle	humble		hungraly	hungrily
huddul	huddle	humbol	humble	hungrely	hungrily
hudel	huddle	humbug		hungrey	hungry
hudil	huddle	humbul	humble	hungrily	
hudle	huddle	hume	whom	hungroly	hungrily
hudol	huddle	humen	human	hungruly	hungrily
hudul	huddle	humer	humor	hungry	
hue		humess	humus	hungur	hunger
hueman	human	humid		hunk	
huemid	humid	humidity		hunt	
huemility	humility	humiliate		hunter	

huny	honey	hurtil	hurtle	huvir	hover
hupe	hoop	hurtle		huvol	hovel
hupe	whoop	hurtol	hurtle	huvor	hover
hur	her	hurtul	hurtle	huvul	hovel
huracane	hurricane	hurucane	hurricane	huvur	hover
hurah	hurrah	hury	hurry	Huwaii	Hawaii
hurass	harass	husal	hustle	huzband	husband
hurb	herb	husband		huze	whose
hurd	herd	husbandry		hy	high
hurdal	hurdle	husbend	husband	hyacinth	
hurdel	hurdle	husbind	husband	hybrid	
hurdil	hurdle	husbond	husband	hydragen	hydrogen
hurdle		husbund	husband	hydrant	
hurdol	hurdle	husck	husk	hydraphobia	hydrophobia
hurdul	hurdle	huse	whose	hydregen	hydrogen
hurecane	hurricane	husel	hustle	hydrent	hydrant
huredity	heredity	hush		hydrephobia	hydrophobia
huricane	hurricane	husil	hustle	hydrigen	hydrogen
hurizon	horizon	husk		hydrint	hydrant
hurl		huskiness		hydriphobia	hydrophobia
hurmit	hermit	huskiniss	huskiness	hydrogen	
hurocane	hurricane	husky		hydront	hydrant
hurracane	hurricane	huskyness	huskiness	hydrophobia	
hurrah		husol	hustle	hydrugen	hydrogen
hurrass	harass	hussal	hustle	hydrunt	hydrant
hurray		hussel	hustle	hydruphobia	hydrophobia
hurrecane	hurricane	hussil	hustle	hyeana	hyena
hurricane		hussol	hustle	hyeena	hyena
hurried		hussul	hustle	hyena	
hurriedly		hustle		hyfan	hyphen
hurrocane	hurricane	husul	hustle	hyfen	hyphen
hurrucane	hurricane	hut		hyfin	hyphen
hurry		hute	hoot	hufon	hyphen
hurryd	hurried	huval	hovel	hyfun	hyphen
hurs	hers	huvar	hover	hygeane	hygiene
hurt		huvel	hovel	hygeene	hygiene
hurtal	hurtle	huver	hover	hygeine	hygiene
hurtel	hurtle	huvil	hovel	hygene	hygiene

hygiene		hyphen		hypocrite	
hyicinth	hyacinth	hyphenate		hypucrite	hypocrite
hym	hymn	hyphin	hyphen	hyroglyphic	hieroglyphic
hymn		hyphon	hyphen	hystearia	hysteria
hyocinth	hyacinth	hyphun	hyphen	hysteeria	hysteria
hypacrite	hypocrite	hypicrate	hypocrite	hysteria	
hypecrate	hypocrite	hypocrisy		hysterical	
hyphan	hyphen	hypocrit	hypocrite	hyucinth	hyacinth

I

I		idal	idle	idle	
i	eye	idal	idol	idle	idol
iadine	iodine	idea		idleness	
iarn	iron	ideal		idleniss	idleness
Iawa	Iowa	idear	idea	idley	idly
ice		ideel	ideal	idly	
iceberg		ideer	idea	Idoho	Idaho
icebirg	iceberg	Ideho	Idaho	idol	
iceburg	iceberg	ideit	idiot	idol	idle
ice cream		idel	idle	Iduho	Idaho
ice creem	ice cream	idel	idol	idul	idle
ice creme	ice cream	idele	ideal	idul	idol
iceing	icing	identical		iedine	iodine
ice kream	ice cream	identification		ier	ire
icey	icy	identify		iern	iron
ich	itch	identity		Iewa	Iowa
icicle		ideot	idiot	if	
icickle	icicle	idere	idea	ifemeral	ephemeral
icikle	icicle	idiet	idiot	iffect	effect
icing		Idiho	Idaho	ifficient	efficient
iclipse	eclipse	idil	idle	iglew	igloo
iconomy	economy	idil	idol	igloo	
icy		idiot		iglue	igloo
I'd		idiotic		ignarant	ignorant
Idaho		idition	edition	igneous	

ignerant	ignorant	ill		ilongate	elongate
ignious	igneous	Illanois	Illinois	ilope	elope
ignirant	ignorant	illastrate	illustrate	il-tempered	ill-tempered
ignite		illeagal	illegal	ilude	elude
ignition		illedgible	illegible	iluminate	illuminate
ignoar	ignore	illeegal	illegal	ilund	island
ignoble		illegal		ilusion	illusion
ignorance		illegible		ilustrate	illustrate
ignorant		illejible	illegible	I'm	
ignore		Illenois	Illinois	imaciated	emaciated
ignurant	ignorant	illestrate	illustrate	imaculate	immaculate
iguana		illewminate	illuminate	image	
igwana	iguana	illewsion	illusion	imaginable	
ikwator	equator	Illinois		imaginary	
ikwip	equip	illipse	ellipse	imagination	
ikwivalent	equivalent	illistrate	illustrate	imaginative	
I'l	I'll	illiterate		imagine	
il	ill	ill-natured		imajine	imagine
ilaborate	elaborate	illness		imancipate	emancipate
iland	island	illniss	illness	imatate	imitate
ilapse	elapse	illogical		imature	immature
ilastic	elastic	illojical	illogical	imbacile	imbecile
ilated	elated	Illonois	Illinois	imbecile	
ile	aisle	illoominate	illuminate	imbed	
ile	isle	illoosion	illusion	imbicile	imbecile
ilect	elect	illostrate	illustrate	imbocile	imbecile
ilectric	electric	ill-tempered		imbucile	imbecile
ilegal	illegal	illuminate		imeasurable	immeasurable
ilegible	illegible	illumination		imediate	immediate
ilend	island	Illunois	Illinois	imege	image
ilet	eyelet	illusion		imemorial	immemorial
ileven	eleven	illustrate		imense	immense
ilicit	elicit	illustration		imerge	emerge
iliminate	eliminate	illustrious		imergency	emergency
ilind	island	il-natured	ill-natured	imerse	immerse
Ilinois	Illinois	ilness	illness	imetate	imitate
iliterate	illiterate	ilogical	illogical	imige	image
I'll		ilond	island	imigrate	immigrate

iminent	imminent
imit	emit
imitate	
imitation	
immackulate	immaculate
immaculate	
immagrate	immigrate
immakulate	immaculate
immamorial	immemorial
immanent	imminent
immature	
immeadiate	immediate
immeasurable	
immediate	
immediately	
immeediate	immediate
immegrate	immigrate
immemorial	
immenent	imminent
immense	
immensely	
immerse	
immesurable	immeasurable
immeture	immature
immewn	immune
immezurable	immeasurable
immigrant	
immigrate	
immigration	
immimorial	immemorial
imminent	
immirse	immerse
immiture	immature
immograte	immigrate
immomorial	immemorial
immonent	imminent
immoovable	immovable
immoral	

immortal	
immortality	
immoture	immature
immovable	
immugrate	immigrate
immumorial	immemorial
immune	
immunent	imminent
immunity	
immurse	immerse
immuture	immature
immuvable	immovable
imoge	image
imoral	immoral
imortal	immortal
imotate	imitate
imotion	emotion
imovable	immovable
imp	
impackt	impact
impact	
impair	
impakt	impact
impalite	impolite
imparceptible	imperceptible
impare	impair
imparshal	impartial
impart	
impartial	
impasable	impassable
impashent	impatient
impashoned	impassioned
impasive	impassive
impassable	
impassioned	
impassive	
impatience	
impatient	

impatus	impetus
impeach	
impead	impede
impearial	imperial
impearious	imperious
impechuous	impetuous
impede	
impediment	
impeech	impeach
impeed	impede
impeerial	imperial
impeerious	imperious
impel	
impelite	impolite
impenetrable	
imperative	
imperceptible	
imperfect	
imperfection	
imperial	
imperil	
imperious	
impersonal	
impertinence	
impertinent	
impetuous	
impetus	
impewdent	impudent
impewnity	impunity
impewr	impure
impilite	impolite
impious	
impirceptible	imperceptible
impirfect	imperfect
impirsonal	impersonal
impirtinent	impertinent
impitus	impetus
implament	implement

implement		imprivise	improvise	inacksessible	inaccessible
impliment	implement	imprizon	imprison	inacktive	inactive
imploar	implore	improbable		inackurate	inaccurate
imploment	implement	improodent	imprudent	inacsessible	inaccessible
implore		improove	improve	inactive	
implument	implement	improper		inacurate	inaccurate
imply		improve		inadequate	
impoart	import	improvement		inadvisable	
impoase	impose	improvise		inaffectual	ineffectual
impolite		imprudant	imprudent	inaffensive	inoffensive
imporceptible	imperceptible	imprudent		inafficient	inefficient
import		impruve	improve	inaksessible	inaccessible
importance		impruvise	improvise	inaktive	inactive
important		impudence		inakurate	inaccurate
importation		impudent		inamel	enamel
impose		impulite	impolite	inappropriate	
imposible	impossible	impulse		inapropriate	inappropriate
imposing		impulsive		inar	inner
impossibility		impunity		inasmuch	
impossible		impurceptible	imperceptible	inatentive	inattentive
impostor		impure		inattentive	
impotus	impetus	impurety	impurity	inaugurate	
impoverish		impurfect	imperfect	inauguration	
impoze	impose	impurity		inavate	innovate
impracktical	impractical	impursonal	impersonal	inawgurate	inaugurate
impractical		impurtinent	impertinent	inasmuch as	
impraktical	impractical	imputus	impetus	inborn	
impravise	improvise	imuge	image	incanceivable	inconceivable
impregnable		imulsion	emulsion	incansiderate	inconsiderate
impres	impress	imune	immune	incansistent	inconsistent
impreshon	impression	imutate	imitate	incanspicuous	inconspicuous
impress		in		incanvenient	inconvenient
impression		in	inn	incapable	
impressive		inability		incarrect	incorrect
imprevise	improvise	inaccessible		incedent	incident
imprint		inaccuracy		incense	
imprison		inaccurate		incentive	
imprisonment		inacent	innocent	incessant	

inch		increse	increase	independent		
incident		incum	income	inderect	indirect	
incidental		incumplete	incomplete	indescribable		
incidentally		incunceivable	inconceivable	indestry	industry	
incipient		incunsiderate	inconsiderate	indeted	indebted	
incisor		incunsistent	inconsistent	indevidual	individual	
incite		incunspicuous	inconspicuous	indevisible	indivisible	
incizor	incisor	incunvenient	inconvenient	indews	induce	
inck	ink	incur		index		
inclement		incurable		India		
inclewd	include	incureable	incurable	Indian		
inclination		incurrect	incorrect	Indiana		
incline		incwire	inquire	indicate		
inclined		indacate	indicate	indication		
inclood	include	indagestion	indigestion	indicator		
include		indago	indigo	indifatigable	indefatigable	
inclusion		indalent	indolent	indiferent	indifferent	
inclusive		indarect	indirect	indifference		
income		indastry	industry	indifferent		
incomparable		indavidual	individual	indigenous		
incompetent		indavisible	indivisible	indigestible		
incomplete		Indea	India	indigestion		
incomprehensible		indead	indeed	indignant		
inconceivable		indebted		indignation		
inconsiderate		indecate	indicate	indignity		
inconsistent		indecks	index	indigo		
inconspicuous		indede	indeed	indijenous	indigenous	
inconstant		indeed		indijestion	indigestion	
inconvenience		indefatigable		indikate	indicate	
inconvenient		indefinite		indilent	indolent	
incorporate		indegestion	indigestion	indipendent	independent	
incorrect		indego	indigo	indirect		
increase		indeks	index	indiscreet		
increasingly		indelent	indolent	indiscretion		
incredible		indelible				
incredibly		indellible	indelible	indiscribable	indescribable	
incredulous		indent		indispensable		
increese	increase	independence		indisposed		
				indistinct		

indistry	industry	inebility	inability	inevate	innovate
individual		inecent	innocent	inevitable	
individuality		ineckscusable	inexcusable	inexact	
individually		inecksorable	inexorable	inexaustible	inexhaustible
indivisible		ineckspensive	inexpensive	inexcusable	
indocate	indicate	inecksperience	inexperience	inexhaustible	
indogestion	indigestion	inecksplicable	inexplicable	inexorable	
indogo	indigo	inecscusable	inexcusable	inexpensive	
indolence		inecsorable	inexorable	inexperience	
indolent		inecspensive	inexpensive	inexperienced	
indomitable		inecsperience	inexperience	inexplicable	
indooce	induce	inecsplicable	inexplicable	inexsorable	inexorable
indoor		inecwolity	inequality	infadel	infidel
indoors		inedible		infalible	infallible
indoose	induce	inedvisable	inadvisable	infallible	
indorect	indirect	inefectual	ineffectual	infamous	
indostry	industry	ineffectual		infancy	
indovidual	individual	ineffensive	inoffensive	infanite	infinite
indovisible	indivisible	inefficient		infant	
inducate	indicate	ineficient	inefficient	infantcy	infancy
induce		inegsact	inexact	infantile	
inducement		inegsaustible	inexhaustible	infantry	
induckt	induct	inegzact	inexact	infantsy	infancy
induct		inegzaustible	inexhaustible	infarmation	information
indugestion	indigestion	inekscusable	inexcusable	infeald	infield
indugo	indigo	ineksorable	inexorable	infearior	inferior
indukt	induct	inekspensive	inexpensive	infeckt	infect
indulent	indolent	ineksperience	inexperience	infect	
indulge		ineksplicable	inexplicable	infection	
indulgence		inekwolity	inequality	infectious	
indulgent		ineppropriate	inappropriate	infedel	infidel
indurect	indirect	inept		infeeld	infield
induse	induce	inequality		infeerior	inferior
industrial		iner	inner	infeild	infield
industrious		inert		infekt	infect
industry		inesmuch	inasmuch	infemous	infamous
induvidual	individual	inestimable		infenite	infinite
induvisible	indivisible	inettentive	inattentive	infent	infant

infentry	infantry	inflooence	influence	Ingland	England
infer		influence		ingot	
inference		influential		ingrashiate	ingratiate
inferior		infodel	infidel	ingratiate	
inferiority		infomous	infamous	ingratitude	
inferm	infirm	infonite	infinite	ingreadient	ingredient
infermation	information	infont	infant	ingredient	
infernal		infontry	infantry	ingreedient	ingredient
infest		inform		ingut	ingot
infewriate	infuriate	informal		inhabit	
infidel		information		inhabitant	
infield		infreakwent	infrequent	inhail	inhale
infimous	infamous	infreaquent	infrequent	inhale	
infinite		infreekwent	infrequent	inhearent	inherent
infinitely		infreequent	infrequent	inheerent	inherent
infint	infant	infrekwent	infrequent	inherent	
infintry	infantry	infrequent		inherit	
infir	infer	infringe		inheritance	
infirm		infudel	infidel	inhewman	inhuman
infirmation	information	infumous	infamous	inhospitable	
infirmity		infunite	infinite	inhuman	
infirnal	infernal	infunt	infant	inibility	inability
inflaim	inflame	infuntry	infantry	inicent	innocent
inflait	inflate	infur	infer	inicwity	iniquity
inflamable	inflammable	infuriate		inidvisable	inadvisable
inflamation	inflammation	infurm	infirm	iniffectual	ineffectual
inflame		infurmation	information	iniffensive	inoffensive
inflammable		infurnal	infernal	inifficient	inefficient
inflammation		infuse		inigma	enigma
inflate		infuze	infuse	inikwity	iniquity
inflecksible	inflexible	ingat	ingot	ining	inning
inflecsible	inflexible	ingeanious	ingenious	inippropriate	inappropriate
infleksible	inflexible	ingeenious	ingenious	iniquality	inequality
inflewence	influence	ingenious		iniquity	
inflexible		ingenuity		inir	inner
inflickt	inflict	inget	ingot	inirt	inert
inflict		inginuity	ingenuity	inishiate	initiate
inflikt	inflict	ingit	ingot	inismuch	inasmuch

initial	
initiate	
initiation	
initiative	
inittentive	inattentive
inivate	innovate
injanuity	ingenuity
injar	injure
injeckt	inject
inject	
injection	
injekt	inject
injenious	ingenious
injenuity	ingenuity
injenuous	ingenuous
injer	injure
injinuity	ingenuity
injir	injure
injonuity	ingenuity
injor	injure
injuncktion	injunction
injunction	
injunktion	injunction
injunuity	ingenuity
injure	
injureous	injurious
injurey	injury
injurious	
injury	
injustice	
ink	
inkanceivable	inconceivable
inkansiderate	inconsiderate
inkansistent	inconsistent
inkanspicuous	inconspicuous
inkanvenient	inconvenient
inkapable	incapable
inkarrect	incorrect

inkenceivable	inconceivable
inkensiderate	inconsiderate
inkensistent	inconsistent
inkenspicuous	inconspicuous
inkenvenient	inconvenient
inker	incur
inkerrect	incorrect
inkinceivable	inconceivable
inkinsiderate	inconsiderate
inkinsistent	inconsistent
inkinspicuous	inconspicuous
inkinvenient	inconvenient
inkir	incur
inkirrect	incorrect
inklement	inclement
inkline	incline
inkling	
inklude	include
inkome	income
inkomparable	incomparable
inkompetent	incompetent
inkomplete	incomplete
inkompre-hensible	incompre-hensible
inkonceivable	inconceivable
inkonsiderate	inconsiderate
inkonsistent	inconsistent
inkonspicuous	inconspicuous
inkonstant	inconstant
inkonvenient	inconvenient
inkorporate	incorporate
inkorrect	incorrect
inkrease	increase
inkredible	incredible
inkreese	increase
inkrese	increase
inkum	income
inkumplete	incomplete

inkunceivable	inconceivable
inkunsiderate	inconsiderate
inkunsistent	inconsistent
inkunspicuous	inconspicuous
inkunvenient	inconvenient
inkur	incur
inkurable	incurable
inkureable	incurable
inkurrect	incorrect
inkwire	inquire
inlade	inlaid
inlaid	
inland	
inlet	
inmait	inmate
inmate	
inmost	
inn	
innacent	innocent
innar	inner
innavate	innovate
innecent	innocent
inner	
innermost	
innert	inert
innevate	innovate
innewmerable	innumerable
innicent	innocent
inning	
innir	inner
innivate	innovate
innockuous	innocuous
innoculate	inoculate
innocuous	
innokuous	innocuous
innoomerable	innumerable
innor	inner
innosent	innocent

innovate	
innovation	
innucent	innocent
innumerable	
innur	inner
innuvate	innovate
inobility	inability
inocent	innocent
inockulate	inoculate
inockuous	innocuous
inoculate	
inoculation	
inocuous	innocuous
inodvisable	inadvisable
inofensive	inoffensive
inoffectual	ineffectual
inoffensive	
inofficient	inefficient
inogurate	inaugurate
inokulate	inoculate
inokuous	innocuous
inoomerable	innumerable
inoppropriate	inappropriate
inor	inner
inormous	enormous
inosmuch	inasmuch
inottentive	inattentive
inough	enough
inovate	innovate
inquier	inquire
inquire	
inquirey	inquiry
inquiry	
inquisitive	
inquizitive	inquisitive
inroad	
inrode	inroad
insadent	incident

insain	insane
insalate	insulate
insalent	insolent
insane	
insanety	insanity
insanity	
insarrection	insurrection
insashable	insatiable
insatiable	
inscrewtable	inscrutable
inscribe	
inscribtion	inscription
inscription	
inscrootable	inscrutable
inscrutable	
inseckt	insect
insect	
insedent	incident
insekt	insect
inselate	insulate
inselent	insolent
insense	incense
insensible	
insensitive	
insentive	incentive
inseparable	
insergent	insurgent
inserrection	insurrection
insert	
insertion	
insessant	incessant
inshoor	insure
inshur	insure
inside	
insidious	
insight	
insignia	
insignificant	

insilate	insulate
insilent	insolent
insincere	
insinsere	insincere
insinuate	
insipient	incipient
insirgent	insurgent
insirrection	insurrection
insirt	insert
insisor	incisor
insist	
insistence	
insistent	
insite	incite
insite	insight
inskribe	inscribe
inskrutable	inscrutable
insodent	incident
insolate	insulate
insolence	
insolent	
insoluble	
insorrection	insurrection
inspeckt	inspect
inspect	
inspection	
inspector	
inspekt	inspect
inspier	inspire
inspiration	
inspire	
install	
installment	
instance	
instanse	instance
instant	
instantaneous	
instantly	

instatute	institute	insulent	insolent	intarstate	interstate
instead		insult		intartwine	intertwine
insted	instead	insurance		intarval	interval
instent	instant	insure		intarvene	intervene
instep		insurection	insurrection	intarview	interview
instetute	institute	insurence	insurance	intarwoven	interwoven
instill		insurgent		intearior	interior
instinckt	instinct	insurjent	insurgent	inteerior	interior
instinct		insurrection		integrity	
instinctive		insurt	insert	intelect	intellect
instinkt	instinct	intackt	intact	inteligent	intelligent
instint	instant	intact		intellect	
institute		intaik	intake	intellectual	
institution		intake		intelligence	
instont	instant	intakt	intact	intelligent	
instotute	institute	intallect	intellect	intelligible	
instrament	instrument	intamate	intimate	intemate	intimate
instrement	instrument	intangible		intemperance	
instriment	instrument	intanjible	intangible	intemperate	
instroment	instrument	intarcede	intercede	intence	intense
instruckt	instruct	intarcept	intercept	intend	
instruct		intarchange	interchange	intense	
instruction		intarcourse	intercourse	intensefy	intensify
instructive		intarest	interest	intensify	
instructor		intarfere	interfere	intensive	
instrukt	instruct	intarject	interject	intent	
instrument		intarlock	interlock	intention	
instrumental		intarloper	interloper	intentional	
instunt	instant	intarlude	interlude	intentionally	
instutute	institute	intarmediate	intermediate	intents	intense
insudent	incident	intarmingle	intermingle	inter	
insuferable	insufferable	intarmission	intermission	intercede	
insufferable		intarmittent	intermittent	intercept	
insufficient		intarnational	international	intercession	
insuficient	insufficient	intarpose	interpose	interchange	
insulate		intarrupt	interrupt	interchangeable	
insulation		intarsect	intersect	intercourse	
insulator		intarsperse	intersperse	interest	

interested		intillect	intellect	intoksicate	intoxicate
interesting		intimacy		intolerable	
interfere		intimate		intolerant	
interference		intimation		intollect	intellect
interior		intimidate		intomate	intimate
interject		intir	inter	intorcede	intercede
interjection		intircede	intercede	intorcept	intercept
interlock		intircept	intercept	intorchange	interchange
interloper		intirchange	interchange	intorcourse	intercourse
interlude		intircourse	intercourse	intorest	interest
intermedeate	intermediate	intirest	interest	intorfere	interfere
intermediate		intirfere	interfere	intorject	interject
interminable		intirject	interject	intorlock	interlock
intermingle		intirlock	interlock	intorloper	interloper
intermission		intirloper	interloper	intorlude	interlude
intermittent		intirlude	interlude	intormediate	intermediate
internal		intirmediate	intermediate	intormingle	intermingle
internally		intirminable	interminable	intormission	intermission
international		intirmingle	intermingle	intormittent	intermittent
interpose		intirmission	intermission	intornational	international
interpret		intirmittent	intermittent	intorpose	interpose
interpretation		intirnal	internal	intorrupt	interrupt
interpreter		intirnational	international	intorsect	intersect
interrogate		intirpose	interpose	intorsperse	intersperse
interrogation		intirpret	interpret	intorstate	interstate
interrupt		intirrogate	interrogate	intortwine	intertwine
interruption		intirrupt	interrupt	intorval	interval
intersect		intirsect	intersect	intorvene	intervene
intersection		intirspirse	intersperse	intorview	interview
intersperse		intirstate	interstate	intorwoven	interwoven
interstate		intirtwine	intertwine	intoxicate	
intertwine		intirval	interval	intoxicating	
interval		intirvene	intervene	intoxication	
intervene		intirview	interview	intracate	intricate
intervention		intirwoven	interwoven	intraduce	introduce
interview		into		intreague	intrigue
interwoven		intocksicate	intoxicate	intrecate	intricate
intestine		intocsicate	intoxicate	intreduce	introduce

intreegue	intrigue	inturnal	internal	invariably	
intregue	intrigue	inturnational	international	invasion	
intrepid		inturpose	interpose	invazion	invasion
intrest	interest	inturpret	interpret	invelid	invalid
intrewd	intrude	inturrogate	interrogate	invent	
intricate		inturrupt	interrupt	invention	
intriduce	introduce	intursect	intersect	inventive	
intrigue		intursperse	intersperse	inventor	
introcate	intricate	inturstate	interstate	inventory	
introduce		inturtwine	intertwine	invert	
introduction		inturval	interval	invertebrate	
introductory		inturvene	intervene	invest	
introod	intrude	inturview	interview	investigate	
intrucate	intricate	inturwoven	interwoven	investigation	
intrude		inubility	inability	investigator	
intruder		inucent	innocent	investment	
intruduce	introduce	inudvisable	inadvisable	investor	
intrusion		inuf	enough	invigorate	
intrust		inuffectual	ineffectual	invilid	invalid
intruzion	intrusion	inuffensive	inoffensive	invincible	
intullect	intellect	inufficient	inefficient	invinsible	invincible
intumate	intimate	inumerable	innumerable	invintory	inventory
intur	inter	inumerate	enumerate	invirt	invert
inturcede	intercede	inunciate	enunciate	invirtebrate	invertebrate
inturcept	intercept	inundate		invisible	
inturchange	interchange	inundation		invitation	
inturcourse	intercourse	inuppropriate	inappropriate	invite	
inturest	interest	inur	inner	inviteing	inviting
inturfere	interfere	inurt	inert	inviting	
inturgect	interject	inusmuch	inasmuch	invizible	invisible
inturlock	interlock	inuttentive	inattentive	invoak	invoke
inturloper	interloper	inuvate	innovate	invocation	
inturlude	interlude	invade		invokation	invocation
inturmediate	intermediate	invader		invoke	
inturminable	interminable	invaid	invade	involid	invalid
inturmingle	intermingle	invalid		involuntarily	
inturmission	intermission	invaluable		involuntary	
inturmittent	intermittent	invantory	inventory	involve	

invontory	inventory	iresolute	irresolute	irritate	
invulid	invalid	iretate	irritate	irritation	
invuntory	inventory	ireverent	irreverent	irrizistible	irresistible
invurt	invert	irezistible	irresistible	irrogate	irrigate
invurtebrate	invertebrate	irezolute	irresolute	irrotate	irritate
inward		irge	urge	irrugate	irrigate
inwardly		irgent	urgent	irrutate	irritate
inwerd	inward	irigate	irrigate	irugate	irrigate
inwird	inward	iriny	irony	iruny	irony
inwood	inward	iris		irupt	erupt
inword	inward	Irish		irutate	irritate
inwud	inward	irisistible	irresistible	is	
inwurd	inward	iritate	irritate	isalate	isolate
iodine		irizistible	irresistible	ise	ice
iorn	iron	irksome		iselate	isolate
Iowa		irksum	irksome	ishew	issue
iphemeral	ephemeral	Irland	Ireland	ishoo	issue
iquator	equator	irn	urn	ishue	issue
iquip	equip	irode	erode	isickle	icicle
iquivalent	equivalent	irogate	irrigate	isicle	icicle
iradicate	eradicate	iron		isikle	icicle
iragate	irrigate	irony		isilate	isolate
irait	irate	irotate	irritate	island	
irany	irony	irragate	irrigate	islander	
irase	erase	irratate	irritate	isle	
iratate	irritate	irrate	irate	ismas	isthmus
irate		irratic	erratic	ismess	isthmus
irb	herb	irregate	irrigate	ismis	isthmus
irban	urban	irregular		ismos	isthmus
irchin	urchin	irregularity		ismus	isthmus
ire		irresistible		isn't	
irect	erect	irretate	irritate	isolate	
iregate	irrigate	irreverent		isolation	
iregular	irregular	irrezistible	irresistible	Israel	
irekt	erect	irrezolute	irresolute	Israeli	
Ireland		irrigate		Isreal	Israel
ireny	irony	irrigation		Isreel	Israel
iresistible	irresistible	irrisistible	irresistible	Isrele	Israel

issue		itherial	etherial	ivary	ivory
isthmus		itiet	idiot	I've	
isulate	isolate	Itily	Italy	ivent	event
it		itim	item	iventual	eventual
Italian		itiot	idiot	ivery	ivory
italic		Itoly	Italy	ivey	ivy
italicize		itom	item	iviry	ivory
itallic	italic	it's		ivoke	evoke
Italy		its		ivolve	evolve
Italyan	Italian	itself		ivory	
itam	item	Ituly	Italy	ivury	ivory
itch		itum	item	ivy	
Itely	Italy	iudine	iodine	iz	is
item		iurn	iron	izn't	isn't
itemize		Iuwa	Iowa	Izrael	Israel
iteot	idiot	ivacuate	evacuate	Izreal	Israel
iternal	eternal	ivade	evade	Izreel	Israel
		ivaporate	evaporate		

J

jab		jackel	jackal	jaggad	jagged
jabar	jabber	jacket		jagged	
jabbar	jabber	jackil	jackal	jaggid	jagged
jabber		jackit	jacket	jaggod	jagged
jabbir	jabber	jackol	jackal	jaggud	jagged
jabbor	jabber	jackot	jacket	jagid	jagged
jabbur	jabber	jackul	jackal	jagod	jagged
jaber	jabber	jackut	jacket	jaguar	
jabir	jabber	jacol	jackal	jagud	jagged
jabor	jabber	jacot	jacket	jagwar	jaguar
jabur	jabber	jacul	jackal	jaid	jade
jacat	jacket	jacut	jacket	jail	
jack		jade		jailer	
jackal		jagad	jagged	jailor	
jackat	jacket	jaged	jagged	jak	jack

jakal	jackal	jay		jeology	geology
jakat	jacket	jaywalker		jeometry	geometry
jakel	jackal	jaz	jazz	jeopardy	
jaket	jacket	jazz		jeoperdy	jeopardy
jakil	jackal	jealos	jealous	jeopirdy	jeopardy
jakit	jacket	jealous		jeopordy	jeopardy
jakol	jackal	jealousy		jeopurdy	jeopardy
jakot	jacket	jealus	jealous	Jepan	Japan
jakul	jackal	jeans		jepardy	jeopardy
jakut	jacket	jeanz	jeans	jepe	jeep
jale	jail	jeap	jeep	jeperdy	jeopardy
jam		jear	jeer	jepirdy	jeopardy
janator	janitor	jeens	jeans	jepordy	jeopardy
janetor	janitor	jeenz	jeans	jepurdy	jeopardy
jangal	jangle	jeep		jeranium	geranium
jangel	jangle	jeer		jere	jeer
jangil	jangle	Jeesus	Jesus	jerk	
jangle		Jeezus	Jesus	jerky	
jangol	jangle	Jehovah		jerm	germ
jangul	jangle	jelatin	gelatin	jernal	journal
janitor		jellous	jealous	jerney	journey
janotor	janitor	jelly		jersey	
January		jelous	jealous	jersy	jersey
janutor	janitor	jely	jelly	jerzey	jersey
Japan		jem	gem	jest	
Japanese		jeneral	general	jester	
jar		jenerate	generate	jesture	gesture
jaspar	jasper	jenerous	generous	Jesus	
jasper		jenes	jeans	jet	
jaspir	jasper	jenez	jeans	jetty	
jaspor	jasper	jenial	genial	jety	jetty
jaspur	jasper	jenie	genie	Jew	
jaunt		jenius	genius	jewal	jewel
jaunty		jentile	gentile	jewbilant	jubilant
javelin		jentility	gentility	jewce	juice
javlin	javelin	jentle	gentle	jewdicial	judicial
jaw		jenuine	genuine	jewel	
jawnt	jaunt	jeography	geography	jeweler	

jewelry		jingel		jolt	
jewil	jewel	jingil		joly	jolly
Jewish		jingle		jonckwil	jonquil
Jewn	June	jingol	jingle	jonkwil	jonquil
jewnior	junior	jingul	jingle	jonqual	jonquil
jewnyor	junior	jinjer	ginger	jonquel	jonquil
jewol	jewel	jinrikisha		jonquil	
Jewpiter	Jupiter	Jipan	Japan	jonquol	jonquil
jewse	juice	jipsy	gypsy	jont	jaunt
jewt	jute	jiraffe	giraffe	Joo	Jew
jewul	jewel	jirk	jerk	joobilant	jubilant
jewvenile	juvenile	jirnal	journal	jooce	juice
Jezus	Jesus	jirney	journey	joodicial	judicial
jiant	giant	jirsey	jersey	jool	jewel
jibe	gibe	joak	joke	Joon	June
jiffy		joalt	jolt	joonior	junior
jify	jiffy	joavial	jovial	joonyor	junior
jig		job		Joopiter	Jupiter
jigal	jiggle	jockey		joose	juice
jigantic	gigantic	jocky	jockey	joot	jute
jigel	jiggle	jog		joovenile	juvenile
jiggal	jiggle	jogal	joggle	Jopan	Japan
jiggel	jiggle	jogel	joggle	jore	jaw
jiggil	jiggle	joggal	joggle	josal	jostle
jiggle		joggel	joggle	josel	jostle
jiggol	jiggle	joggil	joggle	josil	jostle
jiggul	jiggle	joggle		josle	jostle
jigil	jiggle	joggol	joggle	josol	jostle
jigle	jiggle	joggul	joggle	jossal	jostle
jigol	jiggle	jogil	joggle	jossel	jostle
jigsaw		jogle	joggle	jossil	jostle
jigsore	jigsaw	jogol	joggle	jossle	jostle
jigul	jiggle	jogul	joggle	jossol	jostle
Jihovah	Jehovah	join		jossul	jostle
jill	gill	joint		jostle	
jimnasium	gymnasium	jointly		josul	jostle
jin	gin	joke		jot	
jingal	jingle	jolly		jounce	

jounse	jounce	judicious		jumper	
journal		judishal	judicial	junck	junk
journalism		juditial	judicial	junckcher	juncture
journalist		Jue	Jew	junckshun	junction
journel	journal	juebilant	jubilant	juncktion	junction
journey		juedicial	judicial	junckture	juncture
journil	journal	juel	jewel	juncshun	junction
journol	journal	jug		junction	
journul	journal	jugal	juggle	juncture	
journy	journey	juge	judge	June	
joust		jugel	juggle	jungal	jungle
joveal	jovial	juggal	juggle	jungel	jungle
jovial		juggel	juggle	jungil	jungle
jowl		juggil	juggle	jungle	
jownce	jounce	juggle		jungol	jungle
jowst	joust	juggler		jungul	jungle
joy		juggol	juggle	junior	
joyas	joyous	juggul	juggle	junk	
joyess	joyous	jugil	juggle	junkcher	juncture
joyful		jugle	juggle	junkshun	junction
joyis	joyous	jugol	juggle	junktion	junction
joyn	join	jugul	juggle	junkture	juncture
joynt	joint	jugular		junyar	junior
joyos	joyous	juice		junyer	junior
joyous		juicey	juicy	junyir	junior
joyus	joyous	juicy		junyor	junior
jual	jewel	juil	jewel	junyur	junior
jubalant	jubilant	juise	juice	juol	jewel
jubelant	jubilant	jule	jewel	Jupan	Japan
jubilant		July		Jupater	Jupiter
jubilee		jumbal	jumble	Jupeter	Jupiter
jubolant	jubilant	jumbel	jumble	Jupiter	
jubulant	jubilant	jumbil	jumble	Jupoter	Jupiter
juce	juice	jumble		Juputer	Jupiter
judge		jumbo		jurer	juror
judgement	judgment	jumbol	jumble	jurk	jerk
judgment		jumbul	jumble	jurnal	journal
judicial		jump		jurney	journey

juror		justice		jut	
jursey	jersey	justifiable		jute	
jury		justification		juvanile	juvenile
juse	juice	justify		juvenile	
just		justis	justice	juvinile	juvenile
just	joust	justofy	justify	juvonile	juvenile
justafy	justify	justufy	justify	juvunile	juvenile
justefy	justify			jymnasium	gymnasium

K

kab	cab	kalf	calf	kandy	candy
kabbage	cabbage	kalico	calico	kane	cane
kabin	cabin	kalidoscope	kaleidoscope	kangaroo	
kabinet	cabinet	kall	call	kangeroo	kangaroo
kable	cable	kallous	callous	kangiroo	kangaroo
kaboose	caboose	kallus	callus	kangoroo	kangaroo
kache	cache	kalm	calm	kanguroo	kangaroo
kacki	khaki	kalorie	calorie	kanine	canine
kackle	cackle	kamel	camel	kanker	canker
kacky	khaki	kameleon	chameleon	kanned	canned
kactus	cactus	kamera	camera	kannibal	cannibal
kadence	cadence	kamono	kimono	kannon	cannon
kadet	cadet	kamouflage	camouflage	kanny	canny
kafe	cafe	kamp	camp	kanoe	canoe
kafeteria	cafeteria	kampaign	campaign	kanon	canon
kaffeine	caffeine	kamphor	camphor	kanopy	canopy
kage	cage	kan	can	Kansas	
kake	cake	kanal	canal	Kanses	Kansas
kaky	khaki	kanary	canary	Kansis	Kansas
kalamity	calamity	kancel	cancel	Kansos	Kansas
kalcium	calcium	kancer	cancer	Kansus	Kansas
kalculate	calculate	kandid	candid	kantaloupe	cantaloupe
kaldron	caldron	kandidate	candidate	kantankerous	cantankerous
kaleidoscope		kandle	candle	kanteen	canteen
kalendar	calendar	kandor	candor	kanter	canter

Kantucky	Kentucky	kargo	cargo	katechism	catechism
kanvas	canvas	karnage	carnage	kater	cater
kanyon	canyon	karnation	carnation	katerpillar	caterpillar
Kanzas	Kansas	karnival	karnival	kathedral	cathedral
Kanzes	Kansas	karnivorous	carniverous	kattle	cattle
Kanzis	Kansas	karol	carol	kaught	caught
Kanzos	Kansas	karp	carp	kauliflower	cauliflower
Kanzus	Kansas	karpenter	carpenter	Kaurea	Korea
kaos	chaos	karpet	carpet	kause	cause
kap	cap	karriage	carriage	kaution	caution
kapability	capability	karry	carry	kavalcade	cavalcade
kapable	capable	kart	cart	kavalier	cavalier
kapacity	capacity	kartilage	cartilage	kavalry	cavalry
kape	cape	karton	carton	kave	cave
kaper	caper	kartoon	cartoon	kavern	cavern
kapillary	capillary	kartridge	cartridge	kavity	cavity
kapital	capital	karve	carve	kavort	cavort
kapricious	capricious	kascade	cascade	Kawrea	Korea
kapsize	capsize	kase	case	kayac	kayak
kapsule	capsule	kash	cash	kayack	kayak
kaptain	captain	kashew	cashew	kayak	
kaption	caption	kashier	cashier	kea	key
kaptivate	captivate	kashmere	cashmere	keal	keel
kaptive	captive	kask	cask	kealo	kilo
kapture	capture	kasket	casket	kean	keen
kar	car	kasm	chasm	keap	keep
karacter	character	kasserole	casserole	kee	key
karamel	caramel	kast	cast	kee	quay
karavan	caravan	kaste	caste	keel	
karbine	carbine	kastle	castle	keelo	kilo
karbohydrate	carbohydrate	kasual	casual	keen	
karbon	carbon	kasualty	casualty	keeness	keenness
karcass	carcass	kat	cat	keeniss	keenness
kard	card	katalogue	catalogue	keenness	
kardinal	cardinal	katapult	catapult	keenniss	keenness
kare	care	kataract	cataract	keep	
kareer	career	katastrophe	catastrophe	keeper	
karess	caress	katch	catch	keeping	

keepsaik	keepsake			kilegram	kilogram
keepsake		kerusene	kerosene	kileidoscope	kaleidoscope
keg		ketal	kettle	kilemeter	kilometer
kele	keel	ketchup		kilidoscope	kaleidoscope
keleidoscope	kaleidoscope	ketel	kettle	kiligram	kilogram
kelidoscope	kaleidoscope	ketil	kettle	kilimeter	kilometer
kelo	kilo	ketle	kettle	kill	
kelp		ketol	kettle	kill	kiln
kemist	chemist	kettal	kettle	killer	
kemono	kimono	kettel	kettle	kiln	
ken		kettil	kettle	kilo	
kenal	kennel	kettle		kilogram	
kene	keen	kettol	kettle	kilometer	
kenel	kennel	kettul	kettle	kilt	
kenil	kennel	ketul	kettle	kilugram	kilogram
kennal	kennel	kew	cue	kilumeter	kilometer
kennel		kew	queue	kimono	
kennil	kennel	key		kin	
kennol	kennel	key	quay	kinck	kink
kennul	kennel	khaki		kind	
kenol	kennel	khaky	khaki	kindagarten	kindergarten
Kentucky		kichan	kitchen	kindal	kindle
Kentuky	Kentucky	kichen	kitchen	kindargarten	kindergarten
kenul	kennel	kichin	kitchen	kindegarten	kindergarten
kepe	keep	kichon	kitchen	kindel	kindle
kept		kichun	kitchen	kindergarten	
kerasene	kerosene	kick		kindharted	kindhearted
kercheif	kerchief	kid		kindhearted	
kerchief		kidnap		kindigarten	kindergarten
kerchif	kerchief	kidnea	kidney	kindil	kindle
keresene	kerosene	kidnee	kidney	kindirgarten	kindergarten
kerisene	kerosene	kidney		kindle	
kernal	kernel	kidny	kidney	kindliness	
kernel		kik	kick	kindling	
kernel	colonel	kil	kill	kindly	
kernil	kernel	kil	kiln	kindlyness	kindliness
kernol	kernel	kilagram	kilogram	kindness	
kernul	kernel	kilameter	kilometer	kindniss	kindness

kindogarten	kindergarten	kitun	kitten	klever	clever		
kindol	kindle	kity	kitty	klick	click		
kindorgarten	kindergarten	kiyak	kayak	klient	client		
kindred		klad	clad	kliff	cliff		
kindrid	kindred	klaim	claim	klimate	climate		
kindugarten	kindergarten	klam	clam	klimax	climax		
kindul	kindle	klammy	clammy	klimb	climb		
kindurgarten	kindergarten	klamor	clamor	klinch	clinch		
king		klamp	clamp	kling	cling		
kingdam	kingdom	klan	clan	klip	clip		
kingdem	kingdom	klap	clap	klique	clique		
kingdim	kingdom	klarify	clarify	kloak	cloak		
kingdom		klarinet	clarinet	klock	clock		
kingdum	kingdom	klarion	clarion	klod	clod		
kink		klarity	clarity	klog	clog		
kinship		klash	clash	kloister	cloister		
Kintucky	Kentucky	klasp	clasp	klose	close		
kirchief	kerchief	klass	class	kloset	closet		
kirnel	kernel	klassic	classic	klot	clot		
kis	kiss	klassify	classify	kloth	cloth		
kiss		klatter	clatter	klothe	clothe		
kit		klause	clause	kloud	cloud		
kitan	kitten	klaw	claw	klout	clout		
kitchan	kitchen	klay	clay	klove	clove		
kitchen		klean	clean	klover	clover		
kitchin	kitchen	kleanliness	cleanliness	klown	clown		
kitchon	kitchen	klear	clear	klub	club		
kitchun	kitchen	kleat	cleat	klue	clue		
kite		kleave	cleave	klump	clump		
kiten	kitten	kleek	clique	klumsy	clumsy		
kitin	kitten	klef	clef	klung	clung		
kiton	kitten	kleft	cleft	kluster	cluster		
kittan	kitten	klemency	clemency	klutch	clutch		
kitten		klench	clench	klutter	clutter		
kittin	kitten	klense	cleanse	knack			
kitton	kitten	klergy	clergy	knaive	knave		
kittun	kitten	klerical	clerical	knak	knack		
kitty		klerk	clerk	knapsack			

knapsak	knapsack	knok	knock	kobweb	cobweb
knave		knole	knoll	kock	cock
knea	knee	knoll		kockpit	cockpit
knead		knoo	knew	kockroach	cockroach
kneal	kneel	knot		kocky	cocky
knede	knead	know		kocoa	cocoa
knee		knowing		koconut	coconut
kneed	knead	knowingly		kocoon	cocoon
kneel		knowledge		kod	cod
knel	knell	knowlege	knowledge	koddle	coddle
knele	kneel	knowlidge	knowledge	kode	code
knell		knowlige	knowledge	kodger	codger
knelt		known		koerce	coerce
knew		knuckal	knuckle	koffee	coffee
knickars	knickers	knuckil	knuckle	koffin	coffin
knickers		knuckle		kog	cog
knickerz	knickers	knuckol	knuckle	koil	coil
knickirs	knickers	knuckul	knuckle	koin	coin
knickknack		knue	knew	koincide	coincide
knickknak	knickknack	knukal	knuckle	koke	coke
knicknack	knickknack	knukel	knuckle	kold	cold
knicknak	knickknack	knukil	knuckle	koleidoscope	kaleidoscope
knickors	knickers	knukle	knuckle	kolera	colera
knickurs	knickers	knukol	knuckle	kolidoscope	kaleidoscope
knife		knukul	knuckle	kollapse	collapse
knight		koach	coach	kollar	collar
knikers	knickers	koagulate	coagulate	kolleague	colleague
knikerz	knickers	koal	coal	kollect	collect
knikknack	knickknack	koala		kollege	college
knit		koarse	coarse	kollide	collide
knite	knight	koast	coast	kollie	collie
knives		koat	coat	kolon	colon
knivez	knives	koax	coax	kolonel	colonel
kno	know	kob	cob	kolonial	colonial
knoal	knoll	kobalt	cobalt	kolony	colony
knob		kobbler	cobbler	kolor	color
knock		kobblestone	cobblestone	kolossal	colossal
knoe	know	kobra	cobra	kolt	colt

kolumn	column	kompel	compel	koncise	concise
komb	comb	kompensate	compensate	konclude	conclude
kombat	combat	kompete	compete	koncoct	concoct
kombine	combine	kompetent	competent	koncord	concord
kombustion	combustion	kompile	compile	koncourse	concourse
kome	come	komplacent	complacent	koncrete	concrete
komedy	comedy	komplain	complain	koncur	concur
komely	comely	komplement	complement	koncussion	concussion
komet	comet	komplete	complete	kondemn	condemn
komfort	comfort	komplex	complex	kondense	condense
komic	comic	komplexion	complexion	kondescend	condescend
komma	comma	komplicate	complicate	kondition	condition
kommand	command	komply	comply	konduct	conduct
kommemorate	commemorate	kompose	compose	kone	cone
kommence	commence	komposure	composure	konfederate	confederate
kommend	commend	kompound	compound	konfer	confer
komment	comment	komprehend	comprehend	konfess	confess
kommerce	commerce	komprehen-sive	comprehen-sive	konfide	confide
kommission	commission	kompress	compress	konfine	confine
kommit	commit	komprise	comprise	konfirm	confirm
kommittee	committee	kompromise	compromise	konfiscate	confiscate
kommodious	commodious	kompulsion	compulsion	konflagration	conflagration
kommodity	commodity	kompute	compute	konflict	conflict
kommon	common	komrade	comrade	konform	conform
kommotion	commotion	kon	con	konfound	confound
kommunicate	communicate	koncave	concave	konfront	confront
kommuion	communion	konceal	conceal	konfuse	confuse
kommunity	community	koncede	concede	kongeal	congeal
kommute	commute	konceit	conceit	kongenial	congenial
komono	kimono	konceive	conceive	kongested	congested
kompact	compact	koncentrate	concentrate	kongratulate	congratulate
kompanion	companion	koncept	concept	kongregate	congregate
kompany	company	koncern	concern	kongress	congress
kompare	compare	koncert	concert	konjecture	conjecture
kompartment	compartment	koncerto	concerto	konjunction	conjunction
kompass	compass	koncession	concession	konjure	conjure
kompassion	compassion	konciliate	conciliate	konnect	connect
kompatible	compatible			konquer	conquer

konscience	conscience	kontemplate	contemplate	kookie	cookie
konscious	conscious	kontemporary	contemporary	kool	cool
konsecrate	consecrate	kontempt	contempt	koolie	coolie
konsecutive	consecutive	kontend	contend	koop	coop
konsent	consent	kontent	content	kooperate	cooperate
konsequence	consequence	kontention	contention	koordinate	coordinate
konservative	conservative	kontest	contest	kope	cope
konserve	conserve	kontinent	continent	kopious	copious
konsider	consider	kontinue	continue	kopper	copper
konsiderable	considerable	kontinuity	continuity	kopy	copy
konsiderate	considerate	kontort	contort	koral	coral
konsign	consign	kontour	contour	kord	chord
konsist	consist	kontraband	contraband	kord	cord
konsistent	consistent	kontract	contract	kordial	cordial
konsole	console	kontradict	contradict	korduroy	corduroy
konsolidate	consolidate	kontralto	contralto	kore	core
konsonant	consonant	kontrary	contrary	Korea	
konsort	consort	kontrast	contrast	kork	cork
konspicuous	conspicuous	kontribute	contribute	korn	corn
konspire	conspire	kontrite	contrite	kornea	cornea
konstable	constable	kontrive	contrive	korner	corner
konstant	constant	kontrol	control	kornice	cornice
konstellation	constellation	kontroversy	controversy	kornucopia	cornucopia
konsternation	consternation	Kontucky	Kentucky	koronation	coronation
konstituent	constituent	konvalesce	convalesce	koronet	coronet
konstitute	constitute	konvene	convene	korporal	corporal
konstrain	constrain	konvenient	convenient	korporation	corporation
konstrict	constrict	konvent	convent	korps	corps
konstruct	construct	konventional	conventional	korpse	corpse
konstrue	construe	konverse	converse	korpulent	corpulent
konsul	consul	konvert	convert	korpuscle	corpuscle
konsult	consult	konvex	convex	korral	corral
konsume	consume	konvey	convey	korrect	correct
konsummate	consummate	konvict	convict	korrespond	correspond
kontact	contact	konvince	convince	korridor	corridor
kontagious	contagious	konvoy	convoy	korroborate	corroborate
kontain	contain	konvulse	convulse	korrode	corrode
kontaminate	contaminate	kook	cook	korrugate	corrugate

korrupt	corrupt	kovet	covet	kream	cream
korsage	corsage	kovey	covey	krease	crease
korset	corset	kow	cow	kreate	create
korus	chorus	kowala	koala	kreature	creature
kosmetic	cosmetic	koward	coward	kredit	credit
kosmic	cosmic	kower	cower	kredulous	credulous
kosmos	cosmos	kowl	cowl	kreed	creed
kost	cost	koxswain	coxswain	kreek	creek
kostume	costume	koy	coy	kreep	creep
kosy	cosy	koyote	coyote	kreepy	creepy
kot	cot	kozy	cozy	krepe	crepe
kottage	cottage	krab	crab	krescent	crescent
kotton	cotton	krack	crack	krest	crest
kouch	couch	kracker	cracker	krestfallen	crestfallen
kougar	cougar	krackle	crackle	krevice	crevice
kough	cough	kradle	cradle	krew	crew
kould	could	kraft	craft	krib	crib
kouncil	council	krafty	crafty	kricket	cricket
kounsel	counsel	krag	crag	krime	crime
kount	count	kram	cram	krimson	crimson
kountenance	countenance	kramp	cramp	kringe	cringe
kounter	counter	kranberry	cranberry	krinkle	crinkle
kounterfeit	counterfeit	krane	crane	kripple	cripple
kountess	countess	kranium	cranium	krisanthe-	chrysanthe-
kountry	country	krank	crank	mum	mum
kounty	county	kranky	cranky	krisis	crisis
kouple	couple	krape	crape	krisp	crisp
koupon	coupon	krape	crepe	krisscross	crisscross
kourage	courage	krash	crash	kristen	christen
kourier	courier	krate	crate	kritic	critic
kourse	course	krater	crater	kroak	croak
kourt	court	kravat	cravat	krochet	crochet
kourtesy	courtesy	krave	crave	krock	crock
kourtship	courtship	krawl	crawl	krocodile	crocodile
kousin	cousin	krayon	crayon	krocus	crocus
kove	cove	kraze	craze	kromium	chromium
kovenant	covenant	krazy	crazy	kronic	chronic
kover	cover	kreak	creak	krony	crony

krook	crook	kull	cull	kuticle	cuticle
krooked	crooked	kulminate	culminate	kutlass	cutlass
kroon	croon	kulpable	culpable	kutlery	cutlery
krop	crop	kulprit	culprit	kwack	quack
kroquet	croquet	kultivate	cultivate	kwadruped	quadruped
kroquette	croquette	kulture	culture	kwadruplet	quadruplet
kross	cross	kulvert	culvert	kwaff	quaff
krotch	crotch	kumbersome	cumbersome	kwaik	quake
krouch	crouch	kumono	kimono	Kwaiker	Quaker
kroup	croup	kunning	cunning	kwail	quail
krow	crow	Kuntucky	Kentucky	kwaint	quaint
krowd	crowd	kup	cup	kwaiver	quaver
krown	crown	Kupid	Cupid	kwake	quake
krucial	crucial	kur	cur	Kwaker	Quaker
krucifix	crucifix	kurator	curator	kwale	quail
krude	crude	kurb	curb	kwalify	qualify
kruel	cruel	kurchief	kerchief	kwality	quality
kruet	cruet	kurd	curd	kwam	qualm
kruise	cruise	kure	cure	kwantity	quantity
kruller	cruller	kurfew	curfew	kwarantine	quarantine
krumb	crumb	kurious	curious	kwarrel	quarrel
krumble	crumble	kurl	curl	kwarry	quarry
krumple	crumple	kurnel	kernel	kwaver	quaver
krunch	crunch	kurrant	currant	kwean	queen
krusade	crusade	kurrent	current	kwear	queer
krush	crush	kurry	curry	kweary	query
krust	crust	kurse	curse	kween	queen
krutch	crutch	kurt	curt	kweer	queer
krysanthe-mum	chrysanthe-mum	kurtail	curtail	kweery	query
kucumber	cucumber	kurtain	curtain	kwell	quell
kud	cud	kurtsy	curtsy	kwench	quench
kuddle	cuddle	kurve	curve	kwene	queen
kudgel	cudgel	kushion	cushion	kwere	queer
kue	cue	kustard	custard	kwerey	query
kuff	cuff	kustody	custody	kwest	quest
kuleidoscope	kaleidoscope	kustom	custom	kwestion	question
kulidoscope	kaleidoscope	kut	cut	kwick	quick
		kute	cute	kwiet	quiet

kwik	quick	kwoata	quota	kworter	quarter
kwill	quill	kwodruped	quadruped	kworts	quartz
kwilt	quilt	kwodruplet	quadruplet	kwortz	quartz
kwinine	quinine	kwoit	quoit	kwoshent	quotient
kwintet	quintet	kwolify	qualify	kwota	quota
kwire	choir	kwolity	quality	kwote	quote
kwit	quit	kwom	qualm	kwotient	quotient
kwite	quite	kwontity	quantity	kwoyt	quoit
kwiver	quiver	kworantine	quarantine	kue	queue
kwiz	quiz	kworrel	quarrel	kyak	kayak
kwoat	quote	kworry	quarry	kyote	coyote
		kwort	quart		

L

labal	label	labur	labor	lad	
labar	labor	laburatory	laboratory	ladal	ladle
labaratory	laboratory	laburinth	labyrinth	ladan	laden
labarinth	labyrinth	labyrinth		ladar	ladder
label		lace		laddar	ladder
laber	labor	lacerate		ladder	
laberatory	laboratory	lacey	lacy	laddir	ladder
laberinth	labyrinth	lach	latch	laddor	ladder
labil	label	lacirate	lacerate	laddur	ladder
labir	labor	lack		lade	laid
labiratory	laboratory	lacker	lacquer	ladel	ladle
labirinth	labyrinth	lackey		laden	
labol	label	lacking		lader	ladder
labor		lackquer	lacquer	ladil	ladle
laboratory		lacks	lax	ladin	laden
laborer		lacky	lackey	ladir	ladder
laborinth	labyrinth	lacquar	lacquer	ladle	
laborious		lacquer		ladol	ladle
labratory	laboratory	lacquir	lacquer	ladon	laden
labretto	libretto	lacquor	lacquer	lador	ladder
labul	label	lacy		ladul	ladle

ladun	laden	lament		lare	lair		
ladur	ladder	lamentable		lareat	lariat		
lady		lamentation		large			
laf	laugh	lamp		lariat			
laff	laugh	lance		larincks	larynx		
lag		lanck	lank	larinks	larynx		
lagewn	lagoon	land		larinx	larynx		
lagitimate	legitimate	landing		lark			
lagoon		landmark		larriat	lariat		
lagune	lagoon	landscaipe	landscape	larsany	larceny		
laibel	label	landscape		larseny	larceny		
laibor	labor	landskape	landscape	larsiny	larceny		
laice	lace	lane		larsony	larceny		
laid		lane	lain	larsuny	larceny		
laiden	laden	language		larva			
laidle	ladle	languid		larynks	larynx		
laidy	lady	languige	language	larynx			
laike	lake	languish		lasarate	lacerate		
laim	lame	langwage	language	lase	lace		
lain		langwid	languid	laserate	lacerate		
lain	lane	langwish	languish	lash			
lainth	length	lank		lasie	lassie		
lair		lanoleum	linoleum	lasirate	lacerate		
laise	lace	lanse	lance	laso	lasso		
lait	late	lantarn	lantern	lasorate	lacerate		
laith	lathe	lantern		lass			
laizy	lazy	lantirn	lantern	lassie			
lajitimate	legitimate	lantorn	lantern	lasso			
lak	lack	lanturn	lantern	lassy	lassie		
lake		lap		last			
laker	lacquer	lapce	lapse	lasting			
lakey	lackey	lapel		lasurate	lacerate		
laks	lax	lapse		lasy	lazy		
laky	lackey	laquer	lacquer	Latan	Latin		
lam	lamb	larceny		latar	latter		
lama	llama	larciny	larceny	lataral	lateral		
lamb		larck	lark	latatude	latitude		
lame		lard		latch			

late		laugheble	laughable	lawn	
lately		laughible	laughable	lawnch	launch
Laten	Latin	laughoble	laughable	lawnder	launder
lateral		laughtar	laughter	lawrel	laurel
latetude	latitude	laughter		lawyer	
lathar	lather	laughtir	laughter	lax	
lathe		laughtor	laughter	laxaty	laxity
lather		laughtur	laughter	laxety	laxity
lathir	lather	laughuble	laughable	laxity	
lathor	lather	launch		laxoty	laxity
lathur	lather	launder		laxuty	laxity
latice	lattice	launderess	laundress	lay	
Latin		laundery	laundry	layar	layer
latir	later	laundress		laybel	label
latir	latter	laundriss	laundress	laybor	labor
latiral	lateral	laundry		layer	
latis	lattice	laural	laurel	layir	layer
latitude		laurel		layman	
Laton	Latin	lauril	laurel	layor	layer
lator	later	laurol	laurel	layur	layer
lator	latter	laurul	laurel	laziness	
latoral	lateral	lava		laziniss	laziness
latotude	latitude	lavander	lavender	lazy	
lattar	latter	lavatory		lazyness	laziness
latter		lavender		lea	
lattice		lavetory	lavatory	lea	lee
lattir	latter	lavinder	lavender	leach	leech
lattis	lattice	lavish		lead	
lattor	latter	lavitory	lavatory	leader	
lattur	latter	lavonder	lavender	leadership	
Latun	Latin	lavotory	lavatory	leaf	
latur	latter	lavunder	lavender	leaflet	
latural	lateral	lavutory	lavatory	leaflit	leaflet
latutude	latitude	law		leagal	legal
laud		lawd	laud	leage	liege
laud	lord	lawful		leagen	legion
laugh		lawless		leagin	legion
laughable		lawliss	lawless	leagion	legion

league		leech		legicy	legacy
leak		leed	lead	legil	legal
leak	leek	leef	leaf	legind	legend
leakage		leegal	legal	legings	leggings
leakige	leakage	leege	liege	legion	
lean		leegen	legion	legislate	
leanient	lenient	leegin	legion	legislation	
leanyent	lenient	leegion	legion	legislative	
leap		leegue	league	legislator	
lear	leer	leek	leak	legislature	
learn		leen	lean	legitimate	
learned		leenient	lenient	legocy	legacy
learnid	learned	leenyent	lenient	legol	legal
learning		leep	leap	legoon	lagoon
lease		leese	lease	legucy	legacy
leash		leesh	leash	legue	league
least		leest	least	legul	legal
leasure	leisure	leesure	leisure	legune	lagoon
leathar	leather	leeve	leave	leige	liege
leather		leever	lever	leisure	
leathery		leeward		leisurely	
leathir	leather	leewood	leeward	leizure	leisure
leathor	leather	leewud	leeward	lejable	legible
leathur	leather	leezure	leisure	lejan	legion
leave		lefe	leaf	lejand	legend
leaver	lever	left		leje	liege
leazure	leisure	leg		lejeble	legible
lebretto	libretto	legacy		lejen	legion
leckcher	lecture	legal		lejend	legend
leckture	lecture	legasy	legacy	lejible	legible
lecture		legeble	legible	lejin	legion
lecturer		legecy	legacy	lejind	legend
led		legel	legal	lejislate	legislate
led	lead	legend		lejitimate	legitimate
lede	lead	legendary		lejoble	legible
ledge		leggings		lejon	legion
lee		leggingz	leggings	lejond	legend
lee	lea	legible		lejuble	legible

lejun	legion	leopurd	leopard	let	
lejund	legend	lepar	leper	letar	letter
lekcher	lecture	lepard	leopard	leter	letter
leke	leak	lepe	leap	lether	leather
lekture	lecture	lepel	lapel	letice	lettuce
leman	lemon	leper		letir	letter
lemen	lemon	leperd	leopard	letis	lettuce
lement	lament	lepir	leper	letor	letter
lemin	lemon	lepird	leopard	let's	
lemon		lepor	leper	lettar	letter
lemonade		lepord	leopard	letter	
lemun	lemon	leppard	leopard	lettice	lettuce
lend		leprasy	leprosy	lettir	letter
lene	lean	lepresy	leprosy	lettis	lettuce
length		leprisy	leprosy	lettor	letter
lengthen		leprosy		lettuce	
lengthwise		leprusy	leprosy	lettur	letter
lengthwize	lengthwise	lepur	leper	lettus	lettuce
lengthy		lepurd	leopard	letuce	lettuce
lenient		lerch	lurch	letur	letter
lenkth	length	lerk	lurk	letus	lettuce
lenoleum	linoleum	lern	learn	leval	level
lens		les	less	levar	lever
Lent		lesan	lesson	leve	leave
lent		lese	lease	levee	
lental	lentil	lesen	lesson	level	
lentel	lentil	lesin	lesson	lever	
lenth	length	leson	lesson	levey	levee
lentil		less		levey	levy
lentle	lentil	lessan	lesson	levil	level
lentol	lentil	lessen		levir	lever
lentul	lentil	lessen	lesson	levol	level
lenyent	lenient	lesser		levor	lever
lenz	lens	lessin	lesson	levul	level
leopard		lesson		levur	lever
leoperd	leopard	lessun	lesson	levy	
leopird	leopard	lest		levy	levee
leopord	leopard	lesun	lesson	lew	lieu

lewbricate	lubricate	liburty	liberty	ligiment	ligament
lewcid	lucid	licarice	licorice	ligitimate	legitimate
lewdicrous	ludicrous	lice		ligoment	ligament
Lewisiana	Louisiana	licence	license	ligoon	lagoon
Lewiziana	Louisiana	license		ligument	ligament
lewkwarm	lukewarm	licince	license	ligune	lagoon
lewm	loom	licinse	license	lik	lick
lewminous	luminous	lick		likable	
lewn	loon	licker	liquor	like	
lewnar	lunar	lickorice	licorice	likeable	
lewp	loop	lickwid	liquid	likeing	liking
lewr	lure	licorice		likelihood	
lewse	loose	licurice	licorice	likely	
lewsid	lucid	lid		likelyhood	likelihood
lewt	loot	lie		liken	
lewt	lute	lie	lye	likeness	
lewtenant	lieutenant	lieble	liable	likeniss	likeness
li	lie	liege		liker	liquor
li	lye	lieing	lying	likewise	
liable		lien		likewize	likewise
lian	lion	lien	lion	liking	
liar		lier	liar	likorice	licorice
libaral	liberal	liesure	leisure	likwid	liquid
libarty	liberty	lieu		lilac	
liberal		lieutenant		lilak	lilac
liberate		liezure	leisure	lilly	lily
liberty		life		lilt	
libiral	liberal	lifeboy	lifebuoy	lily	
libirty	liberty	lifebuoy		lim	limb
liboral	liberal	lifeless		limated	limited
liborty	liberty	lifeliss	lifeless	limb	
librarian		lift		limbar	limber
library		ligament		limber	
libraryan	librarian	ligement	ligament	limbir	limber
librerry	library	light		limbor	limber
librery	library	lighten		limbur	limber
libretto		lightening	lightning	lime	
libural	liberal	lightning		liment	lament

limestone	
limeted	limited
limf	lymph
limit	
limited	
limitid	limited
limoted	limited
limp	
limph	lymph
limpid	
limuted	limited
linan	linen
linch	lynch
linck	link
lincks	lynx
line	
lineage	
lineing	lining
linen	
liner	
lingar	linger
linger	
lingir	linger
lingor	linger
lingur	linger
liniage	lineage
linin	linen
lining	
link	
links	
links	lynx
linoleum	
linon	linen
lint	
linun	linen
linx	links
linx	lynx
lioble	liable

lion	
lioness	
lioniss	lioness
lionness	lioness
lionniss	lioness
lip	
lipel	lapel
liquar	liquor
liquefy	
liquer	liquor
liquid	
liquify	liquefy
liquir	liquor
liquor	
lirch	lurch
liric	lyric
lirick	lyric
lirik	lyric
lirk	lurk
lirn	learn
lisan	listen
lisance	license
lisanse	license
lise	lice
lisen	listen
lisence	license
lisense	license
lisin	listen
lisince	license
lisinse	license
lison	listen
lisonce	license
lisonse	license
lisp	
lissan	listen
lissen	listen
lissin	listen
lisson	listen

lissun	listen
list	
listen	
listener	
listless	
listliss	listless
lisun	listen
lisunce	license
lisunse	license
lit	
lital	little
litar	litter
litarally	literally
litarary	literary
lite	light
litel	little
liter	litter
literally	
literary	
literate	
literature	
lithe	
litil	little
litir	litter
litirally	literally
litirary	literary
litle	little
litmas	litmus
litmes	litmus
litmis	litmus
litmos	litmus
litmus	
litol	little
litor	litter
litorally	literally
litorary	literary
littal	little
littar	litter

littel	little	lizord	lizard	location	
litter		lizurd	lizard	lock	
littil	little	lizzard	lizard	locker	
littir	litter	lizzerd	lizard	locket	
little		lizzird	lizard	lockit	locket
littol	little	lizzord	lizard	lockjaw	
littor	litter	lizzurd	lizard	locksmith	
littul	little	llama		locol	local
littur	litter	lo	low	locomotion	
litul	little	load		locomotive	
litur	litter	loaf		locost	locust
liturally	literally	loam		locul	local
liturary	literary	loan		locumotion	locomotion
liuble	liable	loan	lone	locust	
liun	lion	loap	lope	lode	load
livar	liver	loar	lore	lodge	
live		loashun	lotion	lodgeing	lodging
liveing	living	loath		lodgic	logic
livelihood		loath	loathe	lodging	
liveliness		loathe		lofe	loaf
lively		loation	lotion	loft	
livelyhood	livelihood	loaves		lofty	
livelyness	liveliness	loavs	loaves	log	
liven		loavz	loaves	loge	lodge
liver		lobby		logic	
lives		lobretto	libretto	logical	
livestock		lobstar	lobster	logitimate	legitimate
livestok	livestock	lobster		logoon	lagoon
livez	lives	lobstir	lobster	logune	lagoon
livid		lobstor	lobster	loin	
living		lobstur	lobster	loitar	loiter
livir	liver	loby	lobby	loiter	
livlihood	livelihood	locait	locate	loitir	loiter
livor	liver	local		loitor	loiter
livur	liver	locality		loitur	loiter
lizard		locamotion	locomotion	lojic	logic
lizerd	lizard	locast	locust	lojitimate	legitimate
lizird	lizard	locate		lok	lock

lokait	locate	longetude	longitude	loser	
lokal	local	longing		loshun	lotion
lokamotion	locomotion	longitude		loss	
lokast	locust	longitudinal		lost	
lokate	locate	lonjatude	longitude	lot	
lokel	local	lonjetude	longitude	lotary	lottery
lokemotion	locomotion	lonjitude	longitude	lotery	lottery
lokest	locust	lonjotude	longitude	lothe	loathe
loket	locket	lonjutude	longitude	lotion	
lokil	local	lonoleum	linoleum	lotiry	lottery
lokimotion	locomotion	loobricate	lubricate	lotory	lottery
lokist	locust	loocid	lucid	lottary	lottery
lokit	locket	loodicrous	ludicrous	lottery	
lokol	local	Looisiana	Louisiana	lottiry	lottery
lokomotion	locomotion	Looiziana	Louisiana	lottory	lottery
lokost	locust	look		lottury	lottery
lokul	local	lookwarm	lukewarm	lotury	lottery
lokumotion	locomotion	loom		louce	louse
lokust	locust	loominous	luminous	loud	
lol	loll	loon		loudly	
lolipop	lollipop	loonar	lunar	Louisiana	
loll		loop		Louiziana	Louisiana
lollipop		loor	lure	lounge	
lollypop		loorid	lurid	louse	
lolypop	lollipop	loose		lovable	
lome	loam	loosen		love	
loment	lament	loosid	lucid	loveable	lovable
lone		loot		loveble	lovable
lone	loan	loot	lute	loveing	loving
loneliness		lop		loveley	lovely
lonely		lope		loveliness	
lonelyness	loneliness	lopel	lapel	lovely	
lonesam	lonesome	lopsided		lovelyness	loveliness
lonesem	lonesome	Lord		lover	
lonesim	lonesome	lord		loving	
lonesome		lore		low	
lonesum	lonesome	los	loss	lowce	louse
long		lose		lowd	loud

lower		luesid	lucid	lunchin	luncheon
lownge	lounge	luetenant	lieutenant	lunchon	luncheon
lowse	louse	lug		lunchun	luncheon
loyal		lugage	luggage	lune	loon
loyally		luggage		luner	lunar
loyalty		lugitimate	legitimate	lung	
loyaly	loyally	lugoon	lagoon	lunge	
loyel	loyal	lugune	lagoon	lunir	lunar
loyer	lawyer	Luisiana	Louisiana	lunoleum	linoleum
loyil	loyal	Luiziana	Louisiana	lunor	lunar
loyn	loin	lujitimate	legitimate	lunur	lunar
loyol	loyal	luk	luck	lupe	loop
loytar	loiter	lukewarm		lupel	lapel
loyter	loiter	luksury	luxury	lurch	
loytir	loiter	lul	lull	lure	
loytor	loiter	lulaby	lullaby	lurid	
loytur	loiter	lull		lurk	
loyul	loyal	lullaby		lurn	learn
lubracate	lubricate	lulleby	lullaby	luscious	
lubrecate	lubricate	lulliby	lullaby	luse	loose
lubretto	libretto	lulloby	lullaby	luse	lose
lubricant		lulluby	lullaby	lushas	luscious
lubricate		lumbar	lumber	lushess	luscious
lubrikant	lubricant	lumber		lushis	luscious
lubrocate	lubricate	lumbir	lumber	lushos	luscious
lubrucate	lubricate	lumbor	lumber	lushus	luscious
luce	loose	lumbur	lumber	lusid	lucid
lucid		lume	loom	lustar	luster
luck		lument	lament	luster	
luckily		luminous		lusterous	lustrous
lucksury	luxury	lump		lustir	luster
lucky		lunar		lustor	luster
luckyly	luckily	lunartic	lunatic	lustrous	
ludicrous		lunatic		lustur	luster
lue	lieu	lunch		lusty	
luebricate	lubricate	lunchan	luncheon	lute	
luecid	lucid	lunchen	luncheon	lute	loot
luedicrous	ludicrous	luncheon		lutenant	lieutenant

luv	love	**ly**	lie	**lynx**	
luxshury	luxury	**ly**	lye	lyric	
luxuriant		lye		lyrical	
luxurious		lying		**lyrickal**	lyrical
luxury		**lymf**	lymph	**lyrik**	lyric
luze	lose	lymph		**lyrric**	lyric
		lynch			

M

ma	may	**mackontosh**	mackintosh	madam	
macanaw	mackinaw	**mackorel**	mackerel	**madamoiselle**	mademoiselle
macanic	mechanic	**macksam**	maxim	madcap	
macantosh	mackintosh	**macksamum**	maximum	made	
macarel	mackerel	**macksem**	maxim	**made**	maid
macaroni		**macksemum**	maximum	**madem**	madam
macaroon		**macksim**	maxim	mademoiselle	
mach	match	**macksimum**	maximum	**madim**	madam
machanic	mechanic	**macksom**	maxim	**madimoiselle**	mademoiselle
machine		**macksomum**	maximum	**madkap**	madcap
machinery		**macksum**	maxim	madly	
machinest	machinist	**macksumum**	maximum	madness	
machinist		**mackunaw**	mackinaw	**madniss**	madness
machure	mature	**mackuntosh**	mackintosh	**madom**	madam
mackanaw	mackinaw	**mackurel**	mackerel	**madomoiselle**	mademoiselle
mackantosh	mackintosh	**maconaw**	mackinaw	Madonna	
mackarel	mackerel	**macontosh**	mackintosh	**madum**	madam
mackaroni	macaroni	**macorel**	mackerel	**madumoiselle**	mademoiselle
mackaroon	macaroon	**macoroni**	macaroni	**magat**	maggot
mackenaw	mackinaw	**macoroon**	macaroon	magazine	
mackentosh	mackintosh	**macunaw**	mackinaw	**magestic**	majestic
mackerel		**macuntosh**	mackintosh	**maget**	maggot
mackinaw		**macurel**	mackerel	**magezine**	magazine
mackintosh		**macuroni**	macaroni	**maggat**	maggot
mackirel	mackerel	**macuroon**	macaroon	**magget**	maggot
mackonaw	mackinaw	mad		**maggit**	maggot

maggot		maibe	maybe	maitren	matron
maggut	maggot	maibey	maybe	maitrin	matron
magic		maiby	maybe	maitron	matron
magical		maid		maitrun	matron
magician		maid	made	maize	
magik	magic	maidan	maiden	maize	maze
magistrate		maiden		majestic	
magit	maggot	maidin	maiden	majestically	
magizine	magazine	maidon	maiden	majesty	
magnafy	magnify	maidun	maiden	majic	magic
magnatude	magnitude	maik	make	majik	magic
magneasium	magnesium	mail		majistrate	magistrate
magneesium	magnesium	mail	male	majority	
magnefy	magnify	maim		makanaw	mackinaw
magnesium		main		makanic	mechanic
magnet		main	mane	makantosh	mackintosh
magnetic		Maine		makarel	mackerel
magnetism		mainger	manger	makaroni	macaroni
magnetize		maingir	manger	makaroon	macaroon
magnetude	magnitude	mainia	mania	make	
magnificence		mainjer	manger	makenaw	mackinaw
magnificent		mainland		makentosh	mackintosh
magnify		mainly		maker	
magnit	magnet	mainstay		makerel	mackerel
magnitude		maintain		makinaw	mackinaw
magnoalia	magnolia	maintainance	maintenance	makintosh	mackintosh
magnofy	magnify	maintanance	maintenance	makirel	mackerel
magnolia		maintane	maintain	makonaw	mackinaw
magnotude	magnitude	maintenance		makontosh	mackintosh
magnufy	magnify	maintinance	maintenance	makorel	mackerel
magnutude	magnitude	maintonance	maintenance	maksam	maxim
magot	maggot	maintunance	maintenance	maksamum	maximum
magozine	magazine	maiple	maple	maksem	maxim
magpie		mair	mare	maksemum	maximum
magpy	magpie	maisa	mesa	maksim	maxim
magut	maggot	maison	mason	maksimum	maximum
maguzine	magazine	mait	mate	maksom	maxim
mahogany		maitran	matron	maksomum	maximum

162

maksum	maxim	malnootrition	malnutrition	manage	
maksumum	maximum	malnuetrition	malnutrition	management	
makunaw	mackinaw	malnutrition		manager	
makuntosh	mackintosh	malody	malady	managerie	menagerie
makurel	mackerel	malord	mallard	manajerie	menagerie
malady		malt		manar	manner
malard	mallard	maltreat		manar	manor
malaria		maltreet	maltreat	mandable	mandible
malasses	molasses	maltrete	maltreat	mandait	mandate
male		maludy	malady	mandalin	mandolin
male	mail	malurd	mallard	mandate	
maleable	malleable	mama		mandeble	mandible
maledy	malady	mamal	mammal	mandelin	mandolin
malerd	mallard	mamath	mammoth	mandible	
malest	molest	mame	maim	mandilin	mandolin
malet	mallet	mamel	mammal	mandoble	mandible
maliable	malleable	mameth	mammoth	mandolin	
malice		mamil	mammal	manduble	mandible
maliceous	malicious	mamith	mammoth	mandulin	mandolin
malicious		mamma		mane	
malidy	malady	mammal		mane	main
malign		mammath	mammoth	Mane	Maine
malignant		mammel	mammal	manea	mania
maline	malign	mammeth	mammoth	manecure	manicure
malird	mallard	mammil	mammal	manefest	manifest
malis	malice	mammith	mammoth	manefold	manifold
malit	mallet	mammol	mammal	manetain	maintain
mallard		mammoth		manetane	maintain
malleable		mammul	mammal	maneuver	
mallerd	mallard	mammuth	mammoth	manewr	manure
mallet		mamol	mammal	manewver	maneuver
malliable	malleable	mamorial	memorial	mangal	mangle
mallice	malice	mamoth	mammoth	manganese	
mallird	mallard	mamul	mammal	mangel	mangle
mallis	malice	mamuth	mammoth	mangenese	manganese
mallit	mallet	man		manger	
mallord	mallard	manacure	manicure	mangil	mangle
mallurd	mallard	manafest	manifest	manginese	manganese
malnewtrition	malnutrition	manafold	manifold	mangir	manger

mangle		manshan	mansion	manyooscript	manuscript
mango		manshen	mansion	manyual	manual
mangol	mangle	manshin	mansion	manyufacture	manufacture
mangonese	manganese	manshon	mansion	map	
mangroave	mangrove	manshun	mansion	mapal	maple
mangrove		mansion		mapel	maple
mangul	mangle	mantal	mantel	mapil	maple
mangunese	manganese	mantal	mantle	maple	
manhood		mantel		mapol	maple
manhud	manhood	mantel	mantle	mapul	maple
mania		mantelpiece		mar	
manicure		mantil	mantel	maragold	marigold
manifest		mantil	mantle	maraner	mariner
manifestation		mantion	mansion	marass	morass
manifold		mantle		marathon	
manige	manage	mantle	mantel	maratime	maritime
manipulate		mantol	mantel	marauder	
manir	manner	mantol	mantle	marawder	marauder
manir	manor	mantul	mantel	marbal	marble
manjer	manger	mantul	mantle	marbel	marble
mankind		manual		marbil	marble
manliness		manucure	manicure	marble	
manly		manuer	manure	marbol	marble
manlyness	manliness	manufacture		marbul	marble
mannar	manner	manufacturer		March	
manner		manufest	manifest	march	
mannir	manner	manufold	manifold	marck	mark
mannor	manner	manur	manner	mare	
mannur	manner	manur	manor	marean	marine
manocure	manicure	manure		mareen	marine
manofest	manifest	manuscript		maregold	marigold
manofold	manifold	many		marene	marine
manoor	manure	manyewal	manual	marener	mariner
manoover	maneuver	manyewfac-		mareonette	marionette
manopoly	monopoly	ture	manufacture	marethon	marathon
manor		manyewscript	manuscript	maretime	maritime
manor	manner	manyooal	manual	marewn	maroon
manority	minority	manyoofac-		marey	marry
manotony	monotony	ture	manufacture	margarine	

margen	margin	marotime	maritime	marugold	marigold
margerine	margarine	marow	marrow	marune	maroon
margin		marrage	marriage	maruner	mariner
margirine	margarine	marread	married	maruthon	marathon
maridian	meridian	marrede	married	marutime	maritime
marigold		marreed	married	marval	marvel
Mariland	Maryland	marrege	marriage	marvel	
marine		marriage		marvellous	marvelous
mariner		married		marvelous	
marionette		marrige	marriage	marvil	marvel
marithon	marathon	marro	marrow	marvol	marvel
maritime		marroge	marriage	marvul	marvel
marjan	margin	marrow		mary	marry
marjarine	margarine	marruge	marriage	Maryland	
marjen	margin	marry		Marz	Mars
marjerine	margarine	marryd	married	masa	mesa
marjin	margin	Mars		Masachu-	
marjirine	margarine	marsh		settes	Massachusetts
marjon	margin	marshal		masacre	massacre
marjorine	margarine	marshal	martial	masage	massage
marjun	margin	marshel	marshal	masan	mason
marjurine	margarine	marshel	martial	mascarade	masquerade
mark		marshil	marshal	mascorade	masquerade
marked		marshil	martial	mascot	
market		marshol	marshal	masculine	
markit	market	marshol	martial	mascurade	masquerade
markt	marked	marshul	marshal	masecre	massacre
marmalade		marshul	martial	masen	mason
marmelade	marmalade	marshy		mash	
marmilade	marmalade	mart		mashine	machine
marmolade	marmalade	martar	martyr	masicre	massacre
marmulade	marmalade	marter	martyr	masin	mason
maro	marrow	martial		masive	massive
marogold	marigold	martial	marshal	mask	
maroner	mariner	martir	martyr	maskarade	masquerade
maroon		martor	martyr	maskerade	masquerade
marose	morose	martur	martyr	masketo	mosquito
marothon	marathon	martyr		maskewline	masculine

maskirade	masquerade	matchless		mattriss	mattress
maskorade	masquerade	matchliss	matchless	mattur	matter
maskot	mascot	matchure	mature	matunee	matinee
maskuline	masculine	mate		matur	matter
maskurade	masquerade	matenee	matinee	mature	
masocre	massacre	material		maturety	maturity
mason		maternal		maturity	
masonry		mathamatics	mathematics	maturnal	maternal
masquarade	masquerade	mathematical		maul	
masquerade		mathematician		mausaleum	mausoleum
masquirade	masquerade	mathematics		mauseleum	mausoleum
masquorade	masquerade	mathimatics	mathematics	mausileum	mausoleum
mass		mathomatics	mathematics	mausoleum	
Massachusetts		mathumatics	mathematics	mausuleum	mausoleum
massacre		matinee		mauve	
massage		matir	matter	mawl	maul
massage	message	matirnal	maternal	mawsaleum	mausoleum
massecre	massacre	matonee	matinee	mawseleum	mausoleum
massicre	massacre	matoor	mature	mawsileum	mausoleum
massive		mator	matter	mawsoleum	mausoleum
massocre	massacre	matramony	matrimony	mawsuleum	mausoleum
Massouri	Missouri	matran	matron	mawve	mauve
massucre	massacre	matremony	matrimony	maxam	maxim
Massuri	Missouri	matren	matron	maxamum	maximum
mast		matress	mattress	maxem	maxim
mastar	master	matrimony		maxemum	maximum
master		matrin	matron	maxim	
masterful		matriss	mattress	maximum	
masterpiece		matromony	matrimony	maxom	maxim
mastir	master	matron		maxomum	maximum
mastor	master	matropolis	metropolis	maxum	maxim
mastur	master	matrumony	matrimony	maxumum	maximum
masucre	massacre	matrun	matron	May	
masun	mason	mattar	matter	may	
mat		matter		mayar	mayor
matanee	matinee	mattir	matter	maybe	
matar	matter	mattor	matter	mayby	maybe
match		mattress		mayer	mayor

166

mayir	mayor
maynea	mania
maynia	mania
mayor	
mayple	maple
maysa	mesa
mayson	mason
maytran	matron
maytren	matron
maytrin	matron
maytron	matron
maytrun	matron
mayur	mayor
mayze	maze
maze	
maze	maize
Mazouri	Missouri
Mazuri	Missouri
me	
mead	
meadea	media
meadeate	mediate
meadeocre	mediocre
meadeum	medium
meadia	media
meadiate	mediate
meadieval	medieval
meadiocre	mediocre
meadium	medium
meadow	
meagar	meager
meager	
meagir	meager
meagor	meager
meagur	meager
meak	meek
meal	
mean	

mean	mien
meander	
meaneal	menial
meanial	menial
meaning	
meant	
meantime	
meanwhile	
meanwile	meanwhile
mear	mere
measals	measles
measels	measles
measils	measles
measles	
measols	measles
measuls	measles
measure	
measurement	
meat	
meat	meet
meat	mete
meateor	meteor
meatior	meteor
meazals	measles
meazels	measles
meazils	measles
meazles	measles
meazols	measles
meazuls	measles
meazure	measure
mecanic	mechanic
mechanic	
mechanical	
mechanically	
mechanics	
mechanism	
mechine	machine
mechure	mature

Mecksico	Mexico
medacal	medical
medacine	medicine
medal	
medal	meddle
medallion	
medasine	medicine
medatate	meditate
Medaterran-ean	Mediterran-ean
meddal	meddle
meddel	meddle
meddil	meddle
meddle	
meddlee	medley
meddler	
meddlesome	
meddley	medley
meddo	meadow
meddol	meddle
meddow	meadow
meddul	meddle
mede	mead
medea	media
medeate	mediate
medecal	medical
medecine	medicine
medel	medal
medel	meddle
medeocre	mediocre
medesin	medicine
medetate	meditate
Medeterran-ean	Mediterran-ean
medeum	medium
media	
mediate	
medical	

medicinal		meedia	media
medicine		meediate	mediate
medieval		meedieval	medieval
medil	medal	meediocre	mediocre
medil	meddle	meedium	medium
mediocre		meegar	meager
medisine	medicine	meeger	meager
meditate		meegir	meager
meditation		meegor	meager
Mediterranean		meegur	meager
medium		meek	
medle	meddle	meekness	
medlee	medley	meekniss	meekness
medley		meel	meal
medo	meadow	meen	mean
medocal	medical	meen	mien
medocine	medicine	meeneal	menial
medol	medal	meenial	menial
medol	meddle	meer	mere
Medonna	Madonna	meesals	measles
medosine	medicine	meesels	measles
medotate	meditate	meesils	measles
Medoterran-ean	Mediterran-ean	meesles	measles
medow	meadow	meesols	measles
meducal	medical	meesuls	measles
meducine	medicine	meet	
medul	medal	meet	meat
medul	meddle	meet	mete
medusine	medicine	meeteor	meteor
medutate	meditate	meeting	
Meduterran-ean	Mediterran-ean	meetior	meteor
meed	mead	meezals	measles
meedea	media	meezels	measles
meedeate	mediate	meezils	measles
meedeocre	mediocre	meezles	measles
meedeum	medium	meezols	measles
		meezuls	measles
		megaphone	

megephone	megaphone
meger	meager
megiphone	megaphone
megophone	megaphone
meguphone	megaphone
mehogany	mahogany
mein	mien
mejestic	majestic
mejority	majority
mekanic	mechanic
meke	meek
Meksico	Mexico
melady	melody
melan	melon
melancholy	
melaria	malaria
melasses	molasses
mele	meal
meledy	melody
melen	melon
melencholy	melancholy
melest	molest
melidy	melody
melign	malign
melin	melon
melincholy	melancholy
meline	malign
mellady	melody
mellan	melon
melledy	melody
mellen	melon
mellidy	melody
mellin	melon
mello	mellow
mellody	melody
mellon	melon
mellow	
melludy	melody

mellun	melon	menipulate	manipulate	merciful	
melody		meniss	menace	merciless	
melon		menny	many	mercinary	mercenary
meloncholy	melancholy	menopoly	monopoly	mercury	
melow	mellow	menority	minority	mercy	
melt		menotony	monotony	mercyful	merciful
meludy	melody	menshan	mention	mercyless	merciless
melun	melon	menshen	mention	merder	murder
meluncholy	melancholy	menshin	mention	mere	
memary	memory	menshon	mention	merean	marine
membar	member	menshun	mention	mereen	marine
member		mension	mention	merely	
membership		ment	meant	merene	marine
membir	member	mental		merge	
membor	member	mentally		meridian	
membrain	membrane	mentaly	mentally	Meriland	Maryland
membrane		mentel	mental	merine	marine
membur	member	mentil	mental	merit	
memery	memory	mention		merk	murk
memiry	memory	mentle	mental	merkury	mercury
memorable		mentol	mental	mermade	mermaid
memorial		mentul	mental	mermaid	
memorize		menu		mermur	murmur
memory		menure	manure	meroon	maroon
memury	memory	meny	many	merose	morose
men		menyew	menu	merrily	
menace		menyoo	menu	merriment	
menagerie		meow		merrit	merit
menajerie	menagerie	merass	morass	merry	
menase	menace	merauder	marauder	merryly	merrily
mend		mercenary		merryment	merriment
mene	mean	merchandise		mersanary	mercenary
mene	mien	merchant		mersenary	mercenary
meneal	menial	merchantise	merchandise	mersinary	mercenary
meneuver	maneuver	merchent	merchant	mersonary	mercenary
menew	menu	merchint	merchant	mersunary	mercenary
menial		merchont	merchant	mersy	mercy
menice	menace	merchunt	merchant	merth	mirth

merune	maroon	meteor		mewkas	mucus
mery	merry	meteoric		mewkess	mucus
Meryland	Maryland	meteorite		mewkis	mucus
mesa		meter		mewkos	mucus
mesage	message	meterial	material	mewkus	mucus
mesanger	messenger	meternal	maternal	mewl	mule
mesenger	messenger	methad	method	mewn	moon
mesh		Methadist	Methodist	mewnicipal	municipal
meshine	machine	methed	method	mewnishon	munition
mesige	message	Methedist	Methodist	mewnisipal	municipal
mesinger	messenger	methid	method	mewnition	munition
mesketo	mosquito	Methidist	Methodist	mewr	moor
mesonger	messenger	method		mewral	mural
mess		methodical		mewrel	mural
message		Methodist		mewril	mural
message	massage	methud	method	mewrol	mural
messanger	messenger	Methudist	Methodist	mewrul	mural
messenger		metil	metal	mews	moose
messige	message	metior	meteor	mewsalage	mucilage
messinger	messenger	metir	meter	mewse	muse
messoge	message	metirnal	maternal	mewselage	mucilage
messonger	messenger	metol	metal	mewseum	museum
Messouri	Missouri	metoor	mature	mewsic	music
messunger	messenger	metor	meter	mewsick	music
Messuri	Missouri	metropolis		mewsik	music
messy		metropolitan		mewsilage	mucilage
mesunger	messenger	metul	metal	mewsolage	mucilage
mesure	measure	metur	meter	mewsulage	mucilage
met		meture	mature	mewt	mute
metal		meturnal	maternal	mewtalate	mutilate
metalic	metallic	mewcas	mucus	mewtany	mutiny
metallic		mewce	moose	mewtchual	mutual
metar	meter	mewcelage	mucilage	mewtelate	mutilate
metchure	mature	mewchual	mutual	mewteny	mutiny
mete		mewcilage	mucilage	mewtilate	mutilate
mete	meat	mewcos	mucus	mewtiny	mutiny
mete	meet	mewcus	mucus	mewtolate	mutilate
metel	metal	mewd	mood	mewtony	mutiny

mewtual	mutual
mewtulate	mutilate
mewtuny	mutiny
mewv	move
mewz	muse
mewzeum	museum
mewzic	music
mewzick	music
mewzik	music
Mexaco	Mexico
Mexeco	Mexico
Mexican	
Mexico	
Mexoco	Mexico
Mexuco	Mexico
Mezouri	Missouri
mezure	measure
Mezuri	Missouri
mi	my
miander	meander
mica	
micanic	mechanic
mice	
michanic	mechanic
Michigan	
michine	machine
michure	mature
micks	mix
micraphone	microphone
micrascope	microscope
micrephone	microphone
micrescope	microscope
micriphone	microphone
micriscope	microscope
microab	microbe
microbe	
microphone	
microscope	
microscopic	
micruphone	microphone
micruscope	microscope
mid	
midal	middle
miday	midday
middal	middle
midday	
middel	middle
middil	middle
middle	
middol	middle
middul	middle
middy	
midget	
midgit	midget
midil	middle
midjet	midget
midjit	midget
midland	
midle	middle
midnight	
midnite	midnight
midol	middle
Midonna	Madonna
midshipman	
midst	
midul	middle
midway	
midy	middy
mien	
mier	mire
miget	midget
might	
mightaly	mightily
mightely	mightily
mightily	
mightoly	mightily
mightuly	mightily
mighty	
migit	midget
migraite	migrate
migrant	
migrate	
migration	
migreat	migrate
migrent	migrant
migrint	migrant
migront	migrant
migrunt	migrant
mihogany	mahogany
mijestic	majestic
mijet	midget
mijit	midget
mijority	majority
mika	mica
mikanic	mechanic
mikraphone	microphone
mikrascope	microscope
mikrephone	microphone
mikrescope	microscope
mikriphone	microphone
mikriscope	microscope
mikroab	microbe
mikrobe	microbe
mikrophone	microphone
mikroscope	microscope
mikruphone	microphone
mikruscope	microscope
miks	mix
mil	mill
milage	mileage
milanery	millinery
milaria	malaria
milasses	molasses
milatary	military

milch		millutary	military	mineral
mild		millyan	million	mineret	minaret
mildew		millyen	million	Minesota	Minnesota
mildoo	mildew	millyin	million	miness	minus
mildue	mildew	millyon	million	mineuver	maneuver
mile		millyun	million	mingal	mingle
mileage		milonery	millinery	mingel	mingle
milege	mileage	milotary	military	mingil	mingle
milenery	millinery	milstone	millstone	mingle	
milest	molest	milunery	millinery	mingol	mingle
milestoan	milestone	milutary	military	mingul	mingle
milestone		milyan	million	miniature	
miletary	military	milyen	million	minimum	
milige	mileage	milyin	million	mining	
milign	malign	milyon	million	minion	
miline	malign	milyun	million	minipulate	manipulate
milinery	millinery	mimic		miniral	mineral
milion	million	mimik	mimic	miniret	minaret
militant		mimmic	mimic	minis	minus
military		mimmik	mimic	Minisota	Minnesota
militia		mimorial	memorial	minister	
milk		minagerie	menagerie	ministry	
mill		minajerie	menagerie	minit	minute
millanery	millinery	minamum	minimum	mink	
millatary	military	minarel	mineral	Minnasota	Minnesota
millenery	millinery	minaret		Minnesota	
miller		minas	minus	minnion	minion
milletary	military	Minasota	Minnesota	Minnisota	Minnesota
milliner		mince		minnister	minister
millinery		minck	mink	minno	minnow
million		mind		Minnosota	Minnesota
millionaire		mindful		minnow	
millitary	military	mine		Minnusota	Minnesota
millonery	millinery	mineature	miniature	minnyan	minion
millotary	military	mineing	mining	minnyen	minion
millstoan	millstone	minemum	minimum	minnyin	minion
millstone		miner		minnyon	minion
millunery	millinery	miner	minor	minnyun	minion

mino	minnow	miracle		mirocle	miracle
minomum	minimum	miraculous		mirokle	miracle
minopoly	monopoly	mirakle	miracle	miroon	maroon
minor		mirar	mirror	miror	mirror
minoral	mineral	mirass	morass	mirose	morose
minoret	minaret	mirauder	marauder	mirrar	mirror
minority		mircenary	mercenary	mirrer	mirror
minos	minus	mirchant	merchant	mirrir	mirror
Minosota	Minnesota	mirchent	merchant	mirror	
minotony	monotony	mirchint	merchant	mirrur	mirror
minow	minnow	mirchont	merchant	mirsanary	mercenary
minse	mince	mirchunt	merchant	mirsenary	mercenary
minstral	minstrel	mircinary	mercenary	mirsinary	mercenary
minstrel		mircury	mercury	mirsonary	mercenary
minstril	minstrel	mircy	mercy	mirsunary	mercenary
minstrol	minstrel	mirder	murder	mirsy	mercy
minstrul	minstrel	mire		mirth	
mint		miread	myriad	miruckle	miracle
minuend		mirean	marine	mirucle	miracle
minuet		mireckle	miracle	mirukle	miracle
minumum	minimum	mirecle	miracle	mirune	maroon
minural	mineral	mireen	marine	mirur	mirror
minure	manure	mirekle	miracle	Mis	Miss
minuret	minaret	mirene	marine	mis	miss
minus		mirge	merge	misadventure	
Minusota	Minnesota	miriad	myriad	misage	massage
minute		mirickle	miracle	misal	missile
minyan	minion	miricle	miracle	misalaneous	miscellaneous
minyen	minion	miridian	meridian	misaltoe	mistletoe
minyewend	minuend	mirikle	miracle	misar	miser
minyewet	minuet	mirine	marine	misary	misery
minyin	minion	mirir	mirror	misbehave	
minyon	minion	mirk	murk	misbihave	misbehave
minyooend	minuend	mirkury	mercury	miscelaneous	miscellaneous
minyooet	minuet	mirmade	mermaid	miscellaneous	
minyun	minion	mirmaid	mermaid	mischief	
miow	meow	mirmur	murmur	mischiefous	mischievous
mirackle	miracle	mirockle	miracle	mischievous	

mischif	mischief	misled		missing	
misconduct		mislede	mislead	mission	
mise	mice	misleed	mislead	missionary	
misedventure	misadventure	mismanagement		Missisippi	Mississippi
miselaneous	miscellaneous	misodventure	misadventure	Mississippi	
miself	myself	misol	missile	missjudge	misjudge
miseltoe	mistletoe	misolanous	miscellaneous	misskonduct	misconduct
miser		misoltoe	mistletoe	misslay	mislay
miserable		misor	miser	misslead	mislead
miserably		misory	misery	missmanage-	mismanage-
misery		Misouri	Missouri	ment	ment
misfit		mispell	misspell	missol	missile
misfortune		misplace		missolaneous	miscellaneous
misgiving		misplaice	misplace	missoltoe	mistletoe
mishan	mission	misplase	misplace	Missouri	
mishap		mispranounce	mispronounce	misspell	
mishen	mission	misprenounce	mispronounce	missplace	misplace
Mishigan	Michigan	misprinounce	mispronounce	misspro-	
mishin	mission	mispronounce		nounce	mispronounce
mishine	machine	misprunounce	mispronounce	misstaik	mistake
mishon	mission	Miss		misstake	mistake
mishun	mission	miss		Misster	Mister
misidventure	misadventure	missage	massage	misstook	mistook
misil	missile	missal	missile	misstreat	mistreat
misilaneous	miscellaneous	missalaneous	miscellaneous	misstress	mistress
misiltoe	mistletoe	missaltoe	mistletoe	misstrust	mistrust
mision	mission	missconduct	misconduct	missul	missile
misir	miser	missel	missile	missulaneous	miscellaneous
misiry	misery	misselaneous	miscellaneous	missultoe	mistletoe
Misisippi	Mississippi	misseltoe	mistletoe	missunder-	misunder-
Mississippi	Mississippi	missfit	misfit	stand	stand
misjudge		missfortune	misfortune	Missuri	Missouri
misjuge	misjudge	missgiving	misgiving	missuse	misuse
misketo	mosquito	misshap	mishap	mist	
miskonduct	misconduct	missil	missile	mistaik	mistake
mislay		missilaneous	miscellaneous	mistake	
mislead		missile		mistaken	
misleading		missiltoe	mistletoe	Mistar	Mister

mistary	mystery	mition	mission	moalten	molten
Mister		mitirnal	maternal	moan	
mistery	mystery	mitoor	mature	moap	mope
mistey	misty	mitropolis	metropolis	moar	more
Mistir	Mister	mitt		moarbid	morbid
mistiry	mystery	mittan	mitten	moarn	mourn
mistletoe		mitten		moarning	morning
mistook		mittin	mitten	moarsel	morsel
Mistor	Mister	mitton	mitten	moartal	mortal
mistory	mystery	mittun	mitten	moartar	mortar
mistreat		miture	mature	moartify	mortify
mistreet	mistreat	miturnal	maternal	moasaic	mosaic
mistress		mix		moast	most
mistrete	mistreat			moat	
mistriss	mistress	mixchoor	mixture	moation	motion
mistrust		mixchur	mixture	moative	motive
mistuk	mistook	mixd	mixed	moator	motor
Mistur	Mister	mixed		mob	
mistury	mystery	mixt	mixed	mobeal	mobile
misty		mixtchoor	mixture	mobeel	mobile
misudventure	misadventure	mixtchure	mixture	mobele	mobile
misul	missile	mixture		mobile	
misulaneous	miscellaneous	Miz	Ms.	mocanic	mechanic
misultoe	mistletoe	mizar	miser	mocasin	moccasin
misunderstand		mizary	misery	moccasin	
misunderstanding		mizer	miser	moccosin	moccasin
misunderstood		mizery	misery	moccusin	moccasin
misur	miser	mizir	miser	mochanic	mechanic
misury	misery	miziry	misery	mochine	machine
misuse		mizor	miser	mochure	mature
misuze	misuse	mizory	misery	mock	
mit	mitt	Mizouri	Missouri	mockary	mockery
mitchure	mature	mizur	miser	mockasin	moccasin
mite		Mizuri	Missouri	mockery	
mite	might	mizury	misery	mockingbird	
miterial	material	mo	mow	mockiry	mockery
miternal	maternal	moad	mode	mockory	mockery
mith	myth	moal	mole	mockury	mockery
		moald	mold		

175

mocosin	moccasin	moistcher	moisture	molosk	mollusk
mocusin	moccasin	moisten		molten	
modafy	modify	moisture		molucule	molecule
modal	model	moisun	moisten	molur	molar
modarate	moderate	mojestic	majestic	molusk	mollusk
modarn	modern	mojority	majority	momant	moment
mode		mok	mock	moment	
modefy	modify	mokanic	mechanic	momentarily	
model		mokasin	moccasin	momentary	
moderate		mokingbird	mockingbird	momentous	
moderation		molacule	molecule	momint	moment
modern		molar		momont	moment
modest		molaria	malaria	momorial	memorial
modesty		molask	mollusk	momunt	moment
modification		molasses		monagerie	menagerie
modify		mold		monagram	monogram
modil	model	molding		monajerie	menagerie
modirate	moderate	moldy		monarch	
modirn	modern	mole		monarchy	
modist	modest	moleckule	molecule	monark	monarch
modofy	modify	molecule		monastery	
modol	model	molekule	molecule	monasyllable	monosyllable
Modonna	Madonna	moler	molar	monator	monitor
modorate	moderate	molesk	mollusk	monck	monk
modorn	modern	molest		monckey	monkey
modufy	modify	molicule	molecule	moncky	monkey
modul	model	molign	malign	Monday	
modurate	moderate	moline	malign	mone	moan
modurn	modern	molir	molar	monegram	monogram
Mohamed	Mohammed	molisk	mollusk	monerch	monarch
Mohammed		mollask	mollusk	monerk	monarch
mohogany	mahogany	mollasses	molasses	monestery	monastery
moisan	moisten	mollesk	mollusk	monesyllable	monosyllable
moischer	moisture	mollisk	mollusk	monetor	monitor
moisen	moisten	mollosk	mollusk	moneuver	maneuver
moisin	moisten	mollusk		money	
moison	moisten	molocule	molecule	mongewse	mongoose
moist		molor	molar	mongoose	

mongral	mongrel
mongrel	
mongril	mongrel
mongrol	mongrel
mongrul	mongrel
monguse	mongoose
monigram	monogram
monipulate	manipulate
monirch	monarch
monirk	monarch
monistery	monastery
monisyllable	monosyllable
monitor	
monk	
monkey	
monky	monkey
monogram	
monopoly	
monorch	monarch
monority	minority
monork	monarch
monostery	monastery
monosyllable	
monotonous	
monotony	
monotor	monitor
monsewn	monsoon
monsoon	
monstar	monster
monster	
monsterous	monstrous
monstir	monster
monstor	monster
monstrous	
monstur	monster
monsune	monsoon
Montana	
month	

monthly	
monugram	monogram
monument	
monumental	
monurch	monarch
monure	manure
monurk	monarch
monustery	monastery
monusyllable	monosyllable
monutor	monitor
mony	money
monyewment	monument
monyooment	monument
mooce	moose
mood	
moody	
moon	
moonlight	
moonlit	
moonlite	moonlight
moor	
moorings	
moose	
moove	move
moovey	movie
moovie	movie
moovy	movie
mop	
mope	
moral	
morality	
morallity	morality
morally	
moraly	morally
morass	
morauder	marauder
morbid	
more	

morean	marine
morebid	morbid
moreen	marine
morel	moral
morene	marine
morening	morning
moreover	
moresel	morsel
moretal	mortal
moretar	mortar
moretify	mortify
moridian	meridian
moril	moral
morine	marine
morn	mourn
morning	
morol	moral
moroon	maroon
morose	
morover	moreover
morow	morrow
morro	morrow
morrose	morose
morrow	
morsal	morsel
morsel	
morsil	morsel
morsol	morsel
morsul	morsel
mortafy	mortify
mortal	
mortally	
mortaly	mortally
mortar	
mortefy	mortify
mortel	mortal
morter	mortar
mortification	

mortify		motar	motor	motur	motor
mortil	mortal	motchure	mature	moture	mature
mortir	mortar	mote	moat	moturnal	maternal
mortofy	mortify	moteld	mottled	mound	
mortol	mortal	moter	motor	mount	
mortor	mortar	moterial	material	mountain	
mortufy	mortify	moternal	maternal	mountaineer	
mortul	mortal	moth		mountainous	
mortur	mortar	mothar	mother	mountan	mountain
morul	moral	mother		mounten	mountain
morune	maroon	mothir	mother	mountin	mountain
mos	moss	mothor	mother	mounton	mountain
mosage	massage	mothur	mother	mountun	mountain
mosaic		motild	mottled	mourn	
mosck	mosque	motion		mourner	
moshan	motion	motir	motor	mournful	
moshen	motion	motirnal	maternal	mourning	
moshin	motion	motive		mouse	
moshine	machine	motled	mottled	moustache	
moshon	motion	motley		moustash	mustache
moshun	motion	motly	motley	mouth	
mosion	motion	moto	motto	mouthful	
mosk	mosque	motold	mottled	mouthpeace	mouthpiece
mosketo	mosquito	motoor	mature	mouthpiece	
Moslam	Moslem	motor		movable	
Moslem		motorcycle		move	
Moslim	Moslem	motorist		moveable	
Moslom	Moslem	motropolis	metropolis	moveble	movable
Moslum	Moslem	mottald	mottled	moveing	moving
mosque		motteld	mottled	movement	
mosqueto	mosquito	mottild	mottled	movey	movie
mosquito		mottled		movie	
moss		mottley	motley	moving	
mossage	massage	mottly	motley	movy	movie
Mossouri	Missouri	motto		mow	
Mossuri	Missouri	mottold	mottled	mower	
most		mottuld	mottled	mownd	mound
motald	mottled	motuld	mottled	mownt	mount

mowntain	mountain	muddol	muddle	mugy	muggy
mowntan	mountain	muddul	muddle	muhogany	mahogany
mownten	mountain	muddy		mujestic	majestic
mowntin	mountain	mude	mood	mujority	majority
mownton	mountain	mudel	muddle	muk	muck
mowntun	mountain	mudil	muddle	mukanic	mechanic
mowse	mouse	mudle	muddle	mukas	mucus
mowth	mouth	mudol	muddle	mukess	mucus
mowtor	motor	Mudonna	Madonna	mukis	mucus
moyst	moist	mudul	muddle	mukos	mucus
mozaic	mosaic	mudy	muddy	mukus	mucus
Mozlam	Moslem	muf	muff	mularia	malaria
Mozlem	Moslem	mufal	muffle	mulasses	molasses
Mozlim	Moslem	mufan	muffin	mulberry	
Mozlom	Moslem	mufel	muffle	mulbery	mulberry
Mozlum	Moslem	mufen	muffin	mulch	
Mozouri	Missouri	muff		mule	
Mozuri	Missouri	muffal	muffle	mulesh	mulish
Ms.		muffan	muffin	mulest	molest
mucanic	mechanic	muffel	muffle	mulign	malign
mucas	mucus	muffen	muffin	muline	malign
muce	moose	muffil	muffle	mulish	
mucelage	mucilage	muffin		mullberry	mulberry
much		muffle		mullbery	mulberry
muchanic	mechanic	muffler		multaply	multiply
muchine	machine	muffol	muffle	multatude	multitude
muchual	mutual	muffon	muffin	multeply	multiply
muchure	mature	mufful	muffle	multetude	multitude
mucilage		muffun	muffin	multiple	
muck		mufil	muffle	multiplication	
mucos	mucus	mufin	muffin	multiply	
mucus		mufle	muffle	multitude	
mud		mufol	muffle	multoply	multiply
mudal	muddle	mufon	muffin	multotude	multitude
muddal	muddle	muful	muffle	multuply	multiply
muddel	muddle	mufun	muffin	multutude	multitude
muddil	muddle	mug		mum	
muddle		muggy		mumbal	mumble

mumbel	mumble	murchant	merchant	mursanary	mercenary
mumbil	mumble	murchent	merchant	mursenary	mercenary
mumble		murchint	merchant	mursinary	mercenary
mumbol	mumble	murchont	merchant	mursonary	mercenary
mumbul	mumble	murchunt	merchant	mursunary	mercenary
mummy		murcinary	mercenary	mursy	mercy
mumorial	memorial	murcury	mercury	murth	mirth
mumps		murcy	mercy	murul	mural
mumy	mummy	murdar	murder	murune	maroon
munagerie	menagerie	murder		mus	muss
munajerie	menagerie	murderer		musage	massage
munch		murderous		musal	muscle
munck	monk	murdir	murder	musal	mussel
munckey	monkey	murdor	murder	musalage	mucilage
muncky	monkey	murdur	murder	musant	mustn't
Munday	Monday	mure	moor	muscewlar	muscular
mune	moon	murean	marine	musck	musk
muneuvar	maneuver	mureen	marine	muscle	
muney	money	murel	mural	muscular	
municipal		murene	marine	muse	
municipality		murge	merge	muse	moose
munipulate	manipulate	muridian	meridian	musel	muscle
munishen	munition	muril	mural	musel	mussel
munisipal	municipal	murine	marine	muselage	mucilage
munition		murk		musent	mustn't
munk	monk	murkey	murky	museum	
munkey	monkey	murkury	mercury	mush	
munky	monkey	murky		mushine	machine
munopoly	monopoly	murmade	mermaid	mushroom	
munority	minority	murmaid	mermaid	mushrume	mushroom
munotony	monotony	murmar	murmur	music	
munth	month	murmer	murmur	musical	
munure	manure	murmir	murmur	musically	
muny	money	murmor	murmur	musician	
mural		murmur		musick	music
murass	morass	murol	mural	musik	music
murauder	marauder	muroon	maroon	musil	muscle
murcenary	mercenary	murose	morose	musil	mussel

musilage	mucilage	mustang		mutinous		
musint	mustn't	mustar	muster	mutiny		
musishan	musician	mustard		mutir	mutter	
musk		mustash	mustache	mutirnal	maternal	
musket		muster		mutolate	mutilate	
musketo	mosquito	musterd	mustard	muton	mutton	
muskit	musket	mustir	muster	mutony	mutiny	
muskrat		mustird	mustard	mutoor	mature	
muslan	muslin	mustn't		mutor	mutter	
musle	muscle	mustor	muster	mutropolis	metropolis	
muslen	muslin	mustord	mustard	muttan	mutton	
muslin		mustur	muster	muttar	mutter	
muslon	muslin	musturd	mustard	mutter		
muslun	muslin	musty		muttin	mutton	
musol	muscle	musul	muscle	muttir	mutter	
musol	mussel	musul	mussel	mutton		
musolage	mucilage	musulage	mucilage	muttor	mutter	
musont	mustn't	musunt	mustn't	muttun	mutton	
muss		mutalate	mutilate	muttur	mutter	
mussage	massage	mutan	mutton	mutual		
mussal	muscle	mutany	mutiny	mutually		
mussal	mussel	mutar	mutter	mutulate	mutilate	
mussant	mustn't	mutchual	mutual	mutun	mutton	
mussel		mutchure	mature	mutuny	mutiny	
mussent	mustn't	mute		mutur	mutter	
mussil	muscle	mutelate	mutilate	muture	mature	
mussil	mussel	muten	mutton	muturnal	maternal	
mussint	mustn't	muteny	mutiny	muve	move	
mussol	muscle	muter	mutter	muvey	movie	
mussol	mussel	muterial	material	muvie	movie	
mussont	mustn't	muternal	maternal	muvy	movie	
Mussouri	Missouri	muthar	mother	muzal	muzzle	
mussul	muscle	muther	mother	muze	muse	
mussul	mussel	muthir	mother	muzel	muzzle	
mussunt	mustn't	muthur	mother	muzeum	museum	
Mussuri	Missouri	mutilate		muzic	music	
must		mutin	mutton	muzick	music	
mustache		mutineer		muzik	music	

muzil	muzzle	muzzle		mysteryous	mysterious
muzlan	muslin	muzzol	muzzle	mystify	
muzle	muzzle	muzzul	muzzle	mystiry	mystery
muzlen	muslin	my		mystofy	mystify
muzlin	muslin	myer	mire	mystory	mystery
muzlon	muslin	myread	myriad	mystufy	mystify
muzlun	muslin	myriad		mystury	mystery
muzol	muzzle	myself		myth	
Muzouri	Missouri			mythacal	mythical
muzul	muzzle	mystafy	mystify	mythecal	mythical
Muzuri	Missouri	mystary	mystery	mythical	
muzzal	muzzle	mystefy	mystify	mythocal	mythical
muzzel	muzzle	mysterious		mythology	
muzzil	muzzle	mystery		mythucal	mythical

N

nabar	neighbor	naip	nape	nap	
naber	neighbor	naition	nation	nape	
nabir	neighbor	naitive	native	naphtha	
nabor	neighbor	naiture	nature	napkin	
Nabraska	Nebraska	naival	naval	napsack	knapsack
nabur	neighbor	naive		naptha	naphtha
nachar	nature	naive	knave	narait	narrate
nacher	nature	naivy	navy	narate	narrate
nachir	nature	nak	knack	narcissus	
nachor	nature	naked		narcisus	narcissus
nachural	natural	nakedness		narl	gnarl
nachure	nature	nakid	naked	naro	narrow
nack	knack	nale	nail	narow	narrow
naftha	naphtha	name		narrait	narrate
nag		nameless		narrate	
naibor	neighbor	nameliss	nameless	narrative	
naiked	naked	namely		narro	narrow
nail		namesaik	namesake	narrow	
naim	name	namesake		narsissus	narcissus

narsisus	narcissus	nautucal	nautical	nay	neigh
nasal		nauty	naughty	naybor	neighbor
nasel	nasal	nauzea	nausea	nazal	nasal
nash	gnash	nauzha	nausea	nazel	nasal
nashan	nation	Navada	Nevada	nazil	nasal
nashen	nation	navagate	navigate	nazol	nasal
nashin	nation	naval		nazul	nasal
nashon	nation	naval	navel	ne	knee
nashun	nation	nave	knave	nea	knee
nasil	nasal	navegate	navigate	neace	niece
nasol	nasal	navel		nead	knead
nasty		navel	naval	nead	need
nasul	nasal	navigable		neadal	needle
nat	gnat	navigate		neadel	needle
natchural	natural	navigation		neadil	needle
natchure	nature	navigator		neadl	needle
nation		navil	naval	neadol	needle
national		navil	navel	neadul	needle
nationality		navogate	navigate	Neagro	Negro
nationally		navol	naval	neal	kneel
native		navol	navel	near	
nativity		navugate	navigate	nearby	
natural		navul	naval	nearly	
naturalist		navul	navel	nease	niece
naturalize		navy		neat	
naturally		naw	gnaw	neathar	neither
nature		nawsea	nausea	neather	neither
naught		nawsha	nausea	neathir	neither
naughtiness		nawt	naught	neathor	neither
naughty		nawtacal	nautical	neathur	neither
naughtyness	naughtiness	nawtecal	nautical	neatness	
nausea		nawtical	nautical	neatniss	neatness
nausha	nausea	nawtocal	nautical	Nebraska	
naut	naught	nawtucal	nautical	nece	niece
nautacal	nautical	nawty	naughty	necesary	necessary
nautecal	nautical	nawzea	nausea	necessarily	
nautical		nawzha	nausea	necessary	
nautocal	nautical	nay		necessitate	

necessity		needn't		neighbor	
neck		needol	needle	neighborhood	
neckarchief	neckerchief	needul	needle	neighboring	
neckerchief		needy		neighborly	
neckirchief	neckerchief	Neegro	Negro	neighbur	neighbor
necklace		neel	kneel	neise	niece
necklass	necklace	neer	near	neithar	neither
necklice	necklace	neese	niece	neither	
neckils	necklace	neet	neat	neithir	neither
neckorchief	neckerchief	neethar	neither	neithor	neither
neckst	next	neether	neither	neithur	neither
necktar	nectar	neethir	neither	nek	neck
neckter	nectar	neethor	neither	nekst	next
necktie		neethur	neither	nektar	nectar
necktir	nectar	nefew	nephew	nekter	nectar
necktor	nectar	nefue	nephew	nektir	nectar
necktur	nectar	negative		nektor	nectar
neckty	necktie	negetive	negative	nektur	nectar
neckurchief	neckerchief	negitive	negative	nele	kneel
necst	next	neglagent	negligent	nell	knell
nectar		negleckt	neglect	nephew	
necter	nectar	neglect		nephue	nephew
nectir	nectar	neglegent	negligent	nerce	nurse
nector	nectar	neglekt	neglect	nerchur	nurture
nectur	nectar	negligence		nere	near
nede	knead	negligent		nerse	nurse
nede	need	neglogent	negligent	nertchur	nurture
nee	knee	neglugent	negligent	nerture	nurture
neece	niece	negoshiate	negotiate	nervass	nervous
need		negotiate		nerve	
need	knead	negotive	negative	nervess	nervous
needal	needle	Negro		nerviss	nervous
needel	needle	negutive	negative	nervoss	nervous
needil	needle	neice	niece	nervous	
needle		neigh		nervousness	
needless		neighbar	neighbor	nervus	nervous
needlework		neighber	neighbor	nesal	nestle
needliss	needless	neighbir	neighbor	nese	niece

nesel	nestle	neutrel	neutral	newly	
nesesary	necessary	neutril	neutral	newmaral	numeral
nesessary	necessary	neutrol	neutral	newmatic	pneumatic
nesil	nestle	neutron		New Mecksico	New Mexico
nesol	nestle	neutrul	neutral	New Mecsico	New Mexico
nessal	nestle	Nevada		New Meksico	New Mexico
nessil	nestle	nevar	never	newmeral	numeral
nessle	nestle	never		New Mexaco	New Mexico
nessol	nestle	nevermore		New Mexeco	New Mexico
nessul	nestle	nevertheless		New Mexico	
nest		nevir	never	New Mexoco	New Mexico
nestle		nevor	never	New Mexuco	New Mexico
nesul	nestle	nevur	never	newmiral	numeral
net		new		newmonia	pneumonia
netal	nettle	new	knew	newmoral	numeral
nete	neat	newborn		newmural	numeral
netel	nettle	newce	noose	newn	noon
nethar	neither	newcomer		news	
nether	neither	newcumer	newcomer	newsance	nuisance
nethir	neither	New England		newscast	
nethor	neither	New Hampshire		newse	noose
nethur	neither	New Ham-shire	New Hamp-shire	newskast	newscast
netil	nettle	New Ingland	New England	newspaper	
netivity	nativity	New Jersey		newsstand	
netle	nettle	New Jersy	New Jersey	newstand	newsstand
netol	nettle	New Jerzey	New Jersey	newtral	neutral
nettal	nettle	New Jerzy	New Jersey	newtrel	neutral
nettel	nettle	New Jirsey	New Jersey	newtril	neutral
nettil	nettle	New Jirsy	New Jersey	newtrition	nutrition
nettle		New Jirzey	New Jersey	newtrol	neutral
nettol	nettle	New Jirzy	New Jersey	newtron	neutron
nettul	nettle	New Jursey	New Jersey	newtrul	neutral
netul	nettle	New Jursy	New Jersey	New Yoark	New York
network		New Jurzey	New Jersey	New York	
neumatic	pneumatic	New Jurzy	New Jersey	newz	news
neumonia	pneumonia	newkomer	newcomer	next	
neutral		newkumer	newcomer	nibal	nibble
neutralize				nibbal	nibble

nibbel	nibble	niethur	neither	nikutine	nicotine
nibbil	nibble	nife	knife	Nile	
nibble		nigairdly	niggardly	nilon	nylon
nibbol	nibble	nigardly	niggardly	nimbal	nimble
nibbul	nibble	nigerdly	niggardly	nimbel	nimble
nibel	nibble	niggardly		nimbil	nimble
nibil	nibble	niggerdly	niggardly	nimble	
nible	nibble	niggirdly	niggardly	nimbley	nimbly
nibol	nibble	niggordly	niggardly	nimbly	
Nibraska	Nebraska	niggurdly	niggardly	nimbol	nimble
nibul	nibble	night		nimbul	nimble
nicatine	nicotine	night	knight	nimf	nymph
nice		nightingale		nimph	nymph
nich	niche	nightly		nine	
niche		nightmair	nightmare	nineth	ninth
nick		nightmare		ninety	
nickal	nickel	nigleckt	neglect	ninth	
nickatine	nicotine	niglect	neglect	nip	
nickel		niglekt	neglect	nirce	nurse
nickers	knickers	nigordly	niggardly	nirchur	nurture
nicketine	nicotine	nigoshiate	negotiate	nirse	nurse
nickil	nickel	nigotiate	negotiate	nirtchur	nurture
nickitine	nicotine	nigurdly	niggardly	nirture	nurture
nickknack	knickknack	nik	nick	nirve	nerve
nickle	nickel	nikal	nickel	nise	nice
nickname		nikatine	nicotine	nit	knit
nickol	nickel	nikel	nickel	nite	knight
nickotine	nicotine	nikers	knickers	nite	night
nickul	nickel	niketine	nicotine	nitivity	nativity
nickutine	nicotine	nikil	nickel	nitragen	nitrogen
nicotine		nikitine	nicotine	nitregen	nitrogen
nicutine	nicotine	nikknack	knickknack	nitrigin	nitrogen
niece		nikle	nickel	nitrogen	
niese	niece	niknaim	nickname	nitrugen	nitrogen
niethar	neither	nikname	nickname	Nivada	Nevada
niether	neither	nikol	nickel	nives	knives
niethir	neither	nikotine	nicotine	nivez	knives
niethor	neither	nikul	nickel	no	

no	know
noal	knoll
noar	nor
noarmal	normal
noarth	north
noase	nose
noat	note
noaz	nose
nob	knob
nobal	noble
nobel	noble
nobil	noble
nobility	
noble	
nobleman	
nobley	nobly
nobly	
nobody	
nobol	noble
Nobraska	Nebraska
nobul	noble
noch	notch
nock	knock
nockshus	noxious
nockternal	nocturnal
nocktirnal	nocturnal
nockturnal	nocturnal
nocshus	noxious
nocternal	nocturnal
noctirnal	nocturnal
nocturnal	
nod	
noe	know
Noel	
noise	
noiseless	
noiseliss	noiseless
noisely	noisily

noisey	noisy
noisily	
noisy	
noize	noise
nok	knock
nokshus	noxious
nokternal	nocturnal
noktirnal	nocturnal
nokturnal	nocturnal
nole	knoll
noledge	knowledge
nolege	knowledge
nolidge	knowledge
nolige	knowledge
nolije	knowledge
noll	knoll
nomad	
nomanate	nominate
nome	gnome
nomenate	nominate
nominate	
nomination	
nominee	
nomonate	nominate
nomunate	nominate
noncence	nonsense
noncense	nonsense
noncents	nonsense
nonchalant	
nonchelant	nonchalant
nonchilant	nonchalant
noncholant	nonchalant
nonchulant	nonchalant
none	
none	nun
nonsence	nonsense
nonsense	
nonsents	nonsense

nonshalant	nonchalant
nonshelant	nonchalant
nonshilant	nonchalant
nonsholant	nonchalant
nonshulant	nonchalant
noo	knew
noo	new
nooce	noose
nook	
noomaral	numeral
noomatic	pneumatic
noomeral	numeral
noomiral	numeral
noomonia	pneumonia
noomoral	numeral
noomural	numeral
noon	
noos	news
noosance	nuisance
noose	
nootral	neutral
nootrel	neutral
nootril	neutral
nootrition	nutrition
nootrol	neutral
nootron	neutron
nootrul	neutral
nooz	news
nor	
nor	gnaw
noremal	normal
normal	
normally	
normaly	normally
normel	normal
normil	normal
normol	normal
normul	normal

north		notafy	notify	novul	novel
North America		notch		now	
northarly	northerly	note		now	know
North Carolina		noteable	notable	noware	nowhere
North Dackota	North Dakota	noteble	notable	nowear	nowhere
North Dacota	North Dakota	notebook		nowhere	
North Dakota		notebuk	notebook	nown	noun
northeast		noted		noxious	
northeest	northeast	notefy	notify	noxius	noxious
northerly		notewerthy	noteworthy	noxous	noxious
northern		notewirthy	noteworthy	noxshus	noxious
northeste	northeast	noteworthy		noyse	noise
northirly	northerly	notewurthy	noteworthy	noyze	noise
northirn	northern	nothing		nozal	nozzle
northorly	northerly	notice ·		noze	nose
North Poal	North Pole	noticeable		nozel	nozzle
North Pole		noticeble	noticeable	nozil	nozzle
North Poll	North Pole	notid	noted	nozle	nozzle
northurly	northerly	notify		nozol	nozzle
northurn	northern	notion		nozul	nozzle
northwest		notis	notice	nozzal	nozzle
nose		notivity	nativity	nozzel	nozzle
noshan	notion	notofy	notify	nozzil	nozzle
noshen	notion	notorious		nozzle	
noshin	notion	notufy	notify	nozzol	nozzle
noshon	notion	notwithstanding		nozzul	nozzle
noshun	notion	noun		nu	knew
nosion	notion	nourish		nu	new
nostral	nostril	nourishment		Nubraska	Nebraska
nostrel	nostril	Novada	Nevada	nuce	noose
nostril		noval	novel	nuckel	knuckle
nostrol	nostril	novel		nuckle	knuckle
nostrul	nostril	novelty		nuclear	
not		November		nucleus	
not	knot	novice		nucliess	nucleus
notable		novil	novel	nuclius	nucleus
notabley	notably	novis	novice	nudge	
notably		novol	novel	nue	knew

nue	new	numiral	numeral	nusense	nuisance
nues	news	numonia	pneumonia	nusince	nuisance
nuesance	nuisance	numoral	numeral	nusinse	nuisance
nuez	news	numural	numeral	nusonce	nuisance
nuge	nudge	nun		nusonse	nuisance
nuget	nugget	nun	none	nusunce	nuisance
nugget		nune	noon	nusunse	nuisance
nuggit	nugget	nupshal	nuptial	nut	
nugit	nugget	nupshel	nuptial	nutcracker	
nuisance		nupshil	nuptial	nutcraker	nutcracker
nuisanse	nuisance	nupshol	nuptial	nuthing	nothing
nuk	nook	nupshul	nuptial	nutivity	nativity
nukle	knuckle	nuptial		nutkracker	nutcracker
nukleus	nucleus	nurce	nurse	nutkraker	nutcracker
nukliess	nucleus	nurchur	nurture	nutmeg	
nuklius	nucleus	nurish	nourish	nutral	neutral
num	numb	nursary	nursery	nutrel	neutral
numaral	numeral	nurse		nutril	neutral
numatic	pneumatic	nursery		nutrishon	nutrition
numb		nursiry	nursery	nutrition	
numbar	number	nursory	nursery	nutritious	
number		nursury	nursery	nutrol	neutral
numbir	number	nurtchur	nurture	nutron	neutron
numbor	number	nurture		nutrul	neutral
numbur	number	nurve	nerve	Nuvada	Nevada
numeral		nusance	nuisance	nuze	news
numerator		nusanse	nuisance	nylon	
numerical		nuse	news	nymf	nymph
numerous		nuse	noose	nymph	
		nusence	nuisance		

O

o	oh	oan	own	oasis	
oad	ode	oar		oat	
oak		oar	or	oath	
oald	old	oar	ore	oatmeal	

oatmeel	oatmeal	oboe		obstunate	obstinate
oatmele	oatmeal	obolisk	obelisk	obsulete	obsolete
obalisk	obelisk	obow	oboe	obsurve	observe
obay	obey	obsalete	obsolete	obtain	
obeadient	obedient	obscewr	obscure	obtainable	
obedience		obscure		obtane	obtain
obedient		obscurity		obtewce	obtuse
obeedient	obedient	obselete	obsolete	obtewse	obtuse
obelisk		observance		obtooce	obtuse
obey		observant		obtoose	obtuse
obilisk	obelisk	observation		obtuce	obtuse
objeckt	object	observatory		obtuse	
object		observe		obulisk	obelisk
objection		observeance	observance	obveous	obvious
objectionable		observence	observance	obvious	
objective		observent	observant	obzirve	observe
objekt	object	observer		obzurve	observe
oblagate	obligate	obsilete	obsolete	ocasion	occasion
oblegate	obligate	obsirve	observe	ocassion	occasion
obligate		obskewr	obscure	occaision	occasion
obligation		obskure	obscure	occasion	
oblige		obsolete		occasional	
obligeing	obliging	obstackle	obstacle	occasionally	
obliging		obstacle		occassion	occasion
obliterate		obstakle	obstacle	occewpy	occupy
oblivion		obstanate	obstinate	occident	
oblivious		obstecle	obstacle	occupancy	
oblogate	obligate	obstenate	obstinate	occupant	
oblong		obsticle	obstacle	occupation	
oblugate	obligate	obstinacy		occupy	
obnockshus	obnoxious	obstinate		occur	
obnocshus	obnoxious	obstocle	obstacle	occurence	occurrence
obnokshus	obnoxious	obstonate	obstinate	occurrence	
obnoxious		obstruckt	obstruct	ocean	
obnoxius	obnoxious	obstruct		ocelot	
obnoxous	obnoxious	obstruction		ocilot	ocelot
obnoxshus	obnoxious	obstrukt	obstruct	ocker	occur
obo	oboe	obstucle	obstacle	ockewpy	occupy

Ocklahoma	Oklahoma	octipus	octopus	offen	often
ocks	ox	octive	octave	offence	offense
ocksagen	oxygen	October		offend	
ocksegen	oxygen	octogon	octagon	offender	
ocksford	oxford	octopus		offense	
ocksident	occident	octugon	octagon	offensive	
ocksidize	oxidize	octupus	octopus	offents	offense
ocksigen	oxygen	ocupy	occupy	offer	
ocksogen	oxygen	od	odd	offering	
ocksugen	oxygen	odar	odor	offerring	offering
ocktagon	octagon	odd		offhand	
ocktapus	octopus	oddaty	oddity	office	
ocktave	octave	oddety	oddity	officer	
ocktegon	octagon	oddity		official	
ocktepus	octopus	oddly		officially	
ocktigon	octagon	oddoty	oddity	officient	efficient
ocktipus	octopus	odds		offin	often
ocktive	octave	odduty	oddity	offir	offer
Ocktober	October	oddz	odds	offis	office
ocktogon	octagon	ode		offishal	official
ocktopus	octopus	odeous	odious	offishel	official
ocktugon	octagon	oder	odor	offishil	official
ccktupus	octopus	odious		offishol	official
ockupy	occupy	odir	odor	offishul	official
ockur	occur	odor		offon	often
Oclahoma	Oklahoma	odur	odor	offor	offer
o'clock		of		offset	
o'clok	o'clock	of	off	offshewt	offshoot
ocra	okra	ofan	often	offshoar	offshore
ocsident	occident	ofar	offer	offshoot	
ocsidize	oxidize	ofen	often	offshore	
octagon		ofend	offend	offshute	offshoot
octagonal		ofer	offer	offspring	
octapus	octopus	off		offun	often
octave		offan	often	offur	offer
octegon	octagon	offar	offer	ofice	office
octepus	octopus	offect	affect	ofin	often
octigon	octagon	offect	effect	ofir	offer

ofis	office	okra		omelette	
ofon	often	oks	ox	omen	
ofor	offer	oksagen	oxygen	omenous	ominous
often		oksegen	oxygen	omilet	omelet
ofun	often	oksford	oxford	omin	omen
ofur	offer	oksident	occident	ominous	
ogar	ogre	oksidize	oxidize	omishon	omission
oger	ogre	oksigen	oxygen	omision	omission
ogir	ogre	oksogen	oxygen	omission	
ogor	ogre	oksugen	oxygen	omit	
ogre		oktagon	octagon	omition	omission
ogur	ogre	oktapus	octopus	omlet	omelet
oh		oktave	octave	ommalet	omelet
oh	owe	oktegon	octagon	ommelet	omelet
Ohio		oktepus	octopus	ommilet	omelet
Ohyo	Ohio	oktigon	octagon	ommolet	omelet
oil		oktipus	octopus	ommulet	omelet
oilcloth		oktive	octave	omnipotent	
oiley	oily	Oktober	October	omolet	omelet
oilkloth	oilcloth	oktogon	octagon	omon	omen
oily		oktopus	octopus	omonous	ominous
ointment		oktugon	octagon	omulet	omelet
oistar	oyster	oktupus	octopus	omun	omen
oister	oyster	okupy	occupy	omunous	ominous
oistir	oyster	okur	occur	on	
oistor	oyster	old		once	
oistur	oyster	olden		oncore	encore
okasion	occasion	old-fashioned		one	
oke	oak	oleomargarine		one	won
oker	occur	olimpic	olympic	oneself	
okewpy	occupy	oliomargarine	oleomargarine	one-sided	
Oklahoma		olive		onest	honest
Oklehoma	Oklahoma	ollive	olive	one-way	
Oklihoma	Oklahoma	olympic		onion	
o'klock	o'clock	omalet	omelet	onkore	encore
Oklohoma	Oklahoma	oman	omen	onlooker	
o'klok	o'clock	omanous	ominous	onluker	onlooker
Okluhoma	Oklahoma	omelet		only	

onor	honor
onrush	
onset	
onslaught	
onslaut	onslaught
onslawt	onslaught
ontew	onto
onto	
ontue	onto
onward	
onwerd	onward
onwird	onward
onword	onward
onwurd	onward
onyan	onion
onyen	onion
onyin	onion
onyon	onion
onyun	onion
ooze	
opaik	opaque
opake	opaque
opal	
opan	open
opaque	
opara	opera
oparate	operate
opartunity	opportunity
opasite	opposite
opazite	opposite
opel	opal
open	
opening	
openly	
openning	opening
opera	
operate	
operation	

operator	
opertunity	opportunity
opesite	opposite
opezite	opposite
opil	opal
opin	open
opinion	
opira	opera
opirate	operate
opirtunity	opportunity
opisite	opposite
opium	
opizite	opposite
opoase	oppose
opoaze	oppose
opol	opal
opon	open
oponent	opponent
oponnent	opponent
opora	opera
oporate	operate
oportunity	opportunity
opose	oppose
oposite	opposite
opossum	
oposum	opossum
opoze	oppose
opozite	opposite
oppartunity	opportunity
oppasite	opposite
oppazite	opposite
oppertunity	opportunity
oppesite	opposite
oppezite	opposite
oppirtunity	opportunity
oppisite	opposite
oppizite	opposite
oppoase	oppose

oppoaze	oppose
opponent	
opponint	opponent
opportunity	
oppose	
opposite	
opposition	
oppossum	opossum
opposum	opossum
oppoze	oppose
oppozite	opposite
oppress	
oppression	
oppressive	
oppressor	
oppurtunity	opportunity
oppusite	opposite
oppuzite	opposite
opress	oppress
optacal	optical
optamistic	optimistic
optecal	optical
optemistic	optimistic
optical	
optimistic	
optocal	optical
optomistic	optimistic
optucal	optical
optumistic	optimistic
opul	opal
opun	open
opura	opera
opurate	operate
opurtunity	opportunity
opusite	opposite
opuzite	opposite
or	
or	ore

oracle	
orafice	orifice
oragin	origin
Oragon	Oregon
oragin	origin
oraition	oration
orakle	oracle
oral	
orally	
orange	
orangutan	
oration	
orator	
oratory	
orb	
orbit	
orchard	
orcherd	orchard
orchestra	
orchestral	
orchid	
orchird	orchard
orchistra	orchestra
orchord	orchard
orchurd	orchard
ordain	
ordanance	ordinance
ordanary	ordinary
ordane	ordain
ordar	order
ordeal	
ordeel	ordeal
ordele	ordeal
ordenance	ordinance
ordenary	ordinary
order	
orderly	
ordinance	

ordinarily	
ordinary	
ordir	order
ordonance	ordinance
ordonary	ordinary
ordor	order
ordunance	ordinance
ordunary	ordinary
ordur	order
ore	
ore	oar
orecle	oracle
orefice	orifice
oregin	origin
Oregon	
oreint	orient
orejin	origin
orekle	oracle
orel	oral
oreole	oriole
oretor	orator
orfan	orphan
orfen	orphan
orfin	orphan
orfon	orphan
orfun	orphan
organ	
organdy	
organism	
organist	
organization	
organize	
orgen	organ
orgendy	organdy
orgenism	organism
orgenize	organize
orgin	organ
orgindy	organdy

orginism	organism
orginize	organize
orgon	organ
orgondy	organdy
orgonism	organism
orgonize	organize
orgun	organ
orgundy	organdy
orgunism	organism
orgunize	organize
oricle	oracle
orient	
Orient	
Oriental	
orifice	
origin	
original	
originality	
originally	
originate	
Origon	Oregon
orijin	origin
orikle	oracle
oril	oral
oringe	orange
oriole	
oritor	orator
orkestra	orchestra
orkid	orchid
orkistra	orchestra
ornait	ornate
ornament	
ornamental	
ornate	
ornement	ornament
orniment	ornament
orning	awning
ornoment	ornament

ornument	ornament	ostentatious		outburst	
orocle	oracle	ostrich		outcast	
orofice	orifice	osulot	ocelot	outcome	
orogin	origin	otar	otter	outcry	
Orogon	Oregon	ote	oat	outdew	outdo
orojin	origin	oter	otter	outdo	
orokle	oracle	othar	other	outdone	
orol	oral	othe	oath	outdoors	
orotor	orator	other		outdue	outdo
orphan		otherwise		outer	
orphanage		othir	other	outfit	
orphen	orphan	othor	other	outgrew	
orphin	orphan	othur	other	outgroan	outgrown
orphon	orphan	otir	otter	outgrow	
orphun	orphan	otor	otter	outgrown	
orratic	erratic	ottar	otter	outing	
orthadox	orthodox	otter		outkast	outcast
orthedox	orthodox	ottir	otter	outkome	outcome
orthidox	orthodox	ottor	otter	outkry	outcry
orthodox		ottur	otter	outkum	outcome
orthudox	orthodox	otur	otter	outlast	
orucle	oracle	ouch		outlaw	
orufice	orifice	ought		outlet	
orugin	origin	ounce		outline	
Orugon	Oregon	ounse	ounce	outlive	
orujin	origin	our		outlook	
orukle	oracle	our	hour	outlying	
orul	oral	ours		outnumber	
orutor	orator	ourself		outpost	
osalot	ocelot	ourselves		output	
oselot	ocelot	ourselvz	ourselves	outrage	
oshan	ocean	ourz	ours	outrageous	
oshen	ocean	oust		outraige	outrage
oshin	ocean	out		outright	
oshon	ocean	outberst	outburst	outrite	outright
oshun	ocean	outbirst	outburst	outrun	
osilot	ocelot	outboard		outscurts	outskirts
osolot	ocelot	outbord	outboard	outset	

outside		overcoat		overseas	
outsider		overcome		overseaz	overseas
outskerts	outskirts	overcrowd		oversee	
outskirts		overdew	overdo	oversees	overseas
outskurts	outskirts	overdew	overdue	overseez	overseas
outspoken		overdid		oversight	
outspread		overdo		oversite	oversight
outspred	outspread	overdo	overdue	oversleep	
outstanding		overdone		overslept	
outstretched		overdue		overstep	
outting	outing	overdue	overdo	overtake	
outward		overeat		overtchur	overture
outwardly		overflow		overthrone	overthrown
outwarn	outworn	overgrown		overthrow	
outway	outweigh	overhall	overhaul	overthrown	
outweigh		overhand		overtime	
outwerd	outward	overhaul		overture	
outwit		overhawl	overhaul	overturn	
outworn		overhead		overule	overrule
outwurd	outward	overhear		overun	overrun
ov	of	overhere	overhear	overwait	overweight
oval		overjoyd	overjoyed	overweight	
ovan	oven	overjoyed		overwelm	overwhelm
ovar	over	overkast	overcast	overwhelm	
ovarture	overture	overkoat	overcoat	overwork	
ovary		overkome	overcome	overy	ovary
ovel	oval	overkrowd	overcrowd	ovil	oval
oven		overkum	overcome	ovin	oven
over		overlap		ovir	over
overalls		overlay		ovirture	overture
overate	overrate	overload		oviry	ovary
overbaring	overbearing	overlook		ovol	oval
overbearing		overnight		ovon	oven
overboard		overnite	overnight	ovor	over
overbord	overboard	overpower		ovorture	overture
overbored	overboard	overrate		ovory	ovary
overcast		overrule		ovul	oval
overchur	overture	overrun		ovun	oven

ovur	over	owr	our	oxigen	oxygen
ovurture	overture	owst	oust	oxodize	oxidize
ovury	ovary	owt	out	oxogen	oxygen
owch	ouch	ox		oxsident	occident
owe		oxadize	oxidize	oxsidize	oxidize
oweing	owing	oxagen	oxygen	oxudize	oxidize
owing		oxedize	oxidize	oxugen	oxygen
owl		oxegen	oxygen	oxygen	
own		oxen		oyl	oil
ownce	ounce	oxfard	oxford	oyntment	ointment
owner		oxferd	oxford	oystar	oyster
ownership		oxfird	oxford	oyster	
ownly	only	oxford		oystir	oyster
ownse	ounce	oxfurd	oxford	oystor	oyster
owr	hour	oxident	occident	oystur	oyster
		oxidize			

P

pa	pay	paddel	paddle	pagen	pagan
pace		paddil	paddle	pagent	pageant
pacefy	pacify	paddle		pagint	pageant
pach	patch	paddol	paddle	pagoada	pagoda
Pacific		paddul	paddle	pagoda	
pacific		pade	paid	pagon	pagan
pacify		padel	paddle	pagun	pagan
pack		padestrian	pedestrian	paice	pace
package		padil	paddle	paid	
packet		padle	paddle	paigan	pagan
packige	package	padlock		paige	page
packit	packet	padlok	padlock	paigen	pagan
packt	pact	padol	paddle	paigin	pagan
pact		padul	paddle	paigon	pagan
pad		pagan		paigun	pagan
padal	paddle	page		pail	
paddal	paddle	pageant		pail	pale

pain		palasade	palisade	pallur	pallor
pain	pane	palatable		pallute	pollute
painful		palate		pallzy	palsy
painstaking		palateable	palatable	palm	
paint		palateble	palatable	palor	pallor
painter		pale		palosade	palisade
painting		pale	pail	palpatate	palpitate
painztaking	painstaking	palece	police	palpetate	palpitate
paiper	paper	paleece	police	palpitate	
pair		paleese	police	palpotate	palpitate
pair	pare	paler	pallor	palputate	palpitate
pair	pear	palesade	palisade	palsy	
paise	pace	palese	police	paltry	
paiso	peso	Palestine		palur	pallor
paiste	paste	palet	palette	palusade	palisade
paistry	pastry	palette		palute	pollute
pait	pate	palice	palace	palzy	palsy
paithos	pathos	palice	police	pam	palm
paitient	patient	palid	pallid	pamflet	pamphlet
paitriarch	patriarch	palir	pallor	pamflit	pamphlet
paitriot	patriot	palis	palace	pampar	pamper
paitron	patron	palisade		pampas	
paive	pave	palise	police	pampaz	pampas
pajamas		Palistine	Palestine	pamper	
pajant	pageant	palit	palate	pampes	pampas
pajent	pageant	palit	palette	pampez	pampas
pajint	pageant	palite	polite	pamphlet	
pajont	pageant	palitical	political	pamphlit	pamphlet
pajunt	pageant	pall		pampir	pamper
pak	pack	pallar	pallor	pampis	pampas
pakage	package	paller	pallor	pampiz	pampas
paket	packet	pallet	palette	pampor	pamper
pakige	package	pallette	palette	pampos	pampas
pakit	packet	pallid		pampoz	pampas
pakt	pact	pallir	pallor	pampur	pamper
pal		pallit	palette	pampus	pampas
palace		pallor		pampuz	pampas
palar	pallor	pallsy	palsy	pan	

panal	panel	panthor	panther	parashute	parachute
Panama		panthur	panther	parasite	
panarama	panorama	pantimime	pantomime	parasol	
pancaik	pancake	pantomime		parat	parrot
pancake		pantry		paratrooper	
pancreas		pants		parceive	perceive
pancrias	pancreas	pantumime	pantomime	parcel	
panda		panul	panel	parception	perception
pander	panda	Panuma	Panama	parch	
pane		panurama	panorama	parchment	
pane	pain	panzy	pansy	parcieve	perceive
panel		papa		parcil	parcel
Panema	Panama	papar	paper	parck	park
panerama	panorama	paper		parcussion	percussion
panestaking	painstaking	papewse	papoose	pardan	pardon
paneztaking	painstaking	papir	paper	parden	pardon
pang		papoose		pardin	pardon
panic		papor	paper	pardon	
panik	panic	papur	paper	pardun	pardon
panil	panel	papuse	papoose	pare	
Panima	Panama	par		pare	pair
paninsula	peninsula	parable		pare	pear
panirama	panorama	parachute		pareble	parable
pankaik	pancake	parade		parechute	parachute
pankake	pancake	paradise		paredise	paradise
pankreas	pancreas	paradox		paredox	paradox
pankrias	pancreas	paraffin		pareffin	paraffin
panninsula	peninsula	parafin	paraffin	paregraph	paragraph
panol	panel	paragraph		parekeet	parakeet
Panoma	Panama	paraid	parade	parelel	parallel
panorama		parakeet		parellel	parallel
pansy		paralel	parallel	parelyze	paralyze
pant		parallel		paremount	paramount
pantamime	pantomime	paralysis		parennial	perennial
pantemime	pantomime	paralyze		parent	
panthar	panther	paramount		parentage	
panther		parant	parent	parental	
panthir	panther	parapet		parentheses	

parentheses	parenthesis	parlement	parliament	parret	parrot
parenthesis		parler	parlor	parrey	parry
parepet	parapet	parley		parrit	parrot
pareshute	parachute	parliament		parrot	
paresite	parasite	parliment	parliament	parrut	parrot
paresol	parasol	parlir	parlor	parry	
paret	parrot	parloment	parliament	parsal	parcel
paretrooper	paratrooper	parlor		parsan	parson
parey	parry	parlument	parliament	parsel	parcel
parform	perform	parlur	parlor	parseley	parsley
parhaps	perhaps	parly	parley	parsely	parsley
pariah		parmission	permission	parsen	parson
parible	parable	parmit	permit	parseption	perception
parichute	parachute	parnicious	pernicious	parseve	perceive
paridise	paradise	paroble	parable	parshal	partial
paridox	paradox	parochial		parsil	parcel
pariffin	paraffin	parochute	parachute	parsimmon	persimmon
parigraph	paragraph	parodise	paradise	parsin	parson
parikeet	parakeet	parodox	paradox	parsist	persist
parilel	parallel	paroffin	paraffin	parsley	
parillel	parallel	parograph	paragraph	parsly	parsley
parilyze	paralyze	parokeet	parakeet	parsnip	
parimount	paramount	parokial	parochial	parsol	parcel
parint	parent	parolel	parallel	parson	
paripet	parapet	parollel	parallel	parspective	perspective
parish		parolyze	paralyze	parspire	perspire
parishute	parachute	paromount	paramount	parsuade	persuade
parisite	parasite	paront	parent	parsue	pursue
parisol	parasol	paropet	parapet	parsul	parcel
parit	parrot	paroshute	parachute	parsun	parson
paritrooper	paratrooper	parosite	parasite	parswade	persuade
park		parosol	parasol	part	
parka		parot	parrot	partacle	particle
parker	parka	parotrooper	paratrooper	partaik	partake
parkussion	percussion	parpetuate	perpetuate	partain	pertain
parkway		parplex	perplex	partake	
parlament	parliament	parport	purport	partane	pertain
parlar	parlor	parrat	parrot	partasan	partisan

partecle	particle	parudise	paradise	pashint	patient
partesan	partisan	parudox	paradox	pashon	passion
partial		paruffin	paraffin	pashont	patient
partially		parugraph	paragraph	pashun	passion
partialy	partially	parukeet	parakeet	pashunt	patient
particepate	participate	parulel	parallel	Pasific	Pacific
participant		parullel	parallel	pasify	pacify
participate		parulyze	paralyze	pasinger	passenger
partickle	particle	parumount	paramount	pasition	position
particle		parunt	parent	pasive	passive
particular		parupet	parapet	paso	peso
particularly		paruse	peruse	pasofy	pacify
partikle	particle	parushute	parachute	pasonger	passenger
partikular	particular	parusite	parasite	Pasover	Passover
parting		parusol	parasol	pass	
partisan		parut	parrot	passage	
partisapate	participate	parutrooper	paratrooper	passageway	
partisepate	participate	paruze	peruse	passanger	passenger
partishon	partition	parvade	pervade	passcherize	pasteurize
partision	partition	parvaid	pervade	passchur	pasture
partisipate	participate	parverse	perverse	passed	past
partisopate	participate	parvert	pervert	passenger	
partisupate	participate	pary	parry	passer-by	
partition		pasafy	pacify	passess	possess
partly		pasage	passage	passing	
partnar	partner	pasanger	passenger	passinger	passenger
partner		pascherize	pasteurize	passion	
partnership		paschur	pasture	passionate	
partnir	partner	pase	pace	passive	
partnor	partner	pasefy	pacify	passonger	passenger
partnur	partner	pasenger	passenger	Passover	
partocle	particle	pasess	possess	passpoart	passport
partosan	partisan	pasetry	pastry	passport	
partucle	particle	pashan	passion	passtel	pastel
parturb	perturb	pashant	patient	passunger	passenger
partusan	partisan	pashen	passion	password	
paruble	parable	pashent	patient	past	
paruchute	parachute	pashin	passion	pastar	pastor

pastaral	pastoral	patete	petite	pattirn	pattern
pastcherize	pasteurize	patewnia	petunia	pattor	patter
pastchur	pasture	path		pattorn	pattern
paste		pathetic		pattur	patter
pastel		pathos		patturn	pattern
paster	pastor	pathway		patty	
pasteral	pastoral	patience		patunia	petunia
pasterize	pasteurize	patiense	patience	patunt	patent
pasteurize		patient		patur	patter
pastime		patients	patience	paturn	pattern
pastir	pastor	patint	patent	paturnal	paternal
pastiral	pastoral	patio		paunch	
pastor		patir	patter	paupar	pauper
pastoral		patirn	pattern	pauper	
pastry		patirnal	paternal	paupir	pauper
pasttime	pastime	patishon	petition	paupor	pauper
pastur	pastor	patont	patent	paupur	pauper
pastural	pastoral	pator	patter	pause	
pasture		patorn	pattern	pauze	pause
pasturize	pasteurize	patran	patron	pave	
pasufy	pacify	patrearch	patriarch	paveing	paving
pasunger	passenger	patren	patron	pavement	
pat		patreot	patriot	pavilion	
patant	patent	patriarch		pavillion	pavilion
patar	patter	patrin	patron	paving	
patarn	pattern	patriot		paw	
patato	potato	partriotic		pawn	
patch		patriotism		pawnch	paunch
patchwork		patrol		pawper	pauper
pate		patroleum	petroleum	pawse	pause
pateat	petite	patronage		pawze	pause
pateet	petite	patronize		pay	
patent		patrun	patron	payce	pace
patential	potential	pattar	patter	payed	paid
pateo	patio	pattarn	pattern	paygan	pagan
pater	patter	patter		payge	page
patern	pattern	pattern		paygen	pagan
paternal		pattir	patter	paygon	pagan

paygun	pagan	peanalize	penalize	pebbol	pebble
payle	pale	peano	piano	pebbul	pebble
payment		peanut		pebel	pebble
payne	pain	peany	peony	pebil	pebble
paynt	paint	peap	peep	peble	pebble
payper	paper	peapal	people	pebol	pebble
payse	pace	peapel	people	pebul	pebble
payso	peso	peaple	people	pecan	
payste	paste	peapol	people	pece	peace
paystry	pastry	peapul	people	pece	piece
payte	pate	pear		pechewlant	petulant
paythos	pathos	pear	peer	pechoolant	petulant
paytient	patient	pear	pier	pechulant	petulant
paytriarch	patriarch	pearce	pierce	Pecific	Pacific
paytriot	patriot	peareod	period	peck	
paytron	patron	peariod	period	peculiar	
pazess	possess	pearl		peculiarity	
pazition	position	pearley	pearly	pedagree	pedigree
pea		pearly		pedal	
peacable	peaceable	pearse	pierce	pedal	peddle
peacan	pecan	peasant		peddal	pedal
peace		peasantry		peddal	peddle
peace	piece	pease	peace	peddel	pedal
peaceable		pease	piece	peddel	peddle
peaceble	peaceable	peasent	peasant	peddil	pedal
peaceful		peasint	peasant	peddil	peddle
peach		peasont	peasant	peddle	
peacock		peasunt	peasant	peddle	pedal
peacok	peacock	peat		peddler	
peak		peavish	peevish	peddol	pedal
peak	peek	peazza	piazza	peddol	peddle
peak	pique	pebal	pebble	peddul	pedal
peakan	pecan	pebbal	pebble	peddul	peddle
Peakingese	Pekingese	pebbel	pebble	pedegree	pedigree
peakok	peacock	pebbil	pebble	pedel	pedal
peal		pebble		pedel	peddle
peal	peel	pebbley	pebbly	pedestal	
pean	peon	pebbly		pedestrian	

pedigree		peer	pier	pelican	
pedil	pedal	peerce	pierce	pelice	police
pedil	peddle	peereod	period	pelise	police
pedistal	pedestal	peeriod	period	pelit	pellet
pedle	pedal	peerless		pelite	polite
pedle	peddle	peerliss	peerless	pelitical	political
pedogree	pedigree	peerse	pierce	pellet	
pedol	pedal	peese	peace	pellit	pellet
pedol	peddle	peese	piece	pell-mel	pell-mell
pedometer		peet	peat	pell-mell	
pedugree	pedigree	peevish		pellute	pollute
pedul	pedal	peg		pel-mel	pell-mell
pedul	peddle	pegoda	pagoda	pel-mell	pell-mell
pee	pea	peice	peace	pelocan	pelican
peecan	pecan	peice	piece	pelt	
peece	peace	peiny	peony	pelucan	pelican
peece	piece	peir	pier	pelute	pollute
peech	peach	peirce	pierce	pen	
peecock	peacock	peirse	pierce	penacillin	penicillin
peecok	peacock	peise	piece	penalize	
peek		pejamas	pajamas	penalty	
peek	peak	pek	peck	penance	
peek	pique	pekan	pecan	penanse	penance
peekan	pecan	peke	peak	penant	pennant
Peekingese	Pekingese	peke	peek	penasillin	penicillin
peekok	peacock	peke	pique	penatence	penitence
peel		pekewlar	peculiar	penatentiary	penitentiary
peel	peal	Pekingese		penatrate	penetrate
peenalize	penalize	pekuliar	peculiar	pencel	pencil
peenut	peanut	pelacan	pelican	pencil	
peeon	peon	pele	peal	pendant	
peep		pele	peel	pendent	pendant
peepal	people	pelecan	pelican	pendewlum	pendulum
peepel	people	pelece	police	pending	
peeple	people	eleece	police	pendint	pendant
peepol	people	peleese	police	pendjewlum	pendulum
peepul	people	pelese	police	pendjoolum	pendulum
peer		pelet	pellet	pendjulum	pendulum

204

pendont	pendant	penmunship	penmanship	Pensilvania	Pennsylvania
pendoolum	pendulum	pennance	penance	pensioner	
pendulum		pennant		pensive	
pendunt	pendant	pennent	pennant	pensol	pencil
penecillin	penicillin	pennife	penknife	Pensolvania	Pennsylvania
penelize	penalize	penniless		pensul	pencil
penelty	penalty	penninsula	peninsula	Pensulvania	Pennsylvania
penence	penance	pennint	pennant	Pensylvania	Pennsylvania
penense	penance	pennont	pennant	pent	
penent	pennant	Pennsalvania	Pennsylvania	penthouse	
penesillin	penicillin	Pennselvania	Pennsylvania	pention	pension
penetence	penitence	Pennsilvania	Pennsylvania	penucillin	penicillin
penetentiary	penitentiary	Pennsolvania	Pennsylvania	penulize	penalize
penetrate		Pennsulvania	Pennsylvania	penulty	penalty
penetration		Pennsylvania		penunce	penance
penguin		pennunt	pennant	penunse	penance
pengwin	penguin	penny		penunt	pennant
penicillin		pennyless	penniless	penusillin	penicillin
penife	penknife	penocillin	penicillin	penutence	penitence
penilize	penalize	penolize	penalize	penutentiary	penitentiary
penilty	penalty	penolty	penalty	penutrate	penetrate
penince	penance	penonce	penance	peny	penny
peninse	penance	penonse	penance	peon	
peninsula		penont	pennant	peony	
penint	pennant	penosillin	penicillin	peopal	people
penisillin	penicillin	penotence	penitence	peopel	people
penitence		penotentiary	penitentiary	peopil	people
penitent		penotrate	penetrate	people	
penitentiary		pensal	pencil	peopol	people
penitrate	penetrate	Pensalvania	Pennsylvania	peopul	people
penjewlum	pendulum	pensel	pencil	pep	
penjoolum	pendulum	Penselvania	Pennsylvania	pepar	pepper
penjulum	pendulum	penshan	pension	pepe	peep
penknife		penshen	pension	peper	pepper
penmanship		penshin	pension	pepir	pepper
penmenship	penmanship	penshon	pension	pepor	pepper
penminship	penmanship	penshun	pension	peppar	pepper
penmonship	penmanship	pensil	pencil	pepper	

peppermint		perfarate	perforate	permission	
peppir	pepper	perfect		permit	
peppor	pepper	perfection		permonent	permanent
peppur	pepper	perfectly		permunent	permanent
pepur	pepper	perferate	perforate	pernicious	
per		perfewm	perfume	pernishus	pernicious
perade	parade	perfict	perfect	perochial	parochial
peraid	parade	perfirate	perforate	perol	peril
peral	peril	perforate		peroose	peruse
perascope	periscope	perform		perooze	peruse
perce	purse	performance		peroscope	periscope
perceive		performer		perpal	purple
percent		perfume		perpandicular	perpendicular
percentage		perfurate	perforate	perpas	purpose
perceptible		perge	purge	perpatrate	perpetrate
perceptibly		perhaps		perpechuate	perpetuate
perception		periah	pariah	perpel	purple
perch		peril		perpendicular	
perchance		perilous		perpess	purpose
perchanse	perchance	period		perpetchuate	perpetuate
perchase	purchase	periodic		perpetrate	
perchess	purchase	periodical		perpetual	
perchis	purchase	periodically		perpetually	
perchos	purchase	periscope		perpetuate	
perchus	purchase	perish		perpil	purple
percieve	perceive	perishable		perpindicular	perpendicular
percolate		perk		perpis	purpose
percussion		perkolate	percolate	perpitrate	perpetrate
pere	peer	perkussion	percussion	perple	purple
pere	pier	perl	pearl	perplecks	perplex
perel	peril	perloin	purloin	perpleks	perplex
perennial		permanence		perplex	
perental	parental	permanent		perplexity	
perenthesis	parenthesis	permeate		perpol	purple
pereod	period	permenent	permanent	perpondicular	perpendicular
perescope	periscope	permiate	permeate	perport	purport
perewse	peruse	perminent	permanent	perpos	purpose
perewze	peruse	permishon	permission	perpotrate	perpetrate

perpul	purple	persuade		pese	piece
perpundicular	perpendicular	persuasion		pesel	pestle
perpus	purpose	persuasive		pesemist	pessimist
perputrate	perpetrate	persucute	persecute	pesent	peasant
perr	purr	persue	pursue	pesess	possess
persacute	persecute	persun	person	Pesific	Pacific
persan	person	persuvere	persevere	pesil	pestle
persavere	persevere	perswade	persuade	pesimist	pessimist
perse	purse	pert		pesint	peasant
persecute		pertain		pesition	position
persecution		pertane	pertain	pesle	pestle
persekute	persecute	pertanent	pertinent	peso	
persen	person	pertenent	pertinent	pesol	pestle
persent	percent	perterb	perturb	pesomist	pessimist
perseption	perception	perticular	particular	pesont	peasant
perseve	perceive	pertikular	particular	pessal	pestle
perseverance		pertinent		pessamist	pessimist
persevere		pertirb	perturb	pessel	pestle
persicute	persecute	pertonent	pertinent	pessemist	pessimist
persimmon		pertunent	pertinent	pessess	possess
persimon	persimmon	perturb		pessil	pestle
persin	person	perul	peril	pessimist	
persist		peruscope	periscope	pessimistic	
persistence		peruse		pessle	pestle
persistent		peruze	peruse	pessol	pestle
persivere	persevere	pervade		pessomist	pessimist
persocute	persecute	pervaid	pervade	pessul	pestle
person		perverce	perverse	pessumist	pessimist
personage		perverse		pest	
personal		pervert		pestalence	pestilence
personality		pervirse	perverse	pestelence	pestilence
personally		pervirt	pervert	pester	
persovere	persevere	pervurse	perverse	pestilence	
perspective		pervurt	pervert	pestle	
perspektive	perspective	pesal	pestle	pestolence	pestilence
perspier	perspire	pesamist	pessimist	pestulence	pestilence
perspiration		pesant	peasant	pesul	pestle
perspire		pese	peace	pesumist	pessimist

pesunt	peasant	petycoat	petticoat	pezont	peasant
pet		peuny	peony	pezunt	peasant
petal		pevilion	pavilion	phaise	phase
petato	potato	pevillion	pavilion	phaize	phase
petchewlant	petulant	pevish	peevish	phalanthro-	philanthro-
petchulant	petulant	pew		pist	pist
pete	peat	pewl	pool	phalosophy	philosophy
peteat	petite	pewma	puma	phanetic	phonetic
peteet	petite	pewny	puny	phanomenon	phenomenon
petel	petal	pewpal	pupil	phantam	phantom
petential	potential	pewpel	pupil	phantem	phantom
peternal	paternal	pewpil	pupil	phantim	phantom
petete	petite	pewpol	pupil	phantom	
petewlant	petulant	pewpul	pupil	phantum	phantom
petewnia	petunia	pewr	pure	Pharaoh	
pethetic	pathetic	pewrafy	purify	pharmacist	
peticoat	petticoat	pewraty	purity	pharmacy	
petil	petal	pewray	purée	pharmecy	pharmacy
petishon	petition	pewree	purée	pharmicy	pharmacy
petision	petition	pewrefy	purify	pharmocy	pharmacy
petite		pewrety	purity	pharmucy	pharmacy
petition		pewrify	purify	Pharo	Pharaoh
petol	petal	pewrity	purity	phase	
petrafy	petrify	pewrofy	purify	phaze	phase
petrefy	petrify	pewroty	purity	pheasant	
petrify		pewrufy	purify	pheasent	pheasant
petroaleum	petroleum	pewruty	purity	pheasint	pheasant
petrofy	petrify	pewtar	pewter	pheasont	pheasant
petrol	patrol	pewter		pheasunt	pheasant
petroleum		pewtir	pewter	pheazant	pheasant
petrufy	petrify	pewtor	pewter	phelanthro-	philanthro-
petticoat		pewtrid	putrid	pist	pist
petty		pewtur	pewter	phelosophy	philosophy
pettycoat	petticoat	pezant	peasant	phenetic	phonetic
petul	petal	pezent	peasant	phenomena	
petulant		pezess	possess	phenomenal	
petunia		pezint	peasant	phenomenon	
pety	petty	pezition	position	phesant	pheasant

phezant	pheasant
philanthropic	
philanthropist	
Philipine	Philippine
Philippine	
Phillipine	Philippine
Phillippine	Philippine
philosopher	
philosophic	
philosophical	
philosophy	
phinetic	phonetic
phinomenon	phenomenon
phisique	physique
phizique	physique
phoan	phone
pholanthro-	philanthro-
pist	pist
pholosophy	philosophy
phonagraph	phonograph
phone	
phonegraph	phonograph
phonetic	
phonigraph	phonograph
phonograph	
phonomenon	phenomenon
phonugraph	phonograph
phosforus	phosphorus
phospharus	phosphorus
phospherus	phosphorus
phosphirus	phosphorus
phosphorus	
phosphurus	phosphorus
photagraph	photograph
photegraph	photograph
photigraph	photograph
photo	
photograph	

photographer	
photography	
photugraph	photograph
phraise	phrase
phraize	phrase
phrase	
phraze	phrase
phulanthro-	philanthro-
pist	pist
phulosophy	philosophy
phunetic	phonetic
phunomenon	phenomenon
physacal	physical
physeak	physique
physecal	physical
physeek	physique
physeke	physique
physeque	physique
physical	
physically	
physician	
physicist	
physics	
physiks	physics
physiology	
physishan	physician
physisist	physicist
physocal	physical
physucal	physical
phyzical	physical
phyzics	physics
phyziks	physics
phyzique	physique
pianeer	pioneer
pianist	
piano	
pias	pious
piaty	piety

piaza	piazza
piazza	
picalo	piccolo
pican	pecan
piccalo	piccolo
piccolo	
picculo	piccolo
pich	pitch
Picific	Pacific
pick	
pickal	pickle
pickchur	picture
pickel	pickle
picket	
pickil	pickle
pickit	picket
pickle	
picknic	picnic
picknick	picnic
picknik	picnic
pickol	pickle
pickolo	piccolo
pickpocket	
pickpoket	pickpocket
picksie	pixie
picksy	pixie
picktchur	picture
picktorial	pictorial
pickture	picture
pickul	pickle
picnic	
picnik	picnic
picolo	piccolo
picsie	pixie
picsy	pixie
pictchur	picture
pictorial	
picture	

picturesque		pik	pick	pilfor	pilfer
piculiar	peculiar	pikal	pickle	pilfur	pilfer
piculo	piccolo	pikan	pecan	pilgram	pilgrim
pide	pied	pikchur	picture	pilgrem	pilgrim
pidestrian	pedestrian	pike		Pilgrim	
pidomter	pedometer	pikel	pickle	pilgrim	
pie		piket	picket	pilgrimage	
piece		pikil	pickle	pilgrom	pilgrim
piece	peace	pikit	picket	pilgrum	pilgrim
piecemeal		pikle	pickle	pilice	police
pied		piknic	picnic	pilige	pillage
pieneer	pioneer	piknick	picnic	pilir	pillar
pier		piknik	picnic	pilise	police
pier	pyre	pikol	pickle	pilit	pilot
pierce		pikolo	piccolo	pilite	polite
pierse	pierce	pikpocket	pickpocket	pilitical	political
piese	piece	pikpoket	pickpocket	pill	
piess	pious	piksie	pixie	pillage	
piety		piksy	pixie	pillar	
pig		piktchur	picture	piller	pillar
pigen	pigeon	piktorial	pictorial	pillfar	pilfer
pigeon		pikture	picture	pillfer	pilfer
pigeon-toed		pikul	pickle	pillfir	pilfer
pig-headed		pikuliar	peculiar	pillfor	pilfer
pig-heded	pig-headed	pil	pill	pillfur	pilfer
pigin	pigeon	pilage	pillage	pillgram	pilgrim
pigment		pilar	pillar	pillgrem	pilgrim
pigmy		pilat	pilot	pillgrim	pilgrim
pigoda	pagoda	pile		pillgrom	pilgrim
pigsty		pilece	police	pillgrum	pilgrim
pigtail		pileece	police	pillige	pillage
pigtale	pigtail	pileese	police	pillir	pillar
pijamas	pajamas	piler	pillar	pillor	pillar
pijan	pigeon	pilese	police	pillow	
pijen	pigeon	pilet	pilot	pillur	pillar
pijin	pigeon	pilfar	pilfer	pillute	pollute
pijon	pigeon	pilfer		pilor	pillar
pijun	pigeon	pilfir	pilfer	pilot	

pilow	pillow	pint		pirfict	perfect		
pilur	pillar	pinto		pirforate	perforate		
pilut	pilot	pinucle	pinnacle	pirform	perform		
pilute	pollute	pinufore	pinafore	pirfume	perfume		
pimpal	pimple	pioneer		pirge	purge		
pimpel	pimple	pios	pious	pirhaps	perhaps		
pimpil	pimple	pioty	piety	piriah	pariah		
pimple		pious		piricy	piracy		
pimpol	pimple	pipe		pirimid	pyramid		
pimpul	pimple	pipeing	piping	pirit	pirate		
pin		piper		pirk	perk		
pinacle	pinnacle	piping		pirkolate	percolate		
pinafore		pique		pirkussion	percussion		
pinakle	pinnacle	pir	per	pirl	pearl		
pincers		piracy		pirloin	purloin		
pinch		pirade	parade	pirmanent	permanent		
pinck	pink	piraid	parade	pirmeate	permeate		
pincushion		piramid	pyramid	pirmission	permission		
pine		pirate		pirmit	permit		
pineapple		pirce	purse	pirnicious	pernicious		
pinecle	pinnacle	pirceive	perceive	pirochial	parochial		
pinefore	pinafore	pirception	perception	pirocy	piracy		
pinicle	pinnacle	pirch	perch	piromid	pyramid		
pinifore	pinafore	pirchase	purchase	pirpal	purple		
pininsula	peninsula	pirchess	purchase	pirpas	purpose		
pink		pirchis	purchase	pirpel	purple		
pinkeye		pirchos	purchase	pirpendicular	perpendicular		
pinkushion	pincushion	pirchus	purchase	pirpess	purpose		
pinnacle		pircieve	perceive	pirpetrate	perpetrate		
pinnakle	pinnacle	pircolate	percolate	pirpetuate	perpetuate		
pinnecle	pinnacle	pircussion	percussion	pirpil	purple		
pinnicle	pinnacle	pire	pyre	pirpis	purpose		
pinninsula	peninsula	pirecy	piracy	pirple	purple		
pinnocle	pinnacle	piremid	pyramid	pirplex	perplex		
pinnucle	pinnacle	pirennial	perennial	pirpol	purple		
pinocle	pinnacle	pirental	parental	pirport	purport		
pinofore	pinafore	pirenthesis	parenthesis	pirpos	purpose		
pinsers	pincers	pirfect	perfect	pirpul	purple		

pirpus	purpose	pistel	pistol	piuneer	pioneer
pirr	purr	pisten	piston	pius	pious
pirse	purse	pistil		piuty	piety
pirsecute	persecute	pistil	pistol	pivat	pivot
pirseption	perception	pistin	piston	pivet	pivot
pirseve	perceive	pistol		pivilion	pavilion
pirsevere	persevere	pistol	pistil	pivillion	pavilion
pirsimmon	persimmon	piston		pivit	pivot
pirsist	persist	pistul	pistil	pivot	
pirson	person	pistul	pistol	pivut	pivot
pirspective	perspective	pistun	piston	pixie	
pirspire	perspire	pit		pixy	
pirsuade	persuade	pitato	potato	pizess	possess
pirsue	pursue	pitch		pizition	position
pirswade	persuade	pitcher		pla	play
pirt	pert	pitchfoark	pitchfork	placard	
pirtain	pertain	pitchfork		place	
pirtane	pertain	piteat	petite	placid	
pirticular	particular	piteet	petite	plackard	placard
pirtikular	particular	pitential	potential	plad	plaid
pirtinent	pertinent	piteous		plague	
pirturb	perturb	piternal	paternal	plaice	place
pirucy	piracy	pitete	petite	plaid	
pirumid	pyramid	pitewnia	petunia	plaig	plague
piruse	peruse	pitfall		plain	
piruze	peruse	pith		plain	plane
pirvade	pervade	pithetic	pathetic	plaintive	
pirvaid	pervade	pithon	python	plaise	place
pirverse	perverse	pitiable		plait	plate
pirvert	pervert	pitiful		plakard	placard
pisess	possess	pitious	piteous	plan	
Pisific	Pacific	pitishon	petition	planck	plank
pisition	position	pitrol	patrol	plane	
pissess	possess	pitroleum	petroleum	plane	plain
pistal	pistil	pitty	pity	planet	
pistal	pistol	pitunia	petunia	planetary	
pistan	piston	pityable	pitiable	planetive	plaintive
pistel	pistil	pityful	pitiful	planit	planet

plank		platter		plaza	
plant		plattir	platter	plazer	plaza
plantain		plattor	platter	ple	plea
plantan	plantain	plattur	platter	plea	
plantation		platune	platoon	plead	
planten	plantain	platunum	platinum	pleasant	
plantin	plantain	platupus	platypus	pleasantry	
planton	plantain	platur	platter	please	
plantun	plantain	platypus		pleaseing	pleasing
plase	place	plausable	plausible	pleasent	pleasant
plasid	placid	plauseble	plausible	pleasing	
plastar	plaster	plausible		pleasint	pleasant
plaster		plausoble	plausible	pleasont	pleasant
plastic		plausuble	plausible	pleasunt	pleasant
plastik	plastic	plauzable	plausible	pleasure	
plastir	plaster	plauzeble	plausible	pleat	
plastor	plaster	plauzible	plausible	pleazant	pleasant
plastur	plaster	plauzoble	plausible	pleaze	please
platanum	platinum	plauzuble	plausible	pleazure	pleasure
platapus	platypus	plawsable	plausible	plede	plead
platar	platter	plawseble	plausible	pledge	
plate		plawsoble	plausible	plee	plea
plateau		plawsuble	plausible	pleed	plead
platenum	platinum	plawzable	plausible	pleese	please
platepus	platypus	plawzeble	plausible	pleet	pleat
plater	platter	plawzible	plausible	pleeze	please
platewn	platoon	plawzoble	plausible	plege	pledge
platform		plawzuble	plausible	plentiful	
platinum		play		plenty	
platipus	platypus	player		plentyful	plentiful
platir	platter	playful		plesant	pleasant
plato	plateau	playground		plese	please
platonum	platinum	playgrownd	playground	plesent	pleasant
platoon		playmait	playmate	plesint	pleasant
platopus	platypus	playmate		plesont	pleasant
plator	platter	playright	playwright	plesunt	pleasant
platow	plateau	playwright		plesure	pleasure
plattar	platter	playwrite	playwright	plete	pleat

pletewn	platoon	pliwud	plywood	plundur	plunder
pletoon	platoon	plod		plunge	
pletune	platoon	ploom	plume	plural	
plewm	plume	ploomage	plumage	plurel	plural
plewmage	plumage	plooral	plural	pluril	plural
plewral	plural	ploorel	plural	plurol	plural
plewrel	plural	plooril	plural	plurul	plural
plewril	plural	ploorol	plural	plus	
plewrol	plural	ploorul	plural	plush	
plewrul	plural	plootonium	plutonium	plutewn	platoon
plewtonium	plutonium	plot		plutonium	
plezant	pleasant	plotewn	platoon	plutoon	platoon
pleze	please	plotoon	platoon	plutune	platoon
plezure	pleasure	plotune	platoon	ply	
pli	ply	plow		plywad	plywood
pliable		pluck		plywood	
pliant		plucky		plywud	plywood
pliars	pliers	plug		pneumatic	
pliarz	pliers	pluk	pluck	pneumonia	
plieble	pliable	plum		poach	
plient	pliant	plumage		poak	poke
pliers		plumar	plumber	poaka	polka
plierz	pliers	plumber		poal	pole
plight		plumbing		poal	poll
plioble	pliable	plume		poaltry	poultry
pliont	pliant	plumer	plumber	poam	poem
pliors	pliers	plumige	plumage	Poap	Pope
pliorz	pliers	pluming	plumbing	poar	pore
plite	plight	plumir	plumber	poarcelain	porcelain
plitewn	platoon	plummage	plumage	poarch	porch
plitoon	platoon	plummige	plumage	poarcupine	porcupine
plitune	platoon	plumor	plumber	poark	pork
pliuble	pliable	plump		poart	port
pliunt	pliant	plumur	plumber	poartable	portable
pliurs	pliers	plundar	plunder	poartal	portal
pliurz	pliers	plunder		poartend	portend
pliwad	plywood	plundir	plunder	poartent	portent
pliwood	plywood	plundor	plunder	poarter	porter

poartico	portico	poisan	poison	poletics	politics
poartion	portion	poise		police	
poartly	portly	poisen	poison	policeman	
poartrait	portrait	poisin	poison	policy	
poartray	portray	poison		poligon	polygon
poase	pose	poisonous		polin	pollen
poast	post	poisun	poison	polio	
poaster	poster	poit	poet	poliomyelitis	
poastpone	postpone	poize	poise	polir	polar
poasy	posy	poizon	poison	polise	police
poatent	potent	pojamas	pajamas	polish	
poation	potion	pok	poke	polisy	policy
poaze	pose	poka	polka	polite	
poazy	posy	pokar	poker	politeness	
poche	poach	poke		political	
Pocific	Pacific	poker		politician	
pock		poket	pocket	politics	
pocket		pokey		polka	
pocketbook		pokir	poker	poll	
pockit	pocket	pokit	pocket	pollan	pollen
pod		pokor	poker	pollen	
podestrian	pedestrian	pokur	poker	pollewt	pollute
poem		polacy	policy	polligon	polygon
poet		polan	pollen	pollin	pollen
poetic		polar		pollo	polo
poetical		polasy	policy	pollon	pollen
poetry		polatics	politics	polloot	pollute
pogoda	pagoda	pole		polls	
poim	poem	pole	poll	pollun	pollen
poinsettia		polece	police	pollute	
point		polecy	policy	pollygon	polygon
pointar	pointer	poleece	police	polo	
pointed		poleese	police	polocy	policy
pointer		polen	pollen	polon	pollen
pointid	pointed	poleo	polio	polor	polar
pointir	pointer	poler	polar	polosy	policy
pointor	pointer	polese	police	polotics	politics
pointur	pointer	polesy	policy	poltry	poultry

polucy	policy	ponninsula	peninsula	por	paw
polun	pollen	pontewn	pontoon	por	pore
polur	polar	pontoon		porade	parade
polusy	policy	pontune	pontoon	poraid	parade
polute	pollute	pony		poras	porous
polutics	politics	poodal	poodle	porceive	perceive
polygon		poodel	poodle	porcelain	
pom	palm	poodil	poodle	porception	perception
pomagranate	pomegranate	poodle		porch	
pome	poem	poodol	poodle	porcieve	perceive
pomegranate		poodul	poodle	porcilain	porcelain
pomel	pommel	pool		porcupine	
pomigranate	pomegranate	pooma	puma	porcussion	percussion
pommel		poor		pore	
pomogranate	pomegranate	poorly		porennial	perennial
pomp		pop		porental	parental
pompas	pompous	popcorn		porenthesis	parenthesis
pompess	pompous	Pope		poress	porous
pompis	pompous	popewlar	popular	porform	perform
pompon		popkorn	popcorn	porhaps	perhaps
pompos	pompous	poplan	poplin	poriah	pariah
pompous		poplar		poridge	porridge
pompus	pompous	poplen	poplin	porige	porridge
pomugranate	pomegranate	popler	poplar	poris	porous
poncho		poplin		pork	
pond		poplir	poplar	porkewpine	porcupine
pondar	ponder	poplon	poplin	porkupine	porcupine
pondarous	ponderous	poplor	poplar	porkussion	percussion
ponder		poplun	poplin	permission	permission
ponderous		poplur	poplar	pormit	permit
pondir	ponder	poppy		porn	pawn
pondirous	ponderous	populace		pornicious	pernicious
pondor	ponder	popular		porochial	parochial
pondorous	ponderous	popularity		poros	porous
pondur	ponder	populate		porous	
pondurous	ponderous	population		porpas	porpoise
poney	pony	populous		porper	pauper
poninsula	peninsula	popy	poppy	porpess	porpoise

porpetuate	perpetuate
porpis	porpoise
porplex	perplex
porpoise	
porport	purport
porpos	porpoise
porpus	porpoise
porridge	
porrige	porridge
porsalain	porcelain
porse	pause
porselain	porcelain
porseption	perception
porseve	perceive
porshon	portion
porsilain	porcelain
porsimmon	persimmon
porsist	persist
porsolain	porcelain
porspective	perspective
porspire	perspire
porsuade	persuade
porsue	pursue
porsulain	porcelain
porswade	persuade
port	
portable	
portaco	portico
portain	pertain
portal	
portane	pertain
portar	porter
Porta Rico	Puerto Rico
porteble	portable
porteco	portico
portel	portal
portend	
portent	

porter	
porthole	
portible	portable
portico	
particular	particular
portikular	particular
portil	portal
portion	
portir	porter
portly	
portoble	portable
portoco	portico
portol	portal
portor	porter
Porto Rico	Puerto Rico
portrait	
portrate	portrait
portray	
portuble	portable
portuco	portico
portul	portal
portur	porter
porturb	perturb
porus	porous
poruse	peruse
poruze	peruse
porvade	pervade
porvaid	pervade
porverse	perverse
porvert	pervert
porze	pause
posable	possible
posam	possum
posative	positive
poschur	posture
pose	
poseble	possible
posem	possum

posess	possess
posetive	positive
poshon	potion
posible	possible
Posific	Pacific
posim	possum
position	
positive	
posoble	possible
posom	possum
posotive	positive
possable	possible
possam	possum
posseble	possible
possem	possum
possess	
possession	
possessive	
possessor	
possibility	
possible	
possibly	
possim	possum
possoble	possible
possom	possum
possuble	possible
possum	
post	
postage	
postal	
postar	poster
postchur	posture
postel	postal
poster	
posterity	
postige	postage
postil	postal
postir	poster

postol	postal	pottar	potter	power	
postor	poster	pottary	pottery	powerful	
postpoane	postpone	potter		powerless	
postpone		pottery		powir	power
postscript		pottir	potter	powlo	polo
postskript	postscript	pottiry	pottery	pownce	pounce
postul	postal	pottor	potter	pownd	pound
postur	poster	pottory	pottery	pownse	pounce
posture		pottur	potter	powor	power
posuble	possible	pottury	pottery	powow	powwow
posum	possum	potunia	petunia	powt	pout
posutive	positive	potunt	potent	powur	power
posy		potur	potter	powwow	
pot		potury	pottery	poynsettia	poinsettia
potant	potent	pouch		poynt	point
potar	potter	pouder	powder	poyse	poise
potary	pottery	poultry		poyson	poison
potato		poum	poem	poyze	poise
poteat	petite	pounce		poyzon	poison
poteet	petite	pound		pozative	positive
potentate		pounse	pounce	poze	pose
potential		pour		pozess	possess
poter	potter	pout		pozetive	positive
poternal	paternal	povarty	poverty	pozition	position
potery	pottery	poverty		pozitive	positive
potete	petite	povilion	pavilion	pozotive	positive
potewnia	petunia	povillion	pavilion	pozutive	positive
pothetic	pathetic	povirty	poverty	pozy	posy
potint	potent	povorty	poverty	pracede	proceed
potion		povurty	poverty	praceed	proceed
potir	potter	powar	power	pracession	procession
potiry	pottery	powch	poach	pracktical	practical
potishon	petition	powch	pouch	pracktice	practice
potont	potent	powdar	powder	pracktis	practice
potor	potter	powder		praclaim	proclaim
potory	pottery	powdir	powder	praclame	proclaim
potrol	patrol	powdor	powder	practacal	practical
potroleum	petroleum	powdur	powder	practecal	practical

practicable		praktacal	practical	pratil	prattle
practical		praktecul	practical	pratle	prattle
practically		praktical	practical	pratol	prattle
practice		praktice	practice	prattal	prattle
practis	practice	praktis	practice	prattel	prattle
practocal	practical	praktocul	practical	prattil	prattle
practucal	practical	praktucal	practical	prattle	
pracure	procure	pralific	prolific	prattol	prattle
pradigious	prodigious	pramote	promote	prattul	prattle
praduce	produce	prance		pratul	prattle
praduse	produce	pranck	prank	pravide	provide
prafain	profane	prank		pravision	provision
prafane	profane	pranounce	pronounce	pravoke	provoke
prafeshion	profession	pranounse	pronounce	pray	
prafesor	professor	pranownce	pronounce	pray	prey
prafess	profess	pranse	prance	prayer	
prafession	profession	prapel	propel	prayrie	prairie
prafessor	professor	prapensity	propensity	prayry	prairie
prafewse	profuse	prapitious	propitious	praze	praise
praficient	proficient	praportion	proportion	preach	
prafishent	proficient	prapose	propose	preachar	preacher
prafound	profound	prapoze	propose	preacher	
prafownd	profound	praprietor	proprietor	preachir	preacher
prafuce	profuse	prapriety	propriety	preachor	preacher
prafuse	profuse	prapulsion	propulsion	preachur	preacher
pragress	progress	prare	prayer	prean	preen
prair	prayer	prarie	prairie	preast	priest
prairie		prary	prairie	precarious	
prairy	prairie	prase	praise	precaution	
praise		prasede	proceed	precawtion	precaution
praisewerthy	praiseworthy	praseed	proceed	precede	
praisewirthy	praiseworthy	prasession	procession	precede	proceed
praiseworthy		pratal	prattle	precedent	
praisewurthy	praiseworthy	prate		preceding	
prait	prate	pratect	protect	preceed	precede
praize	praise	pratekt	protect	preceed	proceed
praject	project	pratel	prattle	preceeding	preceding
prajekt	project	pratest	protest	precepice	precipice

precept		predocessor	predecessor	prehistoric	
precession	procession	predominant		preist	priest
precice	precise	predominate		preject	project
precident	precedent	predotory	predatory	prejekt	project
precinct		preduce	produce	prejewdice	prejudice
precinkt	precinct	preducessor	predecessor	prejoodice	prejudice
precios	precious	preduse	produce	prejudice	
precious		predutory	predatory	prekarious	precarious
precipice		preech	preach	prekaution	precaution
precipitate		preen		preklude	preclude
precipitation		preest	priest	prekocious	precocious
precipitous		preface		prelate	
precise		prefain	profane	prelewd	prelude
precisely		prefane	profane	prelific	prolific
precision		prefer		preliminary	
precius	precious	preferable		prelit	prelate
preclaim	proclaim	preferably		prellate	prelate
preclame	proclaim	preference		prellit	prelate
preclewd	preclude	prefeshion	profession	prellude	prelude
preclood	preclude	prefesor	professor	prelood	prelude
preclude		prefess	profess	prelude	
precocious		prefession	profession	premature	
precoshus	precocious	prefessor	professor	premear	premier
precure	procure	prefewse	profuse	premeditate	
predacessor	predecessor	prefface	preface	premeer	premier
predatory		preffis	preface	premeir	premier
predecessor		preficient	proficient	premere	premier
predesessor	predecessor	preficks	prefix	premeture	premature
predetory	predatory	prefics	prefix	premier	
predicament		prefiks	prefix	premiture	premature
predicessor	predecessor	prefis	preface	premote	promote
predickament	predicament	prefishent	proficient	premoture	premature
predict		prefix		premuture	premature
prediction		prefound	profound	prene	preen
predigious	prodigious	prefownd	profound	prenounce	pronounce
predikament	predicament	prefuce	profuse	prenounse	pronounce
predikt	predict	prefuse	profuse	prenownce	pronounce
preditory	predatory	pregress	progress	prepade	prepaid

prepaid	
prepair	prepare
preparation	
prepare	
prepasition	preposition
prepel	propel
prepensity	propensity
preperation	preparation
prepesition	preposition
prepiration	preparation
prepisition	preposition
prepitious	propitious
preporation	preparation
preportion	proportion
prepose	propose
preposition	
preposterous	
prepoze	propose
prepozition	preposition
preprietor	proprietor
prepriety	propriety
prepulsion	propulsion
prepuration	preparation
prepusition	preposition
pres	press
presadent	precedent
presadent	president
presant	present
presapice	precipice
Presbaterian	Presbyterian
Presbeterian	Presbyterian
Presbiterian	Presbyterian
Presboterian	Presbyterian
Presbuterian	Presbyterian
Presbyterian	
prescribe	
prescribtion	prescription
prescription	

presede	precede
presede	proceed
presedent	precedent
presedent	president
preseed	precede
preseed	proceed
presence	
presense	presence
present	
presentable	
presentation	
presently	
presents	presence
presepice	precipice
presept	precept
preservation	
preserve	
preserver	
presession	procession
presewm	presume
preshous	precious
preshure	pressure
presice	precise
preside	
presidency	
president	
president	precedent
presidential	
presinct	precinct
presinkt	precinct
presint	present
presipice	precipice
presipitate	precipitate
presise	precise
preskribe	prescribe
presodent	precedent
presodent	president
presont	present

presoom	presume
presopice	precipice
press	
pressing	
pressteage	prestige
pressteege	prestige
presstege	prestige
presstige	prestige
pressure	
preste	priest
presteage	prestige
presteege	prestige
prestege	prestige
prestige	
presto	
presudent	precedent
presudent	president
presumable	
presumably	
presume	
presumeable	presumable
presumeble	presumable
presumption	
presumptuous	
presumtion	presumption
presunt	present
presupice	precipice
presure	pressure
preteckst	pretext
pretecst	pretext
pretect	protect
pretekst	pretext
pretekt	protect
pretence	pretense
pretend	
pretense	
pretension	
pretensious	pretentious

pretentious		prezadent	president	prickul	prickle
pretest	protest	prezant	present	priclaim	proclaim
pretext		Prezbaterian	Presbyterian	priclame	proclaim
pretsal	pretzel	Prezbeterian	Presbyterian	priclude	preclude
pretsel	pretzel	Prezbiterian	Presbyterian	pricocious	precocious
pretsil	pretzel	Prezboterian	Presbyterian	pricure	procure
pretsol	pretzel	Prezbuterian	Presbyterian	pride	
pretsul	pretzel	Prezbyterian	Presbyterian	pridicament	predicament
pretty		prezedent	president	pridickament	predicament
prety	pretty	prezent	present	pridict	predict
pretzal	pretzel	prezerve	preserve	pridigious	prodigious
pretzel		prezide	preside	pridikament	predicament
pretzil	pretzel	prezident	president	pridikt	predict
pretzol	pretzel	prezint	present	pridominate	predominate
pretzul	pretzel	prezodent	president	priduce	produce
prevail		prezont	present	priduse	produce
prevailing		prezudent	president	pried	pride
prevale	prevail	prezume	presume	prier	prior
prevalence		prezunt	present	priest	
prevalent		priar	prior	priestly	
prevelent	prevalent	pricarious	precarious	prifain	profane
prevent		pricaution	precaution	prifane	profane
prevention		price		prifer	prefer
preventive		pricede	proceed	prifeshon	profession
preveous	previous	priceed	proceed	prifesor	professor
previde	provide	priceless		prifess	profess
previlent	prevalent	priceliss	priceless	prifession	profession
previous		pricession	procession	prifessor	professor
previously		pricice	precise	prifewse	profuse
prevision	provision	pricipitate	precipitate	prificient	proficient
prevoke	provoke	pricise	precise	prifishent	proficient
prevolent	prevalent	prick		prifound	profound
prevulent	prevalent	prickal	prickle	prifownd	profound
prewdent	prudent	prickel	prickle	prifuce	profuse
prewf	proof	prickil	prickle	prifuse	profuse
prewn	prune	prickle		prigress	progress
prewve	prove	prickly		priject	project
prey		prickol	prickle	prijekt	project

prik	prick	princeple	principle	priscribe	prescribe
prikal	prickle	princess		prise	price
prikarious	precarious	principal		prise	prize
prikaution	precaution	principally		prisede	proceed
prikel	prickle	principle		priseed	proceed
prikil	prickle	prinounce	pronounce	prisem	prism
prikle	prickle	prinounse	pronounce	prisen	prison
priklude	preclude	prinownce	pronounce	priserve	preserve
prikocious	precocious	prinsapal	principal	prisession	procession
prikol	prickle	prinsaple	principle	prisice	precise
prikul	prickle	prinse	prince	priside	preside
prilific	prolific	prinsepal	principal	prisim	prism
priliminary	preliminary	prinseple	principle	prisin	prison
prim		prinsipal	principal	prisipitate	precipitate
primar	primer	prinsiple	principle	prisise	precise
primary		prinsopal	principal	priskribe	prescribe
primative	primitive	prinsople	principle	prism	
prime		prinsupal	principal	prisom	prism
primeaval	primeval	prinsuple	principle	prison	
primeeval	primeval	print		prisoner	
primer		printer		prisum	prism
primery	primary	printing		prisume	presume
primetive	primitive	prior		prisun	prison
primeval		priority		pritect	protect
primier	premier	pripair	prepare	pritekt	protect
primir	primer	pripare	prepare	pritend	pretend
primitive		pripel	propel	pritest	protest
primor	primer	pripensity	propensity	pritty	pretty
primote	promote	pripitious	propitious	prity	pretty
primotive	primitive	priportion	proportion	priur	prior
primroase	primrose	pripose	propose	privacy	
primroaze	primrose	priposterous	preposterous	privail	prevail
primrose		pripoze	propose	privait	private
primroze	primrose	priprietor	proprietor	privale	prevail
primur	primer	pripriety	propriety	privalege	privilege
primutive	primitive	pripulsion	propulsion	private	
prince		prisam	prism	privately	
princepal	principal	prisan	prison	privecy	privacy

privelege	privilege	probability		prodegy	prodigy
privent	prevent	probable		prodigal	
privey	privy	probably		prodigious	
privicy	privacy	probation		prodigy	
privide	provide	probe		prodijious	prodigious
privilege		probeble	probable	prodijy	prodigy
privileged		probible	probable	prodogal	prodigal
privision	provision	problam	problem	prodogy	prodigy
privit	private	problem		produce	
privocy	privacy	problim	problem	producer	
privoke	provoke	problom	problem	produckt	product
privolege	privilege	problum	problem	product	
privucy	privacy	proboble	probable	production	
privulege	privilege	probuble	probable	productive	
privy		procede	proceed	produgal	prodigal
prizan	prison	procedes	proceeds	produgy	prodigy
prize		procedure		produkt	product
prizem	prism	proceed		produse	produce
prizen	prison	proceeds		profacy	prophecy
prizerve	preserve	proceedure	procedure	profacy	prophesy
prizide	preside	proceedz	proceeds	profain	profane
prizim	prism	process		profane	
prizin	prison	procession		profanety	profanity
prizm	prism	procewr	procure	profanity	
prizom	prism	procksy	proxy	profar	proffer
prizon	prison	proclaim		profasy	prophecy
prizum	prism	proclaimation	proclamation	profasy	prophesy
prizume	presume	proclame	proclaim	profecy	prophecy
prizun	prison	proclemation	proclamation	profecy	prophesy
pro		proclimation	proclamation	profer	proffer
proab	probe	proclomation	proclamation	profeshon	profession
proabation	probation	proclumation	proclamation	profesor	professor
proafile	profile	procsy	proxy	profess	
proan	prone	procure		profession	
proase	prose	prod		professional	
proaton	proton	prodagal	prodigal	professor	
proatrude	protrude	prodagy	prodigy	profesy	prophecy
proaze	prose	prodegal	prodigal	profesy	prophesy

profewse	profuse
proffar	proffer
proffer	
proffir	proffer
proffor	proffer
proffur	proffer
proficient	
proficy	prophecy
proficy	prophesy
profile	
profir	proffer
profishent	proficient
profisy	prophecy
profisy	prophesy
profit	
profitable	
profitably	
profocy	prophecy
profocy	prophesy
profor	proffer
profosy	prophecy
profosy	prophesy
profound	
profownd	profound
profuce	profuse
profucy	prophecy
profucy	prophesy
profur	proffer
profuse	
profusion	
profusy	prophecy
profusy	prophesy
progeny	
proginy	progeny
program	
progress	
progressive	
prohibit	

prohibition	
projany	progeny
projeckt	project
project	
projectile	
projection	
projector	
projekt	project
projektile	projectile
projektor	projector
projeny	progeny
projiny	progeny
projony	progeny
projuny	progeny
prokewr	procure
proklaim	proclaim
proklame	proclaim
proksy	proxy
prokure	procure
prolific	
prolong	
promanade	promenade
promanent	prominent
promantory	promontory
promenade	
promenent	prominent
promentory	promontory
promice	promise
prominade	promenade
prominence	
prominent	
promintory	promontory
promise	
promiseing	promising
promising	
promoat	promote
promonade	promenade
promonent	prominent

promontory	
promote	
promotion	
prompt	
promunade	promenade
promunent	prominent
promuntory	promontory
prone	
prong	
prononciation	pronunciation
pronoun	
pronounced	
pronounciation	pronunciation
pronounse	pronounce
pronown	pronoun
pronownce	pronounce
pronunciation	
proodent	prudent
proof	
proon	prune
proove	prove
prop	
propaganda	
propagate	
propar	proper
proparty	property
propeganda	propaganda
propegate	propagate
propel	
propeler	propeller
propeller	
propensity	
proper	
properly	
property	
prophecy	
prophesy	
prophet	

prophetic		prosess	process	protrood	protrude
prophit	prophet	prosession	procession	protrude	
propiganda	propaganda	prosicute	prosecute	protuplasm	protoplasm
propigate	propagate	prosocute	prosecute	proud	
propir	proper	prospar	prosper	proudly	
propirty	property	prospect		proul	prowl
propishus	propitious	prospective		provance	province
propitious		prospector		provadence	providence
propoase	propose	prospekt	prospect	provander	provender
propoaze	propose	prospektor	prospector	provanse	province
propoganda	propaganda	prosper		prove	
propogate	propagate	prosperity		provedence	providence
propor	proper	prosperous		proven	
proportion		prospir	prosper	provence	province
proporty	property	prospor	prosper	provender	
proposal		prospur	prosper	provense	province
propose		prostrait	prostrate	proverb	
proposel	proposal	prostrate		provide	
proposition		prosucute	prosecute	provided	
propoze	propose	protaplasm	protoplasm	providence	
proprietor		protean	protein	provident	
propriety		protect		province	
propryety	propriety	protection		provincial	
propuganda	propaganda	protective		provinder	provender
propugate	propagate	protector		provinse	province
propulsion		proteen	protein	provirb	proverb
propur	proper	protein		provision	
propurty	property	protekt	protect	provisional	
prosacute	prosecute	protene	protein	provoak	provoke
prose		proteplasm	protoplasm	provocation	
prosecute		protest		provodence	providence
prosecution		Protestant		provokation	provocation
prosede	proceed	protien	protein	provoke	
prosedes	proceeds	protiplasm	protoplasm	provonce	province
proseed	proceed	Protistant	Protestant	provonder	provender
proseeds	proceeds	proton		provonse	province
proseedz	proceeds	protoplasm		provudence	providence
prosekute	prosecute	protrewd	protrude	provunce	province

provunder	provender	prufound	profound	psychology	
provunse	province	prufownd	profound	psycology	psychology
provurb	proverb	prufuce	profuse	psykology	psychology
prow		prufuse	profuse	public	
prow	pro	prugress	progress	publication	
prowd	proud	pruject	project	publicity	
prowess		prujekt	project	publickly	publicly
prowiss	prowess	prulific	prolific	publicly	
prowl		prumote	promote	publik	public
prown	prone	prune		publish	
proxy		prunounce	pronounce	publisher	
proze	prose	prunounse	pronounce	publisity	publicity
prucede	proceed	prunownce	pronounce	pucar	pucker
pruceed	proceed	prupel	propel	Pucific	Pacific
prucession	procession	prupensity	propensity	puck	
pruclaim	proclaim	prupitious	propitious	puckar	pucker
pruclame	proclaim	pruportion	proportion	pucker	
prucure	procure	prupose	propose	puckir	pucker
prudant	prudent	prupoze	propose	puckor	pucker
prudence		pruprietor	proprietor	puckur	pucker
prudent		prupriety	propriety	pucor	pucker
prudigious	prodigious	prupulsion	propulsion	pucur	pucker
prudint	prudent	prusede	proceed	pudal	poodle
prudont	prudent	pruseed	proceed	pudal	puddle
pruduce	produce	prutect	protect	puddal	puddle
prudunt	prudent	prutekt	protect	puddel	puddle
pruduse	produce	prutest	protest	puddil	puddle
prufain	profane	pruve	prove	pudding	
prufane	profane	pruvide	provide	puddle	
prufe	proof	pruvision	provision	puddol	puddle
prufeshion	profession	pruvoke	provoke	puddul	puddle
prufesor	professor	pry		pudel	poodle
prufess	profess	pryde	pride	pudel	puddle
prufession	profession	pryor	prior	pudestrian	pedestrian
prufessor	professor	psalm		pudil	poodle
prufewse	profuse	psicology	psychology	pudil	puddle
pruficient	proficient	psichology	psychology	puding	pudding
prufishent	proficient	psikology	psychology	pudle	poodle

pudle	puddle	pullute	pollute	pumul	pommel
pudol	poodle	pully	pulley	pumul	pummel
pudol	puddle	pulp		pun	
pudul	poodle	pulpet	pulpit	punch	
pudul	puddle	pulpit		punck	punk
pue	pew	pulsait	pulsate	punctchual	punctual
pueblo		pulsate		punctchuate	punctuate
Puerto Rico		pulse		punctchur	puncture
pueter	pewter	pulute	pollute	punctual	
puff		pulvarize	pulverize	punctuate	
puffy		pulverize		punctuation	
pufy	puffy	pulvirize	pulverize	puncture	
pugnacious		pulvorize	pulverize	puney	puny
pugnashus	pugnacious	pulvurize	pulverize	pungent	
pugoda	pagoda	puly	pulley	pungint	pungent
pujamas	pajamas	puma		puninsula	peninsula
puk	puck	pumal	pommel	punish	
pukar	pucker	pumal	pummel	punishable	
puker	pucker	pumel	pommel	punishment	
pukir	pucker	pumel	pummel	punjant	pungent
pukor	pucker	pumice		punjent	pungent
pukur	pucker	pumil	pommel	punjint	pungent
pule	pool	pumil	pummel	punjont	pungent
pulece	police	pumis	pumice	punjunt	pungent
puleece	police	pummal	pommel	punk	
puleese	police	pummal	pummel	punkchual	punctual
pulese	police	pummel		punkchuate	punctuate
pulet	pullet	pummel	pommel	punkchur	puncture
puley	pulley	pummil	pommel	punktchuate	punctuate
pulice	police	pummil	pummel	punktchur	puncture
pulise	police	pummol	pommel	punktual	punctual
pulit	pullet	pummol	pummel	punktuate	punctuate
pulite	polite	pummul	pommel	punkture	puncture
pulitical	political	pummul	pummel	punninsula	peninsula
pull		pumol	pommel	punt	
pullet		pumol	pummel	puny	
pulley		pump		pup	
pullit	pullet	pumpkin		pupal	pupil

pupel	pupil	purfect	perfect	purpol	purple
pupet	puppet	purfict	perfect	purport	
pupil		purforate	perforate	purpose	
pupit	puppet	purform	perform	purposeful	
pupol	pupil	purfume	perfume	purposely	
puppet		purge		purpul	purple
puppit	puppet	purhaps	perhaps	purpus	purpose
puppy		puriah	pariah	purr	
pupul	pupil	purify		purse	
pupy	puppy	puritan		pursecute	persecute
pur	per	purity		purseption	perception
pur	poor	purk	perk	purseve	perceive
purade	parade	purkolate	percolate	pursevere	persevere
purafy	purify	purkussion	percussion	pursimmon	persimmon
puraid	parade	purl	pearl	pursist	persist
puraty	purity	purloin		purson	person
puray	purée	purloyn	purloin	purspective	perspective
purce	purse	purmanent	permanent	purspire	perspire
purceive	perceive	purmeate	permeate	pursuade	persuade
purception	perception	purmission	permission	pursue	
purch	perch	purmit	permit	pursuer	
purchase		purnicious	pernicious	pursuit	
purchaser		purochial	parochial	pursute	pursuit
purchess	purchase	purofy	purify	purswade	persuade
purchis	purchase	puroty	purity	purt	pert
purchos	purchase	purpal	purple	purtain	pertain
purchus	purchase	purpas	purpose	purtane	pertain
purcieve	perceive	purpel	purple	purticular	particular
purcolate	percolate	purpendicular	perpendicular	purtikular	particular
purcussion	percussion	purpess	purpose	purtinent	pertinent
pure		purpetrate	perpetrate	purturb	perturb
purée		purpetuate	perpetuate	purufy	purify
purefy	purify	purpil	purple	puruse	peruse
purely		purpis	purpose	puruty	purity
purennial	perennial	purple		puruze	peruse
purental	parental	purplesh	purplish	purvade	pervade
purenthesis	parenthesis	purplex	perplex	purvaid	pervade
purety	purity	purplish		purverse	perverse

purvert	pervert	puthetic	pathetic	puzel	puzzle
pus		putir	pewter	puzess	possess
pusess	possess	putir	putter	puzil	puzzle
push		putishon	petition	puzition	position
pushcart		putor	pewter	puzle	puzzle
pushkart	pushcart	putor	putter	puzol	puzzle
Pusific	Pacific	putrid		puzul	puzzle
pusition	position	putrol	patrol	puzzal	puzzle
pussess	possess	putroleum	petroleum	puzzel	puzzle
pussey	pussy	puttar	putter	puzzil	puzzle
pussy		putter		puzzle	
pusy	pussy	puttey	putty	puzzol	puzzle
put		puttir	putter	puzzul	puzzle
putar	pewter	puttor	putter	pwablo	pueblo
putar	putter	puttur	putter	pwayblo	pueblo
putato	potato	putty		pweblo	pueblo
puteat	petite	putunia	petunia	Pwerto Rico	Puerto Rico
puteet	petite	putur	pewter	py	pie
putential	potential	putur	putter	pyer	pyre
puter	pewter	puty	putty	pyety	piety
puter	putter	puvilion	pavilion	pygmy	
puternal	paternal	puvillion	pavilion	pyramid	
putete	petite	puzal	puzzle	pyre	
putewnia	petunia			python	

Q

quack		Quaiker	Quaker	Quakir	Quaker
quadrewped	quadruped	quail		Quakor	Quaker
quadrewplet	quadruplet	quaint		Quakur	Quaker
quadrooped	quadruped	quaiver	quaver	qualafy	qualify
quadrooplet	quadruplet	quak	quack	qualaty	quality
quadruped		quak	quake	quale	quail
quadruplet		Quakar	Quaker	qualefy	qualify
quaff		quake		qualety	quality
quaik	quake	Quaker		qualification	

qualified		quartur	quarter	quicksand	
qualify		quartz		quicksilver	
quality		quarul	quarrel	quick-witted	
qualm		quaruntine	quarantine	quiet	
qualofy	qualify	quary	quarry	quietness	
qualoty	quality	quavar	quaver	quik	quick
qualufy	qualify	quaver		quill	
qualuty	quality	quavir	quaver	quilt	
quam	qualm	quavor	quaver	quinine	
quantaty	quantity	quavur	quaver	quintet	
quantety	quantity	quay		quiot	quiet
quantity		quean	queen	quit	
quantoty	quantity	quear	queer	quite	
quantuty	quantity	queary	query	quiter	quitter
quaral	quarrel	quee	quay	quitter	
quarantine		queen		quiut	quiet
quarentine	quarantine	queer		quivar	quiver
quaril	quarrel	queery	query	quiver	
quarintine	quarantine	quell		quivir	quiver
quarol	quarrel	quench		quivor	quiver
quarontine	quarantine	quene	queen	quivur	quiver
quarral	quarrel	quere	queer	quiz	
quarrel		querey	query	quoat	quote
quarrelsome		query		quoata	quota
quarril	quarrel	queschon	question	quodruped	quadruped
quarrol	quarrel	quest		quodruplet	quadruplet
quarrul	quarrel	questchon	question	quoit	
quarry		question		quolify	qualify
quart		questionable		quolity	quality
quartar	quarter	queue		quom	qualm
quarter		quew	queue	quontity	quantity
quarterback		quey	quay	quorantine	quarantine
quarterly		quiat	quiet	quorrel	quarrel
quartermaster		quick		quorry	quarry
quartet		quicken		quort	quart
quartir	quarter	quickly		quortar	quarter
quartor	quarter	quickness		quorter	quarter
quarts	quartz	quickniss	quickness	quortir	quarter

quortor	quarter	quortz	quartz	quote	quote
quorts	quartz	quoshent	quotient	quotient	quotient
quortur	quarter	quota	quota	quoyt	quoit
		quotation	quotation		

R

rabal	rabble	rack	rack	radocal	radical
rabbal	rabble	racket	racket	raducal	radical
rabbel	rabble	rackewn	raccoon	raft	raft
rabbi	rabbi	rackit	racket	raftar	rafter
rabbil	rabble	rackoon	raccoon	rafter	rafter
rabbit	rabbit	rackune	raccoon	raftir	rafter
rabble	rabble	racoon	raccoon	raftor	rafter
rabbol	rabble	racune	raccoon	raftur	rafter
rabbul	rabble	radacal	radical	rag	rag
rabease	rabies	radar	radar	rage	rage
rabeaze	rabies	rade	raid	raged	ragged
rabees	rabies	redeate	radiate	ragged	ragged
rabeez	rabies	radecal	radical	raggid	ragged
rabel	rabble	radei	radii	ragid	ragged
rabese	rabies	radeo	radio	raibies	rabies
rabeze	rabies	radeum	radium	raice	race
rabi	rabbi	radeus	radius	raid	raid
rabies	rabies	radiance	radiance	raidar	radar
rabil	rabble	radiant	radiant	raidiate	radiate
rabit	rabbit	radiate	radiate	raidium	radium
rable	rabble	radiator	radiator	raige	rage
rabol	rabble	radical	radical	raik	rake
rabul	rabble	radii	radii	rail	rail
raccewn	raccoon	radio	radio	railing	railing
raccoon	raccoon	radioactive	radioactive	railroad	railroad
raccune	raccoon	radioactivity	radioactivity	railrode	railroad
race	race	radish	radish	railway	railway
racewn	raccoon	radium	radium	raiment	raiment
racial	racial	radius	radius	rain	rain

rain	reign	**rakune**	raccoon	range	
rain	rein	**rale**	rail	**rangel**	wrangle
rainbow		rally		ranger	
raincoat		**raly**	rally	**rangil**	wrangle
raincote	raincoat	ram		**rangle**	wrangle
raindear	reindeer	**rambal**	ramble	**rangol**	wrangle
raindeer	reindeer	**rambel**	ramble	**rangul**	wrangle
raindere	reindeer	**rambil**	ramble	rank	
raindrop		ramble		**rankal**	rankle
rainfall		**rambleing**	rambling	**rankel**	rankle
rainge	range	rambling		**rankil**	rankle
rainkoat	raincoat	**rambol**	ramble	rankle	
rainy		**rambul**	ramble	**rankol**	rankle
raipier	rapier	**rament**	raiment	**rankul**	rankle
rair	rare	ramp		ransack	
raisan	raisin	rampart		**ransak**	ransack
raise		ramrod		**ransam**	ransom
raise	raze	ran		**ransem**	ransom
raisen	raisin	ranch		**ransim**	ransom
raisin		**ranck**	rank	ransom	
raison	raisin	**ranckle**	rankle	**ransum**	ransom
raisor	razor	**rancle**	rankle	rap	
raisun	raisin	**randaivous**	rendezvous	**rap**	wrap
rait	rate	**randam**	random	**rapchur**	rapture
raith	wraith	**randavous**	rendezvous	**repeur**	rapier
raive	rave	**randayvous**	rendezvous	rapid	
raiven	raven	**randem**	random	rapidity	
raize	raise	**randim**	random	rapidly	
raize	raze	random		rapier	
raizin	raisin	**randum**	random	rapt	
raizor	razor	**rane**	rain	**raptchur**	rapture
rajah		**rane**	reign	rapture	
rak	rack	**rane**	rein	**raptureus**	rapturous
rake		**ranedear**	reindeer	rapturous	
raket	racket	**ranedeer**	reindeer	rare	
rakewn	raccoon	**ranedere**	reindeer	rarely	
rakit	racket	rang		**rarety**	rarity
rakoon	raccoon	**rangal**	wrangle	rarity	

rasberry	raspberry	ratil	rattle	ravol	ravel
rascal		ratio		ravon	raven
rasckal	rascal	ration		ravonous	ravenous
rascol	rascal	rational		ravul	ravel
rascul	rascal	ratle	rattle	ravun	raven
rase	race	ratofy	ratify	ravunous	ravenous
rase	raise	ratol	rattle	raw	
rase	raze	rattal	rattle	rawcous	raucous
rash		rattel	rattle	rawcus	raucous
rashal	racial	rattil	rattle	rawhide	
rashio	ratio	rattle		rawkous	raucous
rashon	ration	rattlesnake		rawkus	raucous
rashonal	rational	rattol	rattle	rawt	wrought
rasin	raisin	rattul	rattle	ray	
raskal	rascal	ratufy	ratify	raybies	rabies
raskel	rascal	ratul	rattle	raydar	radar
raskil	rascal	raucous		raydiate	radiate
raskol	rascal	raucus	raucous	raydium	radium
raskul	rascal	raukous	raucous	rayment	raiment
rasor	razor	raukus	raucous	rayon	
rasp		ravage		rays	raise
raspberry		raval	ravel	rayth	wraith
rat		ravan	raven	rayze	raise
ratafy	ratify	ravanous	ravenous	rayze	raze
ratal	rattle	rave		razar	razor
rate		ravean	ravine	razberry	raspberry
ratefy	ratify	raveen	ravine	raze	
ratel	rattle	ravel		raze	raise
rateo	ratio	raven		razer	razor
rath	wrath	ravene	ravine	razin	raisin
rathar	rather	ravenous		razir	razor
rathe	wraith	ravige	ravage	razor	
rather		ravil	ravel	razur	razor
rathir	rather	ravin	raven	razz	
rathor	rather	ravine		reach	
rathur	rather	ravinous	ravenous	reackt	react
ratification		ravish		react	
ratify		ravishing		reaction	

read		reath	wreath	receptacle	
read	reed	reazon	reason	reception	
readaly	readily	rebal	rebel	receptive	
readely	readily	rebel		recepy	recipe
reader		rebelion	rebellion	recess	
readily		rebelious	rebellious	receve	receive
readiness		rebellion		rech	wretch
reading		rebellious		reche	reach
readoly	readily	rebewk	rebuke	recieve	receive
readuly	readily	rebil	rebel	recint	recent
ready		rebirth		recipe	
reaf	reef	rebol	rebel	recipient	
reagal	regal	reborn		recipy	recipe
reagent		rebound		recital	
reagent	regent	rebuff		recitation	
reagion	region	rebuild		recite	
reak	reek	rebuke		recitel	recital
reak	wreak	rebul	rebel	reck	wreck
reakt	react	rec	wreck	reckagnize	recognize
real		recagnize	recognize	reckan	reckon
real	reel	recall		reckegnize	recognize
reality		recampense	recompense	recken	reckon
realization		recancile	reconcile	reckignize	recognize
realize		recannoiter	reconnoiter	reckin	reckon
really		recapture		reckless	
realm		recard	record	recklewse	recluse
realy	really	recead	recede	reckliss	reckless
ream		receave	receive	reckloose	recluse
reap		recede		reckluse	recluse
reaper		receed	recede	reckognize	recognize
reappear		receeve	receive	reckollect	recollect
rear		receipt		reckommend	recommend
rearrange		receit	receipt	reckompense	recompense
reason		receive		reckon	
reasonable		receiver		reckoncile	reconcile
reasonably		recent		reckoning	
reasoning		recently		reckonnoiter	reconnoiter
reassure		recepe	recipe	reckord	record

reckreation	recreation	recownt	recount	redemption	
recktangle	rectangle	recreation		redemtion	redemption
recktor	rector	recrewt	recruit	reden	redden
reckugnize	recognize	recriation	recreation	redewce	reduce
reckun	reckon	recroot	recruit	redewse	reduce
reckwisite	requisite	recruit		redily	readily
reclaim		recrute	recruit	rediness	readiness
reclaimation	reclamation	rectafy	rectify	rediscover	
reclamation		rectangle		redish	reddish
reclame	reclaim	rectangular		redooce	reduce
reclewse	recluse	rectar	rector	redoose	reduce
recline		rectefy	rectify	redouble	
recloose	recluse	recter	rector	redoubtable	
recluce	recluse	rectify		redoutable	redoubtable
recluse		rectir	rector	redowtable	redoubtable
recoarse	recourse	rectofy	rectify	redress	
recognition		rector		reduce	
recognize		rectufy	rectify	reducktion	reduction
recoil		rectur	rector	reduction	
recolect	recollect	recugnize	recognize	reduktion	reduction
recollect		recumpense	recompense	reduse	reduce
recollection		recuncile	reconcile	redwood	
recomend	recommend	recunnoiter	reconnoiter	redy	ready
recommend		recur		reech	reach
recommendation		recurd	record	reed	
recompense		recuver	recover	reed	read
reconcile		recwest	request	reef	
reconciliation		recwire	require	reegal	regal
reconnoiter		recwisite	requisite	reegent	regent
reconoiter	reconnoiter	recwit	requite	reegion	region
reconstruct		red		reek	
record		redden		reek	wreak
recorder		reddish		reel	
recorse	recourse	rede	read	reel	real
recount		rede	reed	reelect	
recourse		redeam	redeem	reem	ream
recover		redeem		reenforce	
recovery		redeme	redeem	reenter	

reep	reap	**refrakt**	refract	**regin**	region
reer	rear	**refrane**	refrain	**regint**	regent
reeson	reason	refresh		region	
reestablish		refreshing		register	
reeth	wreath	refreshment		registration	
reezon	reason	refrigerate		**regle**	regal
refaree	referee	refrigerator		**regol**	regal
refe	reef	**refrijerate**	refrigerate	regret	
refer		refuge		**regretable**	regrettable
referee		refugee		regretful	
reference		refund		regrettable	
refewge	refuge	**refur**	refer	**regul**	regal
refewse	refuse	**refuree**	referee	regular	
refewt	refute	refusal		regularity	
refewze	refuse	refuse		regularly	
refill		**refusel**	refusal	regulate	
refine		refute		regulation	
refined		**refuze**	refuse	rehearsal	
refinement		**regail**	regale	rehearse	
refinery		regain		**reherse**	rehearse
refir	refer	regal		**rehirse**	rehearse
refiree	referee	regale		**rehurse**	rehearse
refit		regard		reign	
refleckt	reflect	regarding		**reilize**	realize
reflect		regardless		rein	
reflection		**regata**	regatta	**reindear**	reindeer
reflector		regatta		reindeer	
reflekt	reflect	**regeam**	regime	**reindere**	reindeer
reforee	referee	**regeem**	regime	reinforce	
reforest		**regel**	regal	reinforcement	
reforestation		**regeme**	regime	reiterate	
reform		**regement**	regiment	**rejeckt**	reject
reformation		**regen**	region	reject	
reformatory		regent		rejection	
reformer		**regewlar**	regular	**rejekt**	reject
refract		**regil**	regal	**rejent**	regent
refrackt	refract	regime		**rejiment**	regiment
refrain		regiment		**rejister**	register

rejoice		rekter	rector	reletive	relative
rejoin		rektify	rectify	relevance	
rejon	region	rektir	rector	relevancy	
rejoyce	rejoice	rektofy	rectify	relevant	
rek	wreck	rektor	rector	reliable	
rekagnize	recognize	rektufy	rectify	reliance	
rekan	reckon	rektur	rector	relic	
reke	reek	rekugnize	recognize	relief	
reke	wreak	rekun	reckon	relieve	
rekegnize	recognize	rekur	recur	religion	
reken	reckon	rekuver	recover	religious	
rekignize	recognize	rekwest	request	relijon	religion
rekin	reckon	rekwire	require	relik	relic
reklaim	reclaim	rekwisite	requisite	relinckwish	relinquish
reklame	reclaim	rekwit	requite	relinkwish	relinquish
rekless	reckless	relacks	relax	relinquish	
reklewse	recluse	relait	relate	relish	
rekline	recline	relaks	relax	relitive	relative
rekloose	recluse	relapse		relivant	relevant
rekluse	recluse	relate		rellic	relic
rekognize	recognize	relation		rellik	relic
rekoil	recoil	relationship		rellish	relish
rekollect	recollect	relative		relm	realm
rekommend	recommend	relatively		reload	
rekompense	recompense	relavant	relevant	relotive	relative
rekon	reckon	relax		relovant	relevant
rekoncile	reconcile	relaxation		reluctance	
rekonnoiter	reconnoiter	relay		reluctant	
rekord	record	rele	real	reluktant	reluctant
rekount	recount	rele	reel	relutive	relative
rekourse	recourse	releaf	relief	reluvant	relevant
rekover	recover	release		rely	
rekreation	recreation	releef	relief	remady	remedy
rekruit	recruit	releese	release	remain	
rektafy	rectify	relefe	relief	remainder	
rektangle	rectangle	relent		remane	remain
rektar	rector	relentless		remark	
rektefy	rectify	relese	release	remarkable	

remarkably	
reme	ream
remedy	
remember	
remembrance	
remidy	remedy
remind	
reminder	
remit	
remnant	
remnent	remnant
remnint	remnant
remnont	remnant
remnunt	remnant
remoarse	remorse
remoat	remote
remodel	
remody	remedy
remonstrate	
remorse	
remorseless	
remote	
remove	
remudy	remedy
remuve	remove
ren	wren
renagade	renegade
renavate	renovate
rench	wrench
rend	
rendaivous	rendezvous
rendar	render
rendavous	rendezvous
rendayvous	rendezvous
render	
rendezvous	
rendir	render
rendor	render

rendur	render
renegade	
renevate	renovate
renew	
renewal	
renigade	renegade
renivate	renovate
renogade	renegade
renoo	renew
renoun	renown
renounce	
renounse	renounce
renovate	
renown	
renownce	renounce
renowned	
renownse	renounce
rent	
rental	
rentel	rental
rentil	rental
rentol	rental
rentul	rental
renue	renew
renugade	renegade
renuvate	renovate
Reo Grande	Rio Grande
reolize	realize
reopen	
repaid	
repair	
reparation	
repare	repair
repast	
repatition	repetition
repay	
repe	reap
repeal	

repeat	
repeated	
repeatedly	
repeel	repeal
repeet	repeat
repel	
repele	repeal
repent	
repentance	
repentant	
reperation	reparation
repete	repeat
repetition	
repewdiate	repudiate
repewt	repute
repiration	reparation
repitition	repetition
replaca	replica
replace	
replacement	
repleca	replica
replenish	
replica	
reploca	replica
repluca	replica
reply	
repoase	repose
repoaze	repose
reporation	reparation
report	
reporter	
repose	
repotition	repetition
repoze	repose
represent	
representation	
representative	
represhon	repression

repress		requosite	requisite	resess	recess
repression		rere	rear	reseve	receive
reprewf	reproof	resadue	residue	resewm	resume
reprewve	reprove	resal	wrestle	reside	
reprisent	represent	resalute	resolute	residence	
reproach		resan	reason	resident	
reproche	reproach	resanant	resonant	residential	
reproduce		resant	recent	residue	
reproduction		resapy	recipe	resieve	receive
reproof		resarrect	resurrect	resign	
reprove		rescew	rescue	resignation	
reprufe	reproof	rescue		resigned	
repruve	reprove	rescuer		resil	wrestle
reptal	reptile	research		resilute	resolute
reptel	reptile	reseave	receive	resin	
reptil	reptile	resedue	residue	resinant	resonant
reptile		reseeve	receive	resine	resign
reptol	reptile	reseive	receive	resint	recent
reptul	reptile	resel	wrestle	resipient	recipient
republic		reselution	resolution	resipy	recipe
republican		resemblance		resirch	research
repudiate		resemble		resirrect	resurrect
repulse		resen	reason	resirve	reserve
repulsive		resenant	resonant	resist	
repuration	reparation	resent		resistance	
reputable		resent	recent	resistant	
reputation		resentful		resite	recite
repute		resentment		reskew	rescue
reputed		reseptacle	receptacle	reskue	rescue
repution	repetition	reseption	reception	resle	wrestle
requasite	requisite	reseptive	receptive	resoarce	resource
requesite	requisite	resepy	recipe	resoart	resort
request		reserch	research	resodue	residue
require		reserrect	resurrect	resol	wrestle
requirement		reservation		resolute	
requisite		reserve		resolution	
requisition		reserved		resolve	
requite		reservoir		resolved	

reson	reason	restaurant		**retale**	retail
resonant		**resterant**	restaurant	retaliate	
resont	recent	restful		**retana**	retina
resoon	resume	**restirant**	restaurant	**retane**	retain
resopy	recipe	**restle**	wrestle	**retanue**	retinue
resorce	resource	restless		retard	
resorrect	resurrect	**restliss**	restless	retch	
resort		**restoar**	restore	**retch**	wretch
resound		**restorant**	restaurant	**retena**	retina
resource		restoration		**retenue**	retinue
resourceful		restore		**retern**	return
resownd	resound	restrain		**rethe**	wreath
resparation	respiration	restraint		**retier**	retire
respeckt	respect	**restrane**	restrain	retina	
respect		**restrickt**	restrict	retinue	
respectable		restrict		retire	
respectful		restriction		retired	
respecting		**restrikt**	restrict	retirement	
respective		**resturant**	restaurant	retiring	
respectively		**resudue**	residue	**retirn**	return
respekt	respect	**resul**	wrestle	**retoart**	retort
resperation	respiration	result		**retona**	retina
respiration		**resulute**	resolute	**retonue**	retinue
respiratory		resume		retort	
respit	respite	resumption		retrace	
respite		**resumtion**	resumption	**retrackt**	retract
resplendent		**resun**	reason	retract	
responce	response	**resunant**	resonant	**retrakt**	retract
respond		**resunt**	recent	retreat	
response		**resupy**	recipe	**retreave**	retrieve
responsibility		**resurch**	research	**retreet**	retreat
responsible		resurrect		**retreeve**	retrieve
responsive		resurrection		**retreive**	retrieve
resporation	respiration	**resurve**	reserve	**retrete**	retreat
respuration	respiration	retail		**retreve**	retrieve
rest		retailer		retrieve	
rest	wrest	retain		retriever	
restarant	restaurant	retainer		**retuna**	retina

retunue	retinue	revine	ravine	rewf	roof
return		revinue	revenue	rewin	ruin
reulize	realize	revirberate	reverberate	rewl	rule
reumatism	rheumatism	revirie	reverie	rewm	room
reunion		revirse	reverse	rewmatism	rheumatism
reunite		revise		rewmor	rumor
reval	revel	revival		reword	reward
revalation	revelation	revive		rewral	rural
revaly	reveille	revivel	revival	rewse	ruse
revanue	revenue	revize	revise	rewst	roost
revarie	reverie	revoak	revoke	rewstar	rooster
reveal		revoalt	revolt	rewster	rooster
revear	revere	revoke		rewstir	rooster
reveel	reveal	revol	revel	rewstor	rooster
reveer	revere	revolation	revelation	rewstur	rooster
reveille		revolt		rewt	root
revel		revolution		rewt	route
revelation		revolutionary		rewtene	routine
revele	reveal	revolutionize		rewthless	ruthless
revelle	reveille	revolve		rewtine	routine
revelry		revolver		rezadue	residue
revely	reveille	revoly	reveille	rezalute	resolution
revenge		revonue	revenue	rezan	reason
revengeful		revorie	reverie	rezanant	resonant
revenue		revue	review	rezarrect	resurrect
reverberate		revul	revel	rezedue	residue
revere		revulation	revelation	rezelute	resolute
reverence		revuly	reveille	rezemble	resemble
reverend		revunue	revenue	rezen	reason
reverent		revurberate	reverberate	rezenant	resonant
reverie		revurie	reverie	rezent	resent
reverse		revurse	reverse	rezerrect	resurrect
revert		rew	rue	rezerve	reserve
review		reward		rezide	reside
revil	revel	rewbarb	rhubarb	rezidue	residue
revilation	revelation	rewby	ruby	rezilute	resolute
revile		rewd	rude	rezin	reason
revily	reveille	rewdiment	rudiment	rezinant	resonant

rezine	resign	riact	react	ricipient	recipient
rezirrect	resurrect	riagent	reagent	ricite	recite
rezirve	reserve	riality	reality	rickachet	ricochet
rezist	resist	rialize	realize	rickashet	ricochet
rezoart	resort	riat	riot	rickaty	rickety
rezodue	residue	rib		rickechet	ricochet
rezolute	resolute	riban	ribbon	rickeshet	ricochet
rezolve	resolve	ribban	ribbon	rickets	
rezon	reason	ribben	ribbon	rickety	
rezonant	resonant	ribbin	ribbon	rickichet	ricochet
rezorrect	resurrect	ribbon		rickishet	ricochet
rezort	resort	ribbun	ribbon	rickits	rickets
rezound	resound	ribel	rebel	rickity	rickety
rezownd	resound	ribewk	rebuke	rickochet	ricochet
rezudue	residue	ribin	ribbon	rickoshet	ricochet
rezult	result	ribon	ribbon	rickoty	rickety
rezulute	resolute	ribuff	rebuff	rickshaw	
rezun	reason	ribuke	rebuke	rickuchet	ricochet
rezunant	resonant	ribun	ribbon	rickushet	ricochet
rezurrect	resurrect	ricachet	ricochet	rickuty	rickety
rezurve	reserve	ricashet	ricochet	riclaim	reclaim
rheumatism		rice		riclame	reclaim
rhinoceros		ricead	recede	ricline	recline
rhinoseros	rhinoceros	ricede	recede	ricochet	
Rhode Island		riceed	recede	ricoil	recoil
rhododendron		riceive	receive	ricord	record
rhubarb		riceptacle	receptacle	ricoshet	ricochet
rhyme		riception	reception	ricount	recount
rhytham	rhythm	riceptive	receptive	ricover	recover
rhythem	rhythm	ricess	recess	ricruit	recruit
rhythim	rhythm	rich		ricuchet	ricochet
rhythm		riches		ricur	recur
rhythmic		richez	riches	ricushet	ricochet
rhythmical		richis	riches	ricuver	recover
rhythom	rhythm	richiz	riches	ricwest	request
rhythum	rhythm	richness		ricwire	require
ri	rye	richniss	richness	ricwit	requite
ri	wry	richual	ritual	rid	

ridacule	ridicule	rifel	rifle	rigeam	regime
ridal	riddle	rifer	refer	rigeem	regime
riddal	riddle	rifewse	refuse	rigel	wriggle
riddel	riddle	rifewt	refute	rigeme	regime
riddil	riddle	rifewze	refuse	riger	rigor
riddle		rifil	rifle	riggal	wriggle
riddol	riddle	rifine	refine	riggel	wriggle
riddul	riddle	rifir	refer	riggil	wriggle
ride		rifle		rigging	
rideam	redeem	rifleckt	reflect	riggle	wriggle
ridecule	ridicule	riflect	reflect	riggol	wriggle
rideem	redeem	riflekt	reflect	riggul	wriggle
ridel	riddle	rifol	rifle	right	
rideme	redeem	riform	reform	rightchus	righteous
rider		rifrackt	refract	righteous	
ridewce	reduce	rifract	refract	righteousness	
ridewse	reduce	rifrain	refrain	rightful	
ridge		rifrakt	refract	rightfully	
ridickulous	ridiculous	rifrane	refrain	rightious	righteous
ridicule		rifresh	refresh	rightius	righteous
ridiculous		rifrigerate	refrigerate	rightly	
ridikulous	ridiculous	rifrijerate	refrigerate	rigid	
ridil	riddle	rift		rigil	wriggle
ridle	riddle	riful	rifle	rigime	regime
ridocule	ridicule	rifund	refund	riging	rigging
ridol	riddle	rifur	refer	rigir	rigor
ridooce	reduce	rifuse	refuse	rigle	wriggle
ridoose	reduce	rifute	refute	rigol	wriggle
ridoubtable	redoubtable	rifuze	refuse	rigor	
ridoutable	redoubtable	rig		rigorous	
ridowtable	redoubtable	rigail	regale	rigret	regret
ridress	redress	rigal	wriggle	rigul	wriggle
riduce	reduce	rigale	regale	rigur	rigor
riducule	ridicule	rigar	rigor	rihearse	rehearse
ridul	riddle	rigard	regard	rijeckt	reject
riduse	reduce	rigata	regatta	riject	reject
riet	riot	rigatta	regatta	rijekt	reject
rifal	rifle	rige	ridge	rijid	rigid

rijoice	rejoice	rilation	relation	rind	
rijoyce	rejoice	rilax	relax	rinew	renew
rikachet	ricochet	rilay	relay	ring	
rikashet	ricochet	rileaf	relief	ring	wring
rikaty	rickety	rilease	release	ringleader	
rikechet	ricochet	rileef	relief	ringleder	ringleader
rikeshet	ricochet	rileese	release	ringleeder	ringleader
rikets	rickets	rilefe	relief	ringlet	
rikety	rickety	rilent	relent	ringlit	ringlet
rikichet	ricochet	rilese	release	ringside	
rikishet	ricochet	riliable	reliable	rink	
rikits	rickets	riliance	reliance	rinkal	wrinkle
rikity	rickety	rilief	relief	rinkel	wrinkle
riklaim	reclaim	riligion	religion	rinkil	wrinkle
riklame	reclaim	rilijon	religion	rinkle	wrinkle
rikline	recline	rilinckwish	relinquish	rinkol	wrinkle
rikochet	ricochet	rilinkwish	relinquish	rinkul	wrinkle
rikoil	recoil	rilinquish	relinquish	rinoceros	rhinoceros
rikord	record	riluctant	reluctant	rinoo	renew
rikoshet	ricochet	riluktant	reluctant	rinoseros	rhinoceros
rikoty	rickety	rily	rely	rinoun	renown
rikount	recount	rim		rinounce	renounce
rikover	recover	rimain	remain	rinounse	renounce
rikruit	recruit	rimane	remain	rinown	renown
rikshaw	rickshaw	rimark	remark	rinownce	renounce
rikuchet	ricochet	rime	rhyme	rinownse	renounce
rikur	recur	rimember	remember	rinse	
rikushet	ricochet	rimind	remind	rinue	renew
rikuty	rickety	rimit	remit	Rio Grande	
rikuver	recover	rimoarse	remorse	riot	
rikwest	request	rimoat	remote	riotous	
rikwire	require	rimonstrate	remonstrate	rip	
rikwit	requite	rimorse	remorse	ripair	repair
rilacks	relax	rimote	remote	ripal	ripple
rilait	relate	rimove	remove	ripare	repair
rilaks	relax	rimuve	remove	ripast	repast
rilapse	relapse	rince	rinse	ripe	
rilate	relate	rinck	rink	ripeal	repeal

ripeat	repeat	ripudiate	repudiate	risource	resource
ripeel	repeal	ripul	ripple	risownd	resound
ripeet	repeat	ripulse	repulse	rispeckt	respect
ripel	repel	ripulsive	repulsive	rispect	respect
ripel	ripple	ripute	repute	rispekt	respect
ripele	repeal	riquest	request	risplendent	resplendent
ripen		riquire	require	rispond	respond
ripent	repent	riquite	requite	rist	wrist
ripete	repeat	risck	risk	ristoar	restore
ripewdiate	repudiate	rise		ristore	restore
ripewt	repute	rise	rice	ristrain	restrain
riple	ripple	risearch	research	ristrane	restrain
riplenish	replenish	riseing	rising	ristrickt	restrict
riply	reply	risemble	resemble	ristrict	restrict
ripoase	repose	risent	resent	ristrikt	restrict
ripoaze	repose	riseptacle	receptacle	risult	result
ripol	ripple	riseption	reception	risurch	research
riport	report	riseptive	receptive	risurve	reserve
ripose	repose	riserch	research	rit	writ
ripoze	repose	riserve	reserve	ritain	retain
rippal	ripple	risess	recess	ritaliate	retaliate
rippel	ripple	riside	reside	ritane	retain
rippil	ripple	risign	resign	ritard	retard
ripple		risine	resign	ritchual	ritual
rippol	ripple	rising		rite	
rippul	ripple	risipient	recipient	rite	right
ripreshon	repression	risirch	research	rite	write
ripress	repress	risirve	reserve	ritern	return
ripression	repression	risist	resist	ritewal	ritual
riprewf	reproof	risite	recite	ritham	rhythm
reprewve	reprove	risk		rithe	writhe
riproach	reproach	risky		rithem	rhythm
riproche	reproach	risoarce	resource	rithim	rhythm
riproof	reproof	risoart	resort	rithm	rhythm
riprove	reprove	risolve	resolve	rithom	rhythm
riprufe	reproof	risorce	resource	rithum	rhythm
ripruve	reprove	risort	resort	ritier	retire
ripublic	republic	risound	resound	ritire	retire

ritirn	return	rivine	ravine	rizownd	resound
ritoart	retort	rivir	river	rizult	result
ritort	retort	rivirberate	reverberate	rizume	resume
ritrackt	retract	rivirse	reverse	rizurve	reserve
ritract	retreat	rivise	revise	ro	roe
ritrakt	retract	rivit	rivet	roab	robe
ritreat	retreat	rivive	revive	roabust	robust
ritreave	retrieve	rivize	revise	roach	
ritreet	retreat	rivoak	revoke	road	
ritreeve	retrieve	rivoalt	revolt	road	rode
ritreive	retrieve	rivoke	revoke	roadent	rodent
ritrete	retreat	rivol	rival	roadeo	rodeo
ritreve	retrieve	rivolt	revolt	Road Island	Rhode Island
ritrieve	retrieve	rivolve	revolve	roadside	
ritual		rivor	river	roadway	
riturn	return	rivue	review	roag	rogue
riut	riot	rivul	rival	roal	role
rival		rivulet		roal	roll
rivalry		rivur	river	roam	
rivar	river	rivurberate	reverberate	Roam	Rome
riveal	reveal	rivurse	reverse	Roaman	Roman
rivear	revere	riward	reward	roamance	romance
riveel	reveal	riword	reward	roamanse	romance
riveer	revere	rize	rise	roap	rope
rivel	rival	rizemble	resemble	roar	
rivele	reveal	rizent	resent	roar	raw
rivenge	revenge	rizerve	reserve	roasary	rosary
river		rizewm	resume	roase	rose
riverberate	reverberate	rizide	reside	roast	
rivere	revere	rizine	resign	roat	rote
riverse	reverse	rizirve	reserve	roatate	rotate
riverside		rizist	resist	roatund	rotund
rivet		rizoart	resort	roave	rove
rivewlet	rivulet	rizolve	resolve	roazary	rosary
riview	review	rizoom	resume	roaze	rose
rivil	rival	rizort	resort	rob	
rivile	revile	rizound	resound	roban	robin

robber		roguish		rood	rude
robbery		rok	rock	roodiment	rudiment
robe		roket	rocket	roof	
roben	robin	rokit	rocket	rooin	ruin
rober	robber	role		rool	rule
robin		role	roll	room	
robon	robin	rolicking	rollicking	roomait	roommate
robor	robber	roliking	rollicking	roomate	roommate
robun	robin	roll		roomatism	rheumatism
robust		roll	role	roominess	
roche	roach	roller		roommait	roommate
rock		rollicking		roommate	
rockar	rocker	rolliking	rollicking	roomor	rumor
rocker		Roman		roomy	
rocket		romance		roomyness	roominess
rockit	rocket	romanse	romance	rooral	rural
rocky		romantic		roose	ruse
rod		Rome		roost	
rodadendron	rhododendron	rome	roam	roostar	rooster
rodant	rodent	Romen	Roman	rooster	
rodao	rodeo	Romin	Roman	roostir	rooster
rodayo	rodeo	Romon	Roman	roostor	rooster
rode		romp		roostur	rooster
rode	road	rompars	rompers	root	
rodedendron	rhododendron	romparz	rompers	root	route
Rode Island	Rhode Island	rompers		rootene	routine
rodent		romperz	rompers	roothless	ruthless
rodeo		rompirs	rompers	rootine	routine
rodidendron	rhododendron	rompirz	rompers	rope	
rodint	rodent	rompors	rompers	rore	raw
rodio	rodeo	romporz	rompers	rore	roar
rododendron	rhododendron	rompurs	rompers	rosary	
rodont	rodent	rompurz	rompers	rose	
rodudendron	rhododendron	Romun	Roman	rosery	rosary
rodunt	rodent	rong	wrong	rosey	rosy
rogue		roobarb	rhubarb	rosiry	rosary
roguesh	roguish	rooby	ruby	rosory	rosary

roste	roast	rowdy		rudament	rudiment
rosury	rosary	rownd	round	rudar	rudder
rosy		rowse	rouse	ruddar	rudder
rot		rowt	rout	rudder	
rotait	rotate	rowt	route	ruddir	rudder
rotan	rotten	rowze	rouse	ruddor	rudder
rotar	rotor	royal		ruddur	rudder
rotate		royally		ruddy	
rotation		royalty		rude	
rote		royaly	royally	rudement	rudiment
roten	rotten	royel	royal	rudeness	
roter	rotor	royil	royal	rudeniss	rudeness
rotir	rotor	royol	royal	ruder	rudder
rotor		royul	royal	rudiment	
rotten		rozary	rosary	rudimentary	
rotund		roze	rose	rudir	rudder
rotur	rotor	rozery	rosary	rudoment	rudiment
roudy	rowdy	roziry	rosary	rudor	rudder
rouge		rozory	rosary	rudument	rudiment
rough		rozury	rosary	rudur	rudder
roughly		ruan	ruin	rudy	ruddy
round		rub		rue	
roundabout		rubar	rubber	rueful	
roundish		rubarb	rhubarb	ruematism	rheumatism
rouse		rubbar	rubber	ruen	ruin
rout		rubber		ruf	rough
route		rubber band		rufal	ruffle
routean	routine	rubbir	rubber	rufe	roof
routeen	routine	rubbish		rufean	ruffian
routene	routine	rubbor	rubber	rufel	ruffle
routine		rubbur	rubber	ruff	
rouze	rouse	ruber	rubber	ruffal	ruffle
rove		rubir	rubber	ruffean	ruffian
rover		rubish	rubbish	ruffel	ruffle
rovine	ravine	rubor	rubber	ruffian	
row		rubur	rubber	ruffil	ruffle
row	roe	ruby		ruffle	

ruffol	ruffle	rumpel	rumple	ruset	russet
rufful	ruffle	rumpess	rumpus	rush	
rufian	ruffian	rumpil	rumple	Rusha	Russia
rufil	ruffle	rumpis	rumpus	rusil	rustle
rufle	ruffle	rumple		rusit	russet
rufol	ruffle	rumpol	rumple	rusol	rustle
ruful	ruffle	rumpos	rumpus	russal	rustle
rug		rumpul	rumple	russel	rustle
ruge	rouge	rumpus		russet	
ruged	rugged	rumur	rumor	Russia	
rugged		run		Russian	
ruggid	rugged	runar	runner	russil	rustle
rugid	rugged	runaway		russit	russet
ruin		run-down		russol	rustle
ruinous		runer	runner	russul	rustle
ruinus	ruinous	rung		rust	
rule		rung	wrung	rustic	
ruler		runing	running	rustik	rustic
rum		runir	runner	rustle	
rumage	rummage	runnar	runner	rusty	
rumar	rumor	runner		rusul	rustle
rumbal	rumble	running		rut	
rumbel	rumble	runt		rute	root
rumbil	rumble	runway		rutene	routine
rumble		ruon	ruin	ruthless	
rumbol	rumble	rupchur	rupture	ruthliss	ruthless
rumbul	rumble	ruptchur	rupture	rutine	routine
rume	room	rupture		ruvine	ravine
rumer	rumor	rural		ry	wry
rumige	rummage	rurel	rural	rye	
rumir	rumor	ruril	rural	ryme	rhyme
rummage		rurol	rural	rytham	rhythm
rummige	rummage	rurul	rural	rythem	rhythm
rumor		rusal	rustle	rythim	rhythm
rump		ruse		rythm	rhythm
rumpal	rumple	rusel	rustle	rythom	rhythm
rumpas	rumpus			rythum	rhythm

S

sa	say	sacrafice	sacrifice	sadul	saddle
sabal	sable	sacrament		sadun	sadden
sabar	saber	sacred		safe	
Sabath	Sabbath	sacrefice	sacrifice	safeguard	
Sabbath		sacrement	sacrament	safekeeping	
Sabbeth	Sabbath	sacrid	sacred	safety	
Sabbith	Sabbath	sacrifice		saffice	suffice
Sabboth	Sabbath	sacriment	sacrament	saffire	sapphire
Sabbuth	Sabbath	sacrofice	sacrifice	saffran	saffron
sabel	sable	sacroment	sacrament	saffren	saffron
saber		sacrufice	sacrifice	saffrin	saffron
Sabeth	Sabbath	sacrument	sacrament	saffron	
sabil	sable	sacsophone	saxophone	saffrun	saffron
sabir	saber	sad		safice	suffice
Sabith	Sabbath	sadal	saddle	safire	sapphire
sable		sadan	sadden	safran	saffron
sabol	sable	saddal	saddle	safren	saffron
sabor	saber	saddan	sadden	safrin	saffron
Saboth	Sabbath	saddel	saddle	safron	saffron
sabul	sable	sadden		safrun	saffron
sabur	saber	saddil	saddle	sag	
Sabuth	Sabbath	saddin	sadden	saga	
succeed	succeed	saddle		sagacious	
saccess	success	saddol	saddle	sagacity	
saccessive	successive	saddon	sadden	sagashus	sagacious
saccum	succumb	saddul	saddle	sagasity	sagacity
sachal	satchel	saddun	sadden	sage	
sachel	satchel	sadel	saddle	saggest	suggest
sachil	satchel	saden	sadden	sahm	psalm
sachol	satchel	sadil	saddle	saiber	saber
sachul	satchel	sadin	sadden	saible	sable
sachurate	saturate	sadle	saddle	saicred	sacred
sack		sadness		said	
sackrament	sacrament	sadniss	sadness	saif	safe
sackrifice	sacrifice	sadol	saddle	saige	sage
sacksophone	saxophone	sadon	sadden	saik	sake

sail		salewtary	salutary	sampel	sample
sail	sale	salicit	solicit	sampil	sample
sailboat		salid	salad	sample	
sailer	sailor	salimander	salamander	sampol	sample
saim	same	saliry	salary	sampul	sample
sain	sane	saliva		samun	salmon
saint		salivary		sanatary	sanitary
saintly		sallow		sanaty	sanity
Saitan	Satan	sally		sancktion	sanction
saive	save	salm	psalm	sancshon	sanction
saivor	savor	salmon		sanctaty	sanctity
saivyor	savior	salod	salad	sanctchuary	sanctuary
sak	sack	salomander	salamander	sanctety	sanctity
sake		saloon		sanction	
sakrafice	sacrifice	saloot	salute	sanctity	
sakrament	sacrament	salory	salary	sanctoty	sanctity
sakred	sacred	salow	sallow	sanctuary	
sakrefice	sacrifice	salt		sanctuty	sanctity
sakrement	sacrament	salty		sand	
sakrid	sacred	salud	salad	sandal	
sakrifice	sacrifice	salumander	salamander	sandel	sandal
sakriment	sacrament	salune	saloon	sandil	sandal
sakrofice	sacrifice	salury	salary	sandle	sandal
sakroment	sacrament	salutary		sandol	sandal
sakrufice	sacrifice	salutation		sandpaper	
sakrument	sacrament	salute		sandstorm	
saksophone	saxophone	salution	solution	sandul	sandal
salad		salvage		sandwich	
salamander		salvation		sandwitch	sandwich
salary		salve		sandy	
sale		salvige	salvage	sane	
sale	sail	saly	sally	sanetary	sanitary
saled	salad	saman	salmon	sanety	sanity
salemander	salamander	same		sang	
salery	salary	samen	salmon	sanguine	
salesman		samin	salmon	sangwin	sanguine
salewn	saloon	samon	salmon	sanitarium	
salewt	salute	sampal	sample	sanitary	

sanitation	
sanity	
sank	
sankchuary	sanctuary
sankshon	sanction
sanktion	sanction
sanktity	sanctity
sanktuary	sanctuary
sanotary	sanitary
sanoty	sanity
Santa Claus	
sanutary	sanitary
sanuty	sanity
sap	
saperior	superior
saperlative	superlative
saphire	sapphire
saplant	supplant
sapling	
saply	supply
saport	support
sapose	suppose
sapphire	
sapplant	supplant
sapply	supply
sapport	support
sappose	suppose
sappress	suppress
saprano	soprano
sapreme	supreme
sapress	suppress
sarcasm	
sarcastic	
sarcazm	sarcasm
sardean	sardine
sardeen	sardine
sardene	sardine
sardine	

sarender	surrender
sarene	serene
sargeant	sergeant
sargent	sergeant
sargint	sergeant
sarjent	sergeant
sarkasm	sarcasm
sarkastic	sarcastic
sarkazm	sarcasm
sarmise	surmise
sarmize	surmise
sarmount	surmount
sarmownt	surmount
saround	surround
sarpass	surpass
sarprise	surprise
sarprize	surprise
sarrender	surrender
sarround	surround
sarvay	survey
sarvey	survey
sarvive	survive
saseptible	susceptible
sash	
saspect	suspect
saspekt	suspect
saspend	suspend
saspense	suspense
saspicious	suspicious
saspishous	suspicious
sastain	sustain
sastane	sustain
sat	
satallite	satellite
Satan	
satan	satin
Satarday	Saturday
satchal	satchel

satchel	
satchil	satchel
satchol	satchel
satchul	satchel
satchurate	saturate
satellite	
Saten	Satan
saten	satin
Saterday	Saturday
satillite	satellite
satin	
Satin	Satan
Satirday	Saturday
satisfaction	
satisfactorily	
satisfactory	
satisfy	
satollite	satellite
Saton	Satan
saton	satin
Satorday	Saturday
satullite	satellite
Satun	Satan
satun	satin
saturate	
Saturday	
sauce	
saucepan	
saucer	
saucey	saucy
saucy	
sault	salt
sauntar	saunter
saunter	
sauntir	saunter
sauntor	saunter
sauntur	saunter
sausage	

sause	sauce	sayber	saber	scandil	scandal
sausige	sausage	sayble	sable	scandol	scandal
sav	salve	saycred	sacred	scandul	scandal
savage		saying		scane	skein
savagery		saynor	señor	scant	
savar	savor	saynora	señora	scanty	
save		saynorita	señorita	scar	
saveing	saving	saynt	saint	scarce	
saver	savor	says		scarcely	
savere	severe	Saytan	Satan	scarcety	scarcity
saveyor	savior	sayvor	savor	scarcity	
savige	savage	scab		scare	
saving		scabbard		scarecrow	
savior		scaffold		scarf	
savir	savor	scafold	scaffold	scarlet	
savor		scail	scale	scarlet fever	
savory		scain	skein	scarlit	scarlet
savur	savor	scair	scare	scarse	scarce
savyar	savior	scairce	scarce	scatar	scatter
savyer	savior	scairse	scarce	scate	skate
savyir	savior	scait	skate	scater	scatter
savyor	savior	scald		scatir	scatter
savyur	savior	scale		scator	scatter
saw		scaley	scaly	scattar	scatter
sawce	sauce	scallap	scallop	scatter	
sawdust		scallep	scallop	scattir	scatter
sawnter	saunter	scallip	scallop	scattor	scatter
sawrce	source	scallop		scattur	scatter
sawrse	source	scallup	scallop	scatur	scatter
sawsage	sausage	scalop	scallop	scauld	scald
sawse	sauce	scalp		scavanger	scavenger
sawsige	sausage	scaly		scavenger	
saxaphone	saxophone	scamp		scavinger	scavenger
saxephone	saxophone	scan		scavonger	scavenger
saxiphone	saxophone	scandal		scavunger	scavenger
saxophone		scandalize		sceam	scheme
saxuphone	saxophone	scandalous		scedjule	schedule
say		scandel	scandal	scedule	schedule

sceem	scheme	scissurs	scissors
scejule	schedule	sciunce	science
sceme	scheme	scizors	scissors
scene		scoald	scold
scenec	scenic	scoap	scope
scenek	scenic	scoar	score
scenery		scoarn	scorn
scenic		scoarpion	scorpion
scenik	scenic	scoff	
scent		scolar	scholar
scepter		scold	
scervy	scurvy	scool	school
scewl	school	scooner	schooner
scewner	schooner	scoop	
scewp	scoop	scoot	
scewt	scoot	scootar	scooter
schedule		scooter	
scheme		scootir	scooter
scholar		scootor	scooter
scholarly		scootur	scooter
scholarship		scope	
scholer	scholar	scorch	
scholir	scholar	score	
scholor	scholar	scorn	
scholur	scholar	scornful	
school		scorpean	scorpion
schooner		scorpion	
sciance	science	Scotch	
science		Scotish	Scottish
scientific		Scotland	
scientist		Scottish	
scionce	science	scoul	scowl
scirvy	scurvy	scoundral	scoundrel
scisors	scissors	scoundrel	
scissars	scissors	scoundril	scoundrel
scissers	scissors	scoundrol	scoundrel
scissirs	scissors	scoundrul	scoundrel
scissors		scour	

scourge	
scout	
scouting	
scowl	
scowndrel	scoundrel
scowr	scour
scowt	scout
scrach	scratch
scraipe	scrape
scrall	scrawl
scrambal	scramble
scrambel	scramble
scrambil	scramble
scramble	
scrambol	scramble
scrambul	scramble
scrap	
scrapbook	
scrape	
scratch	
scrawl	
scrawny	
screach	screech
scream	
screan	screen
screche	screech
screech	
screem	scream
screen	
screme	scream
screne	screen
screw	
screwdriver	
screwple	scruple
screwtiny	scrutiny
scribal	scribble
scribbal	scribble
scribbel	scribble

scribbil	scribble	scrutony	scrutiny	scutel	scuttle
scribble		scrutuny	scrutiny	scutil	scuttle
scribbol	scribble	scufal	scuffle	scutle	scuttle
scribbul	scribble	scufel	scuffle	scutol	scuttle
scribe		scuff		scuttal	scuttle
scribel	scribble	scuffal	scuffle	scuttel	scuttle
scribil	scribble	scuffel	scuffle	scuttil	scuttle
scrible	scribble	scuffil	scuffle	scuttle	
scribol	scribble	scuffle		scuttol	scuttle
scribul	scribble	scuffol	scuffle	scuttul	scuttle
scrimage	scrimmage	scufful	scuffle	scutul	scuttle
scrimige	scrimmage	scufil	scuffle	scwab	squab
scrimmage		scufle	scuffle	scwabble	squabble
scrimmige	scrimmage	scufol	scuffle	scwad	squad
script		scuful	scuffle	scwair	square
Scripture		scule	school	scwalid	squalid
scroal	scroll	sculion	scullion	scwall	squall
scrole	scroll	sculk	skulk	scwalor	squalor
scroll		scull	skull	scwander	squander
scroo	screw	scullion		scware	square
scroople	scruple	sculpchur	sculpture	scwash	squash
scrootiny	scrutiny	sculptchur	sculpture	scwat	squat
scrorny	scrawny	sculpture		scwaw	squaw
scrub		sculyan	scullion	scwawk	squawk
scrue	screw	sculyen	scullion	scweak	squeak
scruff		sculyin	scullion	scweal	squeal
scrupal	scruple	sculyon	scullion	scweaze	squeeze
scrupel	scruple	sculyun	scullion	scweek	squeak
scrupewlous	scrupulous	scum		scweel	squeal
scrupil	scruple	scuner	schooner	scweeze	squeeze
scruple		scunk	skunk	scweke	squeak
scrupol	scruple	scupe	scoop	scwele	squeal
scrupul	scruple	scurge	scourge	scwerm	squirm
scrupulous		scurry		scwerrel	squirrel
scrutany	scrutiny	scurvey	scurvy	scwert	squirt
scruteny	scrutiny	scurvy		scweze	squeeze
scrutinize		scutal	scuttle	scwier	squire
scrutiny		scute	scoot	scwint	squint

scwire	squire	sear	sere
scwirm	squirm	search	
scwirrel	squirrel	searchlight	
scwirt	squirt	searial	serial
scwob	squab	searies	series
scwobble	squabble	searious	serious
scwod	squad	searum	serum
scwolid	squalid	seasan	season
scwoll	squall	seasaw	seesaw
scwolor	squalor	sease	cease
scwonder	squander	sease	seize
scwork	squawk	seasen	season
scwosh	squash	seashore	
scwot	squat	seasick	
scwurm	squirm	seaside	
scwurt	squirt	seasin	season
scy	sky	season	
scythe		seasonal	
se	sea	seasoning	
se	see	seasun	season
sea		seat	
sea	see	seathe	seethe
seacret	secret	seaweed	
sead	seed	seaze	seize
seage	siege	seazon	season
seaira	sierra	secand	second
seak	seek	secceed	succeed
seal		seccess	success
seam		seccessive	successive
sean	scene	seccum	succumb
sean	seen	secks	sex
seanior	senior	seckston	sexton
seap	seep	seclewd	seclude
seaport		seclood	seclude
seaquel	sequel	seclude	
seaquence	sequence	secluded	
sear		seclusion	
sear	seer	second	

secondary	
secondhand	
secondly	
secratary	secretary
secreation	secretion
secrecy	
secreet	secrete
secreetion	secretion
secret	
secretary	
secrete	
secretion	
secretly	
secrit	secret
secritary	secretary
secrotary	secretary
secrutary	secretary
secs	sex
secshon	section
secston	sexton
sect	
section	
secund	second
secure	
securety	security
security	
sed	said
sedait	sedate
sedament	sediment
sedan	
sedar	cedar
sedate	
sede	cede
sede	seed
sedement	sediment
sedewce	seduce
sedewse	seduce
sediment	

sedimentary		seffice	suffice	sekwance	sequence
sedoment	sediment	sefice	suffice	sekwel	sequel
sedooce	seduce	sege	siege	sekwence	sequence
sedoose	seduce	seggest	suggest	sekwil	sequel
seduce		segmant	segment	sekwince	sequence
sedument	sediment	segment		sekwol	sequel
seduse	seduce	segmint	segment	sekwonce	sequence
see		segmont	segment	sekwoya	sequoia
see	sea	segmunt	segment	sekwul	sequel
seecret	secret	seige	siege	sekwunce	sequence
seed		seiling	ceiling	seldam	seldom
seedling		seise	seize	seldem	seldom
seege	siege	seive	sieve	seldim	seldom
seek		seize		seldom	
seel	seal	seizure		seldum	seldom
seem		sekand	second	sele	seal
seem	seam	seke	seek	selebrate	celebrate
seemingly		sekend	second	select	
seen		sekewr	secure	selection	
seen	scene	sekind	second	selekt	select
seenior	senior	seklude	seclude	selery	celery
seep		sekond	second	selestial	celestial
seequel	sequel	sekreation	secretion	self	
seequence	sequence	sekreet	secrete	selfish	
seer		sekreetion	secretion	selicit	solicit
seer	sear	sekret	secret	seliva	saliva
seer	sere	sekretary	secretary	sell	
seerial	serial	sekrete	secrete	sell	cell
seeries	series	sekretion	secretion	sellar	cellar
seerious	serious	sekrit	secret	sellophane	cellophane
seerum	serum	seks	sex	sellulose	cellulose
seesaw		sekshon	section	seloon	saloon
seese	seize	sekston	sexton	selute	salute
seeson	season	sekt	sect	selution	solution
seet	seat	sektion	section	semanary	seminary
seethe		sekund	second	semblance	
seeze	seize	sekure	secure	semblanse	semblance
seezon	season	sekwal	sequel	semblence	semblance

semblense	semblance	senseless		sentury	century
semblince	semblance	senseliss	senseless	senyar	senior
semblinse	semblance	sensetive	sensitive	senyer	senior
semblonce	semblance	sensibility		senyir	senior
semblonse	semblance	sensible		senyor	senior
semblunce	semblance	sensibly		senyor	señor
semblunse	semblance	sensitive		senyora	señora
seme	seam	sensoble	sensible	senyorita	señorita
seme	seem	sensotive	sensitive	senyur	senior
semenary	seminary	sensuble	sensible	sepalcher	sepulcher
sement	cement	sensure	censure	separate	
semetery	cemetery	sensus	census	separately	
semicircle		sensutive	sensitive	separation	
semicolon		sent		sepe	seep
semifinal		sent	cent	sepelchur	sepulcher
semikolon	semicolon	sent	scent	seperate	separate
seminary		sentament	sentiment	seperior	superior
semisircle	semicircle	sentance	sentence	seperlative	superlative
semonary	seminary	sentanel	sentinel	sepilcher	sepulcher
semunary	seminary	sentement	sentiment	sepirate	separate
senate		sentence		seplant	supplant
senater	senator	sentenel	sentinel	seply	supply
senator		sentense	sentence	sepolcher	sepulcher
sence	sense	senter	center	seporate	separate
send		sentigrade	centigrade	seport	support
sene	scene	sentiment		sepose	suppose
sene	seen	sentimental		sepplant	supplant
senior		sentince	sentence	sepply	supply
senit	senate	sentinel		sepport	support
señor		sentipede	centipede	seppose	suppose
señora		sentoment	sentiment	seppress	suppress
señorita		sentonce	sentence	seprano	soprano
sensable	sensible	sentonel	sentinel	sepreme	supreme
sensation		sentral	central	sepress	suppress
sensational		sentry		septar	scepter
sensative	sensitive	sentument	sentiment	September	
sense		sentunce	sentence	septer	scepter
senseble	sensible	sentunel	sentinel	septir	scepter

septor	scepter	serge		sertificate	certificate
septur	scepter	serge	surge	sertify	certify
sepulcher		sergeant		serum	
separate	separate	sergery	surgery	serunade	serenade
sequal	sequel	sergiry	surgery	serval	
sequel		serial		serval	servile
sequence		series		servant	
sequense	sequence	serim	serum	servatude	servitude
sequil	sequel	serinade	serenade	servay	survey
sequoia		serious		serve	
sequol	sequel	serly	surly	servel	servile
sequoya	sequoia	serman	sermon	servent	servant
ser	sir	sermen	sermon	servetude	servitude
seram	serum	sermin	sermon	servey	survey
seramics	ceramics	sermise	surmise	service	
seranade	serenade	sermize	surmise	serviceable	
serch	search	sermon		servile	
sere		sermount	surmount	servint	servant
sere	sear	sermownt	surmount	servis	service
sere	seer	sermun	sermon	servitude	
sereal	cereal	sername	surname	servive	survive
sereal	serial	serom	serum	servol	servile
serean	serene	seronade	serenade	servont	servant
sereen	serene	seround	surround	servotude	servitude
sereez	series	serpant	serpent	servul	servile
serem	serum	serpass	surpass	servunt	servant
seremony	ceremony	serpent		servutude	servitude
serenade		serpentine		sery	surrey
serender	surrender	serpint	serpent	seseptible	susceptible
serene		serplus	surplus	seshon	session
serenety	serenity	serpont	serpent	sespect	suspect
serenity		serprise	surprise	sespekt	suspect
sereous	serious	serprize	surprise	sespend	suspend
serese	series	serpunt	serpent	sespense	suspense
sereze	series	serrender	surrender	sespicious	suspicious
serf		serround	surround	sespishous	suspicious
serf	surf	serry	surrey	sessation	cessation
serface	surface	sertain	certain	session	

sestain	sustain	sevor	sever	sfinks	sphinx
sestane	sustain	sevoral	several	sfinx	sphinx
set		sevun	seven	shaby	shabby
setal	settle	sevur	sever	shabby	
setback		sevural	several	shack	
sete	seat	sew		shackal	shackle
setee	settee	sew	sue	shackel	shackle
setel	settle	sewer		shackil	shackle
setil	settle	sewicide	suicide	shackle	
seting	setting	sewing		shackol	shackle
setle	settle	sewn	soon	shackul	shackle
setol	settle	sewp	soup	shade	
settal	settle	sewperb	superb	shadeing	shading
settee		sewperficial	superficial	shadey	shady
settel	settle	sewperfluous	superfluous	shading	
settil	settle	sewperinten-dent	superinten-dent	shado	shadow
setting				shadow	
settle		sewpermarket	supermarket	shadowy	
settlement		sewpernatural	supernatural	shady	
settler		sewpersede	supersede	shaft	
settol	settle	sewperstition	superstition	shaggy	
settul	settle	sewpervise	supervise	shagrin	chagrin
setul	settle	sewt	suit	shagy	shaggy
sevan	seven	sewtable	suitable	shaid	shade
sevar	sever	sewth	soothe	shaik	shake
sevaral	several	sewtor	suitor	shaim	shame
sevear	severe	sewvenir	souvenir	shaip	shape
seveer	severe	sex		shair	share
seven		sextan	sexton	shaise	chaise
sever		sexten	sexton	shaive	shave
several		sextin	sexton	shak	shack
severe		sexton		shakal	shackle
severely		sextun	sexton	shake	
severity		sez	says	shakel	shackle
sevin	seven	seze	seize	shakey	shaky
sevir	sever	sfear	sphere	shakil	shackle
seviral	several	sfeer	sphere	shakle	shackle
sevon	seven	sfere	sphere	shakol	shackle

shakul	shackle	shassis	chassis	sheep	
shaky		shatar	shatter	sheepish	
shalac	shellac	shateau	chateau	sheepskin	
shall		shater	shatter	sheer	
shall	shawl	shatir	shatter	sheer	shear
shallac	shellac	shator	shatter	sheet	
shallow		shattar	shatter	sheeth	sheath
shalow	shallow	shatter		sheeth	sheathe
sham		shattir	shatter	shefe	sheaf
shambal	shamble	shattor	shatter	sheik	
shambel	shamble	shattur	shatter	sheild	shield
shambil	shamble	shatur	shatter	sheke	sheik
shamble		shauffeur	chauffeur	shelac	shellac
shambles		shave		shelf	
shambol	shamble	shaveing	shaving	shell	
shambul	shamble	shaven		shellac	
shame		shaving		shellak	shellac
shameful		shawl		shellfish	
shameless		shawr	shore	sheltar	shelter
shameliss	shameless	shawrt	short	shelter	
shampew	shampoo	she		sheltir	shelter
shampoo		sheaf		sheltor	shelter
shampue	shampoo	sheak	sheik	sheltur	shelter
shamrock		sheald	shield	shelve	
shamrok	shamrock	shean	sheen	shelves	
shanck	shank	sheap	sheep	shelvez	shelves
shandelier	chandelier	shear		shene	sheen
shank		shear	sheer	shepard	shepherd
shanty		shears		shepe	sheep
shape		shearz	shears	sheperd	shepherd
shapeless		sheat	sheet	shepherd	
shapeliss	shapeless	sheath		shepherdess	
shapely		sheathe		shepird	shepherd
sharck	shark	shed		shepord	shepherd
share		sheef	sheaf	shepurd	shepherd
shark		sheek	sheik	sherbat	sherbet
sharp		sheeld	shield	sherbet	
sharpen		sheen		sherbit	sherbet

sherbot	sherbet	shine		shod	
sherbut	sherbet	shiney	shiny	shoe	
shere	shear	shingal	shingle	shoemaker	
shere	sheer	shingel	shingle	shok	shock
sheriff		shingil	shingle	sholac	shellac
sherk	shirk	shingle		sholder	shoulder
sherriff	sheriff	shingol	shingle	shole	shoal
sherry		shingul	shingle	shollac	shellac
shert	shirt	shiny		shone	shown
shery	sherry	ship		shoo	
shete	sheet	shipar	shipper	shoo	shoe
shethe	sheath	shiper	shipper	shood	should
shew	shoe	shiping	shipping	shoogar	sugar
shew	shoo	shipmant	shipment	shook	
shewr	sure	shipment		shoor	sure
shewrety	surety	shipper		shoorety	surety
shewt	shoot	shipping		shoot	
shiek	sheik	shipreck	shipwreck	shop	
shield		shipshape		shoping	shopping
shift		shipwreck		shopkeeper	
shiftless		shipyard		shopping	
shiftliss	shiftless	shirbet	sherbet	shore	
shifty		shirk		short	
shilac	shellac	shirt		shortage	
shiling	shilling	shivalry	chivalry	shortening	
shillac	shellac	shivar	shiver	shortige	shortage
shilling		shiver		shortly	
shimar	shimmer	shivir	shiver	shorton	shorten
shimer	shimmer	shivor	shiver	shorts	
shimir	shimmer	shivur	shiver	shortstop	
shimmar	shimmer	sho	show	shot	
shimmer		shoal		shotgun	
shimmir	shimmer	shoalder	shoulder	should	
shimmor	shimmer	shoan	shown	shouldar	shoulder
shimmur	shimmer	shoar	shore	shoulder	
shimor	shimmer	shoart	short	shouldir	shoulder
shimur	shimmer	shock		shouldor	shoulder
shin		shocking		shouldur	shoulder

shout		shrivil	shrivel	shuful	shuffle
shoval	shovel	shrivol	shrivel	shugar	sugar
shove		shrivul	shrivel	shuk	shook
shovel		shroo	shrew	shuk	shuck
shovil	shovel	shrood	shrewd	shulac	shellac
shovol	shovel	shroud		shullac	shellac
shovul	shovel	shrowd	shroud	shun	
show		shrub		shurbet	sherbet
showar	shower	shrubbery		shurk	shirk
shower		shrubery	shrubbery	shurt	shirt
showir	shower	shrude	shrewd	shut	
shown		shrue	shrew	shutal	shuttle
showor	shower	shrug		shutar	shutter
showt	shout	shuck		shute	chute
showur	shower	shud	should	shute	shoot
showy		shudar	shudder	shutel	shuttle
shrapnal	shrapnel	shuddar	shudder	shuter	shutter
shrapnel		shudder		shutil	shuttle
shrapnil	shrapnel	shuddir	shudder	shutir	shutter
shrapnol	shrapnel	shuddor	shudder	shutle	shuttle
shrapnul	shrapnel	shuddur	shudder	shutol	shuttle
shreak	shriek	shuder	shudder	shutor	shutter
shred		shudir	shudder	shuttal	shuttle
shreek	shriek	shudor	shudder	shuttar	shutter
shreik	shriek	shudur	shudder	shuttel	shuttle
shreke	shriek	shue	shoe	shutter	
shrew		shue	shoo	shuttil	shuttle
shrewd		shufal	shuffle	shuttir	shutter
shrewdness		shufel	shuffle	shuttle	
shrewdniss	shrewdness	shuffal	shuffle	shuttol	shuttle
shriek		shuffel	shuffle	shuttor	shutter
shrill		shuffil	shuffle	shuttul	shuttle
shrimp		shuffle		shuttur	shutter
shrinck	shrink	shuffol	shuffle	shutul	shuttle
shrine		shufful	shuffle	shutur	shutter
shrink		shufil	shuffle	shuv	shove
shrival	shrivel	shufle	shuffle	shuvel	shovel
shrivel		shufol	shuffle	shy	

shyly		sidate	sedate	sight	
shyness		side		sightless	
shyniss	shyness	sidel	sidle	sightliss	sightless
si	sigh	sider	cider	sightseeing	
siance	science	sidetrack		sign	
sicamore	sycamore	sidewalk		signachure	signature
sicceed	succeed	sideways		signafy	signify
siccess	success	sidewce	seduce	signal	
siccessive	successive	sidewse	seduce	signatchure	signature
siccum	succumb	sidil	sidle	signature	
sichuate	situate	sidle		signefy	signify
sick		sidol	sidle	signel	signal
sickal	sickle	sidooce	seduce	signet	
sickel	sickle	sidoose	seduce	signeture	signature
sickil	sickle	siduce	seduce	significance	
sickle		sidul	sidle	significant	
sickly		siduse	seduce	signify	
sickness		siege		signil	signal
sickniss	sickness	sience	science	signit	signet
sickol	sickle	sier	sire	signiture	signature
sicks	six	siera	sierra	signofy	signify
sickul	sickle	sierra		signol	signal
sicle	cycle	siese	seize	signoture	signature
sicle	sickle	siesta		signufy	signify
siclone	cyclone	sieve		signul	signal
siclude	seclude	sieze	seize	signuture	signature
sicology	psychology	sifan	siphon	sik	sick
sicomore	sycamore	sifen	siphon	sikal	sickle
sicreation	secretion	siffice	suffice	sikamore	sycamore
sicreet	secrete	sifice	suffice	sikel	sickle
sicreetion	secretion	sifin	siphon	sikemore	sycamore
sicrete	secrete	sifon	siphon	sikewr	secure
sicretion	secretion	sift		sikil	sickle
sics	six	sifun	siphon	sikimore	sycamore
sicumore	sycamore	sigar	cigar	sikle	sickle
sidait	sedate	sigarette	cigarette	siklude	seclude
sidal	sidle	siggest	suggest	sikol	sickle
sidan	sedan	sigh		sikology	psychology

sikomore	sycamore	silooette	silhouette	simfeny	symphony
sikreation	secretion	siloon	saloon	simfiny	symphony
sikreetion	secretion	silow	silo	simfony	symphony
sikrete	secrete	silt		simfuny	symphony
sikretion	secretion	siluble	syllable	similar	
siks	six	siluette	silhouette	similarity	
sikul	sickle	silunt	silent	similtaneous	simultaneous
sikumore	sycamore	silute	salute	simir	simmer
sikure	secure	silution	solution	simitry	symmetry
sikwoya	sequoia	silvan	sylvan	simmar	simmer
silable	syllable	silvar	silver	simmatry	symmetry
silant	silent	silven	sylvan	simmer	
sileble	syllable	silver		simmetry	symmetry
silect	select	silversmith		simmir	simmer
silekt	select	silverware		simmitry	symmetry
silence		silvery		simmor	simmer
silent		silvin	sylvan	simmotry	symmetry
silents	silence	silvir	silver	simmur	simmer
silewette	silhouette	silvon	sylvan	simmutry	symmetry
silhouette		silvor	silver	simolar	similar
silible	syllable	silvun	sylvan	simoltaneous	simultaneous
silicit	solicit	silvur	silver	simor	simmer
silinder	cylinder	sily	silly	simotry	symmetry
silint	silent	simalar	similar	simpal	simple
siliva	saliva	simaltaneous	simultaneous	simpathy	sympathy
silk		simar	simmer	simpel	simple
silkworm		simatry	symmetry	simpethy	sympathy
silky		simbal	cymbal	simphany	symphony
sill		simbal	symbol	simpheny	symphony
sillable	syllable	simbel	symbol	simphiny	symphony
silleble	syllable	simbil	symbol	simphony	symphony
sillible	syllable	simbol	symbol	simphuny	symphony
silloble	syllable	simbul	symbol	simpil	simple
silluble	syllable	simelar	similar	simpithy	sympathy
silly		simeltaneous	simultaneous	simple	
silo		simer	simmer	simpleton	
siloble	syllable	simetry	symmetry	simplicity	
silont	silent	simfany	symphony	simplify	

simplisity	simplicity	sinful		sip	
simply		sing		siperior	superior
simplyfy	simplify	singal	single	siperlative	superlative
simpol	simple	singar	singer	siphan	siphon
simpothy	sympathy	singe		siphen	siphon
simptam	symptom	singel	single	sipher	cipher
simptem	symptom	singer		siphin	siphon
simptim.	symptom	singewlar	singular	siphon	
simptom	symptom	singil	single	siphun	siphon
simptum	symptom	singir	singer	siplant	supplant
simpul	simple	single		siply	supply
simputhy	sympathy	singlehanded		siport	support
simular	similar	singley	singly	sipose	suppose
simultaneous		singly		sipplant	supplant
simur	simmer	singol	single	sipply	supply
simutry	symmetry	singor	singer	sipport	support
sin		singul	single	sippose	suppose
sinagogue	synagogue	singular		sippress	suppress
sinanym	synonym	singularly		siprano	soprano
sinas	sinus	singur	singer	sipreme	supreme
since		sinigogue	synagogue	sipress	cypress
sincear	sincere	sininym	synonym	sipress	suppress
sinceer	sincere	sinis	sinus	siquoia	sequoia
sincere		sinister		siquoya	sequoia
sincerety	sincerity	sink		sir	
sincerity		sinnamon	cinnamon	siran	siren
sinch	cinch	sinnar	sinner	sirap	syrup
sinck	sink	sinner		sirch	search
sinder	cinder	sinogogue	synagogue	sircle	circle
sine		sinonym	synonym	sircuit	circuit
sine	sign	sinos	sinus	sircuitous	circuitous
sinegogue	synagogue	sinse	since	sircular	circular
sinema	cinema	sinsere	sincere	sirculate	circulate
sinenym	synonym	sinue	sinew	sircumference	circumference
siner	sinner	sinugogue	synagogue	sircumstance	circumstance
siness	sinus	sinunym	synonym	sircumvent	circumvent
sinew		sinus		sircus	circus
sinewy		sionce	science	sire	

siren		siseptible	susceptible	sity	city
sirender	surrender	sisors	scissors	siunce	science
sirene	serene	sispect	suspect	siv	sieve
sirep	syrup	sispekt	suspect	sivere	severe
sirf	serf	sispend	suspend	sivic	civic
sirf	surf	sispense	suspense	sivil	civil
sirface	surface	sispicious	suspicious	sivilian	civilian
sirge	serge	sispishous	suspicious	six	
sirge	surge	sissors	scissors	sixtieth	
sirgery	surgery	sistain	sustain	sixty	
sirgiry	surgery	sistam	system	sixtyeth	sixtieth
sirin	siren	sistane	sustain	sizal	sizzle
sirip	syrup	sistar	sister	size	
sirly	surly	sistem	system	sizel	sizzle
sirmise	surmise	sister		sizil	sizzle
sirmize	surmise	sistern	cistern	sizle	sizzle
sirmon	sermon	sistim	system	sizol	sizzle
sirmount	surmount	sistir	sister	sizors	scissors
sirmownt	surmount	sistom	system	sizul	sizzle
sirname	surname	sistor	sister	sizzal	sizzle
siron	siren	sistum	system	sizzel	sizzle
sirop	syrup	sistur	sister	sizzil	sizzle
siround	surround	sit		sizzle	
sirpass	surpass	sitadel	citadel	sizzol	sizzle
sirpent	serpent	sitation	citation	sizzors	scissors
sirplus	surplus	sitchuate	situate	sizzul	sizzle
sirprise	surprise	site		skab	scab
sirprize	surprise	site	cite	skaffold	scaffold
sirrender	surrender	site	sight	skafold	scaffold
sirround	surround	sitewate	situate	skail	scale
sirry	surrey	sithe	scythe	skain	skein
sirun	siren	siting	sitting	skair	scare
sirvay	survey	sitizen	citizen	skairce	scarce
sirve	serve	sitrus	citrus	skairse	scarce
sirvey	survey	sitting		skait	skate
sirvive	survive	situate		skald	scald
siry	surrey	situated		skale	scale
sise	size	situation		skaley	scaly

skallop	scallop	skeluton	skeleton	skippur	skipper
skalop	scallop	skeme	scheme	skipur	skipper
skalp	scalp	skerge	scourge	skirge	scourge
skaly	scaly	skermish	skirmish	skirmish	
skamp	scamp	skert	skirt	skirt	
skan	scan	skervy	scurvy	skirvy	scurvy
skandal	scandal	sketch		skoald	scold
skandel	scandal	sketchy		skoap	scope
skandil	scandal	skewl	school	skoar	score
skandol	scandal	skewner	schooner	skoarn	scorn
skandul	scandal	skewp	scoop	skoarpion	scorpion
skane	skein	skewt	scoot	skoff	scoff
skant	scant	ski		skolar	scholar
skar	scar	ski	sky	skold	scold
skarce	scarce	skid		skool	school
skare	scare	skies		skooner	schooner
skarf	scarf	skiff		skoop	scoop
skarlat	scarlet	skilet	skillet	skoot	scoot
skarlet	scarlet	skilit	skillet	skope	scope
skarlit	scarlet	skill		skorch	scorch
skarse	scarce	skilled		skore	score
skate		skillet		skorn	scorn
skatter	scatter	skillful		skorpion	scorpion
skavenger	scavenger	skillit	skillet	skotch	scotch
skeam	scheme	skim		Skotland	Scotland
skech	sketch	skimpy		skoul	scowl
skedjule	schedule	skin		skoundrel	scoundrel
skedule	schedule	skinny		skour	scour
skee	ski	skiny	skinny	skourge	scourge
skeem	scheme	skip		skout	scout
skein		skipar	skipper	skowl	scowl
skejule	schedule	skiper	skipper	skowndrel	scoundrel
skelaton	skeleton	skipir	skipper	skowr	scour
skeleton		skipor	skipper	skowt	scout
skeliton	skeleton	skippar	skipper	skrach	scratch
skellton	skeleton	skipper		skraipe	scrape
skeloton	skeleton	skippir	skipper	skrall	scrawl
skelton	skeleton	skippor	skipper	skramble	scramble

skrap	scrap	skule	school	skwele	squeal
skrape	scrape	skulk		skwerm	squirm
skratch	scratch	skull		skwerrel	squirrel
skrawl	scrawl	skullion	scullion	skwert	squirt
skrawny	scrawny	skulpture	sculpture	skweze	squeeze
skreach	screech	skulyon	scullion	skwier	squire
skream	scream	skum	scum	skwint	squint
skrean	screen	skuner	schooner	skwire	squire
skreche	screech	skunk		skwirm	squirm
skreech	screech	skupe	scoop	skwirrel	squirrel
skreem	scream	skurge	scourge	skwirt	squirt
skreen	screen	skurmish	skirmish	skwob	squab
skreme	scream	skurry	scurry	skwobble	squabble
skrene	screen	skurt	skirt	skwod	squad
skrew	screw	skurvy	scurvy	skwolar	squalor
skrewple	scruple	skute	scoot	skwolid	squalid
skrewtiny	scrutiny	skutle	scuttle	skwoll	squall
skribble	scribble	skuttle	scuttle	skwonder	squander
skribe	scribe	skwab	squab	skwork	squawk
skrible	scribble	skwabble	squabble	skwosh	squash
skrimage	scrimmage	skwad	squad	skwot	squat
skrimmage	scrimmage	skwair	square	skwurm	squirm
skript	script	skwalid	squalid	skwurt	squirt
skroal	scroll	skwall	squall	sky	
skrole	scroll	skwalor	squalor	skylark	
skroll	scroll	skwander	squander	skylight	
skroo	screw	skware	square	skyline	
skroople	scruple	skwash	squash	skys	skies
skrootiny	scrutiny	skwat	squat	skyscraper	
skrorny	scrawny	skwaw	squaw	skyskraper	skyscraper
skrub	scrub	skwawk	squawk	sla	slay
skrue	screw	skweak	squeak	sla	sleigh
skruff	scruff	skweal	squeal	slab	
skruple	scruple	skweaze	squeeze	slack	
skrutiny	scrutiny	skweek	squeak	slackan	slacken
skuff	scuff	skweel	squeal	slacken	
skuffle	scuffle	skweeze	squeeze	slackin	slacken
skufle	scuffle	skweke	squeak	slackon	slacken

slacks		sledge		slingshot	
slackun	slacken	sleek		slink	
slacs	slacks	sleep		slip	
slag		sleepless		sliper	slipper
slaik	slake	sleepliss	sleepless	slipery	slippery
slain		sleepy		slipper	
slait	slate	sleet		slippery	
slaive	slave	sleeve		slipshod	
slak	slack	slege	sledge	slir	slur
slake		sleigh		slise	slice
slaks	slacks	sleke	sleek	slit	
slam		slendar	slender	slite	slight
slandar	slander	slender		slivar	sliver
slander		slendir	slender	sliver	
slandir	slander	slendor	slender	slivir	sliver
slandor	slander	slendur	slender	slivor	sliver
slandur	slander	slepe	sleep	slivur	sliver
slane	slain	slept		slo	slow
slang		sler	slur	sloap	slope
slant		slete	sleet	sloath	sloth
slap		sleve	sleeve	slogan	
slash		slew		slogen	slogan
slat		slewp	sloop	slogin	slogan
slate		sli	sly	slogon	slogan
slaughter		slice		slogun	slogan
slave		slick		sloo	slew
slavery		slicker		sloop	
slavesh	slavish	slid		slop	
slavish		slide		slope	
slax	slacks	slight		sloppy	
slay		slightly		slopy	sloppy
slay	sleigh	slik	slick	slorter	slaughter
slayne	slain	slim		slosh	
sleak	sleek	slime		slot	
sleap	sleep	slimey	slimy	sloth	
sleat	sleet	slimy		slothful	
sleave	sleeve	slinck	slink	slouch	
sled		sling		slovenly	

slow		smite	
slowch	slouch	smiten	smitten
sluce	sluice	smith	
slue	slew	smitin	smitten
slug		smiton	smitten
sluggish		smittan	smitten
slugish	sluggish	smitten	
sluice		smittin	smitten
sluise	sluice	smitton	smitten
slum		smittun	smitten
slumbar	slumber	smitun	smitten
slumber		smoak	smoke
slumbir	slumber	smoalder	smolder
slumbor	slumber	smock	
slumbur	slumber	smog	
slump		smok	smock
slung		smoke	
slupe	sloop	smoker	
slur		smokestack	
sluse	sluice	smokey	smoky
slush		smoky	
sluvenly	slovenly	smoldar	smolder
sly		smolder	
slyly		smoldir	smolder
smack		smoldor	smolder
smak	smack	smoldur	smolder
small		smooth	
smart		smothar	smother
smash		smother	
smear		smothir	smother
smeer	smear	smothor	smother
smell		smothur	smother
smelt		smudge	
smelter		smug	
smere	smear	smugal	smuggle
smewth	smooth	smuge	smudge
smile		smugel	smuggle
smitan	smitten	smuggal	smuggle

smuggel	smuggle
smuggil	smuggle
smuggle	
smuggler	
smuggol	smuggle
smuggul	smuggle
smugil	smuggle
smugle	smuggle
smugol	smuggle
smugul	smuggle
smuthe	smooth
smuther	smother
snach	snatch
snack	
snag	
snaike	snake
snail	
snair	snare
snak	snack
snake	
snale	snail
snap	
snappy	
snapshot	
snapy	snappy
snare	
snarl	
snatch	
sneak	
snear	sneer
sneaze	sneeze
sneek	sneak
sneer	
sneeze	
sneke	sneak
snere	sneer
snewp	snoop
snewze	snooze

sneze	sneeze	**snuff**		**sobur**	sober
sniff		snug		so-called	
sniffal	sniffle	**snugal**	snuggle	**soccar**	soccer
sniffel	sniffle	**snugel**	snuggle	**succeed**	succeed
sniffil	sniffle	**snuggal**	snuggle	soccer	
sniffle		**snuggel**	snuggle	**soccess**	success
sniffol	sniffle	**snuggil**	snuggle	**soccessive**	successive
snifful	sniffle	snuggle		**soccir**	soccer
snip		**snuggol**	snuggle	**soccor**	soccer
snipe		**snuggul**	snuggle	**soccum**	succumb
sno	snow	**snugil**	snuggle	**soccur**	soccer
snoar	snore	**snugle**	snuggle	sociable	
snoarkel	snorkel	**snugol**	snuggle	social	
snoart	snort	**snugul**	snuggle	**sociaty**	society
snob		**snupe**	snoop	society	
snoop		**snuze**	snooze	**socioty**	society
snoose	snooze	so		**sociuty**	society
snooze		**so**	sew	sock	
snorcal	snorkel	**so**	sow	**sockar**	soccer
snorcol	snorkel	**soacial**	social	**socker**	soccer
snorcul	snorkel	**soada**	soda	socket	
snore		soak		**sockir**	soccer
snorkal	snorkel	**soal**	sole	**sockit**	socket
snorkel		**soal**	soul	**sockor**	soccer
snorkil	snorkel	**soald**	sold	**sockur**	soccer
snorkol	snorkel	**soaldier**	soldier	sod	
snorkul	snorkel	soap		soda	
snort		soapsuds		**sodar**	solder
snout		soapy		**soder**	solder
snow		soar		**sodir**	solder
snowball		**soar**	sore	**sodor**	solder
snowdrift		**soard**	sword	**sodur**	solder
snowfall		**soashal**	social	sofa	
snowflake		sob		**sofamore**	sophomore
snowstorm		**sobar**	sober	**sofemore**	sophomore
snowt	snout	sober		**soffice**	suffice
snowy		**sobir**	sober	**sofice**	suffice
snub		**sobor**	sober	**sofimore**	sophomore

sofmore	sophomore	solewtion	solution	somebody	
sofomore	sophomore	solice	solace	someday	
soft		solicit		somehow	
softly		solid		someone	
sofumore	sophomore	solidify		somersault	
soggest	suggest	solim	solemn	something	
soggy		solir	solar	sometime	
sogy	soggy	solis	solace	somewear	somewhere
soibean	soybean	solisit	solicit	somewhat	
soil		solitary		somewhere	
soing	sewing	solitude		somirsault	somersault
sojern	sojourn	soliva	saliva	somorsault	somersault
sojirn	sojourn	soljer	soldier	somursault	somersault
sojourn		sollid	solid	son	
sojurn	sojourn	solo		song	
sok	sock	soloist		sonorous	
soke	soak	solom	solemn	soo	sue
soker	soccer	soloon	saloon	sooer	sewer
soket	socket	solootion	solution	sooicide	suicide
sokit	socket	solor	solar	soon	
solace		solotary	solitary	soop	soup
solam	solemn	soluble		sooperb	superb
solar		solum	solemn	sooperficial	superficial
solas	solace	solur	solar	sooperfluous	superfluous
solatary	solitary	solutary	solitary	sooperinten-dent	superinten-dent
sold		solute	salute		
solder		solution		soopermarket	supermarket
soldier		solve		soopernatural	supernatural
soldjer	soldier	som	psalm	soopersede	supersede
sole		somarsault	somersault	sooperstition	superstition
sole	soul	sombar	somber	soopervise	supervise
solely		somber		soot	
solem	solemn	sombir	somber	soot	suit
solemn		sombrairo	sombrero	soothe	
solemnity		sombraro	sombrero	sootor	suitor
soler	solar	sombrero		soovenir	souvenir
soletary	solitary	sombur	somber	sope	soap
solewble	soluble	some		soperior	superior

soperlative	superlative	sorpass	surpass	sourse	source
sophamore	sophomore	sorprise	surprise	south	
sophemore	sophomore	sorprize	surprise	South Africa	
sophimore	sophomore	sorrender	surrender	South America	
sophomore		sorro	sorrow	southarly	southerly
sophumore	sophomore	sorround	surround	southarn	southern
soplant	supplant	sorrow		South Carolina	
soply	supply	sorry		South Dakota	
soport	support	sorsage	sausage	southeast	
sopose	suppose	sorse	sauce	southerly	
sopplant	supplant	sorse	source	southern	
sopply	supply	sorsery	sorcery	southirly	southerly
sopport	support	sorsiry	sorcery	southirn	southern
soppose	suppose	sorsory	sorcery	southorly	southerly
soppress	suppress	sorsury	sorcery	southorn	southern
soprano		sort		southurly	southerly
sopreme	supreme	sorvay	survey	southurn	southern
sopress	suppress	sorvey	survey	southwest	
sor	saw	sorvive	survive	souvanir	souvenir
sorce	sauce	sory	sorry	souvenir	
sorce	source	soseptible	susceptible	souvinir	souvenir
sorcerer		soshal	social	souvonir	souvenir
sorceress		sospect	suspect	souvunir	souvenir
sorcery		sospekt	suspect	sovareign	sovereign
sorciry	sorcery	sospend	suspend	sovere	severe
sord	sword	sospense	suspense	sovereign	
sordid		sospicious	suspicious	sovereignty	
sore		sospishous	suspicious	Soviet Union	
sore	soar	soss	sauce	sovireign	sovereign
sorender	surrender	sostain	sustain	sovoreign	sovereign
sorene	serene	sostane	sustain	sovreign	sovereign
sormise	surmise	sought		sovrin	sovereign
sormize	surmise	soul		sovureign	sovereign
sormount	surmount	sound		sow	
sormownt	surmount	soundproof		sow	sew
soro	sorrow	soup		sownd	sound
soround	surround	sour		sowr	sour
sorow	sorrow	source		sowth	south

soybean		sparce	sparse	speaker	
soybeen	soybean	sparck	spark	spear	
soybene	soybean	spare		specefy	specify
soyl	soil	sparingly		specewlate	speculate
space		spark		speche	speech
spaceship		sparkal	sparkle	special	
spacious		sparkel	sparkle	specialist	
spade		sparkil	sparkle	specialize	
spagetti	spaghetti	sparkle		specially	
spaghetti		sparkol	sparkle	specialty	
spaice	space	sparkul	sparkle	species	
spaicious	spacious	sparow	sparrow	specific	
spaid	spade	sparrow		specification	
Spain		sparse		specify	
spair	spare	spasam	spasm	specimen	
spaise	space	spase	space	speck	
spaishus	spacious	spasem	spasm	speckal	speckle
span		spashus	spacious	speckel	speckle
spanck	spank	spasim	spasm	speckil	speckle
Spane	Spain	spasm		speckle	
spangal	spangle	spasom	spasm	speckol	speckle
spangel	spangle	spasum	spasm	specktacle	spectacle
spangil	spangle	spat		speckter	specter
spangle		spatar	spatter	specktrum	spectrum
spangol	spangle	spater	spatter	speckul	speckle
spangul	spangle	spatir	spatter	speckulate	speculate
Spaniard		spator	spatter	spectacle	
spaniel		spattar	spatter	spectacles	
Spanish		spatter		spectacular	
spank		spattir	spatter	spectar	specter
spanking		spattor	spatter	spectator	
spanyal	spaniel	spattur	spatter	spectecle	spectacle
Spanyard	Spaniard	spatur	spatter	specter	
spanyel	spaniel	spawn		specticle	spectacle
spanyil	spaniel	spazm	spasm	spectir	specter
spanyol	spaniel	speach	speech	spectocle	spectacle
spanyul	spaniel	spead	speed	spector	specter
spar		speak		spectram	spectrum

spectrem	spectrum
spectrim	spectrum
spectrom	spectrum
spectrum	
spectucle	spectacle
spectur	specter
speculate	
speculation	
spede	speed
speech	
speechless	
speechliss	speechless
speecies	species
speed	
speedily	
speedometer	
speedy	
speedyly	speedily
speek	speak
speer	spear
speeshies	species
speghetti	spaghetti
spek	speck
speke	speak
spektacle	spectacle
spekter	specter
spektrum	spectrum
spekulate	speculate
spell	
spellbound	
speller	
spelling	
spend	
spendthrift	
spent	
sper	spur
spere	spear
sperm	

spern	spurn
spert	spurt
spesafy	specify
spesefy	specify
speshal	special
speshies	species
spesify	specify
spesofy	specify
spesufy	specify
spewk	spook
spewl	spool
spewn	spoon
sphear	sphere
sphere	
spheer	sphere
Sphinks	Sphinx
Sphinx	
spi	spy
spice	
spicey	spicy
spicy	
spidar	spider
spider	
spidir	spider
spidor	spider
spidur	spider
spier	spire
spigat	spigot
spiget	spigot
spighetti	spaghetti
spigit	spigot
spigot	
spigut	spigot
spike	
spill	
spin	
spinach	
spinal	

spindal	spindle
spindel	spindle
spindil	spindle
spindle	
spindol	spindle
spindul	spindle
spine	
spinel	spinal
spineless	
spineliss	spineless
spinich	spinach
spinil	spinal
spinol	spinal
spinstar	spinster
spinster	
spinstir	spinster
spinstor	spinster
spinstur	spinster
spinul	spinal
spir	spur
spiral	
spire	
spirel	spiral
spiril	spiral
spirit	
spirited	
spiritual	
spirm	sperm
spirn	spurn
spirol	spiral
spirt	spurt
spirul	spiral
spise	spice
spit	
spite	
spiteful	
splash	
splatar	splatter

splater	splatter	spool		sprinkol	sprinkle
splatir	splatter	spoon		sprinkul	sprinkle
splator	splatter	spoonful		sprite	
splattar	splatter	spore		spritely	sprightly
splatter		sporn	spawn	sprooce	spruce
splattir	splatter	sport		sproose	spruce
splattor	splatter	spot		sprout	
splattur	splatter	spotless		sprowt	sprout
splatur	splatter	spotlight		spruce	
splendar	splendor	spotliss	spotless	spruse	spruce
splender	splendor	spouce	spouse	spry	
splendid		spouse		spughetti	spaghetti
splendir	splendor	spout		spuke	spook
splendor		spowce	spouse	spule	spool
splendur	splendor	spowse	spouse	spunck	spunk
splice		spowt	spout	spune	spoon
splint		spoyl	spoil	spunge	sponge
splinter		sprain		spunk	
splise	splice	sprall	sprawl	spur	
split		sprane	sprain	spurm	sperm
spoak	spoke	sprawl		spurn	
spoar	spore	spray		spurt	
spoart	sport	spread		sputar	sputter
spoghetti	spaghetti	spred	spread	sputer	sputter
spoil		spree		sputir	sputter
spoke		sprewce	spruce	sputor	sputter
spoken		sprewse	spruce	sputtar	sputter
spokesman		spri	spry	sputter	
sponcer	sponsor	sprig		sputtir	sputter
sponcir	sponsor	sprightly		sputtor	sputter
sponge		sprinckle	sprinkle	sputtur	sputter
sponsar	sponsor	spring		sputur	sputter
sponser	sponsor	springboard		spy	
sponsir	sponsor	springtime		spyder	spider
sponsor		sprinkal	sprinkle	squab	
sponsur	sponsor	sprinkel	sprinkle	squabal	squabble
spontaneous		sprinkil	sprinkle	squabbal	squabble
spook		sprinkle		squabbel	squabble

squabbil	squabble	squeek	squeak	stachir	stature
squabble		squeel	squeal	stachoo	statue
squabbol	squabble	squeeze		stachoot	statute
squabbul	squabble	squeke	squeak	stachor	stature
squabel	squabble	squele	squeal	stachue	statue
squabil	squabble	squerm	squirm	stachur	stature
squable	squabble	squerrel	squirrel	stachure	stature
squabol	squabble	squert	squirt	stachute	statute
squabul	squabble	squeze	squeeze	stack	
squad		squier	squire	stade	staid
squadran	squadron	squint		stadeum	stadium
squadren	squadron	squire		stadium	
squadrin	squadron	squirm		staff	
squadron		squirrel		stag	
squadrun	squadron	squirt		stagar	stagger
squair	square	squob	squab	stage	
squalar	squalor	squobble	squabble	stagecoach	
squaler	squalor	squod	squad	stager	stagger
squalid		squolid	squalid	staggar	stagger
squalir	squalor	squoll	squall	stagger	
squall		squolor	squalor	staggir	stagger
squallid	squalid	squonder	squander	staggor	stagger
squalor		squork	squawk	staggur	stagger
squalur	squalor	squosh	squash	stagir	stagger
squandar	squander	squot	squat	stagnant	
squander		sta	stay	stagnent	stagnant
squandir	squander	stab		stagnint	stagnant
squandor	squander	stabal	stable	stagnont	stagnant
squandur	squander	stabel	stable	stagnunt	stagnant
square		stabil	stable	stagor	stagger
squash		stability		stagur	stagger
squat		stable		staible	stable
squaw		stabol	stable	staid	
squawk		stabul	stable	staidium	stadium
squeak		stachar	stature	staige	stage
squeaky		stacher	stature	staik	steak
squeal		stachew	statue	staike	stake
squeaze	squeeze	stachewt	statute	stail	stale

staimen	stamen	stammar	stammer	stark	
stain		stammer		starry	
staiple	staple	stammir	stammer	start	
stair		stammor	stammer	startal	startle
stair	stare	stammur	stammer	startel	startle
staircase		stamon	stamen	startil	startle
stairway		stamor	stammer	startle	
stait	state	stamp		startol	startle
staitus	status	stampead	stempede	startul	startle
staive	stave	stampede		starvation	
stak	stack	stampeed	stampede	starve	
stake		stamun	stamen	stary	starry
stake	steak	stamur	stammer	stashon	station
stalactite		stand		statas	status
stalagmite		standard		statchar	stature
stalaktite	stalactite	standardize		statcher	stature
stale		standerd	standard	statchew	statue
stalion	stallion	standing		statchewt	statute
stalk		standird	standard	statchir	stature
stall		standord	standard	statchoo	statue
stallion		standpoint		statchoot	statute
stallwart	stalwart	standstill		statchor	stature
stalwart		standurd	standard	statchue	statue
stalwert	stalwart	stane	stain	statchur	stature
stalwirt	stalwart	stanza		statchure	stature
stalwort	stalwart	stanzer	stanza	statchute	statute
stalwurt	stalwart	stapal	staple	state	
stalyan	stallion	stapel	staple	stated	
stalyen	stallion	stapil	staple	stately	
stalyin	stallion	staple		statement	
stalyon	stallion	stapol	staple	statesman	
stalyun	stallion	stapul	staple	statesmanship	
staman	stamen	star		statess	status
stamar	stammer	starch		statew	statue
stamen		starchy		static	
stamer	stammer	stare		statik	static
stamin	stamen	stare	stair	station	
stamir	stammer	starfish		stationary	

stationery	
statis	status
statos	status
statuary	
statue	
statuery	statuary
stature	
status	
statute	
staunch	
stave	
stawk	stalk
stawnch	staunch
stay	
stayble	stable
staydium	stadium
stayed	staid
stayge	stage
stayke	stake
staymen	stamen
stayn	stain
stayple	staple
stayshon	station
staytion	station
staytus	status
stead	
stead	steed
steadaly	steadily
steadely	steadily
steadfast	
steadily	
steadiness	
steadoly	steadily
steaduly	steadily
steady	
steadyness	steadiness
steak	
steal	

steal	steel
stealth	
steam	
steamboat	
steamship	
steap	steep
steaple	steeple
stear	steer
sted	stead
stede	steed
steed	
steel	
steel	steal
steem	steam
steep	
steepal	steeple
steepel	steeple
steepil	steeple
steeple	
steepol	steeple
steepul	steeple
steer	
stelactite	stalactite
stelagmite	stalagmite
stele	steal
stele	steel
stelth	stealth
stem	
steme	steam
step	
stepe	steep
stepfather	
stepladder	
steple	steeple
stepmother	
ster	stir
steral	sterile
sterdy	sturdy

stere	steer
sterel	sterile
stergen	sturgeon
stergeon	sturgeon
steril	sterile
sterile	
sterilize	
sterjon	sturgeon
sterling	
stern	
sterol	sterile
sterul	sterile
sterup	stirrup
stethascope	stethoscope
stethescope	stethoscope
stethiscope	stethoscope
stethoscope	
stethuscope	stethoscope
stew	
steward	
stewardess	
stewdent	student
stewdio	studio
stewerd	steward
stewird	steward
stewl	stool
steword	steward
stewp	stoop
stewpefy	stupefy
stewpendous	stupendous
stewpid	stupid
stewpify	stupefy
stewpor	stupor
stewurd	steward
sti	sty
stich	stitch
stick	
sticky	

stif	stiff	stirdy	sturdy	stomach	
stifal	stifle	stirep	stirrup	stomak	stomach
stifel	stifle	stirgen	sturgeon	stomek	stomach
stiff		stirgeon	sturgeon	stomik	stomach
stiffan	stiffen	stiring	stirring	stomok	stomach
stiffen		stirip	stirrup	stomuk	stomach
stiffin	stiffen	stirjon	sturgeon	stone	
stiffon	stiffen	stirling	sterling	stoneware	
stiffun	stiffen	stirn	stern	stoo	stew
stifil	stifle	stirop	stirrup	stooard	steward
stifle		stirrap	stirrup	stood	
stifol	stifle	stirrep	stirrup	stoodent	student
stiful	stifle	stirring		stoodio	studio
stigma		stirrip	stirrup	stool	
stigmer	stigma	stirrop	stirrup	stoop	
stik	stick	stirrup		stoopefy	stupefy
stil	still	stirup	stirrup	stoopendus	stupendous
stilactite	stalactite	stitch		stoopid	stupid
stilagmite	stalagmite	sto	stow	stoopify	stupefy
stile		stoal	stole	stoopor	stupor
stile	style	stoan	stone	stop	
still		stoar	store	stopar	stopper
stillness		stoark	stork	stoper	stopper
stillniss	stillness	stoarm	storm	stopir	stopper
stilt		stoary	story	stopor	stopper
stilted		stoave	stove	stoppar	stopper
stiltid	stilted	stock		stopper	
stimewlate	stimulate	stockade		stoppir	stopper
stimulant		stockaid	stockade	stoppor	stopper
stimulate		stocking		stoppur	stopper
stimulus		stocky		stopur	stopper
sting		stok	stock	storage	
stingy		stokade	stockade	store	
stinjy	stingy	stokaid	stockade	storeage	storage
stink		stolactite	stalactite	storekeeper	
stint		stolagmite	stalagmite	storeroom	
stir		stole		storey	story
stirap	stirrup	stolen		stork	

stork	stalk	straightforward		stratogem	stratagem
storm		strain		stratogy	strategy
stormy		strainer		stratom	stratum
stornch	staunch	strainge	strange	stratosphere	
story		strainth	strength	stratugem	stratagem
stout		strait		stratugy	strategy
stove		strait	straight	stratum	
stow		straitum	stratum	stratusphere	stratosphere
stowaway		strand		straw	
stown	stone	strane	strain	strawberry	
stowt	stout	strangal	strangle	stray	
stra	stray	strange		straytum	stratum
stradal	straddle	strangel	strangle	streak	
straddal	straddle	strangely		stream	
straddel	straddle	stranger		streamar	streamer
straddil	straddle	strangil	strangle	streamer	
straddle		strangle		streamir	streamer
straddol	straddle	strangol	strangle	streamline	
straddul	straddle	strangul	strangle	streamor	streamer
stradel	straddle	stranth	strength	streamur	streamer
stradil	straddle	strap		streat	street
stradle	straddle	straping	strapping	strech	stretch
stradol	straddle	strapping		streek	streak
stradul	straddle	stratagem		streem	stream
stragal	straggle	stratagy	strategy	street	
stragel	straggle	stratam	stratum	streke	streak
straggal	straggle	stratasphere	stratosphere	streme	stream
straggel	straggle	strate	straight	strenewous	strenuous
straggil	straggle	strate	strait	strength	
straggle		strategem	stratagem	strengthen	
straggol	straggle	strategic		strenth	strength
straggul	straggle	strategy		strenuous	
stragil	straggle	stratem	stratum	stress	
stragle	straggle	stratesphere	stratosphere	stretch	
stragol	straggle	stratigem	stratagem	stretcher	
stragul	straggle	stratigy	strategy	strete	street
straight		stratim	stratum	strewn	
straighten		stratisphere	stratosphere	stricken	

strickt	strict	struggol	struggle	stucko	stucco
strict		struggul	struggle	stuco	stucco
stride		strugil	struggle	stud	
stried	stride	strugle	struggle	stud	stood
strife		strugol	struggle	studant	student
strike		strugul	struggle	student	
strikeing	striking	struk	struck	studeo	studio
striken	stricken	strukchur	structure	studeous	studious
striking		strukture	structure	studied	
strikingly		strune	strewn	studint	student
strikt	strict	strung		studio	
string		strut		studious	
stringy		stuard	steward	studont	student
strip		stub		studunt	student
stripe		stubal	stubble	study	
striped		stubarn	stubborn	studyd	studied
strive		stubbal	stubble	stue	stew
stroak	stroke	stubbarn	stubborn	stuff	
stroal	stroll	stubbel	stubble	stuffing	
stroke		stubbern	stubborn	stuffy	
strole	stroll	stubbil	stubble	stuk	stuck
stroll		stubbirn	stubborn	stuko	stucco
strong		stubble		stulactite	stalactite
stronghold		stubbol	stubble	stulagmite	stalagmite
stroon	strewn	stubborn		stule	stool
stror	straw	stubbul	stubble	stumach	stomach
strorberry	strawberry	stubburn	stubborn	stumak	stomach
struck		stubel	stubble	stumbal	stumble
struckchur	structure	stubern	stubborn	stumbel	stumble
struckture	structure	stubil	stubble	stumbil	stumble
structchur	structure	stubirn	stubborn	stumble	
structure		stuble	stubble	stumbol	stumble
strugal	struggle	stubol	stubble	stumbul	stumble
strugel	struggle	stuborn	stubborn	stumek	stomach
struggal	struggle	stubul	stubble	stumik	stomach
struggel	struggle	stuburn	stubborn	stumok	stomach
struggil	struggle	stucco		stump	
struggle		stuck		stumuk	stomach

stun	
stung	
stuning	stunning
stunning	
stunt	
stupar	stupor
stupe	stoop
stupefy	
stupendous	
stuper	stupor
stupid	
stupidity	
stupify	stupefy
stupir	stupor
stupor	
stupur	stupor
stur	stir
sturdy	
sturgen	sturgeon
sturgeon	
sturjon	sturgeon
sturling	sterling
sturn	stern
sturup	stirrup
stutar	stutter
stuter	stutter
stutir	stutter
stutor	stutter
stuttar	stutter
stutter	
stuttir	stutter
stuttor	stutter
stuttur	stutter
stutur	stutter
sty	
style	
stylesh	stylish
stylish	

su	sue
subdew	subdue
subdivide	
subdivision	
subdoo	subdue
subdue	
suberb	suburb
subirb	suburb
subject	
subjekt	subject
subjict	subject
subjikt	subject
sublime	
submarine	
submerge	
submirge	submerge
submisive	submissive
submission	
submissive	
submit	
submurge	submerge
subordinate	
subsaquent	subsequent
subscribe	
subscriber	
subscribtion	subscription
subscription	
subsequent	
subsequently	
subside	
subsiquent	subsequent
subsist	
subsistance	subsistence
subsistence	
subskribe	subscribe
subsoquent	subsequent
substance	
substancial	substantial

substanse	substance
substantial	
substantially	
substatute	substitute
substence	substance
substense	substance
substetute	substitute
substince	substance
substinse	substance
substitute	
substitution	
substonce	substance
substonse	substance
substotute	substitute
substunce	substance
substunse	substance
substutute	substitute
subsuquent	subsequent
subtarranean	subterranean
subterranean	
subtirranean	subterranean
subtle	
subtlety	
subtley	subtly
subtly	
subtorranean	subterranean
subtract	
subtraction	
subtrakt	subtract
subturranean	subterranean
suburb	
suburban	
subway	
succar	succor
succead	succeed
succede	succeed
succeed	
success	

successful		sucum	succumb	suffucate	suffocate
succession		sudan	sudden	suffur	suffer
successive		suddan	sudden	suficate	suffocate
successively		sudden		sufice	suffice
successor		suddin	sudden	suficks	suffix
succewlent	succulent	suddon	sudden	sufics	suffix
succor		suddun	sudden	sufiks	suffix
succor	sucker	suden	sudden	sufir	suffer
succulent		sudin	sudden	sufise	suffice
succumb		sudon	sudden	sufix	suffix
succur	succor	suds		sufocate	suffocate
such		sudun	sudden	sufor	suffer
suck		sudz	suds	sufrage	suffrage
suckar	succor	sue		sufrige	suffrage
suckar	sucker	suede		sufruge	suffrage
suckceed	succeed	suer	sewer	sufucate	suffocate
suckcess	success	sufacate	suffocate	sufur	suffer
suckcessive	successive	sufar	suffer	sugar	
sucker		sufecate	suffocate	suger	sugar
sucker	succor	sufer	suffer	suggest	
suckir	succor	suffacate	suffocate	suggestion	
suckir	sucker	suffar	suffer	suggestive	
suckor	succor	suffecate	suffocate	sugir	sugar
suckor	sucker	suffer		sugjest	suggest
suckseed	succeed	suffering		sugor	sugar
sucksess	success	sufficate	suffocate	sugur	sugar
sucksessive	successive	suffice		suicide	
suckshon	suction	sufficient		suiside	suicide
sucktion	suction	sufficiently		suit	
suckulent	succulent	sufficks	suffix	suitable	
suckum	succumb	suffics	suffix	suitar	suitor
suckur	succor	suffiks	suffix	suitcase	
suckur	sucker	suffir	suffer	suite	
sucor	succor	suffise	suffice	suiter	suitor
sucor	sucker	suffix		suitir	suitor
sucshon	suction	suffocate		suitor	
suction		suffor	suffer	suitur	suitor
suculent	succulent	suffrige	suffrage	suk	suck

sukceed	succeed	sultun	sultan	sumory	summary
sukcess	success	sulun	sullen	sumpchuous	sumptuous
sukcessive	successive	sulute	salute	sumptchuous	sumptuous
sukor	succor	sulution	solution	sumptuous	
sukor	sucker	sum		sumtchuous	sumptuous
sukseed	succeed	sum	some	sumtuous	sumptuous
suksess	success	suman	summon	sumun	summon
suksessive	successive	sumar	summer	sumur	summer
sukshon	suction	sumary	summary	sumury	summary
suktion	suction	sumchuous	sumptuous	sun	
sukulent	succulent	sumen	summon	sun	son
sukum	succumb	sumer	summer	sunburn	
sulan	sullen	sumery	summary	sunck	sunk
sulen	sullen	sumin	summon	sundae	
sulfar	sulfur	sumir	summer	Sunday	
sulfer	sulfur	sumiry	summary	sunday	sundae
sulfir	sulfur	sumit	summit	sundown	
sulfor	sulfur	summan	summon	sundree	sundry
sulfur		summar	summer	sundries	
sulicit	solicit	summarize		sundry	
sulin	sullen	summary		sundrys	sundries
suliva	saliva	summen	summon	sune	soon
sulk		summer		sunflower	
sulky		summery	summary	sung	
sullan	sullen	summin	summon	sunk	
sullen		summir	summer	sunkan	sunken
sullin	sullen	summiry	summary	sunken	
sullon	sullen	summit		sunkin	sunken
sullun	sullen	summon		sunkon	sunken
sulon	sullen	summons		sunkun	sunken
suloon	saloon	summor	summer	sunlight	
sulphur		summory	summary	sunlit	
sultan		summun	summon	sunny	
sulten	sultan	summur	summer	sunrise	
sultin	sultan	summury	summary	sunset	
sulton	sultan	sumon	summon	sunshine	
sultry		sumor	summer	sunstroke	

suny	sunny
sup	
supal	supple
supar	supper
suparficial	superficial
suparinten-dent	superinten-dent
suparmarket	supermarket
suparnatural	supernatural
suparsede	supersede
suparstition	superstition
suparvise	supervise
supe	soup
supearior	superior
supeerior	superior
supel	supple
super	supper
superb	
supercede	supersede
superficial	
superfluous	
superintendent	
superior	
superiority	
superlative	
supermarket	
supernatural	
supersede	
superstition	
superstitious	
supervise	
supervision	
supervisor	
supil	supple
supir	supper
supirb	superb
supirficial	superficial

supirfluous	superfluous
supirinten-dent	superinten-dent
supirlative	superlative
supirmarket	supermarket
supirnatural	supernatural
supirsede	supersede
supirstition	superstition
supirvise	supervise
suplacate	supplicate
suplament	supplement
suplant	supplant
suple	supple
suplecate	supplicate
suplement	supplement
suplicate	supplicate
supliment	supplement
suplocate	supplicate
suploment	supplement
suplucate	supplicate
suplument	supplement
suply	supply
supol	supple
supor	supper
suporficial	superficial
suporinten-dent	superinten-dent
supormarket	supermarket
supornatural	supernatural
suporsede	supersede
suporstition	superstition
suport	support
suporvise	supervise
supose	suppose
suppal	supple
suppar	supper
suppel	supple

supper	
suppil	supple
suppir	supper
supplacate	supplicate
supplament	supplement
supplant	
supple	
supplecate	supplicate
supplement	
supplicate	
supplication	
suppliment	supplement
supplocate	supplicate
supploment	supplement
supplucate	supplicate
supplument	supplement
supply	
suppol	supple
suppor	supper
support	
supporter	
suppose	
supposed	
supposeing	supposing
supposing	
suppoze	suppose
suppress	
suppression	
suppul	supple
suppur	supper
suprano	soprano
supream	supreme
supreem	supreme
supremacy	
supreme	
supremecy	supremacy
supress	suppress

supul	supple	surjery	surgery	suspekt	suspect
supur	supper	surly		suspence	suspense
supurb	superb	surmise		suspend	
supurficial	superficial	surmize	surmise	suspenders	
supurfluous	superfluous	surmon	sermon	suspense	
supurinten-dent	superinten-dent	surmount		suspension	
		surmownt	surmount	suspicious	
supurlative	superlative	surname		suspishous	suspicious
supurmarket	supermarket	suroty	surety	sustain	
supurnatural	supernatural	suround	surround	sustainance	sustenance
supursede	supersede	surownd	surround	sustanance	sustenance
supurstition	superstition	surpass		sustane	sustain
supurvise	supervise	surpent	serpent	sustenance	
sur	sir	surplus		sut	soot
suraty	surety	surprise		sutable	suitable
surch	search	surpriseing	surprising	sutal	subtle
sure		surprising		sutch	such
surely		surprize	surprise	sute	suit
surender	surrender	surrender		sutel	subtle
surene	serene	surrey		suthe	soothe
surety		surround		sutil	subtle
surey	surrey	surroundings		sutle	subtle
surf		surrownd	surround	sutol	subtle
surf	serf	surry	surrey	sutor	suitor
surface		suruty	surety	sutul	subtle
surfase	surface	survay	survey	suvenir	souvenir
surfice	surface	surve	serve	suvere	severe
surfis	surface	survey		swa	sway
surge		surveyor		swab	
surge	serge	survival		swade	suede
surgecal	surgical	survive		swagar	swagger
surgen	surgeon	survivel	survival	swager	swagger
surgeon		surviver	survivor	swaggar	swagger
surgery		survivor		swagger	
surgical		sury	surrey	swaggir	swagger
surgin	surgeon	susceptible		swaggor	swagger
surgiry	surgery	suseptible	susceptible	swaggur	swagger
surity	surety	suspect		swagir	swagger

swagor	swagger	sweeton	sweeten	swine	
swagur	swagger	sweetun	sweeten	swing	
swaid	suede	swell		swirl	
swain		swelling		swirve	swerve
swair	swear	swellter	swelter	swish	
swallow		sweltar	swelter	Swiss	
swalow	swallow	swelter		switch	
swam		sweltir	swelter	Switserland	Switzerland
swamp		sweltor	swelter	Switzerland	
swampy		sweltur	swelter	swoar	swore
swan		swepe	sweep	swob	swab
swane	swain	swept		swolen	swollen
swap		swerl	swirl	swollen	
sware	swear	swerve		swollow	swallow
swarm		swet	sweat	swolow	swallow
swarthy		swetar	sweater	swomp	swamp
swat		swete	suite	swon	swan
swawr	swore	swete	sweet	swoon	
sway		sweter	sweater	swoop	
sweap	sweep	swetir	sweater	swop	swap
swear		swetor	sweater	sword	
sweat		swetur	sweater	swordfish	
sweat	suite	swewn	swoon	swore	
sweat	sweet	swewp	swoop	sworm	swarm
sweatar	sweater	swich	switch	sworn	
sweater		swift		sworthy	swarthy
sweatir	sweater	swiftness		swot	swat
sweator	sweater	swiftniss	swiftness	swum	
sweatur	sweater	swim		swune	swoon
sweep		swimer	swimmer	swung	
sweeper		swimmer		swupe	swoop
sweeping		swindal	swindle	swurl	swirl
sweet		swindel	swindle	swurve	swerve
sweet	suite	swindil	swindle	sycamore	
sweetan	sweeten	swindle		sycle	cycle
sweeten		swindler		syclone	cyclone
sweetheart		swindol	swindle	sycology	psychology
sweetin	sweeten	swindul	swindle	sycomore	sycamore

sycumore	sycamore	symmetry	
sykology	psychology	symmitry	symmetry
sylable	syllable	symmotry	symmetry
sylinder	cylinder	symmutry	symmetry
syllabicate		symotry	symmetry
syllabication		sympathetic	
syllabify		sympathetically	
syllable		sympathize	
sylvan		sympathy	
symatry	symmetry	sympethy	sympathy
symbal	cymbal	symphany	symphony
symbol		sympheny	symphony
symbolize		symphiny	symphony
symetry	symmetry	symphony	
symfany	symphony	symphuny	symphony
symfeny	symphony	sympithy	sympathy
symfiny	symphony	sympothy	sympathy
symfony	symphony	symptam	symptom
symfuny	symphony	symptem	symptom
symitry	symmetry	symptim	symptom
symmatry	symmetry	symptom	
symmetrical		symptum	symptom
		symputhy	sympathy

symutry	symmetry
synagogue	
synanym	synonym
synegogue	synagogue
synenym	synonym
synigogue	synagogue
syninym	synonym
synogogue	synagogue
synonym	
synugogue	synagogue
synunym	synonym
sypress	cypress
syrup	
systam	system
system	
systematic	
systematically	
systim	system
systom	system
systum	system
sythe	scythe
su	sue

T

tabacco	tobacco	tablet	
tabal	table	tablit	tablet
tabarnacle	tabernacle	taboggan	toboggan
tabel	table	tabol	table
tabernacle		tabornacle	tabernacle
tabil	table	tabul	table
tabirnacle	tabernacle	taburnacle	tabernacle
table		tack	
tablecloth		tackal	tackle
tablespoon		tackel	tackle

tackil	tackle
tackle	
tackol	tackle
tacks	tax
tacksi	taxi
tacktics	tactics
tackul	tackle
tacs	tax
tacsi	taxi
tact	

tactful		tale	tail	tampur	tamper
tacticks	tactics	talen	talon	tan	
tactics		talent		tanck	tank
tactiks	tactics	talented		tang	
taday	today	taler	tailor	tangal	tangle
tadpoal	tadpole	talin	talon	tangeble	tangible
tadpole		talint	talent	tangel	tangle
tag		talisman		tangerine	
tagether	together	talk		tangible	
taible	table	talkative		tangil	tangle
taik	take	talketive	talkative	tangirine	tangerine
tail		talkitive	talkative	tangle	
tail	tale	talkotive	talkative	tangol	tangle
tailer	tailor	talkutive	talkative	tangul	tangle
tailor		tall		tanight	tonight
taim	tame	tallow		tanjable	tangible
taint		tally		tanjarine	tangerine
taip	tape	talon		tanjeble	tangible
taiper	taper	talont	talent	tanjerine	tangerine
tair	tear	talor	tailor	tanjible	tangible
taist	taste	talow	tallow	tanjirine	tangerine
tak	tack	talun	talon	tanjoble	tangible
takal	tackle	talunt	talent	tanjorine	tangerine
take		taly	tally	tanjuble	tangible
takel	tackle	tamato	tomato	tanjurine	tangerine
taken		tambarine	tambourine	tank	
take-off		tamberine	tambourine	tankard	
takil	tackle	tambirine	tambourine	tanker	
takle	tackle	tamborine	tambourine	tankerd	tankard
takol	tackle	tambourine		tankird	tankard
taks	tax	tamburine	tambourine	tankord	tankard
taksi	taxi	tame		tankurd	tankard
takt	tact	tamerity	temerity	tantalize	
taktics	tactics	tamorrow	tomorrow	tantelize	tantalize
takul	tackle	tampar	tamper	tantilize	tantalize
talan	talon	tamper		tantolize	tantalize
talant	talent	tampir	tamper	tantram	tantrum
tale		tampor	tamper	tantrem	tantrum

tantrim	tantrum	tarrific	terrific	tatle	tattle
tantrom	tantrum	tarry		tatol	tattle
tantrum		tart		tatoo	tattoo
tantulize	tantalize	tartan		tator	tatter
tap		tartar		tattal	tattle
tapar	taper	tarten	tartan	tattar	tatter
tape		tarter	tartar	tattel	tattle
tapeoca	tapioca	tartin	tartan	tatter	
taper		tartir	tartar	tattered	
tapestry		tarton	tartan	tattew	tattoo
tapeworm		tartor	tartar	tattil	tattle
tapioca		tartun	tartan	tattir	tatter
tapir	taper	tartur	tartar	tattle	
tapistry	tapestry	tary	tarry	tattol	tattle
tapor	taper	tasal	tassel	tattoo	
taps		tasel	tassel	tattor	tatter
tapur	taper	tasil	tassel	tattue	tattoo
tar		task		tattul	tattle
taranchula	tarantula	tasol	tassel	tattur	tatter
tarantula		tassal	tassel	tatue	tattoo
tararium	terrarium	tassel		tatul	tattle
tardy		tassil	tassel	tatur	tatter
tare	tear	tassol	tassel	taught	
tarestrial	terrestrial	tassul	tassel	taunt	
target		taste		taut	
targit	target	tasteful		tavarn	tavern
tariff		tasteless		tavern	
tarific	terrific	tasteliss	tasteless	tavirn	tavern
tarnish		tastey	tasty	tavorn	tavern
tarpalin	tarpaulin	tasty		tavurn	tavern
tarpaulin		tasul	tassel	taward	toward
tarpelin	tarpaulin	tatal	tattle	tawk	talk
tarpilin	tarpaulin	tatar	tatter	tawnt	taunt
tarpolin	tarpaulin	tatel	tattle	tawny	
tarpulin	tarpaulin	tater	tatter	tawrd	toward
tarrarium	terrarium	tatew	tattoo	tawt	taught
tarrestrial	terrestrial	tatil	tattle	tawt	taut
tarriff	tariff	tatir	tatter	tax	

taxashon	taxation	technucal	technical	tel	tell
taxation		tecknical	technical	telacast	telecast
taxi		Tecksas	Texas	telagram	telegram
te	tea	teckst	text	telaphone	telephone
tea		teckstil	textile	telascope	telescope
teach		tecksture	texture	telavise	televise
teacher		tecnical	technical	telecast	
teaching		Tecsas	Texas	telegram	
teacup		tecst	text	telegraph	
teadious	tedious	tecstile	textile	telekast	telecast
teakettle		tecsture	texture	telephone	
team		teday	today	telescope	
team	teem	tedeous	tedious	televise	
teamstar	teamster	tedious		television	
teamster		tee	tea	telicast	telecast
teamstir	teamster	teech	teach	teligram	telegram
teamstor	teamster	teedious	tedious	teliphone	telephone
teamstur	teamster	teem		teliscope	telescope
teamwork		teem	team	telivise	televise
teapee	tepee	teepee	tepee	tell	
teapot		teer	tear	teller	
tear		teer	tier	telltale	
tear	tier	teese	tease	telocast	telecast
teara	tiara	teetar	teeter	telogram	telegram
tearful		teeter		telophone	telephone
tease		teeth		teloscope	telescope
teaspoon		teethe		telovise	televise
teater	teeter	teetir	teeter	telucast	telecast
teath	teeth	teetor	teeter	telugram	telegram
teathe	teethe	teetur	teeter	teluphone	telephone
teaze	tease	teeze	tease	teluscope	telescope
tebacco	tobacco	tegether	together	teluvise	televise
teboggan	toboggan	teir	tier	temato	tomato
teche	teach	teknical	technical	teme	team
technacal	technical	Teksas	Texas	teme	teem
technecal	technical	tekst	text	temerity	
technical		tekstile	textile	temorrow	tomorrow
technocal	technical	teksture	texture	tempal	temple

tempar	temper	temt	tempt	tenight	tonight
temparary	temporary	ten		teniment	tenement
temparate	temperate	tenacious		tenint	tenant
temparature	temperature	tenacity		tenir	tenor
tempel	temple	tenament	tenement	tenis	tennis
temper		tenant		Tennessee	
temperament		tenar	tenor	tennis	
temperamental		tenashus	tenacious	tenoment	tenement
temperance		tenasity	tenacity	tenont	tenant
temperary	temporary	tence	tense	tenor	
temperate		tend		tense	
temperature		tendan	tendon	tenshon	tension
temperment	temperament	tendancy	tendency	tension	
tempeschuous	tempestuous	tendar	tender	tent	
tempest		tenden	tendon	tentacle	
tempestuous		tendency		tentecle	tentacle
tempil	temple	tender		tenth	
tempir	temper	tenderfoot		tenticle	tentacle
tempirary	temporary	tenderness		tentocle	tentacle
tempirate	temperate	tendin	tendon	tents	tense
tempirature	temperature	tendincy	tendency	tentucle	tentacle
tempist	tempest	tendir	tender	tenument	tenement
temple		tendon		tenunt	tenant
tempol	temple	tendoncy	tendency	tenur	tenor
tempor	temper	tendor	tender	tepee	
temporarily		tendral	tendril	tepid	
temporary		tendrel	tendril	terable	terrible
temporate	temperate	tendril		terace	terrace
temporature	temperature	tendrol	tendril	terantula	tarantula
temprament	temperament	tendrul	tendril	terar	terror
temprature	temperature	tendun	tendon	terarium	terrarium
tempt		tenduncy	tendency	terase	terrace
temptation		tendur	tender	teratory	territory
tempul	temple	tenement		terban	turban
tempur	temper	tenent	tenant	terbine	turbine
tempurary	temporary	tener	tenor	terbulent	turbulent
tempurate	temperate	Tenessee	Tennessee	terce	terse
tempurature	temperature	tenfold		tere	tear

tere	tier	terrace		testify	
tereble	terrible	terrar	terror	testiment	testament
terer	terror	terrarium		testimony	
terestrial	terrestrial	terrase	terrace	testofy	testify
teret	turret	terratory	territory	testoment	testament
teretory	territory	terreble	terrible	testufy	testify
terf	turf	terrer	terror	testument	testament
terible	terrible	terrestrial		testy	
terice	terrace	terret	turret	tetanus	
terier	terrier	terretory	territory	tetenus	tetanus
terific	terrific	terrible		teter	teeter
terir	terror	terrice	terrace	tethar	tether
teris	terrace	terrier		tethe	teeth
teritory	territory	terrific		tether	
Terk	Turk	terrify		tethir	tether
terkey	turkey	terrir	terror	tethor	tether
terky	turkey	terris	terrace	tethur	tether
term		territory		tetinus	tetanus
termanal	terminal	terroble	terrible	tetonus	tetanus
termenal	terminal	terrofy	terrify	tetunus	tetanus
terminal		terror		tew	to
terminate		terrorize		tew	too
termination		terrotory	territory	tew	two
terminus		terruble	terrible	tewb	tube
termite		terrur	terror	tewba	tuba
termoil	turmoil	terrutory	territory	tewberculosis	tuberculosis
termonal	terminal	terse		tewition	tuition
termunal	terminal	tertle	turtle	tewl	tool
tern		teruble	terrible	tewlip	tulip
tern	turn	terur	terror	tewm	tomb
ternament	tournament	terutory	territory	tewmult	tumult
ternip	turnip	tese	tease	tewn	tune
teroble	terrible	test		tewna	tuna
teror	terror	testafy	testify	tewnic	tunic
terotory	territory	Testament		tewnik	tunic
terpentine	turpentine	testament		tewr	tour
terquoise	turquoise	testefy	testify	Tewsday	Tuesday
terrable	terrible	testement	testament	tewt	toot

tewth	tooth	thawrn	thorn	there	
tewtor	tutor	thawt	thought	there	their
Texas		thay	they	thereabout	
texchur	texture	the		thereafter	
Texes	Texas	thea	thee	thereby	
Texis	Texas	theaf	thief	therefore	
Texos	Texas	theam	theme	therefour	therefore
text		theary	theory	therein	
textal	textile	theas	these	thereof	
textbook		theater		thermas	thermos
textchur	texture	theatre		thermastat	thermostat
textel	textile	theatrical		thermess	thermos
textil	textile	theaz	these	thermestat	thermostat
textile		thee		thermis	thermos
textol	textile	theef	thief	thermistat	thermostat
textul	textile	theem	theme	thermometer	
texture		theery	theory	thermos	
Texus	Texas	thees	these	thermostat	
teze	tease	theeter	theater	thermus	thermos
tha	they	theez	these	thermustat	thermostat
thach	thatch	thefe	thief	thero	thorough
thair	their	theft		Thersday	Thursday
thair	there	theif	thief	therst	thirst
than		their		therteen	thirteen
thanck	thank	their	there	therty	thirty
thank		theirs		thery	theory
thankful		theiry	theory	Therzday	Thursday
thankless		theirz	theirs	these	
thankliss	thankless	theiter	theater	theter	theater
thanks		them		theury	theory
thanksgiving		theme		theuter	theater
thare	their	themselves		they	
thare	there	themselvz	themselves	theze	these
tharmometer	thermometer	then		thi	thigh
that		theology		thi	thy
thatch		theory		thick	
thaw		theoter	theater	thicken	
thawrax	thorax	therd	third	thicket	

thickit	thicket	tho	though	three	
thickness		thoas	those	thresh	
thickniss	thickness	thoaz	those	threshhold	threshold
thief		thong		threshold	
thiefs	thieves	thor	thaw	thret	threat
thier	their	thoracks	thorax	threw	
thieves		thoracs	thorax	threw	through
thievz	thieves	thoraks	thorax	thrift	
thigh		thorax		thrifty	
thik	thick	thormometer	thermometer	thrill	
thiket	thicket	thorn		thrive	
thikit	thicket	thorny		thro	throw
thimbal	thimble	thorough		throan	throne
thimbel	thimble	thoroughbred		throan	thrown
thimbil	thimble	thoroughfare		throat	
thimble		thoroughly		throb	
thimbol	thimble	thort	thought	throne	
thimbul	thimble	those		throne	thrown
thin		though		throng	
thinck	think	thought		throo	threw
thing		thoughtful		throo	through
think		thoughtless		throtal	throttle
thiology	theology	thoughtliss	thoughtless	throte	throat
third		thousand		throtel	throttle
thirmometer	thermometer	thousend	thousand	throtil	throttle
thirmos	thermos	thousind	thousand	throtle	throttle
thirmostat	thermostat	thousond	thousand	throtol	throttle
thiro	thorough	thousund	thousand	throttal	throttle
Thirsday	Thursday	thouzand	thousand	throttel	throttle
thirst		thowsand	thousand	throttil	throttle
thirsty		thowzand	thousand	throttle	
thirteen		thoze	those	throttol	throttle
thirtene	thirteen	thrall		throttul	throttle
thirtieth		thrash		throtul	throttle
thirty		thread		through	
thirtyeth	thirtieth	threat		throughout	
Thirzday	Thursday	threaten		throw	
this		thred	thread	thrown	

thrue	threw	tickil	tickle	tikel	tickle
thrush		tickit	ticket	tiket	ticket
thrust		tickle		tikil	tickle
thud		ticklesh	ticklish	tikit	ticket
thum	thumb	ticklish		tikle	tickle
thumb		tickol	tickle	tikol	tickle
thump		tickul	tickle	tikul	tickle
thundar	thunder	tidal		til	till
thunder		tiday	today	tile	
thunderbolt		tidbit		till	
thunderstorm		tide		tilt	
thundir	thunder	tidel	tidal	timarous	timorous
thundor	thunder	tidil	tidal	timato	tomato
thundur	thunder	tidiness		timbar	timber
thurd	third	tidings		timber	
thurmometer	thermometer	tidingz	tidings	timbir	timber
thurmos	thermos	tidol	tidal	timbor	timber
thurmostat	thermostat	tidul	tidal	timbur	timber
thuro	thorough	tidy		time	
Thursday		tidyness	tidiness	time	thyme
thurst	thirst	tie		timely	
thurteen	thirteen	tier		timepiece	
thurty	thirty	tier	tire	timerity	temerity
Thurzday	Thursday	tifewn	typhoon	timerous	timorous
thus		tifoid	typhoid	timetable	
thwart		tifoon	typhoon	timid	
thwort	thwart	tifune	typhoon	timidity	
thy		tigar	tiger	timirous	timorous
thyme		tiger		timorous	
ti	tie	tigether	together	timorrow	tomorrow
tiara		tight		timurous	timorous
tiarra	tiara	tighten		tin	
tibacco	tobacco	tightrope		tinacious	tenacious
tiboggan	toboggan	tigir	tiger	tincker	tinker
tick		tigor	tiger	tindar	tinder
tickal	tickle	tigur	tiger	tinder	
tickel	tickle	tik	tick	tindir	tinder
ticket		tikal	tickle	tindor	tinder

tindur	tinder	tirant	tyrant	tishue	tissue
tingal	tingle	tirantula	tarantula	tissue	
tinge		tirarium	terrarium	tital	title
tingel	tingle	tirban	turban	tite	tight
tingil	tingle	tirbine	turbine	titel	title
tingle		tirbulent	turbulent	titil	title
tingol	tingle	tirce	terse	title	
tingul	tingle	tire		titol	title
tinight	tonight	tired		titul	title
tinkal	tinkle	tirenny	tyranny	to	
tinkar	tinker	tirestrial	terrestrial	to	toe
tinkel	tinkle	tiret	turret	to	too
tinker		tirf	turf	to	tow
tinkil	tinkle	tirific	terrific	to	two
tinkir	tinker	tirinny	tyranny	toad	
tinkle		Tirk	Turk	toadstool	
tinkol	tinkle	tirkey	turkey	toaken	token
tinkor	tinker	tirky	turkey	toal	toll
tinkul	tinkle	tirm	term	toald	told
tinkur	tinker	tirminal	terminal	toan	tone
tinsal	tinsel	tirmite	termite	toapaz	topaz
tinsel		tirmoil	turmoil	toar	tore
tinsil	tinsel	tirn	tern	toarch	torch
tinsol	tinsel	tirn	turn	toarment	torment
tinsul	tinsel	tirnament	tournament	toarn	torn
tint		tirnip	turnip	toarnado	tornado
tiny		tironny	tyranny	toarpedo	torpedo
tip		tirpentine	turpentine	toarpid	torpid
tipe	type	tirquoise	turquoise	toartoise	tortoise
tiphewn	typhoon	tirrarium	terrarium	toarture	torture
tiphoid	typhoid	tirrestrial	terrestrial	toast	
tiphoon	typhoon	tirret	turret	toaster	
tiphune	typhoon	tirrific	terrific	toatal	total
tipical	typical	tirse	terse	toatem	totem
tipsy		tirtle	turtle	tobacco	
tiptoe		tirunny	tyranny	tobacko	tobacco
tiptop		tishew	tissue	tobaco	tobacco
tiranny	tyranny	tishoo	tissue	tobako	tobacco

toboggan		tolorant	tolerant	tooition	tuition
tocksic	toxic	tolurant	tolerant	took	
tocsic	toxic	tomahawk		tool	
todal	toddle	tomato		toolip	tulip
today		tomb		toom	tomb
toddal	toddle	tomboy		toomult	tumult
toddel	toddle	tombstone		toon	tune
toddil	toddle	tomcat		toona	tuna
toddle		tomehawk	tomahawk	toonic	tunic
toddol	toddle	tomerity	temerity	toonik	tunic
toddul	toddle	tomihawk	tomahawk	toor	tour
tode	toad	tomohawk	tomahawk	Toosday	Tuesday
todel	toddle	tomorrow		toot	
todil	toddle	tom-tom		tooth	
todle	toddle	tomuhawk	tomahawk	toothache	
todol	toddle	ton		toothbrush	
todul	toddle	tonage	tonnage	toothpick	
toe		tone		tootor	tutor
toenail		tongs		top	
together		tongue		topal	topple
toil		tongue-tied		topaz	
toilet		tongz	tongs	topel	topple
toilit	toilet	tonic		topic	
tokan	token	tonige	tonnage	topik	topic
token		tonight		topil	topple
tokin	token	tonik	tonic	tople	topple
toksic	toxic	tonnage		topol	topple
tokun	token	tonnige	tonnage	toppal	topple
tol	toll	tonsal	tonsil	toppel	topple
tolarant	tolerant	tonsel	tonsil	toppil	topple
told		tonsil		topple	
tole	toll	tonsol	tonsil	toppol	topple
tolerable		tonsul	tonsil	toppul	topple
tolerance		too		topsy-turvy	
tolerant		too	two	topul	topple
tolerate		toob	tube	torant	torrent
tolirant	tolerant	tooba	tuba	torantula	tarantula
toll		tooberculosis	tuberculosis	torarium	terrarium

torch		totaly	totally	tousle	
torchur	torture	totam	totem	touzle	tousle
tord	toward	totar	totter	tow	
tore		totel	total	tow	toe
torent	torrent			towal	towel
torestrial	terrestrial	totem		towar	tower
torid	torrid	toter	totter	toward	
torific	terrific	totil	total	towards	
torint	torrent	totim	totem	towel	
torment		totir	totter	tower	
torn		totol	total	towering	
tornado		totom	totem	towil	towel
tornament	tournament	totor	totter	towir	tower
tornt	taunt	tottar	totter	towl	towel
torny	tawny	totter		town	
toront	torrent	tottir	totter	towol	towel
torpedo		tottor	totter	towor	tower
torpid		tottur	totter	towsle	tousle
torrant	torrent	totul	total	towul	towel
torrarium	terrarium	totum	totem	towur	tower
torrent		totur	totter	towzle	tousle
torrestrial	terrestrial	touch		toxic	
torrid		touchdown		toy	
torrific	terrific	touching		toyl	toil
torrint	torrent	touchy		toylet	toilet
torront	torrent	tough		toylit	toilet
torrunt	torrent	toughen		tra	tray
tort	taught	tour		trace	
tort	taut	tourist		traceing	tracing
tortchur	torture	tournament		trachea	
tortoise		tournaquet	tourniquet	trachia	trachea
torture		tournement	tournament	tracing	
torunt	torrent	tournequet	tourniquet	track	
toss		tourniment	tournament	tract	
toste	toast	tourniquet		tractar	tractor
tot		tournoment	tournament	tracer	tractor
total		tournoquet	tourniquet	tractir	tractor
totally		tournument	tournament	tractor	
		tournuquet	tourniquet		

tractur	tractor
trade	
trademark	
trader	
tradishon	tradition
tradition	
traditional	
traffic	
traffik	traffic
trafic	traffic
trafik	traffic
tragady	tragedy
tragedy	
tragic	
tragidy	tragedy
tragik	tragic
tragody	tragedy
tragudy	tragedy
traice	trace
traide	trade
traikea	trachea
trail	
trailer	
train	
trainer	
training	
traise	trace
trait	
traitar	traitor
traiter	traitor
traitir	traitor
traitor	
traitorous	
traitur	traitor
trajady	tragedy
trajedy	tragedy
trajidy	tragedy
trajody	tragedy

trajudy	tragedy
trak	track
trakea	trachea
trakia	trachea
trakt	tract
traktor	tractor
trale	trail
tramp	
trampal	trample
trampel	trample
trampil	trample
trample	
trampol	trample
trampul	trample
trance	
trancwil	tranquil
trane	train
trankwil	tranquil
tranqual	tranquil
tranquel	tranquil
tranquil	
tranquility	
tranquillity	
tranquol	tranquil
transact	
transaction	
transakt	transact
transam	transom
transcontinental	
transe	trance
transem	transom
transfawrm	transform
transfer	
transfewsion	transfusion
transfir	transfer
transform	
transformation	
transfur	transfer

transfusion	
transfuzion	transfusion
transgress	
transhent	transient
transient	
transim	transom
transit	
transition	
translait	translate
translate	
translation	
translewcent	translucent
transloocent	translucent
translucent	
translusent	translucent
transmishon	transmission
transmission	
transmit	
transmiter	transmitter
transmitter	
transom	
transparent	
transplant	
transport	
transportation	
transum	transom
transverse	
transvirse	transverse
transvurse	transverse
tranzact	transact
tranzakt	transact
tranzient	transient
tranzition	transition
trap	
trapeaze	trapeze
trapeez	trapeze
traper	trapper
trapeze	

trapings	trappings	treasun	treason	tremer	tremor
trapper		treasure		tremir	tremor
trappings		treasurer		tremor	
trase	trace	treasurey	treasury	tremulous	
trash		treasury		tremur	tremor
tratar	traitor	treat		trench	
trate	trait	treatise		trend	
trater	traitor	treatment		treo	trio
tratir	traitor	treaty		trepadation	trepidation
trator	traitor	treazon	treason	trepedation	trepidation
tratur	traitor	treazure	treasure	trepeze	trapeze
travail		trebal	treble	trepidation	
traval	travel	trebel	treble	trepodation	trepidation
travale	travail	trebil	treble	trepudation	trepidation
travel		treble		tres	tress
traveler		trebol	treble	tresal	trestle
traveller		trebul	treble	tresel	trestle
traverse		trecherous	treacherous	tresil	trestle
travil	travel	treck	trek	tresle	trestle
travirse	traverse	tred	tread	tresol	trestle
travol	travel	tredition	tradition	treson	treason
travul	travel	tredle	treadle	trespass	
travurse	traverse	tree		trespess	trespass
tray		treeson	treason	trespis	trespass
tre	tree	treet	treat	trespos	trespass
treacharous	treacherous	treetise	treatise	trespus	trespass
treacherous		treezon	treason	tress	
treachery		trek		tressal	trestle
treachirous	treacherous	trelis	trellis	tressel	trestle
treachorous	treacherous	trellis		tressil	trestle
treachurous	treacherous	tremar	tremor	tressle	trestle
tread		trembal	tremble	tressol	trestle
treadle		trembel	tremble	tressul	trestle
treadmill		trembil	tremble	trestle	
treasan	treason	tremble		tresul	trestle
treasen	treason	trembol	tremble	tresure	treasure
treasin	treason	trembul	tremble	trete	treat
treason		tremendous		tretise	treatise

trew	true	trickul	trickle	tril	trill
trewant	truant	trickury	trickery	trile	trial
trewce	truce	tricky		trill	
trewp	troop	tricolor		trim	
trewp	troupe	triculor	tricolor	trimendous	tremendous
trewse	truce	tricycle		triming	trimming
trewth	truth	tridant	trident	trimming	
trezon	treason	trident		trincket	trinket
trezure	treasure	tridint	trident	trinckit	trinket
tri	try	tridition	tradition	trinket	
trial		tridont	trident	trinkit	trinket
triangle		tridunt	trident	trio	
triangular		tried		triol	trial
tribal		triel	trial	trip	
tribe		trifal	trifle	tripal	triple
tribel	tribal	trifel	trifle	tripe	
tribewlation	tribulation	trifil	trifle	tripel	triple
tribewnal	tribunal	trifle		tripeze	trapeze
tribewt	tribute	trifol	trifle	tripil	triple
tribewtary	tributary	triful	trifle	triple	
tribil	tribal	trigar	trigger	triplet	
tribol	tribal	triger	trigger	triplit	triplet
tribul	tribal	triggar	trigger	tripod	
tribulation		trigger		tripol	triple
tribunal		triggir	trigger	tripul	triple
tributary		triggor	trigger	trisicle	tricycle
tribute		triggur	trigger	trisycle	tricycle
tricicle	tricycle	trigir	trigger	triul	trial
trick		trigor	trigger	triumf	triumph
trickal	trickle	trigur	trigger	triumph	
trickary	trickery	trik	trick	triumphal	
trickel	trickle	trikal	trickle	triumphant	
trickery		trikel	trickle	triveal	trivial
trickil	trickle	trikil	trickle	trivial	
trickiry	trickery	trikle	trickle	troal	troll
trickle		trikol	trickle	trod	
trickol	trickle	trikul	trickle	trodition	tradition
trickory	trickery	trikulor	tricolor	trof	trough

trofy	trophy
trole	troll
troley	trolley
troll	
trolley	
trolly	trolley
troly	trolley
tromboan	trombone
trombone	
troo	true
trooant	truant
trooce	truce
troop	
troop	troupe
trooper	
trooper	trouper
troose	truce
trooth	truth
tropeze	trapeze
trophy	
tropical	
tropics	
tropiks	tropics
trot	
troth	
troubal	trouble
troubel	trouble
troubil	trouble
trouble	
troublesome	
troubol	trouble
troubul	trouble
trough	
trounce	
trounse	trounce
troup	troop
troupe	
trouper	

trouper	trooper
trousers	
trout	
trouzers	trousers
trowal	trowel
trowel	
trowil	trowel
trowl	trowel
trownce	trounce
trownse	trounce
trowol	trowel
trowsers	trousers
trowt	trout
trowul	trowel
trowzers	trousers
truant	
trubal	trouble
trubel	trouble
trubil	trouble
truble	trouble
trubol	trouble
trubul	trouble
truce	
truck	
trudge	
trudition	tradition
true	
truely	truly
truent	truant
truge	trudge
truint	truant
truk	truck
truly	
trumpet	
trumpeter	
trumpit	trumpet
trunck	trunk
trundal	trundle

trundel	trundle
trundil	trundle
trundle	
trundol	trundle
trundul	trundle
trunk	
truont	truant
trupe	troop
trupe	troupe
truper	trooper
truper	trouper
trupeze	trapeze
trus	truss
truse	truce
truss	
trust	
trustee	
trusting	
trustworthy	
trusty	
trusty	trustee
truth	
truthful	
try	
trycicle	tricycle
trycycle	tricycle
tryd	tried
trying	
tryout	
trysicle	tricycle
trysycle	tricycle
tub	
tuba	
tubacco	tobacco
tube	
tuberculosis	
tubirculosis	tuberculosis
tuboggan	toboggan

tuburculosis	tuberculosis
tuch	touch
tuck	
tuday	today
tue	to
tue	too
tue	two
Tuesday	
Tuezday	Tuesday
tuf	tough
tuft	
tug	
tugboat	
tugether	together
tuition	
tuk	took
tuk	tuck
tule	tool
tulip	
tumato	tomato
tumbal	tumble
tumbel	tumble
tumbil	tumble
tumble	
tumbler	
tumbol	tumble
tumbul	tumble
tume	tomb
tumerity	temerity
tumorrow	tomorrow
tumulchuous	tumultuous
tumult	
tumultuous	
tun	ton
tuna	
tunal	tunnel
tundra	

tune	
tunel	tunnel
tung	tongue
tungstan	tungsten
tungsten	
tungstin	tungsten
tungston	tungsten
tungstun	tungsten
tunic	
tunight	tonight
tunik	tunic
tunil	tunnel
tunnal	tunnel
tunnel	
tunnil	tunnel
tunnol	tunnel
tunnul	tunnel
tunol	tunnel
tunul	tunnel
turantula	tarantula
turarium	terrarium
turban	
turben	turban
turbewlent	turbulent
turbin	turban
turbine	
turbon	turban
turbulent	
turbun	turban
turce	terse
turcwoise	turquoise
ture	tour
turestrial	terrestrial
turet	turret
turf	
turific	terrific
turit	turret

Turk	
turkee	turkey
Turkesh	Turkish
Turkey	
turkey	
Turkish	
turkwoise	turquoise
turky	turkey
turm	term
turminal	terminal
turmite	termite
turmoil	
turmoyl	turmoil
turn	
turnament	tournament
turnap	turnip
turnep	turnip
turnip	
turniquet	tourniquet
turnop	turnip
turnout	
turnpike	
turnstile	
turnup	turnip
turpantine	turpentine
turpentine	
turpintine	turpentine
turpontine	turpentine
turpuntine	turpentine
turquoise	
turrarium	terrarium
turrestrial	terrestrial
turret	
turrific	terrific
turrit	turret
turse	terse
turtal	turtle

turtel	turtle	twenty		twitir	twitter
turtil	turtle	twentyeth	twentieth	twitor	twitter
turtle		twerl	twirl	twittar	twitter
turtol	turtle	twice		twitter	
turtul	turtle	twich	twitch	twittir	twitter
tusal	tussle	twidal	twiddle	twittor	twitter
Tuseday	Tuesday	twiddal	twiddle	twittur	twitter
tusel	tussle	twiddel	twiddle	twitur	twitter
tusil	tussle	twiddil	twiddle	two	
tusk		twiddle		twurl	twirl
tusle	tousle	twiddol	twiddle	twylight	twilight
tusle	tussle	twiddul	twiddle	ty	tie
tusol	tussle	twidel	twiddle	tyfewn	typhoon
tussal	tussle	twidil	twiddle	tyfoid	typhoid
tussel	tussle	twidle	twiddle	tyfoon	typhoon
tussil	tussle	twidol	twiddle	tyfune	typhoon
tussle		twidul	twiddle	typacal	typical
tussle	tousle	twig		type	
tussol	tussle	twil	twill	typecal	typical
tussul	tussle	twilight		typefy	typify
tusul	tussle	twill		typewriter	
tutar	tutor	twin		typhewn	typhoon
tute	toot	twinckle	twinkle	typhoid	
tuter	tutor	twine		typhoon	
tuthe	tooth	twinge		typhune	typhoon
tutir	tutor	twinkal	twinkle	typical	
tutor		twinkel	twinkle	typify	
tutur	tutor	twinkil	twinkle	typocal	typical
twang		twinkle		typucal	typical
twead	tweed	twinkol	twinkle	tyrannical	
twede	tweed	twinkul	twinkle	tyranny	
tweed		twirl		tyrant	
twelfth		twise	twice	tyrenny	tyranny
twelve		twist		tyrinny	tyranny
twelvth	twelfth	twitar	twitter	tyronny	tyranny
twentieth		twitch		tyrunny	tyranny
		twiter	twitter		

U

u	you
ucalyptus	eucalyptus
udar	udder
uddar	udder
udder	
uddir	udder
uddor	udder
uddur	udder
uder	udder
udir	udder
udor	udder
udur	udder
uffect	effect
ufficient	efficient
ugliness	
ugly	
uglyness	ugliness
ukalyptus	eucalyptus
ultamate	ultimate
ultemate	ultimate
ultimate	
ultomate	ultimate
ultumate	ultimate
umbrela	umbrella
umbrella	
umpier	umpire
umpire	
unable	
unaccented	
unaccountable	
unaccustomed	
unacorn	unicorn
unaform	uniform
unafy	unify
unaided	
unanimous	

unanimously	
unarmed	
unason	unison
unassuming	
unattended	
unavailing	
unaversal	universal
unaversity	university
unavoidable	
unaware	
unbearable	
unbecoming	
unbend	
unbiased	
unbolt	
unborn	
unbound	
unbuckle	
unbutton	
uncal	uncle
uncalled-for	
uncanny	
uncany	uncanny
unceasing	
uncertain	
uncertainty	
unchain	
unchanged	
uncivilized	
unckle	uncle
unclasp	
uncle	
unclean	
uncoil	
uncol	uncle
uncomfortable	

uncommon	
uncommonly	
uncompromising	
unconcerned	
unconditional	
unconquerable	
unconscious	
unconsciously	
unconstitutional	
uncooth	uncouth
uncouth	
uncover	
uncul	uncle
uncultivated	
uncurl	
uncuth	uncouth
undar	under
undaunted	
undecided	
undeniable	
under	
underbrush	
underclothes	
underfed	
underfoot	
undergarment	
undergo	
underground	
undergrowth	
underhand	
underhanded	
underline	
undermine	
underneath	
underpass	
underrate	

undershirt		uneasy		ungainly
understand		unecorn	unicorn	ungodly
understanding		uneek	unique	ungracious
understood		uneform	uniform	ungrateful
undertake		unefy	unify	unguarded
undertaker		uneke	unique	unguent
undertaking		unemployed		ungwent unguent
undertone		unemployment		unhand
undertook		unending		unhappily
underwear		unequal		unhappiness
underwent		unequaled		unhappy
undesirable		uneque	unique	unhealthful
undewlate	undulate	unerring		unhealthy
undid		uneson	unison	unheard-of
undignified		uneven		unhesitatingly
undir	under	uneventful		unhinge
undisputed		uneversal	universal	unhitch
undisturbed		uneversity	university	unhook
undjewlate	undulate	unexpected		unicorn
undjulate	undulate	unexpectedly		uniform
undo		unfailing		uniformity
undoing		unfair		uniformly
undone		unfaithful		unify
undoolate	undulate	unfamiliar		unikorn unicorn
undor	under	unfasten		unimportant
undoubted		unfavorable		uninhabited
undoubtedly		unfeeling		unintelligible
undress		unfinished		union
undue		unfit		unique
undulate		unflinching		unison
unduly		unfold		unit
undur	under	unforeseen		unite
undying		unforgettable		United Nations
uneak	unique	unfortunate		United States
unearth		unfounded		unity
unearthly		unfriendly		universal
uneasily		unfurl		universally
uneasiness		unfurnished		universe

university

unjewlate   undulate
unjoolate   undulate
unjulate   undulate
unjust

unkal   uncle
unkanny   uncanny
unkany   uncanny
unkel   uncle
unkempt

unkewth   uncouth
unkil   uncle
unkind
unkindly
unkindness

unkle   uncle
unknown

unkol   uncle
unkooth   uncouth
unkul   uncle
unkuth   uncouth
unlace
unlawful
unlearned
unless
unlike
unlikely
unlimited
unload
unlock
unlucky
unmarried
unmask
unmerciful
unmindful
unmistakable
unmixed
unmolested

unmoved
unnatural
unnecessary
unnerve
unnoticed
unobserved
unoccupied
unocorn   unicorn
unofficial
unoform   uniform
unofy   unify
unoson   unison
unoversal   universal
unoversity   university
unpack
unpaid
unparalleled
unpin
unpleasant
unpopular
unprecedented
unprepared
unprincipled
unprofitable
unquestionable
unquestionably
unravel
unreal
unreasonable
unremitting
unreservedly
unrest
unrestrained
unrivaled
unroll
unruly
unsaddle
unsafe

unsaid
unsatisfactory
unsatisfied
unscrew
unscrupulous
unseal
unseat
unseemly
unseen
unselfish
unsettle
unsettled
unshaken
unsheathe
unsightly
unskilled
unskillful
unsophisticated
unsound
unspeakable
unspeakably
unstable
unsteady
unstressed
unsuccessful
unsuitable
unsuspected
unthinkable
untidy
untie
until
untimely
untiring
unto
untold
untouched
untoward
untrained

untried		unyun	union
untrue		up	
untruth		upar	upper
unucorn	unicorn	upbrade	upbraid
unuform	uniform	upbraid	
unufy	unify	uper	upper
unused		upheld	
unuson	unison	uphill	
unusual		uphoalster	upholster
unusually		uphold	
unuversal	universal	upholester	upholster
unuversity	university	upholster	
unveil		upholstery	
unwary		upir	upper
unwelcome		upkeep	
unwell		uplift	
unwholesome		upon	
unwieldy		upor	upper
unwilling		uppar	upper
unwillingly		upper	
unwillingness		uppermost	
unwind		uppir	upper
unwise		uppor	upper
unwisely		uppur	upper
unwittingly		upraise	
unworthy		upright	
unwound		uprightness	
unwrap		uprising	
unyan	onion	uproar	
unyan	union	uproot	
unyen	onion	upset	
unyen	union	upshot	
unyielding		upside	
unyin	onion	upstairs	
unyin	union	upstart	
unyon	onion	upstream	
unyon	union	up-to-date	
unyun	onion	upturn	

upur	upper
upward	
urainium	uranium
uran	urine
uraneum	uranium
uranium	
uraynium	uranium
urb	herb
urban	
urben	urban
urbin	urban
urbon	urban
urbun	urban
urchan	urchin
urchen	urchin
urchin	
urchon	urchin
urchun	urchin
uren	urine
urge	
urgent	
urgint	urgent
urin	urine
urinate	
urine	
urjant	urgent
urjent	urgent
urjint	urgent
urjont	urgent
urjunt	urgent
urksome	irksome
urn	
uron	urine
Urope	Europe
urratic	erratic
urun	urine
us	
usable	

usage		usurp		uttar	utter
use		Utah		uttarly	utterly
useable	usable	utalize	utilize	utter	
useage	usage	utar	utter	utterance	
used		utarly	utterly	utterly	
useful		utelize	utilize	uttir	utter
usefulness		utensil		uttirly	utterly
useless		uter	utter	uttor	utter
user		uterly	utterly	uttorly	utterly
userp	usurp	uther	other	uttur	utter
ushar	usher	utility		utturly	utterly
usher		utilize		utulize	utilize
ushir	usher	utir	utter	utur	utter
ushor	usher	utirly	utterly	uturly	utterly
ushur	usher	utmost		uv	of
usige	usage	utolize	utilize	uven	oven
usirp	usurp	utor	utter	uze	ooze
usual		utorly	utterly	uze	use
usually				uzurp	usurp

V

vacancy		vacilate	vacillate	vacuum	
vacant		vacillate		vagabond	
vacantsy	vacancy	vacinity	vicinity	vagebond	vagabond
vacashon	vacation	vacksine	vaccine	vagibond	vagabond
vacate		vacont	vacant	vagobond	vagabond
vacation		vacseen	vaccine	vagrant	
vacceen	vaccine	vacsene	vaccine	vagrent	vagrant
vaccene	vaccine	vacsine	vaccine	vagrint	vagrant
vaccinate		vacuam	vacuum	vagront	vagrant
vaccination		vacuem	vacuum	vagrunt	vagrant
vaccine		vacuim	vacuum	vagubond	vagabond
vace	vase	vacume	vacuum	vague	
vacelate	vacillate	vacunt	vacant	vaicant	vacant
vacellate	vacillate	vacuom	vacuum	vaig	vague

vaigrant	vagrant	valit	valet	vanilla	
vail	vale	valiunt	valiant	vanish	
vail	veil	valley		vanity	
vain		vallid	valid	vankwish	vanquish
vain	vane	vallt	vault	vanoty	vanity
vain	vein	vally	valley	vanquish	
vainly		valocity	velocity	vanuty	vanity
vaipor	vapor	valontine	valentine	vapar	vapor
vairy	vary	valor		vaper	vapor
vaise	vase	valuable		vapir	vapor
vakant	vacant	valuation		vapor	
vakcine	vaccine	value		vapur	vapor
vakent	vacant	valueble	valuable	varacious	voracious
vakint	vacant	valuminous	voluminous	varanda	veranda
vakont	vacant	valuntine	valentine	varey	vary
vaksine	vaccine	valur	valor	variable	
vakume	vacuum	valve		variance	
vakunt	vacant	valy	valley	variation	
vakuum	vacuum	valyant	valiant	varied	
valantine	valentine	valyent	valiant	variety	
valar	valor	valyint	valiant	various	
valay	valet	valyont	valiant	varmillion	vermillion
vale		valyunt	valiant	Varmont	Vermont
vale	veil	van		varnish	
valees	valise	vanaty	vanity	vary	
valentine		vancwish	vanquish	varyable	variable
valer	valor	vandal		varyance	variance
valese	valise	vandel	vandal	varyation	variation
valet		vandil	vandal	varyd	varied
valew	value	vandol	vandal	varyous	various
valey	valley	vandul	vandal	vasal	vassal
valiant		vane		vasallate	vacillate
valid		vane	vain	vase	
valient	valiant	vane	vein	vasel	vassal
valintine	valentine	vanety	vanity	vasellate	vacillate
valiont	valiant	vangard	vanguard	vasil	vassal
valir	valor	vanguard		vasillate	vacillate
valise		vanila	vanilla	vasinity	vicinity

vasol		vegetation		Venas	Venus		
vasollate	vacillate	vegitable	vegetable	venason	venison		
vassal		vegtable	vegetable	venchur	venture		
vassel	vassal	vehemence		vend			
vassil	vassal	vehement		vender	vendor		
vassol	vassal	vehicle		vendor			
vassul	vassal	vehikle	vehicle	venem	venom		
vast		veicle	vehicle	venerable			
vastly		veil		veneson	venison		
vastness		veiment	vehement	Veness	Venus		
vastniss	vastness	vein		vengeance			
vasul	vassal	vejatable	vegetable	vengence	vengeance		
vasullate	vacillate	vejetable	vegetable	vengince	vengeance		
vat		vejitable	vegetable	venilla	vanilla		
vault		vejotable	vegetable	venim	venom		
vawlt	vault	vejtable	vegetable	venirable	venerable		
vaycant	vacant	vejutable	vegetable	Venis	Venus		
vayg	vague	veks	vex	venison			
vaygrant	vagrant	velam	vellum	venjance	vengeance		
vaypor	vapor	vele	veal	venjence	vengeance		
vayse	vase	velem	vellum	venjince	vengeance		
vaze	vase	velim	vellum	venjonce	vengeance		
vea	via	velise	valise	venjunce	vengeance		
veacle	vehicle	vellam	vellum	venom			
veal		vellem	vellum	venomous			
veament	vehement	vellim	vellum	venorable	venerable		
Veanus	Venus	vellom	vellum	Venos	Venus		
vear	veer	vellum		venoson	venison		
veato	veto	velocity		vent			
vecinity	vicinity	velom	vellum	ventalate	ventilate		
vecks	vex	velosity	velocity	ventchur	venture		
vecs	vex	velum	vellum	ventelate	ventilate		
veel	veal	veluminous	voluminous	ventilate			
Veenus	Venus	velvet		ventilation			
veer		velvety		ventilator			
veeto	veto	velvit	velvet	ventolate	ventilate		
vegetable		venam	venom	ventulate	ventilate		
vegetarian		venarable	venerable	venture			

venturesome		verman		vermin		vesinity	vicinity
venum	venom	vermen		vermin		vesol	vessel
venurable	venerable	vermillion				vessal	vessel
Venus		vermin				vessel	
venuson	venison	vermon	vermin			vessil	vessel
veocle	vehicle	Vermont				vessol	vessel
veoment	vehement	vermun	vermin			vessul	vessel
veracious	voracious	verofy	verify			vest	
verafy	verify	verotable	veritable			vestabule	vestibule
veranda		verry	very			vestebule	vestibule
veratable	veritable	versatile				vestibule	
verb		verse				vestige	
verbal		versed				vestment	
verbally		versetile	versatile			vestobule	vestibule
verbel	verbal	version				vestubule	vestibule
verbil	verbal	versitile	versatile			vesul	vessel
verbol	verbal	versotile	versatile			vetaran	veteran
verbul	verbal	versutile	versatile			vetarinary	veterinary
verce	verse	vertabra	vertebra			veteran	
verchual	virtual	vertacal	vertical			veterinarian	
verchue	virtue	vertchue	virtue			veterinary	
verdant		vertebra				vetiran	veteran
verdent	verdant	vertecal	vertical			vetirinary	veterinary
verdict		vertibra	vertebra			veto	
verdikt	verdict	vertical				vetoran	veteran
verdint	verdant	vertobra	vertebra			vetorinary	veterinary
verdont	verdant	vertocal	vertical			veturan	veteran
verdunt	verdant	vertual	virtual			veturinary	veterinary
vere	veer	vertubra	vertebra			veucle	vehicle
verefy	verify	vertucal	vertical			veument	vehement
veretable	veritable	vertue	virtue			vew	view
verge		verufy	verify			vex	
vergen	virgin	verutable	veritable			vexation	
vergin	virgin	very				vi	vie
Verginia	Virginia	verzion	version			via	
veriety	variety	vesal	vessel			viaduct	
verify		vesel	vessel			vial	
veritable		vesil	vessel			vialate	violate

vialent	violent	victur	victor	vile	
vialet	violet	vicur	vicar	vile	vial
vialin	violin	vie		vilen	villain
viand		vieduct	viaduct	vilent	violent
vibrait	vibrate	viel	vial	viler	villa
vibrant		vielate	violate	vilet	violet
vibrate		vielent	violent	vilige	village
vibration		vielet	violet	vilin	villain
vibrent	vibrant	vielin	violin	vilin	violin
vibrint	vibrant	viend	viand	vilise	valise
vibront	vibrant	view		villa	
vibrunt	vibrant	viewpoint		village	
vicar		vigar	vigor	villager	
vice		vigel	vigil	villain	
vice	vise	viger	vigor	villainous	
viceroy		vigil		villainy	
vice versa		vigilance		villan	villain
vicinity		vigilant		villen	villain
vicious		vigir	vigor	viller	villa
vickar	vicar	vigor		villige	village
vicksen	vixen	vigorous		villin	villain
vicktim	victim	vigur	vigor	villon	villain
vicktor	victor	vijal	vigil	villun	villain
vicor	vicar	vijel	vigil	vilocity	velocity
vicount	viscount	vijil	vigil	vilon	villain
vicownt	viscount	vijol	vigil	viluminous	voluminous
vicsen	vixen	vijul	vigil	vilun	villain
victam	victim	vikar	vicar	vilun.	violon
victar	victor	viking		vim	
victem	victim	vikount	viscount	vinagar	vinegar
victer	victor	vikownt	viscount	vindacate	vindicate
victim		viksen	vixen	vindecate	vindicate
victir	victor	viktim	victim	vindicate	
victom	victim	viktor	victor	vindication	
victor		vila	villa	vindictive	
victorious		vilage	village	vindocate	vindicate
victory		vilain	villain	vinducate	vindicate
victum	victim	vilan	villain	vine	

vinegar		virgen	virgin	vise versa	vice versa
vineyard		virgin		visewal	visual
vinigar	vinegar	Virginia		vishas	vicious
vinilla	vanilla	Virgin Islands		vishess	vicious
vinogar	vinegar	viriety	variety	vishis	vicious
vintage		viris	virus	vishos	vicious
vintige	vintage	virjan	virgin	vishous	vicious
vinugar	vinegar	virjen	virgin	vishus	vicious
vinyard	vineyard	virjin	virgin	visibility	
viola		Virjinia	Virginia	visible	
violate		virjon	virgin	visibly	
violation		virjun	virgin	visige	visage
violator		virmillion	vermillion	visinity	vicinity
violence		virmin	vermin	vision	
violent		Virmont	Vermont	visionary	
violently		viros	virus	visir	visor
violet		virsatile	versatile	visit	
violin		virse	verse	visitor	
violinist		virsion	version	visoble	visible
vipar	viper	virtchual	virtual	visor	
viper		virtchue	virtue	vista	
vipir	viper	virtebra	vertebra	vister	vista
vipor	viper	virtical	vertical	visual	
vipur	viper	virtual		visuble	visible
vioduct	viaduct	virtually		visur	visor
viol	vial	virtue		vital	
viond	viand	virtuous		vitality	
viracious	voracious	virus		vitals	
viranda	veranda	visable	visible	vitamin	
viras	virus	visage		vitel	vital
virb	verb	visar	visor	vitemin	vitamin
virce	verse	visa versa	vice versa	vitil	vital
virchual	virtual	viscount		vitimin	vitamin
virchue	virtue	vise		vitol	vital
virdant	verdant	vise	vice	vitomin	vitamin
virdict	verdict	viseble	visible	vitul	vital
viress	virus	viser	visor	vitumin	vitamin
virge	verge	viseroy	viceroy	viuduct	viaduct

viul	vial	voakation	vocation	volume	
viulate	violate	voalt	volt	voluminous	
viulent	violent	voat	vote	voluntarily	
viulet	violet	vocabulary		voluntary	
viulin	violin	vocal		volunteer	
viund	viand	vocation		volutile	volatile
vivacious		vociferous		voly	volley
vivacity		vocinity	vicinity	vomit	
vivashous	vivacious	vocol	vocal	vonilla	vanilla
vivasity	vivacity	vocul	vocal	voracious	
vivid		vogue		voranda	veranda
vixan	vixen	voice		vorashous	voracious
vixen		void		voriety	variety
vixin	vixen	voise	voice	vormillion	vermillion
vixon	vixen	vokabulary	vocabulary	Vormont	Vermont
vixun	vixen	vokal	vocal	vosiferous	vociferous
vizable	visible	vokation	vocation	vosinity	vicinity
vizage	visage	volanteer	volunteer	vote	
vizar	visor	volatile		voter	
vizeble	visible	volcanic		vouch	
vizer	visor	volcano		vouchsafe	
vizewal	visual	volenteer	volunteer	vow	
vizible	visible	voletile	volatile	vowal	vowel
vizige	visage	volewble	voluble	vowch	vouch
vizion	vision	volewm	volume	vowel	
vizir	visor	volewminous	voluminous	vowil	vowel
vizit	visit	voley	volley	vowol	vowel
vizoble	visible	volinteer	volunteer	vowul	vowel
vizor	visor	volise	valise	voyage	
vizual	visual	volitile	volatile	voyager	
vizuble	visible	volkano	volcano	voyce	voice
vizur	visor	volley		voyd	void
voacabulary	vocabulary	volly	volley	voyige	voyage
voacal	vocal	volocity	velocity	voyse	voice
voacation	vocation	volonteer	volunteer	vu	view
voag	vogue	volotile	volatile	vucinity	vicinity
voakabulary	vocabulary	volt		vue	view
voakal	vocal	voluble		vulchur	vulture

vulgar		vuluminous	voluminous	vurmillion	vermillion
vulgarity		vunilla	vanilla	vurmin	vermin
vulger	vulgar	vuracious	voracious	Vurmont	Vermont
vulgir	vulgar	vuranda	veranda	vursatile	versatile
vulgor	vulgar	vurb	verb	vurse	verse
vulgur	vulgar	vurce	verse	vursion	version
vulise	valise	vurchual	virtual	vurtchue	virtue
vulnarable	vulnerable	vurchue	virtue	vurtebra	vertebra
vulnerable		vurdant	verdant	vurtical	vertical
vulnirable	vulnerable	vurdict	verdict	vurtual	virtual
vulnorable	vulnerable	vurge	verge	vurtue	virtue
vulnurable	vulnerable	vurgen	virgin	vurzion	version
vulocity	velocity	vurgin	virgin	vusinity	vicinity
vultchur	vulture	Vurginia	Virginia	vy	vie
vulture		vuriety	variety	vying	

W

wa	way	wadle	waddle	waful	waffle
wa	weigh	wafal	waffle	wafur	wafer
wa	whey	wafar	wafer	wag	
wabble		wafe	waif	wagan	wagon
wac	whack	wafel	waffle	wage	
wach	watch	wafer		wagen	wagon
wack	whack	waffal	waffle	wager	
wacks	wax	waffel	waffle	waggish	
wacs	wax	waffil	waffle	wagin	wagon
wad		waffle		wagish	waggish
wadal	waddle	waffol	waffle	wagon	
waddal	waddle	wafful	waffle	wagun	wagon
waddel	waddle	wafil	waffle	waid	wade
waddil	waddle	wafir	wafer	waif	
waddle		wafle	waffle	waifer	wafer
waddol	waddle	wafol	waffle	waige	wage
waddul	waddle	wafor	wafer	waik	wake
wade		waft		wail	

wail	whale	walress	walrus	wardon	warden
wain	wane	walris	walrus	wardrobe	
wainscot		walros	walrus	wardun	warden
wainskot	wainscot	walrus		ware	
wair	ware	waltz		ware	wear
wair	wear	wampum		ware	where
wair	where	wan		warehouse	
wairy	wary	wand		waren	warren
waist		wandar	wander	warent	warrant
waist	waste	wander		wareor	warrior
waistcoat		wanderer		warey	wary
wait		wandir	wander	warf	wharf
waiter		wandor	wander	warfair	warfare
waiting		wandur	wander	warfare	
waitress		wane		warily	
waitriss	waitress	wanescot	wainscot	warin	warren
waive		waneskot	wainscot	wariness	
waive	wave	want		warint	warrant
wak	whack	wantan	wanton	warior	warrior
wake		wanten	wanton	warlike	
waken		wantin	wanton	warm	
waks	wax	wanting		warmblooded	
wale	wail	wanton		warmth	
wale	whale	wantun	wanton	warn	
walet	wallet	war		warn	worn
walit	wallet	waran	warren	warning	
walk		warant	warrant	waron	warren
wall		warbal	warble	waront	warrant
wallet		warbel	warble	warp	
wallit	wallet	warbil	warble	warpath	
wallnut	walnut	warble		warran	warren
wallow		warbler		warrant	
wallpaper		warbol	warble	warren	
wallrus	walrus	warbul	warble	warrent	warrant
walltz	waltz	ward		warreor	warrior
walnut		wardan	warden	warrin	warren
walow	wallow	warden		warrint	warrant
walras	walrus	wardin	warden	warrior	

warron	warren	waterway		weapan	weapon
warront	warrant	watery		weapen	weapon
warrun	warren	watir	water	weapin	weapon
warrunt	warrant	wator	water	weapon	
warship		watt		weapun	weapon
wart		watur	water	wear	
warun	warren	wave		weard	weird
warunt	warrant	waver		wearer	
wary		wavey	wavy	wearily	
waryly	warily	wavy		weariness	
waryness	wariness	wax		wearisome	
was		waxen		weary	
wash		way		wearyly	wearily
washer		way	weigh	wearyness	weariness
washing		way	whey	wearysome	wearisome
Washington		wayfer	wafer	weasal	weasel
wasn't		wayge	wage	weasel	
wasp		waylay		weasil	weasel
waste		wayside		weasol	weasel
wastecoat	waistcoat	wayward		weasul	weasel
wasteful		waz	was	weat	wheat
wat	watt	we		weathar	weather
wat	what	we	wee	weather	
watar	water	wead	weed	weathervane	
watch		weadle	wheedle	weathir	weather
watchdog		weak		weathor	weather
watchful		weak	week	weathur	weather
watchman		weaken		weave	
watchtower		weakling		weaver	
watchword		weakly		weavil	weevil
wate	wait	weakness		weaze	wheeze
wate	weight	weakniss	weakness	weazel	weasel
water		weal	wheel	web	
waterfall		weald	wield	webbed	
waterfront		wealth		webed	webbed
watermelon		wealthy		wed	
waterproof		wean		wedding	
watertight		weap	weep	wede	weed

wedge		weird		wepin	weapon
weding	wedding	weke	weak	wepon	weapon
wedle	wheedle	weke	week	wept	
wedlock		wel	well	wepun	weapon
Wednesday		welcome		wer	were
wee		welcum	welcome	wer	whir
weed		weld		werce	worse
weedle	wheedle	wele	wheel	werd	word
week		welfair	welfare	were	
week	weak	welfare		werey	weary
weekday		welkum	welcome	werk	work
weekend		well		werl	whirl
weekly		well-being		werld	world
weel	wheel	well-bred		werm	worm
weeld	wield	wellcome	welcome	werry	worry
ween	wean	wellcum	welcome	werse	worse
weep		wellfair	welfare	wership	worship
weerd	weird	wellfare	welfare	werst	worst
weery	weary	well-known		werth	worth
weesal	weasel	wellkum	welcome	wery	weary
weesel	weasel	welp	whelp	wery	worry
weesil	weasel	welt		west	
weesol	weasel	weltar	welter	westarn	western
wessul	weasel	welter		westerly	
weet	wheat	welth	wealth	western	
weeval	weevil	weltir	welter	westirn	western
weeve	weave	weltor	welter	westorn	western
weevel	weevil	weltur	welter	westurn	western
weevil		wen	when	West Virginia	
weevol	weevil	wench		westward	
weevul	weevil	wend		wet	
weeze	wheeze	wene	wean	wet	whet
weezel	weasel	Wensday	Wednesday	wete	wheat
weft		went		wethar	weather
wege	wedge	Wenzday	Wednesday	wether	weather
weigh		wepan	weapon	wether	whether
weight		wepe	weep	wethir	weather
weild	wield	wepen	weapon	wethor	weather

wethur	weather	while		who	
weve	weave	whim		whoa	
wevil	weevil	whimpar	whimper	whoal	whole
wew	woo	whimper		whoever	
wewnd	wound	whimpir	whimper	whole	
weze	wheeze	whimpor	whimper	wholehearted	
whack		whimpur	whimper	wholesale	
whale		whimsical		wholesome	
wharf		whimzical	whimsical	wholey	wholly
what		whine		wholly	
whatever		whinny		whom	
whatsoever		whip		whoop	
wheat		whippoorwill		whooping cough	
wheedal	wheedle	whir		whoos	whose
wheedel	wheedle	whirl		whooz	whose
wheedil	wheedle	whirlpool		whose	
wheedle		whirlwind		whupe	whoop
wheedol	wheedle	whisk		why	
wheedul	wheedle	whiskar	whisker	wi	why
wheel		whisker		wic	wick
wheelbarrow		whiskey		wich	which
wheeze		whiskir	whisker	wich	witch
whelp		whiskor	whisker	wick	
when		whiskur	whisker	wickar	wicker
whenever		whisky	whiskey	wicked	
where		whispar	whisper	wickedness	
whereabouts		whisper		wicker	
whereas		whispir	whisper	wicket	
whereby		whispor	whisper	wickid	wicked
wherein		whispur	whisper	wickir	wicker
whereof		whistle		wickit	wicket
whereupon		white		wickor	wicker
wherever		whiten		wickur	wicker
whet		whitewash		wide	
whether		whither		widely	
whey		whitle	whittle	widen	
which		whittle		widespread	
whiff		whiz		wido	widow

widow		wildfire	windstorm
widower		wildly	windy
width		**wildorness** wilderness	wine
wield		**wildurness** wilderness	**wine** whine
wier wire		wile	**winer** winner
wierd weird		**wile** while	wing
wife		**wiley** wily	winged
wiff whiff		will	**wingid** winged
wig		**willdirness** wilderness	**wining** winning
wigal wiggle		willful	wink
wigel wiggle		willing	winner
wiggal wiggle		willingly	winning
wiggel wiggle		willingness	**winny** whinny
wiggil wiggle		**willo** willow	**winsam** winsome
wiggle		willow	**winse** wince
wiggol wiggle		**wilo** willow	**winsem** winsome
wiggul wiggle		**wilow** willow	**winsim** winsome
wigil wiggle		wilt	**winsom** winsome
wigle wiggle		wily	winsome
wigol wiggle		**wim** whim	**winsum** winsome
wigul wiggle		**wiman** women	**wintar** winter
wigwam		**wimen** women	winter
wigwom wigwam		**wimin** women	wintergreen
wik wick		**wimon** women	wintertime
wikar wicker		**wimper** whimper	**wintery** wintry
wiked wicked		**wimsical** whimsical	**wintir** winter
wiker wicker		**wimun** women	**wintor** winter
wiket wicket		**wimzical** whimsical	wintry
wikir wicker		win	**wintur** winter
wikit wicket		wince	**winy** whinny
wikor wicker		wind	**Wioming** Wyoming
wikur wicker		windfall	**wip** whip
wil will		windmill	wipe
wild		**windo** window	**wippoorwill** whippoorwill
wildarness wilderness		window	**wir** were
wildcat		windpipe	**wir** whir
wilderness		windshield	**wirce** worse

wird	word	wissal	whistle	withstood	
wire		wissel	whistle	withur	wither
wireing	wiring	wissil	whistle	witil	whittle
wireless		wissol	whistle	witle	whittle
wirey	wiry	wissul	whistle	witless	
wiring		wisteria		witliss	witless
wirk	work	wistful		witness	
wirl	whirl	wistle	whistle	witniss	witness
wirld	world	wisul	whistle	witol	whittle
wirm	worm	wit		wittal	whittle
wirry	worry	wital	whittle	wittel	whittle
wirse	worse	witch		wittil	whittle
wirship	worship	witchary	witchery	wittle	whittle
wirst	worst	witchcraft		wittol	whittle
wirth	worth	witchery		wittul	whittle
wiry		witchiry	witchery	witty	
wiry	worry	witchory	witchery	wity	witty
wisal	whistle	witchury	witchery	wives	
Wisconsin		wite	white	wivez	wives
wisdam	wisdom	witel	whittle	wiz	whiz
wisdem	wisdom	with		wizard	
wisdim	wisdom	with	width	wizdam	wisdom
wisdom		withar	wither	wizdem	wisdom
wisdum	wisdom	withdraw		wizdim	wisdom
wise		withdrawal		wizdom	wisdom
wisel	whistle	withdrawl	withdrawal	wizdum	wisdom
wish		withdrawn		wize	wise
wishbone		withdrew		wizerd	wizard
wisil	whistle	wither		wizird	wizard
wisk	whisk	wither	whither	wizord	wizard
wisker	whisker	withheld		wizurd	wizard
wiskey	whiskey	withhold		wo	whoa
Wiskonsin	Wisconsin	within		wo	woe
wisky	whiskey	withir	wither	woak	woke
wisol	whistle	withor	wither	woar	wore
wisp		without		woave	wove
wisper	whisper	withstand		wobal	wobble

wobbal	wobble	won		wool	
wobbel	wobble	won	one	woolan	woolen
wobbil	wobble	won	wan	woolen	
wobble		wonce	once	woolin	woolen
wobbley	wobbly	wond	wand	woolon	woolen
wobbly		wondar	wander	woolun	woolen
wobbol	wobble	wondar	wonder	woond	wound
wobbul	wobble	wonder		worble	warble
wobel	wobble	wonder	wander	worce	worse
wobil	wobble	wonderful		word	
woble	wobble	wonderous	wondrous	word	ward
wobol	wobble	wondir	wander	wording	
wobul	wobble	wondir	wonder	wordy	
woch	watch	wondor	wander	wore	
wod	wad	wondor	wonder	worf	wharf
woe		wondrous		work	
woeful		wondrus	wondrous	workbench	
woffle	waffle	wondur	wander	workbook	
wofle	waffle	wondur	wonder	worker	
woke		wont		working	
wolet	wallet	wont	want	workmanship	
wolf		woo		workout	
wolit	wallet	wood		workshop	
wollet	wallet	wood	would	world	
wollit	wallet	woodchuck		worldly	
wollow	wallow	woodcutter		worm	
wolow	wallow	wooded		worm	warm
wolverine		wooden		wormy	
wolves		woodid	wooded	worn	
wolvez	wolves	woodland		worn	warn
woman		woodpecker		worn-out	
womanly		woods		worp	warp
women		woodshed		worry	
womin	woman	woodwind		worse	
womon	woman	woodwork		worship	
wompum	wampum	woodz	woods	worshiper	
womun	woman	woof		worst	

327

worsted		wreck	wreak	wry	
wort	wart	wreckage		wud	wood
worth		wrecker		wud	would
worthiness		wreckige	wreckage	wue	woo
worthless		wreeth	wreath	wuf	woof
worthliss	worthless	wrek	wreck	wul	wool
worthwhile		wreke	wreak	wulf	wolf
worthy		wren		wulverine	wolverine
worthyness	worthiness	wrench		wuman	woman
wory	worry	wrest		wun	one
wosh	wash	wrestle		wun	won
wosp	wasp	wrestler		wunce	once
wot	watt	wrestling		wund	wound
wot	what	wretch		wundar	wonder
wotch	watch	wretched		wunder	wonder
wott	watt	wretchedness		wundir	wonder
would		wretchid	wretched	wundor	wonder
wouldn't		wrethe	wreath	wundur	wonder
wound		wriggle		wur	were
wove		wring		wur	whir
woven		wringer		wurce	worse
wraith		wrinkle		wurd	word
wrangle		wrist		wurk	work
wrap		writ		wurl	whirl
wraper	wrapper	write		wurld	world
wraping	wrapping	writeing	writing	wurm	worm
wrapper		writen	written	wurry	worry
wrapping		writer		wurse	worse
wrath		writhe		wurship	worship
wrathe	wraith	writing		wurst	worst
wrathful		written		wurth	worth
wrayth	wraith	wrong		wury	worry
wreak		wrongdoing		wusted	worsted
wreath		wrongful		wuz	was
wrec	wreck	wrote		wy	why
wreck		wrought		Wyoming	
		wrung			

X

xilaphone	xylophone	**Xmas**		**xylaphone**	xylophone
xilephone	xylophone	**Xmes**	Xmas	**xylephone**	xylophone
xiliphone	xylophone	**Xmis**	Xmas	**xyliphone**	xylophone
xilophone	xylophone	**Xmos**	Xmas	xylophone	
xiluphone	xylophone	**Xmus**	Xmas	**xyluphone**	xylophone
		X-ray			

Y

ya	yea	**yeald**	yield	**yestarday**	yesterday
yac	yak	year		**yeste**	yeast
yacht		yearbook		yesterday	
yachting		yearling		**yestirday**	yesterday
yachtsman		yearly		**yestorday**	yesterday
yack	yak	yearn		**yesturday**	yesterday
yak		yearning		yet	
yall	yawl	yeast		**yew**	you
yam		**yeeld**	yield	**Yekon**	Yukon
yanck	yank	**yeer**	year	**yewl**	yule
Yangtze		**yeest**	yeast	**yews**	use
yank		**yeild**	yield	**yewsual**	usual
Yankee		**yel**	yell	**yewsurp**	usurp
Yankey	Yankee	yell		**yewth**	youth
Yanky	Yankee	**yello**	yellow	**yewz**	use
yap		yellow		**yewzual**	usual
yard		Yellowstone		yield	
yardstick		**yelo**	yellow	yielding	
yarn		**yelow**	yellow	**yirn**	yearn
yat	yacht	yelp		**yoadel**	yodel
yawl		yen		**yoak**	yoke
yawn		yeoman		**yoak**	yolk
yawr	your	**yere**	year	**yoar**	your
yay	yea	**yern**	yearn	**yodal**	yodel
yea		yes		yodel	

yodil	yodel	young		yuletide	
yodol	yodel	youngstar	youngster	yunanimous	unanimous
yodul	yodel	youngster		yung	young
yoke		youngstir	youngster	yunicorn	unicorn
yoke	yolk	youngstor	youngster	yuniform	uniform
yolk		youngstur	youngster	yunify	unify
yoman	yeoman	your		yunion	union
yondar	yonder	your	you're	yunique	unique
yonder		you're		yunison	unison
yondir	yonder	yours		yunit	unit
yondor	yonder	yourself		yunite	unite
yondur	yonder	yourselves		yuniversal	universal
yoo	you	yourselvez	yourselves	yuniversity	university
Yookon	Yukon	yourz	yours	yunyon	union
yool	yule	youth		yuranium	uranium
yoos	use	youthful		yurine	urine
yoosual	usual	yowl		yurn	yearn
yoosurp	usurp	yu	you	yuse	use
yooth	youth	yuca	yucca	yusual	usual
yooz	use	yucca		yusurp	usurp
yoozual	usual	yucka	yucca	Yutah	Utah
yore	your	yue	you	yutensil	utensil
yorn	yawn	Yuekon	Yukon	yuth	youth
Yosemite		yuka	yucca	yutilize	utilize
yot	yacht	Yukon		yuze	use
you		yule		yuzual	usual

Z

zar	czar	zealis	zealous	zeanith	zenith
zeabra	zebra	zealit	zealot	zearo	zero
zeal		zealos	zealous	zebra	
zealas	zealous	zealot		zeebra	zebra
zealat	zealot	zealous		zeel	zeal
zealess	zealous	zealus	zealous	zeenith	zenith
zealet	zealot	zealut	zealot	zeero	zero

zefer	zephyr	zew		zoo	
zele	zeal	zewm		zoom	
zellot	zealot	Zews		Zeus	
zellous	zealous	Zian		Zion	
zelot	zealot	Zien		Zion	
zelous	zealous	zigzag			
zenith		zinc			
zepalin	zeppelin	zinck	zinc		
zepelin	zeppelin	zinea	zinnia		
zephar	zephyr	zinia	zinnia		
zepher	zephyr	zink	zinc		
zephir	zephyr	zinnea	zinnia		
zephor	zephyr	zinnia			
zephur	zephyr	Zion			
zephyr		Zionism			
zepilin	zeppelin	zip			
zepolin	zeppelin	zipar	zipper		
zeppalin	zeppelin	ziper	zipper		
zeppelin		zipir	zipper		
zeppilin	zeppelin	zipor	zipper		
zeppolin	zeppelin	zippar	zipper		
zeppulin	zeppelin	zipper			
zepulin	zeppelin	zippir	zipper		
zero		zippor	zipper		
zest		zippur	zipper		
Zeus		zipur	zipper		

zithar	zither
zither	
zithir	zither
zithor	zither
zithur	zither
Ziun	Zion
zoadiac	zodiac
zoan	zone
zodeac	zodiac
zodiac	
zone	
zoo	
zoological	
zoologist	
zoology	
zoom	
Zoos	Zeus
zu	zoo
zue	zoo
zume	zoom
Zuse	Zeus
zweaback	zwieback
zweback	zwieback
zweeback	zwieback
zweiback	zwieback
zwieback	